THE PEDAGOGY OF WISDOM

SERIES EDITOR

John Russon

REREADING ANCIENT PHILOSOPHY

THE PEDAGOGY OF WISDOM

An Interpretation of Plato's *Theaetetus*

GREGORY KIRK

NORTHWESTERN UNIVERSITY PRESS • EVANSTON, ILLINOIS

Northwestern University Press
www.nupress.northwestern.edu

Printed in the United States of America

10 9 8 7 6 5 4 3 2 1

Library of Congress Cataloging-in-Publication Data

Kirk, Gregory, 1977– author.
The pedagogy of wisdom : an interpretation of Plato's Theaetetus / Gregory Kirk.
pages cm. — (Rereading ancient philosophy)
ISBN 978-0-8101-3176-7 (pbk. : alk. paper) — ISBN 978-0-8101-3100-2 (cloth : alk. paper) — ISBN 978-0-8101-3101-9 (ebook)
1. Plato. Theaetetus. 2. Knowledge, Theory of. I. Title. II. Series: Rereading ancient philosophy.
B386.K57 2015
831—dc23
2015017551

∞ The paper used in this publication meets the minimum requirements of the American National Standard for Information Sciences—Permanence of Paper for Printed Library Materials, ANSI Z39.48–1992.

To Alice Kirk

CONTENTS

ACKNOWLEDGMENTS

I am grateful to many people for helping me with this project, as well as for helping me to develop my thinking about Plato, and for helping me to understand better what it is that one is accomplishing in doing philosophy. Regarding all of these, and particularly the latter, most of all I am grateful to John Russon. I am also grateful to Anna Bekerman for her love and support and for having a keen editor's eye toward my sometimes convoluted sentences.

I want to thank Whitney Howell and Joseph Arel for being great friends and essential dialogue partners; Peter Manchester for the inspiring creativity of his thinking; Ed Casey, Patricia Locke, and David Allison for their thoughtful and challenging comments on my work; Mitchell Miller and Eric Sanday for making themselves available to discuss with me and others the immensely difficult final section of the *Theaetetus*; and Jeff Epstein and Emiliano Diaz for their invaluable insights during our Plato reading group.

I would also like to thank the philosophy departments of the University of Guelph and Stony Brook University, my colleagues at Northern Arizona University, and (in no apparent order) David Ciavatta, Shannon Hoff, Kirsten Jacobson, Patricia Fagan, Tim Fitzjohn, Kym Maclaren, Gregory Recco, Jared Babin, Susan Bredlau, Eve Rabinoff, Laura McMahon, Simon Rice, Matthew Drake, Allan Kirk, and Janet Kirk.

THE PEDAGOGY OF WISDOM

INTRODUCTION

Human Life as the Occasion for the Possibility of Knowledge

This book is an attempt to interpret Plato's *Theaetetus* as a whole. It is an attempt to do so by attending to the context within which the particular conversations that are portrayed occur. These interpretive decisions have led me to conclude that the conversation that occurs between the central characters—Socrates, Theaetetus and Theodorus—is a demonstration of Socrates's pedagogy, which is to say, his practice of striving to aid in the cultivation of a philosophical orientation in certain young men of Athens. This demonstration is placed within the context of a lengthy discussion of *epistēmē*, or knowledge. The explicit content of the discussion of knowledge that Socrates has with Theaetetus relates to Socrates's practice of philosophical education, sometimes in a harmonious, sometimes in a discordant manner. I take part of the responsibility in interpreting the dialogue to involve highlighting ways in which the explicit conversation lives up to, and fails to live up to, its subject matter, particularly in light of the continuities and discontinuities between what is explicitly stated about knowledge and how Theaetetus's learning process unfolds. This sometimes involves demonstrating how the education that Theaetetus is undergoing with Socrates shows us characteristics of the nature of knowledge that are underdeveloped in their conversation about knowledge. As a reader and an interpreter of this dialogue, I take myself and anyone else seeking to reap the considerable benefits of reading Plato's *Theaetetus* to be a distinct kind of interlocutor, one who benefits from being at a distance from the conversation, and one who must attend to what is said and to what is unsaid in order to think for oneself in fresh terms about the nature of knowledge.

Though philosophical education is a theme central to the Platonic corpus as a whole, as well as to specific dialogues, I take the *Theaetetus* to offer readers a unique opportunity to reflect on this practice. This is due to its juxtaposition of its dramatization of philosophical education, its explicit reflection on the nature of knowledge, its presentation (through the mouth of Socrates himself in his "midwife speech") of Socrates's own practice, and its meditation on what it is to be a philosopher. In the *Republic* we are presented with a rigorous presentation of philosophical education. In several other dialogues, we are given a dramatic presentation of Socrates's practice of trying to influence young men to pursue philosophy. What the *Theaetetus* offers is the opportunity to reflect on a dramatic presentation of the learning process while simultaneously reflecting on what the presumptive accomplishment of that learning process is.

Plato's *Theaetetus* presents a documented conversation Socrates is said to have had with his acquaintance, the mathematician and teacher, Theodorus, along with Theodorus's promising student, Theaetetus. The documented conversation is presented to us as having been written by a student of Socrates, or at least an admirer of Socrates, named Euclides. Euclides instructs his slave to read the documented conversation to him and his acquaintance, Terpsion, on the occasion of the impending death of Theaetetus many years after the death of Socrates. It is as a result of thinking about Theaetetus dying that Euclides is reminded of the conversation he recorded shortly before Socrates himself had died. Euclides is motivated to have his recording of the reported conversation read to both him and Terpsion, who brought him the news of Theaetetus's impending death, both because the impending death of Theaetetus reminds Euclides of the death of Socrates, and because he considers the document itself to be of intrinsic ongoing interest.

The recorded conversation begins with a short speech by Socrates that contextualizes the lengthy conversation that follows. Socrates tells Theodorus that he cares about the young men of Athens talented in philosophy. He both makes a point of searching on his own, and goes around to the older men around whom young men congregate in large numbers, so that he can find the young men that stand out as talented in philosophy in order to examine them and discover for himself their abilities. Socrates does not specify to Theodorus beyond this to what end he examines the young men, instead merely noting that Theodorus is one such man around whom the young congregate, and is therefore someone from whom he would find out with pleasure which young men are remarkable. Theodorus does not ask Socrates what his purpose might be, but rather tells Socrates with great enthusiasm that Theaetetus is not only such a talented young man, but also a young man of great character.

In the conversation that immediately follows this, Socrates tells the young Theaetetus that he wants to examine his soul, since he is reputed by his teacher, Theodorus, to be so remarkable. Socrates asks Theaetetus to attempt to answer the question "What is knowledge?" Theaetetus proposes (sometimes with Socrates's prompting) three definitions of knowledge: that knowledge is perception, that knowledge is true opinion, and that knowledge is true opinion with an account. Each of these is examined and shown to be inadequate. Over the course of that conversation, Socrates does not merely passively observe, nor does his participation take the form of merely testing the merits of Theaetetus's intellect or character. He is not a mere examiner. Rather, Socrates proves himself to be invested in the transformation and improvement of Theaetetus, in response to what he observes in Theaetetus's behavior. Thus, implicitly, Socrates shows that he does not merely care most of all about assessing those reputed to be excellent for the purpose of deciding whether they are in fact excellent. Socrates wants to find the excellent so that he can influence them. Theaetetus, in Socrates's estimation at several later points in the dialogue, *does* in fact show himself to be excellent (148b1–3; 185e3–9; 199e8). Socrates seeks young men excellent in philosophy for the purpose of shaping them further, so that they, like he, can lead a philosophical life. He appears to see in Theaetetus the potential for such a life.

I argue in the chapters that follow that Socrates seeks out the young who are best prepared for education in philosophy and offers himself as a guide through that process. I argue that this pedagogical commitment on Socrates's part, and the dramatic presentation of that commitment in (what ultimately only amounts to) a preliminary lesson with Theaetetus near the end of Socrates's life, deeply informs the implicit account of knowledge underlying the explicit discussion of Theaetetus's three proposed definitions of knowledge. In other words, it is from this context, and according to these motivations on the part of Socrates, that Socrates and Theaetetus, with substantial contributions from Theodorus, embark on a complex and ultimately inconclusive pursuit of the answer to the question, "What is knowledge?"

Within this study, I consider my major contributions to scholarship on Plato in general, and on the *Theaetetus* in particular, to be my emphasis on the interpersonal dynamics between the interlocutors. Some scholars have focused on the arguments for each of the three definitions of knowledge presented in the dialogue, and derive from the relative merit of those arguments what is taken to be Plato's own account of knowledge;[1] some focus attention on Plato's literary method, and the philosophical significance of that method;[2] some emphasize the educational value of the experience of *aporia* in the dialogue.[3] Each of these points of emphasis I take to be important to a strong interpretation of the dialogue, and, indeed, I take my own approach to be making use of these three interpretive decisions. I also, however, attend closely to the personalities of the participants of the dialogue, and to the ways in which the interaction between those personalities affects how one should interpret the claims characters make, as well as how to interpret how the dynamics between characters inform their conversational choices. I take my approach, therefore, to give equal consideration to the variety of demands unique to the Platonic text, and apply them to the production of an original interpretation of the *Theaetetus*. In the remainder of this introduction, I will describe what I take to be the key insights into the nature of knowledge to take away from the *Theaetetus*.

I take there to be three crucial insights concerning knowledge that are central to understanding what is accomplished in the text. These insights are to be derived not only from the issues explicitly discussed by the characters, but also from the interpersonal dynamics that develop between them. Insofar as the dialogue is not only about the relative merits of three definitions of knowledge, but also about the contextualizing examination and education of Theaetetus, the means by which those arguments are elaborated is as important as the explicit content of the discussion. Further, the insights I emphasize here are related both to the nature of knowledge and to the education of the soul; indeed, the nature of knowledge and the education of the soul turn out to be inextricable from one another.

1. Life Is the Context of Knowledge

The first insight to be taken from the dialogue is that knowledge only ever occurs within the context of a life, and is therefore limited in specific respects by the conditions of human life. While this might appear to be a patently obvious point, it entails the notion that discussions of the nature of knowledge ought to be *grounded* in the reality of human life.[4] The implications of this insight ought to, but do not, govern the discussion of knowledge between Socrates and Theaetetus. It is not because Socrates neglects this fact that he and Theaetetus fail to ground their discussion appropriately. Rather, because their discussion is governed by the need to educate Theaetetus into the practice of cultivating a philosophical orientation to the world, Socrates is guided—in his guidance of Theaetetus—by the needs of Theaetetus in his philosophical education, rather than by the fundamental nature of knowledge. That Socrates is oriented primarily by the education of Theaetetus is demonstrated throughout, but is made explicit on at least two occasions. On each of these occasions, Socrates avoids allowing the conversation to follow a digression—first, concerning the nature of justice in the political domain (172c1–2), second, concerning the ideas of Parmenides (183d12–184b2).

In the first case, he expresses concern that the conversation at hand will get away from them if they follow the digression; the matter from which they would be getting away is the education of Theaetetus. In the second case, he refuses to allow the digression to continue on the grounds that this would divert them from the course of tending to Theaetetus. Socrates is not concerned primarily with the question of knowledge, but rather with the education of Theaetetus. The dialogue is about knowledge to the extent that questions of knowledge are related to questions concerning the education of the soul, concerning the shaping of a human life. To recognize that knowledge occurs within the context of human life means to acknowledge that it emerges from a situation of ignorance, from a necessarily limited perspective on the world, and from a perspective that must integrate it with a web of accumulated dogmatically held presumptions that require a lifetime of dedication to examine. Though the explicit arguments of the conversation that Socrates and Theaetetus have do not particularly take this fact into account, Socrates's treatment of the education of Theaetetus does. Socrates is therefore more responsive to the rootedness of knowledge in human life than is the explicit discussion in which he participates with Theaetetus and Theodorus. I address the significance and implications of this particular insight in chapters 1 and 2.

In chapter 1, I argue that the opening discussion between Terpsion and Euclides introduces themes central both to our ability to think about the nature of knowledge, and to our thinking about philosophical education. The themes introduced direct us pointedly to important characteristics of the ways of the human soul. These include the fact that we are capable of functioning understandingly in the world without active reflection; the fact that we have a peculiar kind of knowledge of our own deaths; the fact that our lifetime of actions shape a determinate character; the fact that we are reliant upon memory, a capacity toward which we have a significantly passive disposition; and the fact that our limited perspective, combined with the relentlessness of our need to act, together place the burden and responsibility upon us to make interpretations with inadequate understanding. These themes draw our attention to the very personal manner in which Socrates discusses issues of philosophical importance with his two interlocutors, and particularly with Theaetetus.

In chapter 2, I deal directly with Socrates's approach to interacting with Theaetetus, his explicitly outlined method, and its desired results. I take as the centerpiece of this chapter, first, Socrates's characterization of what (and whom) he cares about, and, second, his characterization of his life's vocation of midwifery. I claim that Socrates's project consists in the activity of compelling young men to articulate their thoughts. It turns out, for those young men, that the thoughts that they articulate and had previously taken for granted as understood were grounded upon presumptions that had remained unexamined. Socrates's questioning therefore draws attention not only to one's ignorance, but also to the fact that one had thought one had known what one had not, as well as to the fact that one had accumulated presumptions without consciously deciding to do so. I argue more generally that the aim of the teacher of philosophy is to generate in the student the recognition of the intrinsic desirability of the project of rational inquiry, a recognition that is at the same time tempered by the further recognition that life has the character of generating prejudices requiring persistent questioning. I claim that the mature result of this set of recognitions constitutes wisdom. This chapter first announces Socrates's intellectual midwifery as the principle around which my interpretation of the dialogue as a whole is oriented. I read this account he gives of himself, and what this account presents as a necessary part of the process of education, *against* the accounts of knowledge that are explicitly presented in the dialogue itself.

Socrates's intellectual midwifery emphasizes the fact that human beings live with tacit presumptions about the world, presumptions that are inevitably accumulated in living. It emphasizes this fact and attempts to respond to it by addressing the necessarily accumulated obstructions to the accomplishment of the human need to strive to know. These accumulated presumptions in a certain sense provide us with the means by which to live according to the conventions by which people around us normally live; they take a form that appears to facilitate living. Due to the fact that they are unexamined, we inevitably find situations in which we are confronted with the recognition that this or that presumption contradicts some insight about the world by which we are struck. This is the moment of intellectual pregnancy—the moment of "conception"—that is Socrates's "professional" concern. The experience of wonder in such moments is fragile, though, because we can be, and often are, swept back into the activity of life that rests comfortably on those presumptions. Socrates finds people in that state of pregnancy and strives to force them to maintain that state such that they can build insights on top of the delivery of their confused ideas, insights that generate momentum leading toward a life *governed* by the kind of inquisitiveness distinctive of that moment of pregnancy.

The structure of human life that underlies Socrates's educational project bears explicitly outlining. Human beings in principle begin already in the midst of responding to the world in a way that tacitly accumulates presumptions, many of which presumptions are false, and few of which are explicitly considered and evaluated on their own merits. It is from out of this process of accumulating unreflected-upon know-how that we become able to develop knowledge of any kind. It is therefore essential to the true account of knowledge to recognize its emergence from out of ignorance, as well as to recognize the fact that it is circumscribed by ignorance.

Merely to recognize that knowledge is something that emerges from out of ignorance does not tell us anything significant about the problems with the mode of inquiry that Socrates and Theaetetus undertake together. It does, however, orient us toward thinking about the human circumstances in which knowledge is pursued. Attending to the matters of human life will therefore tell us something about the character of knowledge. The first two chapters—and the opening sections of the *Theaetetus* to which they are addressed—deal with the fact that knowledge occurs within the context of human life. In consequence of this, the first lesson to be learned by Theaetetus, discussed in chapter 2, is that he must begin the process of articulating his own thoughts for the purpose of subjecting them to examination. This is the necessary first step in turning his soul to philosophy.

2. Perception and Reflection Are Mutually Mediating, Inextricable, and Transformational

The second crucial insight about knowledge is the fact that while our immediate apprehension of the world in perception appears to precede and provide resources for reflection, it, too, is dependent upon the processes of thought, and is therefore subject to the same demand for examination that exists for our consciously articulated ideas, as well as for our implicit ideas. To engage immediately with the world around us in perception is already to be involved in intellectual commitments demanding questioning. The lesson for Theaetetus that coincides with this insight is that he must engage in the process of thinking his ideas through thoroughly, which means to recognize implications not readily apparent to him in his immediate adoption of an idea as his own. Further, to recognize that perception is the domain that manifests our intellectual, as well as our sensory, perspective on the world is to recognize that our thinking and reflective examination will of necessity be one step behind the perceptual resources with which we think. To reflect well on perception, to learn the lesson about the way in which implications of one's ideas about the world permeate one's immediate apprehension of the world, is therefore to recognize that one is not entirely in control of one's perspective on the world. Indeed, recognition of the extent to which the shaping of our perception of the world lies outside of our control brings with it an implicit imperative to participate as actively as possible in the cultivation of our future perception.

I address this theme in my treatment of the analysis of the first definition of knowledge—that knowledge (*epistēmē*) is perception (*aisthēsis*)—in chapters 3 and 4, articulating its implications both for the concept of knowledge and for the educational experience of Theaetetus. In chapter 3, I focus on the articulation, the "delivery," of the idea that knowledge is perception, focusing first on the process of articulation, and, second, on Socrates's initial presentation of an account of perception as the product of the coupling of perceiver and perceptible object. Though perception, on first consideration, appears to consist in the immediate apprehension that precedes and provides the material for thinking, it, too, turns out to be grounded in thinking. In chapter 4, I develop this notion through the discussion centered on Socrates's account of the philosopher. Because thought is a mediating force in how we perceive, we must consider the fact that how we perceive is shaped and conditioned, and must, indeed, actively participate in the shaping and conditioning of our future perceptions. To reflect on the shaping of our perception is, further, to experience the demand that we undergo existential and personal transformation, because it is an experience of the recognition that our understanding is something not entirely our own, but rather something that we have to make our own.

It is with this in mind that I therefore develop not only the theme of the mediation inherent within perception, but also the theme of the personal transformation that Socrates is trying to help initiate in Theaetetus. Specifically, I take the discussion of the first definition of knowledge to be a long lesson for Theaetetus in coming to recognize, first, that his perspective is tethered to a set of implications that might not be evident in the immediate entertainment of given ideas, and second, that, as a consequence of that first lesson, he is ultimately responsible for those implications despite not having yet reflected on them. Learning to think his ideas through—which is to say, to come to understand the actual character and quality of his own thoughts—has the purpose of making Theaetetus (or anyone habituated into such a practice) more readily able to immediately apprehend the world. The model of cultivated perception to be aimed at in this pursuit is presented in the apparent digression concerning the philosopher (172c3–177c7). This set of lessons has the potential to transform Theaetetus's immediate apprehension of the world in the specific sense of inclining him to inquire into the implications of what appears as immediate in his experience, in essence making him experience reality as indicating something beyond what previously appeared to have been immediately apprehended.

3. Knowledge Is a Relational Identity, the Offspring of the Soul's Capacities

The third crucial insight regarding knowledge is the fact that one cannot attribute knowledge to any one particular power human beings have, but must rather understand it as a relational attribute that emerges as something more than the sum of its parts. What emerges, however, in the process of knowing, is imbued with each of the limitations to be found in the individual capacities themselves. Knowledge is something that emerges out of the interrelation of our capacities. Thus, the abstraction of any of the particular powers humans have (to perceive, to opine, or to use rational discourse, for example) will fail to explain adequately what knowledge is. This insight into the nature of knowledge insinuates the need for the fundamental transformation of how we conceive of knowledge, and is the third lesson for Theaetetus.

This third lesson consists in the fact that recognition of the context from which knowledge emerges, and recognition of knowledge as an emergent phenomenon born of the integrated whole of human capacities, involves coming to terms with the various examples of the passive aspect to knowledge I have mentioned in the summaries of the first three chapters: our passivity in relation to memory, our passivity in relation to the accumulated prejudices governing our everyday lives, and our passivity in the relationship between our perceptual apprehension and the more agent-like reflection to which we are capable of subjecting that apprehension. Coming to terms with this passivity requires the reorientation of our assumptions about knowledge, insofar as it must be understood to be rooted in something of which we cannot achieve complete control, but must rather cede the presumption of agency to the shared domain of dialogue.

In chapters 5 and 6, I present these claims by examining the second and third definitions of knowledge, respectively; I treat them as demonstrating two sides of the same point. Specifically, in chapter 5 I argue that the discussion of the second definition—that knowledge is true opinion—illustrates that the abstraction of specific human powers for the purpose of examination independent of their participation in the integrated whole of the human soul has the effect of obscuring their true nature. Socrates and Theaetetus first abstract true opinion from learning and forgetting—which is to say from two of the characteristic activities by which any given opinion comes to be or passes away—and then later, during the presentation of the two images of true opinion (the "wax image" and the "bird cage"), abstract the activity of consciously acquiring or failing to acquire knowledge from the passive receptivity that informed the discussion of perception. In each case opinion is presented in such a way that it fails to reflect accurately the reality in which it actually occurs. This, I argue, provides an implicit critique of the kind of mathematical conception of knowledge that deeply informs Theaetetus's presumptions.

In chapter 6, I subsequently argue that the discussion of the third definition of knowledge illustrates that the only proper way to understand human capacities is to recognize that the integrated, organized whole of those powers generates something larger than the sum of its parts. This argument picks up on the theme of parts and wholes that dominates the latter part of the discussion of the third definition. It is here that we begin to see the need to recognize sufficiently the ontological status of relational identity, that is, to recognize that from the relationship between particular things—which is to say from the organization of things according to their interrelations with others—emerges a whole that is generated from, rather than merely the aggregate of, its parts (i.e., the interrelating things). Specifically, the interrelation of the parts of the soul generates a whole that is related to, and responsive to, the world. This whole that is related to and responsive to the world ought to measure its perceptions, opinions, thoughts and expressions against the manner in which that world imposes itself on that whole. Further, it must do so in a way that uses the (reported) perceptions, opinions, thoughts, and expressions of others as a part of that measure.

The integrated whole of these two definitions of knowledge has the effect of drawing attention to the fact that philosophical inquiry into the nature of knowledge reorients our understanding of what knowledge is. It turns out that what we want to insist knowledge to be is typically some kind of harmony between true opinion and objective external guarantee of that opinion. This proves to be an erroneous approach. The inquiry has the effect of displacing this notion of knowledge in favor of one that takes the form of the gradual cultivation of deeper insight into reality, occasionally resting in the comfort (and dangerously false certainty) of opinion, and always opened onto the uncertain terrain of interpersonal, dialogical scrutiny.

Socrates is educating Theaetetus into the adoption of a more active role in shaping his own way of perceiving the world. This more active role curiously results from giving up the presumption of the possibility of achieving a complete grasp by oneself, while simultaneously encouraging the pursuit as though one could achieve such a grasp, provided that one does so through dialogue with others. Philosophical education from Socrates is at its heart an erotic education, recognizing that one needs to maintain distance from something in order to desire it, while never giving up on the underlying meaning of that desire, which is in some sense to become one with the object. Socrates wants Theaetetus to recognize that the world shows itself to him as something demanding that he try better to know it. He also wants Theaetetus to understand better his own nature as something that is unable to complete the project that the world beckons him to pursue. This latter message is also the one that tells Socrates that he must therefore seek out others with whom to consort in undergoing that, in some sense, incompletable, yet intrinsically desirable, pursuit. To live in accordance to these various demands—to be able to navigate their apparent contradictions—is to live wisely.

CHAPTER 1

Preparing an Introduction to the Question of Knowledge (142a–143c)

> Now the path of investigation must lie from what is more immediately cognizable and clear to us, to what is clearer and more intimately cognizable in its own nature; for it is not the same thing to be directly accessible to our cognition and to be intrinsically intelligible.
>
> —Aristotle, *Physics*, I.1 184a17–19

> What I don't advise is that we remain as we are.
>
> —Plato, *Laches*, 201a7

Introduction

Platonic Beginnings

Plato's *Theaetetus* portrays Socrates initiating Theaetetus into philosophical education. Philosophical education, like all kinds of education, must begin. To think about education requires of us that we also think about both the fact that it begins, and how it begins. To think about education as it is presented in the *Theaetetus*, we must think both about the education that occurs within the drama, and also about the education that we undergo as readers. To think about our own education as readers, we must consider the manner in which the text begins. Introductions within the texts of the Platonic corpus are pregnant with meaning, often conspicuously so; on a first reading, we might have the impression that there is deeper meaning to what is said, but only if we decide to read it in anticipation of the unknown discussion that follows. On subsequent readings, we are invited to begin to interpret in light of what we know will follow. Thus, in subsequent readings, it is suggested to us that we had not been prepared for the introduction when it actually functioned as an introduction. This is one of the characteristics of the beginning of philosophical education: We begin before we are sufficiently equipped to understand what we are beginning to do, and are only in retrospect able to identify the significance of what came before.

It is easy to list examples of conspicuous and provocative openings in the Platonic corpus, about which we can retrospectively identify their significance. In the *Symposium*, Apollodorus, while responding to a question to which we are given no access, relates to an unknown interlocutor his experience of the previous day, in which he had related to Glaucon a story Apollodorus himself had heard from Aristodemus: one night, decades prior, Socrates had engaged in an evening of speeches concerning *erōs*. Thus the story of an evening in which people present speeches concerning desire—a species of longing for what one does not have—is contextualized by rumor and myth, inaccessible to us and made into an object of desire. Similarly, in the *Republic*, Socrates recounts, again, to an unknown interlocutor, his having gone "down to the Piraeus" to say a prayer to the new goddess introduced to Athens. The metaphor of descent is repeated when he famously relates the allegory of the cave, while the theme of new gods reminds us both of the accusation against Socrates in the *Apology* and the suspicion of novelty in his city in speech. Each of these introductions is provocative in that it refers to important themes in the dialogue that follows, and anticipates interpretive decisions that the reader ought to but might not otherwise pursue, and probably will not pursue the first time through.

Each of these particular examples is also provocative—and in the same fashion that the *Theaetetus* is—insofar as each portrays one person reporting a long conversation that either other people or they themselves had had previously. This literary technique denies us access to a contrived, objective standpoint on the conversation, and thus places the accuracy of the reported conversation in the hands of a person—and indeed sometimes more than one person, with each person at a further degree of remove from the original conversation—who has his own motivations and interests. In other words, Plato has provocatively chosen, in each of these dialogues, to place the original event beyond the grasp of certainty, and explicitly within a personal, rather than an impersonal, context. The issue of perspective is thus importantly present in interpreting Plato, and, as we shall discuss below, made especially significant in the *Theaetetus*, whose explicit theme is the question of the nature of knowledge.

Other dialogues open provocatively in ways that correspond differently to the opening of the Theaetetus. The *Gorgias*—a dialogue explicitly concerned with the power and danger of oratory to manipulate public opinion and shape conventional wisdom—begins with Socrates's belligerent interlocutor, Callicles, taunting him with the conventional wisdom concerning bravery and manliness. The *Phaedo* begins with Phaedo being asked whether he had himself been to visit Socrates the day he died. The dialogue that follows, which Phaedo recounts, is partially concerned with whether or not the soul continues, and continues as self-same, after one dies. In each of these dialogues, Plato puts in the mouths of his characters utterances rich with meaning relevant to the themes that are to be realized in what follows, themes that cannot be anticipated in advance of that realization. It is likewise the case with the *Theaetetus*.

The *Theaetetus*, like the *Symposium* and *Phaedo* in particular, begins years later than the conversation it recounts. Like the *Phaedo*, it is initially framed by a conversation outside of Athens, and as characters do in the *Phaedo*, the characters in the *Theaetetus* revive the old conversation in part to revive their memories of the dead (in the case of the *Theaetetus*, the dead are Socrates and Theaetetus).[1] As characters in the *Symposium* did, in the *Theaetetus*, the character Euclides consults Socrates in the refinement of the story of the conversation.

In this chapter, I will carefully attend to the introduction to the *Theaetetus*. Plato begins the *Theaetetus* by preceding and contextualizing the discussion between Socrates, Theodorus, and Theaetetus with a conversation taking place several years later, between Terpsion and Euclides. Inspired by the imminent death of Theaetetus, they decide to have read to them by a slave the transcribed version of a conversation about the nature of knowledge Theaetetus had had with Socrates before Socrates's own death. In providing the context for that discussion, the introduction gathers together the themes of beginning, the continuity of character, death, reflection, memory, and interpretation, suggesting to the attentive reader their relevance to the question of the nature of knowledge.[2]

We must begin by considering the question of beginning, as we are invited to do by the text itself. We will do so by reflecting on the activity of learning. Specifically, we will begin by discussing in general terms why it is that, in considering a given topic, we find it important to say or write words of preparation. At the very least, this phenomenon draws attention to something that occurs regardless of our preparation. In order to come to know, it must begin. Knowing is temporal; it emerged, is emerging, or will emerge. Beginnings are therefore always essential to the process of knowing. Let us briefly consider beginnings generally, before ourselves beginning to examine the opening moments of the dialogue.

The Epistemological Significance of the Problem of Beginning

An introduction sets up the context of what is to be discussed. In crafting an introduction, one typically aims, not to do the work to be accomplished in the discussion that follows, but to prepare the reader in some way. This preparation can take the form of clearly delineating the author's aims, such that the reader is not forced to concern herself with the aims of the author during the discussion itself. For example, in a particularly difficult text, it might be undesirable for the reader not to know in advance the purpose of the discussion. If she is confused in her reading, she might disproportionately emphasize the salience of passages she understood at the expense of more difficult ones. The preparation need not be so prosaic, however. An introduction can serve the more seductive purpose of arousing the reader's curiosity, eliciting in her the desire to turn with anticipation to the material that follows. In this case, clarity might be precisely what is not aimed at, because the confused reader will more eagerly turn to the text for answers. An introduction might also serve a more explicitly rhetorical purpose. Perhaps the text allows for a variety of interpretations, and the author of the introduction (who need not have been the author of the text the reader is being prepared for) aims at persuading the reader to adopt his particular interpretation.[3] There are surely other specific purposes for an introduction as well. In each case, however, we might ask ourselves the following question: what am I being prepared for?

To ask this question of oneself, though, during one's first encounter with the introduction is to ask someone not properly qualified to answer. Insofar as it is preparing something one has not read, one cannot answer it except by continuing to read. One can answer this question more profitably only by returning to it and reading in a way that anticipates what one already knows will follow. In returning, however, one is no longer engaging with the introduction as a beginning, as something that precedes an unknown text that follows. The productive analysis of an introduction's effectiveness as a beginning can only occur when it no longer performs its function. The beginning, as an experience of something preceding and preparing what follows cannot be analyzed from within, but only from an artificial standpoint.

What has been extracted from this opening passage cannot be derived from an initial reading. While in a straightforward sense, this passage is the beginning of the dialogue, and is indeed an introduction insofar as it is, from a narrative standpoint, independent of the conversation that follows from it, in another sense it is not the beginning. In fact, there is no beginning; at least not in the sense of something that remains as a beginning. On the contrary, from the standpoint of what is available for us to reflect upon, the beginning exists only as the obscure past perspective that existed for the purpose of producing our current standpoint, which latter standpoint has the character of having permanently discarded that beginning. Thus, while I began with the claim that all education has to begin, and that we are witnessing the beginning of Theaetetus's philosophical education, it now turns out, retrospectively, to be the case that there is no beginning to whose experiential standpoint we can return; it can only be identified as a beginning when framed by what follows from it, and what follows cannot be anticipated with certainty during the process of beginning.

I will argue in this chapter that the "beginning" of the *Theaetetus* introduces the reader to the most important themes of the text—including the theme of introduction—in an introduction whose significance cannot be understood without having both read the text as a whole already, and having thought about the explicit theme independently. The introductory scene of the *Theaetetus*, in fact, has a dual function. On a first reading, in which the reader is not adequately situated to be consciously prepared for the complicated discussion of the nature of knowledge that follows, the introductory scene gives almost nothing by way of preparation, while simultaneously providing what seems to be an interesting yet incidental, straightforward dramatic context for our access to the dialogue. It performs the role of setting the scene. On subsequent readings, however, this scene provides the reader with themes that, should she be attentive, will reorient her reading significantly. The introduction functions most effectively—that is, reveals that it is dealing with the puzzles surrounding the problem of knowledge and the education of the soul—when it is no longer introducing. What at first appeared immediately accessible, only after the fact emerged as having not been fully accessed to begin with.[4] Before performing a serious analysis of the introductory dialogue between Euclides and Terpsion, however, let us briefly introduce ourselves to it in greater detail by plotting the drama it depicts.

The *Theaetetus* begins with a short preface which takes place either in 391, between 390–387 or in 369 B.C.E, which is to say that it takes place many years after the death of Socrates.[5] It dramatizes a conversation between Euclides and Terpsion, two former students or disciples of Socrates. Euclides is independently known either to have initiated or to have been instrumental in initiating what is called the Megarian school, a philosophical school inspired by Socrates, yet possessed of tenets either original to Euclides or at least certainly independent of what we would call explicitly "Socratic" philosophy.[6] The conversation appears to open with Euclides responding to something said by Terpsion, seemingly that Terpsion had been searching for him, or simply that Terpsion had returned to (or arrived in) Megara. Euclides explains his (perhaps unusual) absence from the marketplace where Terpsion had (we think) been looking for him, and informs Terpsion that he had been on his way toward the harbor when he saw that Theaetetus was being brought back to Megara on the verge of death, from either wounds or dysentery or both. They discuss what fine character Theaetetus had, how Socrates had presciently identified what fine character he would eventually come to have, and how Socrates had done so shortly before his own death. Euclides then mentions that he had coincidentally documented a conversation between Socrates and Theaetetus shortly before Socrates died, and that it would be well worth reading. After briefly discussing Euclides's editorial decisions in creating the textual reproduction of the dialogue, they decide to have a slave read it to them, at which point our perspective is permanently shifted from them to the dialogue documented by Euclides. The remainder of the dialogue, in others words, is depicted as having been written by Euclides.[7]

Having plotted the scene, let us now examine it more deeply, from the beginning.

1. The Inadequate Starting Point, or Starting Points as Inadequacy (142a1)

The first sentence of the *Theaetetus* refuses to exploit the preparatory advantages of introduction. Plato has the reader arrive too late to hear the beginning of the conversation between Euclides and Terpsion: "Just now, Terpsion, or a long time ago from the country?"[8] Though it is the first sentence, it reads unmistakably as though following an unmentioned previous utterance. Plato could just as easily have chosen to begin at the start of the conversation. Why force the reader to read further into the text before learning what was meant? In other words, why force the reader to do what introductory remarks would typically avoid, namely, having the reader's attention directed at alleviating confusion rather than at what the argument or narrative is addressing? While the first reading momentarily creates that confusion, we are invited, on a subsequent reading, to think about what we do intuitively as readers, and, upon reflection, what this intuitive behavior means.

Anyone who reads these lines cannot help reading into them that there were previous words spoken by someone else (who turns out to be Terpsion). We also cannot help having a general notion of what those remarks concerned. More striking still, we cannot keep ourselves from presuming those opening remarks, despite neither being able to, nor needing to, provide content to them with any certainty. We are able to read these first written words and to impose the meaning of the absent ones preceding them, without needing to have the concrete, particular words implied by the meaning of the absent previous remark. The tacitly presumed meaning is sufficient for us to continue. We do not require complete knowledge of what has been said to be capable of understanding—in a loose, general, though functionally adequate sense—Euclides's response. Moreover, we are denied such complete knowledge.

While our ability to comprehend quite well without the absolute presence of the content of the conversation is quite striking upon reflection, it would be just as easy to be compelled to take a skeptical stance as it would be to be impressed by the seemingly natural human ingenuity in the face of inadequate information. In other words, the apparent and de facto success of this interpolation of meaning (i.e., the ability to understand both that Terpsion began the conversation with remarks we do not have access to, and to understand in a functionally adequate sense the content of those remark), perhaps ought equally to compel us to insist that we do not, and cannot, know what was said, and cannot therefore know what the conversation is about. From this skeptical standpoint, it would seem that we are burdened with the need to use a range of strategies—all insufficiently grounded, from a strictly skeptical standpoint—to derive any meaning whatsoever. We must retain several as yet unidentified objects of thought, while we read ahead in anticipation that those objects will eventually be identified. We are forced to do this if we wish to access the material in what is in fact only an inadequate sense. It is these strategies that make possible what was described in the previous paragraph, namely, the tendency to interpolate meaning that had not been made explicit, to be unproblematically natural. If we fixate on those strategies, we are forced into a skeptical position that chooses to ignore the functionality of our worldly operations.

Let us examine specifically some of what is implicitly required for us to understand the opening line. Identifying what we impose on the experience of reading, we will be able to explain why we function successfully in the world, and why, in truth, the skeptical standpoint too strictly ignores what Aristotle—in the epigraph to this chapter—calls the "immediately cognizable." To understand the opening line—"Just now, Terpsion, or a long time ago in the country"—we must (1) assume something has occurred at some time whose temporal situation (i.e., now or long ago) is being questioned by Euclides; (2) assume something whose spatial location depends in some way upon how it is to be temporally situated; (3) assume that there is a reason why the spatial and temporal locations of the as-yet-unknown entity are relevant to Euclides; (4) seek in the text that follows answers to the question "of what nature is this "something?" While we are forced by these opening lines to retain contentless assumptions of "sometime" "someplace," and "something"—which essentially function as questions we ask of the text—in this particular case, we should also note other concepts-as-questions we must retain regardless of how the dialogue has begun. We must also ask (5) who these people named Euclides and Terpsion are; (6) what their relationship to each other might be; and (7) what their relevance to the project of the author, Plato, is. We do not, of course, typically *consciously* negotiate such a variety of questions as we read that first sentence. We certainly do not consciously do so our first time reading it (which is to say the time when these questions are most relevant to our epistemic predicament). Nonetheless, in order for that first sentence to compel us to follow through with the ensuing discussion these issues must be implicitly understood as having been announced by that first sentence, and must be experienced as compelling our interest. All of these issues must emerge as questions for us, which, we either hope or assume, will be answered. Further, in some sense at least, we have to care that answers be provided by what follows. This means that, for us to be able to read at all, and more generally to engage with our world, we must relate to these objects questioningly, as interested students.

Plato's dialogue is crafted for students. It is important that we remember that Plato wrote the opening of the dialogue in this way. Let us briefly note what is demonstrated in this opening: in rereading, and in knowing that the dialogue will concern knowledge, we can reflect upon our—typically unconscious–tendency to impose on what is given to us information that it did not provide, and we can also reflect upon the fact that that tendency is often essential to our ability to continue reading. This revelation, however, is not merely relevant to situations in which a written work begins representing a conversation after its implied start, or even more generally to situations in which relevant information is conspicuously excluded by the author of a text. Indeed, were the dialogue to have begun with an ostensibly clear statement of all relevant information, the same insight that we impose information to fill in epistemic gaps would have applied; the only difference would have been that our imposition of information, and our tentative faith that information would be filled in, would not have been as conspicuously available for us to notice. We are being afforded the opportunity—again, upon a reflective rereading of the text—to attend to something we always do. Had we begun the dialogue with a pretense of certainty—for example, had the dialogue begun at the beginning of the conversation, creating an artificial beginning to the fictional world presented to us—the illusion would have been created that all information relevant to our understanding of the dramatic context was present and accounted for. It would have been as though whatever occurred prior to that moment within the drama never existed, and thus nothing relevant to our formulation of judgments was absent.

The illusion that one has all necessary information is the result of disengaged and unconscious reading. As I have already implied, the reader that makes these discoveries about the text must actively extract them for herself; Plato does not make it explicit, because Plato does not speak through his own voice. The reader must extract these insights and must do so while anticipating to some degree the themes of the dialogue. She must be thoughtful, and somewhat familiar with the text. None of these insights is transmitted to the reader by force of necessity or by direct transmission of the explicit meaning of words. The *Theaetetus*, like so many other Platonic texts, does not dissemble, but nonetheless rewards active reading. Thus, not only does the engagement with a text depend upon a reader who imposes her anticipatory interpretive questions on what follows, but, by virtue of this fact, learning what the dialogue has to offer depends upon the extent of active engagement by the reader. More specifically, in order for the reader to understand what is being shown to her by beginning the dialogue in mid-conversation, she must be attuned to the themes that will be under discussion in what follows; she must therefore have read it before.

From prior reading, we know that the discussion between Socrates and Theaetetus was unable to fix on a satisfactory definition of knowledge; the question of the nature of knowledge was elusive to Theaetetus in his first attempt. We—as readers rereading—note that the withholding of information here, the fact that Plato initiated us into a conversation about the nature of knowledge having from the start deprived us of sufficient information for us to have precise knowledge of what was happening, suggests that we should assume that this is connected to the question of knowledge itself. It is in the nature of our experience to be presented with objects whose meaning was being demonstrated before our arrival, and the experience of which meaning always arrives after the demonstration has already begun.

What I have described here about the process of reading the opening of the dialogue applies generally to our experience of the world. In particular, it is surely the case that we can continue to live as though the information given to us in our immediate understanding is adequate, and as a result can take for granted and tacitly consent to presumptions we have not consciously evaluated. In life, the analogue to rereading consists in reflection on the information provided by the world, and what we illicitly derive from that information. Reflection upon our derivations ends up with the result that we ourselves become the object of reflection, just as we as readers become the object in critical rereading of the dialogues. We will discuss this particular issue of self-reflection in chapter 2, and will find that this activity of self-reflection is what Socrates is attempting to initiate in his "midwifery."

One final note regarding this opening sentence: the characters in the dialogue speak with one another "naturally," which is to say without explicit awareness of, and thus regard for the needs of, a third party. They do not appear to provide information for our benefit—providing, for example, to accommodate our late arrival—but rather only for each other's benefit. We have to consider what is happening in the world of the characters Euclides and Terpsion (and of course later Socrates, Theodorus, and Theaetetus), which is to say that we have to consider them within the framework in which they operate, but we must also consider them as objects of thought in a work being crafted for the reader. The fact is that, despite Plato's having written dialogue intended to appear as though the people dramatized as speaking it are doing so without regard for a third party, the dialogue is precisely for a third party. This conversation meant to appear as though not having been crafted for us, was crafted for us; further, it was crafted for us to appear as though its having been crafted for us was intended to appear as not having been crafted for us. It was crafted to compel us to consider its having been crafted. Our need to consider its having been crafted requires us also to consider the theme of education on two distinct orders that I have previously mentioned. First, we must consider Socrates's methods in educating Theaetetus philosophically. Second, we must consider also Socrates's methods in relation to the methods of Plato's philosophical education of his readers. We are forced to relate to the dialogue as reality and as fiction for our own education. This, too, will turn out to be relevant to the nature of knowledge.

2. Knowing Our Way to Death (142a9–b1, 142c6)

Once we catch up with the content of that opening remark, we learn that Terpsion has been looking for Euclides. We never learn why, perhaps because of the significance of the news Euclides brings. Euclides had been down at the harbor, and had seen that Theaetetus was on the verge of death, having contracted dysentery, and having suffered severe battle wounds. We do not know yet, but will soon find out, that the dialogue between Socrates and Theaetetus which Euclides has documented took place days or weeks prior to Socrates's death. It is only later that we learn that it takes place on the day that Socrates first meets the charges against him that will lead to his death, as depicted in the *Euthyphro*, *Apology*, *Crito*, and *Phaedo*. The *Theaetetus*—the main content of which we soon find out is to be understood as having been written by Euclides—is thus between two people—that is, Socrates and Theaetetus—on the verge of death, and whose deaths are separated by years and perhaps decades. It is only because of the contrivance of the discussion between Euclides and Terpsion that the conversation depicted implies the death of its two primary interlocutors; we would not otherwise know this conversation to be an epitaph to the dead, just as the participants themselves did not. Of course, any dialogue depicted between actual human beings is necessarily between dead people if we wait long enough before reading it. These two dead people died at very different times under very different circumstances. The text, however, contrives it so that the fact of their respective deaths coincide, juxtaposing the specter of death with the discussion of the nature of knowledge.[9] Euclides has inadvertently produced an epitaph to the lives of Theaetetus and Socrates, and we, the readers, inherit and perpetuate the memory of their lives in studying them.

The relevance of death to the question of knowledge presents itself here: the actual knowledge that both Socrates and Theaetetus had is lost to us.[10] The remnants of their knowledge come to us as an inheritance, but in the deeply mediated form of Euclides's epitaph. In the dialogue, both Theaetetus and Socrates are on the verge of death, Theaetetus in the preface, and Socrates in the dialogue proper. Why might it be important for us to consider the approach of death in performing an inquiry into the nature of knowledge? It is certain that, at the time when Euclides and Terpsion sit down and have the slave read Euclides's book, Theaetetus is at that moment afforded the opportunity to reflect on the imminence of his own death, to think about the time when he no longer will be. Perhaps as he talks to Theaetetus weeks before his own death, Socrates, too, is thinking about that possibility. Each faces an event that neither of them—nor any other person—knows. If there is anything mature human beings have the very real potential to fully grasp, it is that we face an event about which we cannot know. If there is knowledge of any kind, it is of our ignorance of death. We are invited, by this opening juxtaposition, to reflect on that most intimate moment about which we cannot know, but about our ignorance of which we can.

All of our pursuits, including knowledge, are circumscribed by (among other things) time. One of the agents of that circumscription is death. It appears that Socrates forged this relationship to Theaetetus because he cares about the young Athenians, because he wants to know who among them will "prove good and able" (143d6). We know, though, that Socrates will not be given adequate time either to develop that relationship or to find out that Theaetetus did indeed prove good and able, though not in philosophy, as he might have hoped. This particular instance of his life's work of eliciting ideas from people, and particularly from the young, will not reach mature development. He could neither control nor anticipate the events that precipitated his death, and thus the interruption of his life's work.

The consideration of the question of knowledge is necessarily connected to the consideration of the nature of human life, of death, and of the question of the education of the soul. To come to know is to be educated. In the broadest sense, human beings can never extricate themselves from their education. We are always in the process of coming to know; that process of coming to know is the consistency, the context, of life. The *Theaetetus*, a dialogue about the nature of knowledge, is therefore also a dialogue about the nature of human life, about the nature of education, about a lifetime, and about death. As a temporal phenomenon, knowledge is an activity. Knowledge is, when considered from the experiential standpoint, participial. We are know*ing*; we *are* knowingly, and are knowingly only temporally and temporarily.

The question of knowledge is, from this standpoint the question of one's life's work, of one's lifetime. It is the question of development, of cultivation, of coming to be and of passing away. The question of knowledge is the question of something that I in some sense have, but which, in so far as I will cease to be, I do not and cannot permanently retain. If it is true that we at some point have knowledge, it is also true that our knowledge emerges, which is to say that whatever knowledge I possess I once did not possess. However, knowledge is not *simply* at one time absent and then at another time present. Rather, knowledge takes shape, develops in time, over time. Our temporality is in fact demonstrated in the experience of coming to know something, and that it takes time to know something demonstrates our finitude.

3. Knowing: The Continuity of Character (142b6–d4)

When Euclides announces to Terpsion that Theaetetus is on the verge of death, first Terpsion, and then Euclides, is compelled to reflect on the quality of Theaetetus's life, and on the quality of his character. Theaetetus is presented as having been both "beautiful and good," and having conducted himself bravely in battle (142b7–8). Indeed, Terpsion points out that there is, in a sense, nothing remarkable about the fact that Theaetetus conducted himself bravely in battle, but rather that it would have been remarkable had he behaved otherwise.[11] After a brief discussion of Theaetetus's desire to return home after battle, Euclides remembers how Socrates had prophetically spoken highly of him years earlier. Within a few lines, our attention is drawn to the continuity of Theaetetus's character, first, from Terpsion—that it is no surprise that Theaetetus's excellence displays itself in action—and second, from Euclides—that it is surprising that its continuity would be demonstrated over such a long period of time. Again, Terpsion notices that a person will usually, and unsurprisingly, behave in ways that are expected of them (presumably by people with keen insight into a person's character), or at least that the excellent Theaetetus did so. Conversely, Euclides registers surprise at the very same phenomenon, when it is stretched out over the span of time between the discussion with Socrates and Theatetus's death. Euclides is impressed by the ability of Socrates to note that Theaetetus was to become someone of considerable virtue; Terpsion is unimpressed by the fact that Theaetetus displayed great virtue because his character indicated he would.

Of course, what differentiates these two instances is time, which is to say the maturity of the development of Theaetetus's character. That an adult would behave in continuity with his or her character is nothing remarkable, while for Socrates to predict that a young and impressionable man of perhaps eighteen years would grow up and realize the potential he had exhibited is remarkable. This is so because the shape one's character typically takes is governed to a great extent by one's actions. The young have so much still to develop, while the mature adult has already developed so much. As was said already, the first words recorded by Euclides in his documentation of the dialogue between Socrates and Theaetetus consist in Socrates's remark that he cares most about the young men of Athens, and that he likes to spend his time finding teachers around whom the young congregate, finding the most remarkable among them, and befriending them (143d1–9). He does so because he cares about the young of his city, and wants to participate in the care for their souls.

Here, in the introduction, we are given clues regarding why the care for the souls of the young might be so important to Socrates. We are also given clues regarding why it might be so important to the consideration of the nature of knowledge. Let us consider these in turn.

In youth, character is a far less settled issue. The kind of person one will become consists in a set of possibilities. To speak of a young person's character—to speak in general about how a young person will behave—is always to speculate, because it is by no means certain what kind of adult that young person will become. Such speculation, however, is not unwarranted; when we identify patterns of behavior in someone, this observation lends itself to the prediction of that person's likely future behavior, which is appropriate in light of our observation of the characteristics of youth. When we talk about what kind of person someone is, we typically mean by this a mixture of the kinds of actions that person has undertaken in the past and the kinds of actions we imagine they are likely to undertake in the future. Put differently, the meaning implicit in what we call "character" is the momentum of that person's future possibilities. To be this or that kind of person, to have this or that kind of character, is to be a person who will act in this or that way. To have character—which is, in a certain sense, to say "to be a person"—is to have an identifiable set of likely future actions. When we say, "she is an honest person," what we mean by that is that her character has the kind of momentum that will drive her into the unknown and unknowable future in such a way that her actions typically will be honest. To be a person, to have character, is to have the kind of momentum that drives toward a given set of actions, and in a way potentially recognizable by others.[12]

There is much more to be said about the mechanisms at work in creating and cultivating this momentum, as well as what it means to include the essentially human variable of consciousness of one's own character, and this will be discussed at length over the course of the consideration of education. Indeed, in chapter 2, we will discuss in detail why certain stages of the development of character are more appropriate for philosophical education than others. For now, however, let it suffice to say that what characterizes youth is that it is a state in which momentum has begun to build, but neither to the same extent, nor with the same force that it has in mature adulthood. To be young involves being more susceptible to shifts in momentum. Character in youth remains unsettled.

By contrast, adulthood is marked by the increase in momentum, the predictability of actions, and a more sharply defined character. We can say with more confidence about an adult that she or he will behave in this or that way. Should an adult deviate from predictability, we are surprised. Indeed, we are perhaps more likely to call into question the merit of our original assessment of their character than to presume that the person has changed. We might say, for example, "I did not know her as well as I thought." Euclides and Terpsion, it seems, know Theaetetus, and it would therefore be utterly surprising for Euclides to report to Terpsion that Theaetetus had cowered in the face of the enemy on the battlefield, because it would be, as we say in English, "out of character."

That mature character sets parameters of expected actions for adulthood is worth bearing in mind, both as an important means of fostering harmonious and fluid social (as well as economic, political, and interpersonal) activity, and as demonstrated in our prima facie and typical attitude toward education, that is, that it is something undergone in youth, and that it is for the purpose of shaping kinds of people fulfilling kinds of roles in society. Consider the obvious fact that we populate our essential vocations in social and political life primarily, indeed almost exclusively, with adults. Political life depends to a very large extent upon the reliability of character, and the possibility of reliance upon others depends on the phenomenon of continuity in the fully developed soul. We are selective about the people who work for us and who work with us, as well as the people with whom we keep company. The preferences we have in our strictly instrumental political interactions (i.e., our dealings with people performing social and political institutional roles) typically preclude people in childhood or youth. While there are surely roles in society granted to young people, and while, indeed, to be young in part involves the increasing insistence to be taken seriously and recognized as a reliable actor, the granting of this recognition is typically accompanied with reticence. In comparison to adults, we typically feel less certain that the youth or adolescent will act in the way that her character indicates she will. Yet she will at some point be recognized in the continuity of her character, and will be relied upon by others to perform a narrow or wide range of roles in the various domains of the adult sphere. Were she not able to be relied upon—were it the case that the soul did not have the nature of building the momentum of recognizable and generally predictable behavior—the domains of the adult sphere would not be possible. The adult world—and human society as we know it—would be impossible without the fact that the soul shapes into something of continuity, that is, without character.

These facts about the nature of the human soul indicate the privileges and responsibilities that necessarily accompany the ushering in of adulthood. Adults have the responsibility to participate in the web of activities that are of primary importance to the shaping of human culture, technology, knowledge, and so on. But these attributes of adulthood are typically also confining. To be relied upon is also to be confined to a given set of expectations; not only is the adult subjected to the responsibilities that accompany being relied upon; she is also subjected to the identification of her character and to the momentum of that identification. She is expected to behave in accordance with her character. Terpsion indicates that it would have been surprising had Theaetetus not acted bravely on the battlefield. Whenever Theaetetus goes out to battle, others expect of him acts of military excellence and, crucially, organize their behavior around that expectation.

The fact that we generally organize our behavior toward adults around the expectation that they will behave according to their character, and that we do not do so to the same degree around the young, has serious consequences for how we behave toward young people, in contrast to how we behave around adults. Young people are greater sites of possibility than adults. Therefore, in addition to the apprehension the adult world has in bestowing responsibility on the young, there is also a sense of excitement. Young people may or may not live up to the expectations we have of them, but they might also exceed those expectations. Indeed, they might—and many in fact do—transform the very adult world into which we initiate them. This means, on the one hand, that young people threaten the very fabric of the adult world by not yet being predictable members of it, but, on the other hand, that they can much more readily be relied upon than fellow adult members of social life for the transformation of the worst, most unjust aspects of that world. This fact about the structure of character is surely not lost on Socrates. He cares most of all about those who show great ability because he cares most about Athens. They will be the vehicle of transformation, and it is by no means certain whether or not they will transform it for the better.

It is extraordinarily important that we develop an understanding of the nature of Socrates's interest in the young, and in youth in general, if we are to understand his pedagogical methods. It appears that Socrates embraces the revolutionary potential of youth. It seems that he does not want to contain it, which is to say, to force youth to conform to the existing framework of Athenian society. Socrates arguably *shared* the revolutionary spirit of youth. However, his interest in the young ought not to be understood as a wholesale embrace of revolution for its own sake. It is clear that Socrates had ideas both about how to shape youth and about the danger of youth. We will have the chance to talk about this at much greater length in the following chapter.

For now, let it suffice to mention that Socrates recognizes that the nature of character is relevant to the political domain. The structure of the human soul and the phenomenon of the continuity of character oblige us to attend to education, because education will inform the way that our experiences of the world take shape. The claims that Socrates makes in initiating the conversation with Theodorus (not to mention the conspicuous difference between his way of relating to the much older Theodorus and his way of relating to the younger Theaetetus) indicate that he has a keen awareness of this importance. It indicates that he recognizes that excellence of character in youth is a valuable but fragile thing, requiring thoughtful attention.

Finally, it should be noted that yet another way in which knowledge is circumscribed is by character. Knowledge emerges from the kind of person one has become. Mathematical knowledge, for example, is manifested and deployed differently in the obtuse geometer Theodorus, the warrior Theaetetus, and the lover of wisdom Socrates. Plato produced the complex and sophisticated epistemological arguments of this dialogue amid the very messy terrain of the personal dynamics between these three very distinct characters. We will see later that this helps illustrate the ultimately subordinate importance of the question of knowledge to the cultivation of wisdom, and to the education of character.

4. Knowledge, Memory, and Recollection (142c2–5, 142d4–143a9)

Thus far, we have accumulated three of the most essential aspects of the nature of human life, in our discussion of the interpretive framework of the dialogue. (1) We begin with a constitution that inclines us, first, toward comprehension of its world, and second, toward questioning of that comprehension. This is the structure that makes possible the activity of learning. (2) We are directed toward a death that we cannot know, but about our ignorance of which we can have concrete knowledge. (3) We develop in such a way that our actions become consistently identifiable as a reflection of our identity, and we call this our character. An additional dimension of human life that makes those I have mentioned possible is memory; it plays a central role in the opening of the dialogue, and in a way that highlights its relevance to the process of education, as well as revealing a passive dimension at the heart of education.

We have seen that, during his discussion with Terpsion, Euclides is reminded of Socrates's prophetic observation that, should Theaetetus reach maturity, he would achieve renown, and that Socrates expressed great admiration for him (142c4–8). He is reminded of this immediately after Terpsion's remark that Theaetetus was a great man, and therefore a difficult man to lose. Euclides's recollection appears, in other words, to have been compelled by events in the conversation. The fact that Theaetetus is dying, coupled with remarks regarding his character, seems to have had the productive force to draw from Euclides the recollection of an experience from many years before. The contingent circumstances of the conversation draw from Euclides the recollection of his own past experience. It seems as though Euclides somehow, in some way, retains these past experiences, and is not exactly in control of when and how they are expressed. How does past experience emerge from the reservoir of the soul that we call memory? Looking ahead to our main topic of education, if indeed the education of the soul is of such importance, how is it possible if memory lies (even only to some extent) outside of our conscious control?

The phenomenon of recollection implies that the only domain within which knowledge occurs is one not fully within our control. Euclides, having performed the labor of documenting the conversation between Socrates and Theaetetus, based on Socrates's account, possesses that experience somehow available in reserve, awaiting whatever configuration of events that would trigger its discharge into his conscious awareness.[13] Was it the doubtlessly labor-intensive activity of documenting the conversation that etched it into Euclides's reserve of memories, or was it simply by virtue of having had the experience that it will always be available for recollection? It would be easy to assume that the more intense experiences we have are somehow—but how?—more readily on reserve for our recall. However, regardless of the mechanism by which a hierarchy of recollections functions, whether or not there is an order to the kinds of experiences that can be recalled, Euclides's conscious decision-making cannot be solely responsible for remembering. Contingent circumstances beyond his control play a central, active role in the recall of those significant experiences. In this case, were it not for Theaetetus's imminent death and for the contingencies of Euclides's conversation with Terpsion, that documented conversation between Socrates and Theaetetus would have remained forgotten in Euclides's home. Having the document on hold for potential future reading is insufficient (though necessary) for provoking those future readings.

Before drawing out the implications of this lack of control at the heart of memory, let us consider the very real potential for conscious agency in remembering, particularly, the document itself that Euclides wrote. Why would anyone write such a thing? We know of Euclides that he was in some sense connected to Socrates, and was influenced to a considerable degree by Socrates's thinking.[14] It was presumably important to Euclides to hear what his great teacher had to say about important philosophical issues. This is something that Euclides shares with serious students of any kind. In our time, students often record lectures and conversations of their best teachers. The significant difference for Euclides is that his recording device requires more time and effort, and in this particular case—in which Euclides was not present for the conversation—required the testimony of the teacher himself.

If we speculate that Euclides was motivated by the desire to have more or less permanent access to the thoughts of his teacher concerning the question of knowledge, this slightly alters our claim regarding the phenomenon of recollection in this particular case: Euclides may not have had control over the contingencies of conversation that compelled him to remember; he did, however, prepare himself, many years beforehand, with important conditions making this recall possible. Euclides was a good student who took thorough notes. To take notes, to record words from conversations of interest is, among other things, to prepare oneself for the opportunity to recall those thoughts in the indeterminate future. To take notes is also implicitly to anticipate that those ideas will be relevant to the indeterminate future. Indeed, taking notes *imposes* the relevance of those ideas on an indeterminate future. We record in order to play a role in determining that future. Euclides knew that Socrates had ideas worthwhile not only for his immediate edification, but also potentially for activities and engagements he did not yet know. He, in an important sense, decided to make the ghost of Socrates haunt him after Socrates's death.

We should note that the structure of this activity—that is, taking notes because of anticipated interest—bears an important resemblance to the activity we readers perform when we first encounter Euclides's first line of the dialogue: we cannot know for certain that the ideas we are in the midst of retaining are going to find a satisfactory future use; we nonetheless hold onto them because we anticipate that they will be a guiding force at some future time.

The themes of memory, recollection, and anticipation are thus intimately connected to the nature of beginning. We begin not with a complete set of information to be discharged into the reality of experience, but rather with sensations and thoughts that are gathered and selectively retained as resources to be deployed in an indefinite and indeterminate future. That future is further constituted by contingencies that participate intimately in the compulsion of recall. Euclides had, nine years prior, seen the opportunity to engage with Socrates in an activity that would facilitate his ability to recall some important insights and stimulating conversation in an as yet undisclosed future. It is, in part, because he felt so compelled that the opportunity to sit with Terpsion while the slave reads the dialogue comes to realization for us (if, of course, we place ourselves within the narrative context). It is also, however, because of the convergence of circumstances—Theaetetus dying, Terpsion looking for him, Terpsion reflecting admiringly on Theaetetus's character, and so on—that that labor found this moment as a realization of its purpose.

Memory—called by Socrates "the mother of the muses"[15] (191d3–4)—is made possible in part by the tacit prescription of potential, unanticipated future significance in the preparatory activity of documenting. It was not the desire for knowledge alone that motivated Euclides to hold on to Socrates's fascinating conversation, but rather the desire to impose on himself a future consisting in part in the recall of Socrates's thought, a future in which those thoughts would mix well—it is hoped—with the unknown. We do not therefore control the discharge of memory—we cannot *make* ourselves remember things without contingent circumstances calling on us to remember; nor can we know what the moment we hope to retain will mean to future experiences. We do, however, as do our educators, have a role to play in the preparation of memories, thereby creating some of the material conditions with which the future will take shape.

5. Representation, Interpretation, and Reliability (143b6–c8)

Immediately after revealing that he had recorded a conversation between Socrates and Theaetetus just before Socrates died, Euclides begins to tell us some of what was involved in the documenting. The method of documentation, we shall see, shifts our attention from the phenomenon of memory, to that of interpretation, from which neither memory, nor the three previous attributes of the soul discussed above, nor anything concerned with knowledge, can be extracted. First, we find out that Socrates narrated the conversation to him when Euclides visited Athens. The discussion was, according to Euclides, "well worth hearing." Having had the conversation advertised to him, Terpsion asks Euclides if he would be willing to recite it. Euclides notes that he would not be able to recall it from memory. It was in part as a result of the difficulty of remembering an entire conversation that Euclides had compelled by his interest in the discussion to write down "reminders" when he returned home (143a2). Later at his "leisure," Euclides took more extensive notes to fill in the gaps (143a3). He did this last part from memory. Euclides then, "as often as [he] returned to Athens" from Megara, asked Socrates questions concerning the conversation (143a4). After doing this "repeatedly," Euclides had finally cobbled together a version of the conversation, so that "pretty nearly the entire speech" had been written by Euclides (143a4–7). We should note thus far that the dialogue we are about to hear represented depends on Euclides having had a kind of friendship with Socrates, on his memory, on his having had considerable leisure, on the rigor of his note-taking, and on him having been satisfied at some point short of having documented the entire speech.[16]

Before Euclides completes his account of this process by which he produced the dialogue, Terpsion points out that he had remembered Euclides talking about the written dialogue before, but that he had never been compelled to ask Euclides to show it to him until now. He then urges Euclides to take him to the document to show it to him, so that he can hear it read, because he is tired. When it turns out that Euclides too is tired, Terpsion agrees that they ought to sit and listen to it read by the slave boy.[17]

At this point, the events in the drama between Euclides and Terpsion appear to be edited. Immediately following the agreement between them, Euclides says "Here's the book" (143b5). It had been indicated that they were going to Euclides's home, and now it appears that not only are they already inside Euclides's home, but he has already retrieved or had someone else retrieve the book. Plato has not only chosen to neglect to dramatize the walk to the house and the search for the book, either through expository dialogue or through narrative interpolation; he has also chosen to draw the reader's attention to this fact. We have already been informed that the dialogue we are about to read has been filtered through several layers of reliance on memory, perhaps as well as Euclides's own selective interest in the conversation. Why is *this* document, the one between Euclides and Terpsion, the one whose ostensibly omniscient author remains unknown—in contrast to the dialogue that follows, whose (fictional) author is Euclides—displaying evidence of editorial artifice? We are presented with a reminder that we cannot legitimately rely upon this as a transparent representation of a conversation between two people.

Once they arrive at his home, Euclides explains yet another aspect of the process of crafting the dialogue that they are about to hear. After having taken perhaps judicious notes of Socrates's account of his conversation, and after having sought out Socrates for verification so that he had "pretty nearly" the whole conversation written down (143a6), Euclides decided to remove the narration and to present the dialogue in the form of direct speech.[18] He did so, he says, "in order that the narration between the speeches might not cause trouble in the writing" (143b9–c1). It is difficult to understand what Euclides means by this.[19] What sort of difficulty would it cause to include the narration? Is it simply a matter of quantity of words? Is it because the inclusion of the narrator's observations remembered by Socrates (or by Euclides in his original notes) draw attention to the fact that they offer only a partial account of who has spoken? In other words, is Plato drawing our attention to the fact that Euclides conceals those narrative elements which would draw attention to the fact that not all narrative elements were documented? Regardless of the unclear motivations Euclides had,[20] we are, by the end of this introduction, highly conscious of the activity of documentary writing—what it includes and what it excludes; what is remembered and forgotten; that it must either be recognized as merely partial, or understood as something other than a representation of reality.[21] It is, rather, as we have already discussed, a means for Euclides to craft a memory to impose upon his own future. We are the beneficiaries of his need to influence his own future; we are also, however, potentially the victims of his imposition if we make the mistake of taking for granted the transparency of the document. Let us look more closely at each of the details of Euclides's account of his production.

Socrates somehow felt compelled to recount his conversation to Euclides. We do not know what circumstances motivated this. Based on the information we are given, the conversation would have taken several hours to complete. There is precedent for this impressive recounting within the

Platonic corpus itself. In the *Republic*, it appears that Socrates recounts in great detail a conversation that would have taken many hours, and does so on the same day that he completed the conversation. Thus, while it is not clear to what extent and with what detail Socrates recounted the conversation (or why), it is consistent with the portrayal of Socrates in the Platonic corpus to imagine him having done so. Socrates is thus portrayed as having had an astonishing memory, if we are to assume that he recounts his conversations accurately.

Euclides, too, relied upon his memory, this time a memory not of an event, but of a description of an event: He presents himself as having filled in the gaps between details of Socrates's description later on and "at his leisure" (143a3). Here, too, we find the representation of the conversation relies on memory, and again with what we can reasonably assume to be a diminishing return in accuracy, or at least a disproportionate emphasis on certain aspects of the conversation over others. Euclides later returns to Athens periodically to check details with Socrates (143a4–5). Note that, since Socrates would be dead within a few weeks of the event transcribed, these periodic visits would have taken place both at regular intervals and while Socrates awaited his own death. The editorial refinement of this dialogue would likely have been done at intervals between Socrates's reflections on his own death, for example, between the events portrayed in the *Crito* and in the *Phaedo*.

Putting aside Euclides's puzzling and inaccessible motivations for editorially removing any narration from his version of the dialogue, we can nonetheless account for the implications of that decision on our access to the conversation, and more importantly, to the implications *this* dramatic choice on the part of Plato has for our understanding of the question of knowledge: Euclides denies us access to a report of how people behaved in saying what they said. Without that information, we are left having to fill in interpretive gaps in order even to portray for ourselves at all what happens in the dialogue. Were there moments where any of the characters grew silently frustrated with the things others were saying? In what tone did Theaetetus give voice to his agreement with Socrates on this or that point? We do not know, because Euclides removed the information with which we might have come to know. Nonetheless, when we read the text, we surely use the words in our reading to indicate *likely* tones of voice, and we use the information we are given about each character to build a rough sketch of how they might conduct themselves, because we have to. Plato has the characters engage in far more than mere purely rational disputation on the nature of knowledge. The discussion is rich with characterization, and yet the fullness (and accuracy) of that characterization is not accessible.

There is a tension here. On the one hand, we are supposed to recognize that the elimination of narration requires of us that we be conscious of our ignorance, and of the interpretive restraints we harbor in reading the text. On the other hand, the text itself *insists* that it be read according to interpretive commitments we have no license to make. We cannot legitimately make assumptions about the behavior of the characters and the tone of their interactions. We *must* make assumptions about them, nonetheless.[22]

To summarize: we are inclined throughout reading the dialogue—as we are with any dramatic text—to add to the words we read the emotional force behind them, in order to give to ourselves a complete picture. Having learned from Euclides that the way in which the words were spoken has been editorially removed, however, we ought to be aware that our additions are an epistemologically uncertain imposition of our own interpretive choices—we are in a sense no different from Euclides. We are invited by Plato to discover the fact that we fill in the meaning—because we cannot help filling in the meaning to be capable of engaging with the text at all—despite the fact that in a certain sense we *ought not* to do so. In a dialogue concerned with knowledge, this is of profound philosophical importance. It indicates to us that the information of which we are given certain knowledge in our experience of the world is insufficient to the demands imposed by our need to engage with the world. We must reach beyond what we are given epistemological license to presume we know in order to relate to the text at all. Further, our activity of reaching beyond is typically performed without our giving conscious consideration of how we do so. Were we to be conscious of it, the manner of our reaching beyond would be transformed. The name given to that transformation is wisdom. In closely examining the relationship between Socrates and Theaetetus, and the relationship between Plato and the reader in the chapters that follow, we will give shape to the attributes of wisdom.

Conclusion

In this chapter, I have presented the themes addressed in the preface of the *Theaetetus*. I have argued that, when gathered together, these themes form the foundation of an inquiry into the nature of human knowledge. Specifically, the themes of the opening dialogue consist of the following: (1) We are naturally equipped to adopt an understanding attitude toward the world but are also able to reflect on and criticize our inclination to adopt that attitude. (2) We develop toward a standpoint where we are able to come to recognize—and have knowledge of—the fact that we die, as well as the obscure nature of our deaths. (3) Our development is toward a kind of continuity of activity that we call character. (4) That development of character—informed by the way in which it comes to know the world in which it acts—is conditioned by memory; memory, itself is determined not only by the conscious decisions concerning what one wishes to retain, but also by the contingent circumstances under which those educative projections are awakened in the indeterminate future. (5) The circumstances in which we act are always based upon limited access to the world, yet we are nonetheless forced to act on what would, upon reflection, be considered insufficient information. These are the conditions that both produce and demand interpretation.

I have claimed that this account of the lived conditions in which knowledge emerges is to be taken from the introductory scene, but that it cannot be derived without having returned to the material a second time, and without having consciously chosen to find within that scene what one anticipates from what follows from it. I take this need for rereading to be deeply relevant to a proper understanding of what philosophy is, and therefore to what Socrates's project is. Insight into these characteristics of the soul allow us to see the importance of the project of cultivating the activity of reflection upon what appears to us as transparent, and therefore as requiring no reflection. Such insight calls us to adopt a new attitude toward all of our experiences, one which seeks to identify objects of experience as inherently worthy of reflection. The activity of reflection, we will see, is aiming at instituting an erotic structure within the soul in its attitude toward the world. Let us now turn to the drama of this philosophical education as it is demonstrated in the relationship between Socrates and Theaetetus.

CHAPTER 2

The Teacher (143d1–151d3)

> If it really resides in you, it provides a sense of its presence, by means of which you would form an opinion not only that you have it but of what sort it is.
>
> —*Charmides*, 159a2–4

> None of the gods loves wisdom or wants to become wise—for they are wise . . . what's especially difficult about being ignorant is that you are content with yourself, even though you are neither beautiful and good nor intelligent. Those who love wisdom fall between those two extremes.
>
> —*Symposium*, 204a1–b4

Introduction

The introductory discussion between Euclides and Terpsion has highlighted for us several features of the soul which together produce the framework within which the activity of knowing emerges. Let us briefly review what those features are, and how they are interrelated. We are forced to commit to actions based on interpretations that we make without sufficient knowledge to ground those interpretations. Out of the process of making commitments, patterns of behavior take shape that eventually produce a kind of character, with the result that we begin to develop a relatively stable interpretive framework. The patterns of behavior that develop into character initially develop passively—which is to say that they develop without our taking a conscious role in choosing them—but these patterns over time progressively, and potentially increasingly, involve our active, self-conscious participation. In other words, as we grow and develop, we become more capable of making choices that project the kind of person we want to become. Even within the development of the ability to consciously participate in the shaping of our character, however, we depend upon structures of memory—themselves projections of future behavior—that rely upon the uncontrollable external world for their deployment. In other words, even within the self-conscious projection of our future selves, we find an aspect of passivity which shapes who we are. As we develop over the course of a lifetime, we become capable of recognizing the certainty of death, but that certainty takes the form of certainty of absolute and necessary ignorance, insofar as we cannot, properly speaking, experience our death. These attributes of our experience of the world together illustrate, first, the dependence of action upon interpretations, and second, the intermingling of knowledge and ignorance in the very fabric of the soul's activity. No complete and true account of knowledge can be performed without taking these into account.

It was with these attributes in mind that I claimed near the end of the chapter that wisdom is the primary aim of philosophical education, and that it ought to be the primary aim of education in general. I take wisdom to consist in having cultivated the kind of character that is reconciled to the fact that how one chooses to act is always necessarily situated within a context of uncertainty, and the kind of character that chooses how to act conscious of that uncertainty.[1] The pursuit of knowledge for the wise person is directed at something the wise person knows will never be accomplished to his or her satisfaction. Thus, the wise person's knowledge of the world is always situated alongside knowledge of herself, and of her limitations. The kind of education that a human being requires in order to be wise therefore must as much involve learning about the nature of the soul as it does learning the nature of the world.[2] I take it that the *Theaetetus* provides us with a demonstration of Socrates initiating Theaetetus into this kind of education.

In this chapter, I will examine the process of philosophical education as it is dramatized in the *Theaetetus* with particular attention to what is involved in being a teacher. I pay particular attention to the role of the teacher in the process of education, due to the fact that the initial passages of the *Theaetetus* are strikingly oriented around Socrates's claims about himself: First, his claim that he cares most of all about the young men of Athens talented in philosophy (143d1–e4), and, second, his claim that he is a psychological midwife (150a8–151d3). These two distinct though related topics constitute the first two large sections of the chapter.

In section 1, I claim that what Socrates cares for most of all is the activity of philosophical education, and, because he possesses human wisdom, and has thus reconciled himself to the nature of the soul, has chosen appropriate circumstances in which, and people with whom, to engage in that activity.

To demonstrate this, first, I unpack the political significance of that claim, specifically arguing that, for Socrates, the project of philosophical education is a political responsibility as much as an instrumental, moral, and pleasurable activity. I argue that the fact that the demands of political life produce social mechanisms that inevitably impose themselves perniciously on education creates the need for Socrates to participate in the shaping of the young. This shaping consists in encouraging the young to develop a standpoint that examines the context within which their given field of study is situated. Second, I interpret Socrates's specification that it is with young men on the cusp of maturity that he wants most of all to spend his time. I argue that young adulthood is the best time for philosophical education, and that the reasons for this are built on claims I made in chapter 1 concerning the stages of character development. Young adulthood is a time at which one is most likely not to have yet developed the wide range of prejudices associated with the habits and responsibilities of adult life. One is therefore more likely to be able to allow philosophical discussion to lead one in unpredictable directions. In young adulthood, one is likely to have developed sufficient agency to have ownership over one's own opinions and how to spend one's time.

In section 2, I discuss the methods that Socrates uses in his favored activity. I divide his process into two distinct phases, the first consisting in preparing the student for an interrogation of his character, and the second consisting in that interrogation. The preparation consists, first, in getting the student to begin to distinguish authority from expertise, and second, in extracting the student from specialization in narrow, disciplinary education. The essence of the preparation is to foster the student's recognition that she or he can learn from people other than those with whom she or he has become familiar, and can learn things with more universal application.

The second phase of Socrates's process consists in interrogating the student. The interrogation itself consists in demanding of the student that he give account of his ideas. This "Socratic" method is typically characterized as being aimed at demonstrating that the student did not know what he thought he knew. I argue, however, that this characterization fails to pay attention to the psychologically transformational character of the imperative for the student to give account of his presumed knowledge. Theaetetus is made to recognize, first, that it is difficult to provide an account of one's tacitly held opinions, and second, that he might not have previously known what his tacitly held opinions actually were, and third, that he was not as much in control of himself as he thought, insofar as he had been operating under presumptions he was not consciously aware of, and finally, fourth, that it takes time and effort to be capable of giving an account well. In this section, I show that

Socrates's method of philosophical discussion demonstrates the formative character of one's tacit, unconscious philosophical commitments, which is to say that Socrates demonstrates that doing philosophy means doing psychology, which is also to say that philosophy is soul care.

In the third and final section of the chapter, I present and interpret Socrates's midwife speech. I here argue that what is significant about Socrates's claim is that philosophical education consists in bringing to the student's attention the tacitly understood, yet never critically reflected upon, ideas that govern his life and shape his character. I further argue that the significance of Socrates's barrenness lies in his constant engagement in the dialectical activity of articulating and criticizing his own presumptions. As a result, I claim that Socrates presents an implicit characterization of himself as a student, as well as demonstrating himself to be a teacher.

One thing that we must keep in mind in the discussion that follows is that being a teacher in the sense that I present Socrates to be means trying to cause change in the soul of one's student. Philosophical education focuses primarily on the "medium" of knowledge, which is to say that it focuses on the soul.[3] Even while being explicitly concerned with a particular topic, philosophical education is implicitly concerned with the life of the person undergoing the inquiry. Socrates is trying to compel Theaetetus to engage in an activity the result of which will be that he is changed by it. The fact that teaching in the way that Socrates does means trying to provoke transformation of the medium through which the student learns—as opposed to providing something new for that medium to consider—means that his kind of teaching is of a different order than that of a typical educator. Let us now consider, first what motivates this kind of teaching, and second, how it is done.

1. What Socrates Cares About (143d1–e4)

a. Interpersonal Dynamics

The conversation between Euclides and Terpsion that opens the *Theaetetus* ends with a slave being asked to read the book Euclides wrote as a document of the reported conversation between Socrates, Theodorus, and Theaetetus (143c7). Just as the dialogue as a whole opened without explaining how the context of the conversation between Euclides and Terpsion was initiated, likewise, Euclides's book begins without explaining why the characters talk to each other under these specific circumstances. His book simply begins with Socrates speaking. We do not know what purpose brought Socrates to this conversation with Theodorus. We have only the things that he says to Theodorus, and later to Theaetetus, to learn from. Before we begin to interpret his opening speech, however, we should consider once again the significance of the fact that we have no access either to the interior thoughts of the characters or to an exterior narrator's perspective. We should do so, first, because it once again draws our attention to the epistemic limitations we face both as readers of the text and as interpreters of our own interpersonal landscape, that is, we have no narrator to give us an interpretive commentary on the context of our interactions with others, nor do we have access to the interior experiences of those with whom we are interacting. Second, we should consider the fact that we are denied access to interior thoughts and narration because being conscious of the distinction between words uttered and the implicit motivations as we read will make us better able to interpret, for example, the extent to which the speaker is trying to communicate transparently his own actual thoughts, and the extent to which he is trying to produce a specific response in his audience. It will also make us better able to consider how characters tailor their speech with one another, and to ask why they tailor their speech as they do. It will also give us occasion to reconsider what is involved in what is typically presumed to be "transparently communicating" thoughts.[4]

With these interpretive demands in mind, let us set the stage for the conversation. Socrates has approached Theodorus, the geometry teacher and authority figure, at an undescribed location. At first, the students are at a distance from the two men as they begin to talk. Theaetetus eventually comes to them because he has been called over (144d7). It appears that a crowd of some other students comes by to witness the elaborate discussion as it unfolds.[5]

It is important that we consider the fact that Socrates is here engaging in a conversation with two unique people, Theodorus and Theaetetus. Each of these people has character traits that strongly influence the way in which he articulates himself. Taking account of this fact is an interpretive demand implicit in all of Plato's dialogues. Consider what it would be like, for example, if a history professor were to explain, as accurately as possible, the causes of the French Revolution to her academic colleague, her best friend, and her curious nine-year-old son. No doubt the details of the explanation would be most elaborate in the first case, with questions from the interlocutor focused on finer points of analysis. In the case of her best friend, one could imagine the events being more broadly described, perhaps with more forceful and less precisely substantiated claims, depending on the nature of the relationship between them. In the third case, no doubt the account would be shorter and simpler, with more basic context, and with questions of a very general nature coming from her interlocutor. Her answers would vary dramatically from one another, if she were to be an effective communicator. More importantly, were we to read, say, the explanation given to the nine-year-old, taking it for granted as transparently representing the professor's views on the French Revolution, rather than accounting for the fact that she has carefully crafted those views to meet the needs of a specific listener, we would surely misjudge her expertise. Accounting, therefore, for the traits of characters and the dynamics between characters is essential to our ability to recognize that particular claims are made for the purpose of eliciting a specific response in a specific person, and, particularly in the case of Socrates, not necessarily for the purpose of declaring his exhaustive, rigorous position on a given topic.

Whether we are aware of doing so or not, we ourselves tailor our speech to meet the needs and expectations of our audience, no matter how transparent or objective we strive to be. If we consider the interpersonal dynamics of the characters in Platonic dialogues, it will be readily apparent to us that issues of the sort I am describing are very much at play. We must therefore consider some of the salient characteristics of his interlocutors as they are presented in the dialogue, and discuss some of the possible ways in which those characteristics influence Socrates's speech. Let us therefore briefly examine Theodorus and Theaetetus, and some of the details about their respective relationships to him, as well as their relationship to one another, in order to see how these relationships set the terms for the ways in which the characters express themselves.

Theodorus is probably fairly close to Socrates's age, though a few years younger.[6] He is a geometry teacher. Though Socrates begins by complimenting him for meriting the considerable crowd of young men whom he teaches, and though Theaetetus will shortly claim that Theodorus is expert in all the aspects of philosophy (145a9), it becomes clear as the dialogue unfolds that Theodorus's intellectual interests are strikingly narrow and not very adaptable. He consistently resists directly engaging in the discussion on the grounds that he is unaccustomed to such forms of conversation, this despite the fact that it is quite clear that Theaetetus, too, is unaccustomed to such conversations, and is not offered the choice to opt out (146b1–7). There could be a number of causes of Theodorus's behavior having to do with his relationship to philosophical discussion. He could be somewhat intellectually lazy, and therefore not willing to attempt to struggle through difficult reasoning. He could be cowardly, fearing the possibility of being proven less discursively able than the others. Related to being cowardly, he could be intellectually vain, and therefore concerned more with his appearance and reputation than with the issues being discussed. He could be simply not very interested in this, or perhaps any, serious philosophical discussion. In contrast to these possible ways of interpreting his obstinacy, it could be the case that Socrates has indecorously subjected Theodorus and Theaetetus to a socially awkward situation, and that Theodorus evades participation because he is angry or uncomfortable with Socrates's behavior. Regardless, Theodorus's unwillingness to commit to positions that might turn out, under scrutiny, to be erroneous provides a stark contrast with Socrates's willingness to do so. Socrates openly and enthusiastically subjects his own ideas, along with those of others, to scrutiny, and explicitly acknowledges their shortcomings when appropriate. It is strongly insinuated in the dynamics of the conversation as it unfolds and as Theodorus becomes increasingly obstinate that he is someone Socrates finds quite irritating.

We must bear these dynamics in mind as we reconsider the context of the discussion. Socrates is talking to someone he knows at least reasonably well. He appears not to regard Theodorus to be particularly insightful outside of his field of geometry. We should also be aware that Socrates is approaching Theodorus with what we discover to be the intention to steal the attention and interest of his best student away from him. Perhaps Socrates is trying to mitigate the damage that this bad teacher (of philosophy, anyway) is doing to a good student. At the outset, Theodorus has something Socrates wants, though Socrates does not yet know what specifically it is; he knows merely that, since many students congregate around Theodorus, some might be very good (143e1–4). Socrates did not merely wander through the streets and happen to run into Theodorus; he has arrived there with a purpose. Though that purpose is made explicit at the outset, it is presented along with complimentary language the sincerity of which is at least dubious.

Theaetetus, a meeting with whom is the unanticipated purpose of that approach, is much younger than Socrates. He is perhaps in his early twenties, and at least in his late teens.[7] Once he is subjected to Socrates's examination, his youth, perhaps among other characteristics of his personality, leads him occasionally to be distracted, no doubt in part as a result of boredom, and surely as a result of being simultaneously confused and shy about acknowledging his confusion. At the very least, his evident discomfort at the outset of the conversation is at least comprehensible due to his comparative lack of experience conversing in the company of highly esteemed older men. He comes from a family that Socrates holds in high regard and which until recently had a great deal of property that has apparently been squandered by Theaetetus's guardian (144c5–d4). As Theodorus advertises, Theaetetus is an excellent geometry student, having apparently already made a significant contribution to that field (147d3–148b3). We will discover that his accomplishment involved solving a problem that contributed to the development of the typology of numbers, and that this went beyond what Theodorus had presented to him. These attributes imply a student of great potential.

This last point ought to shed light on our interpretation of Theodorus's praise, as well as on his relationship with Theaetetus. It is certainly possible that he is to be regarded as highly as Theodorus says he is. However, it is also the case that someone like Theodorus might want to diminish his own sense of embarrassment at having been bested by his student in his own discipline, and to do so by over-inflating the extent of his student's ability; if Theaetetus is indeed so exceptional, Theodorus might reason, then the teacher is merely a victim of the contingent circumstance that he was given a prodigiously talented student to teach. He might also reason that Theaetetus's accomplishment is his own as well, by virtue of the fact that it was accomplished by his student. In either case, Theodorus might have complicated or conflicting motivations for his praise of Theaetetus, due to the familiar tension between admiration and envy.[8]

As we will discuss in greater detail below, it is important that we keep in mind the under-presented dynamics between Theaetetus and Theodorus, particularly to understanding both how Socrates relates to teachers of specialized fields (in contrast to how he relates to philosophers), and how he relates specifically to Theaetetus as a specialist. Theodorus appears to have won uncritical admiration from Theaetetus. Because of the fact that he seems to be the principle intellectual role model thus far in the young man's life, Theaetetus has developed some false notions of Theodorus's capabilities, regarding him, falsely, it will turn out, as skilled in all areas of education. The need to recognize that Theodorus's authority in geometry does not guarantee expertise generally will be one of the first lessons Socrates has for Theaetetus.

The method by which Socrates imposes his lessons on Theaetetus often involves pointedly forcing him to give answers to questions the subtlety of which he is clearly not equipped to understand. Often we might feel compelled to sympathize with Theaetetus, to think that perhaps Socrates is miscalculating Theaetetus's maturity in forcing these questions on such a young student, and under circumstances that Theaetetus did not enter into entirely by choice. In light of the consideration of these interpersonal dynamics, however, we can see that Socrates is actually trying to do Theaetetus a great service: Socrates forces Theaetetus to speak with his own voice, to give account of himself, and therefore to recognize his accomplishments (and failures) to be distinct from those of his teacher, from whom he has apparently been insufficiently extricated. We will have occasion in section 2 to discuss in more detail the virtues of forcing Theaetetus to give account of himself.

In his attempt to compel Theaetetus to speak with his own voice, we see an instance of Socrates's preference for the company of young men.[9] He appears to find them most readily while they undertake various forms of training from other men closer to his age. Here, Socrates explicitly claims that he wants to meet the best of them in order to see if they are capable of engaging in philosophical discussions (143e3–4). It seems that Socrates likes to find young men under the influence of popular teachers of a given craft, in order to "harvest" them, lest they become like overripe fruit. An overripe fruit that has not been plucked from the tree serves the purpose only of carrying the seed, in the hopes of germinating and growing into a new tree like the one from which it fell. Likewise, the overripening of Theaetetus under Theodorus could produce yet another geometry teacher specializing in an intellectual field without interest in or consideration of its own underlying principles. Either that, or Socrates can help Theaetetus identify new pursuits that will properly frame his lessons up to that point, thereby turning him away, ultimately, from specialization without context.

b. Socrates's First Account of Himself

The first words of Euclides's book consist in a speech by Socrates, which turns out to be delivered to Theodorus. It is a general description of what he cares about most of all. He declares that if he were from Cyrene, where Theodorus is from, he would care most of all about the young of Cyrene. But he is not from Cyrene. He is from Athens, and is therefore a friend to Athenians first (143d1–6). Thus, he cares most of all about the young men of Athens.[10] For Socrates, to live somewhere, anywhere, would mean caring for that city's talented young people. There is an important point worth noting here: Socrates cares about the young of his city because they are the young of his city, not (a) because they happen to be Athenian or (b) because they are talented in philosophy.[11] The fact that Socrates is from Athens and spends most of his time there makes him a friend to the Athenians. The implicit idea in Socrates's interest in the young is that there are, for him, social responsibilities inherent to living in a city; the city does not have to earn Socrates's friendship.[12] If it were merely the case that Socrates spent time around the young men because it was fun for him, he would care most of all about young men without qualification. That Socrates qualifies his interest in the young by tying it to the practical political obligations of caring about the development of fellow citizens implies that he considers himself to be obligated to apply his personal interest in philosophical discussion with young men—which is not necessarily itself, without qualification, a pursuit of pleasure—to the public good of his city. Let us consider some of the reasons why Socrates might feel such a sense of obligation.

(1) The Call from the City. A political system can function without its citizens engaging in philosophical questioning. Most of the time political systems do function without critical engagement. One of the reasons for this is the fact that human beings do not typically realize that the institutions that make up a political system are in part the product of deliberation and decision-making by people like themselves, and are therefore appropriate subject matter for their own deliberation.[13] This has to do with the fact that human beings die, and are perpetually replaced by people who take up existing systems as though they were always in place. When new laws are instituted, they are a live issue for deliberation. However, as soon as those laws have survived the generation of their authors, they tend to disappear as issues. Once the people who were present for the institution of that new policy are dead, the evidence of its having been instituted need no longer be present. Instead, the policy can easily appear as part of the foundation of the terms of social life.[14] The situation of political life is one in which there is always a threat of having forgotten, not merely this or that given change in policy, but much more importantly the fact that many of the terms of political life are a product of human design and open to being changed. The phenomena associated with our political life—those which are intimately formative of who we are as individuals and as citizens of a given community—happen to be capable of compelling us to forget something central to our very nature, namely, that we are collectively the architects of that political life.

A similar structure of forgetting can occur at the level of our individual, vocationally specialized practices, and in a way that is very much connected to this greater political phenomenon. In part as a result of the need for the proper functioning of political institutions, individuals have a tendency to participate in one particular aspect of the city as part of their professional life. In so doing, people can develop a narrowly articulated perspective from which to interpret their world. Concerns of theirs related to their narrowly articulated perspective are then treated as the ground from which they make all political decisions. Someone working in a particular industry might decide to support policies that serve the interests of their industry, regardless of how this might affect the society as a whole. The danger of allowing one's concerns to be oriented around one's chosen vocation is thus that one ceases to be capable of reflecting on the underlying principles that make possible one's vocation.

Socrates's activity in the city is directed at making citizens aware of such underlying principles, and to draw them outside of their narrow world. He draws people's attention to the questions that are no longer being considered. He reminds people of their nature, which is to say that he reminds them that they are capable of thinking about the things that they take for granted. In the *Apology*, he compares himself to a gadfly, whose responsibility is to wake people up from their metaphorical slumber (*Apology*, 31a-b). This famous analogy presents Socrates as someone responding to the insight that if we fail to ask questions and to give consideration to the basic assumptions governing our lives, we are no longer governing our lives, but are rather being led by forces of which we are not aware, and in directions not of our choosing.

We can, then, understand why Socrates would be interested in targeting the young men with talent in philosophy to converse with him. It is they who are immediately inheriting the demands of political life (typically alongside the powers of political life), and doing so typically while having been poorly prepared to remember the responsibilities of participation in political life.[15] Let us now turn to a more focused discussion of the stages of life, and particularly to the question of Socrates's preference for young men.

(2) The Time for Philosophy. Why is it young men in particular with whom Socrates wishes to engage? We saw in chapter 1 that one of the typical characteristics of adulthood is the fact that we begin to develop patterns of behavior that are predictable, such that our spontaneous actions accord with the identity we have developed, and are typically perceived by others as characteristic of who we are. We saw just now that adulthood is also, and in a related manner, characterized by a tendency to fall into social and political roles that have the effect of compelling us to forget one of the attributes most essential to human nature, which is political self-determination. In chapter 1, we also discussed, by contrast, how one of the things that distinguish youth from adulthood is the fact that in youth we are still much more subject to dramatic and even revolutionary transformations in our character. I claimed that this demonstrated that it is natural to human beings for life to have stages.

It is no doubt true that the duration of stages in people's lives varies significantly from person to person, and that circumstances will influence those durations, requiring some to make the transition into a more fixed set of behavior patterns at an early age, and requiring others to take much more time to do so. It is nonetheless the case that these stages occur by nature, due to the fact that we develop from infancy, and grow in accordance—or at least in response to—the demands and situations of our specific environments.

It is highly relevant to Socrates's agenda to discern the stage at which the young men to whom he is introduced have reached.[16] On the one hand, once people have reached a certain stage of adulthood, depending on the circumstances of their development, they might be ill-equipped to commit to the kind of conversation Socrates wants. Specifically, Socrates's way of conversing involves serious reflection on the things we might take for granted that govern the way that we live. Calling those things into question implicitly anticipates a commitment to *changing one's life* according to the conclusions drawn concerning those governing presumptions. Being adult members of a community, by contrast, as was discussed in chapter 1, depends upon a kind of predictability of character. On the other hand, students who are too early in their educational development lack the equipment to engage in serious philosophical conversations. They are also at an age where it is in a certain sense not yet clear what kind of person they will be. Let us look further at the kinds of limits that each of these stages of life sets against free philosophical inquiry, by examining how Socrates interacts, first with a middle-aged man in the *Euthyphro*, and second, with young boys in the *Lysis*.

While it is true that in the Platonic corpus Socrates is portrayed interacting with people of wide-ranging character, age, and intellectual ability from various parts of Greece, it would be false to assume that this demonstrates his equal eagerness to have philosophical discussions with anyone. One might be given the impression that he is equally eager in all discussions, not only from the sheer range of types of interlocutors, but also from the way in which Socrates characterizes himself in the *Apology*.[17] However, if we pay attention to the circumstances and tone of those conversations, it becomes clear, first, that in some cases Socrates is essentially an unwilling participant, and second that in those cases, his strategies and aims are something less than the cultivation of philosophical wisdom. In other words, he sometimes is doing something less than "what he cares for most of all." An illuminating example of this occurs later the same day portrayed in the *Theaetetus*, in Socrates's conversation with Euthyphro on the steps of the king archon. The fact that this conversation even occurs, given both the circumstances of Socrates's presence there and the fact that Socrates arrives having completed a complex discussion of several hours, no doubt demonstrates Socrates's insatiability for philosophical dialogue. It also, however, demonstrates the limits to what can be accomplished by conversing with people who are neither particularly intelligent, nor at the appropriate age to be initiated into philosophical discourse.

Euthyphro is probably in his mid-forties at the time of their meeting.[18] He is a diviner, whose craft is the interpretation of signs from the gods, and whose expertise consists of, ostensibly, knowing what it is that pleases the gods. The conversation begins with Socrates describing the case being brought against him, focusing first on the charge that he corrupts the young, and second on the charge that he creates new gods while not believing in the old ones (*Euthyphro*, 2c2–3b2) After showing support for Socrates in his case—curiously, in light of what follows, acknowledging that religious matters are easily misrepresented (*Euthyphro*, 3b5–7)—Euthyphro informs Socrates that he himself is performing an action typically construed as paradigmatically impious, namely, prosecuting his own father for murder. Socrates claims that surely only those who are most wise would be capable of doing such a thing without in some way doing it badly (*Euthyphro*, 4a9). Euthyphro says that those who claim he is being impious do not understand piety and impiety as he does (*Euthyphro*, 4e1–5a2). When Socrates asks if indeed Euthyphro does consider himself expert in an area as inscrutable as piety to the gods, Euthyphro responds confidently: "I should be of no use, Socrates, and Euthyphro would not be superior to the majority of men, if I did not have accurate knowledge of all such things" (*Euthyphro*, 4e8–5a2). Socrates indicates that it is fortuitous that he should come into contact with someone expert in piety, as he can either use Euthyphro's expertise to demonstrate his innocence of impiety, or willingly learn what piety actually is and correct his actions accordingly. When Euthyphro agrees to help him, over the course of ten minutes or so, Socrates demonstrates that Euthyphro in fact does not know what piety is at all, and is only able to parrot received information about it. After four attempts at defining piety, and after inadvertently circling back on the original definition, Euthyphro is challenged by Socrates to start over and try one more time, having learned from his mistakes on the previous attempts (which Euthyphro evidently had not done in returning to his original definition). Euthyphro suddenly claims that he is in a hurry, and that it is time for him to go. He leaves abruptly before the natural end of the conversation.

The failure to demonstrate knowledge of piety is a significant embarrassment for Euthyphro because he binds his identity, and indeed his otherwise unjustifiable willingness to prosecute his own father, to his expertise in that very subject.[19] He would thus certainly be reluctant to acknowledge to others or even to himself his own ignorance on that matter. He is entrenched in a life that cannot persist as it is if he takes seriously his own ignorance. More to the point, his life cannot persist as it is if he takes seriously the activity of examining it, since examination implies uncertainty that he wishes not to convey. It is thus understandable that he would depart abruptly before his conversation with Socrates comes to its natural end; it is quite possible that Euthyphro is humiliated at having had it demonstrated to him that he does not have the very knowledge for which his vocation would have it that he be sought by the community—that is, concerning which actions will please the gods.[20]

Euthyphro has committed himself to a particular kind of life, and doing so makes it increasingly difficult for him to permit himself to engage in philosophical discussion. This is so much the case that each time Socrates demonstrates that his definitions of piety are completely wrong, he is convinced that the next one is right. He will not allow himself to show, and might not even acknowledge to himself, that he does not know what he is talking about. The idea that the life he has chosen, with which he has inflated his sense of his own worth, is founded upon falsehoods is an idea he will not entertain.

This example of willful ignorance, of the hubris required to think one knows what pleases the gods, is not typical of most human beings. However, most human beings cultivate opinions about the world rooted in their various commitments to their jobs and to their families. Most do not consider themselves to be in a position to have the luxury to subject themselves to the transformational project of serious philosophical conversation. In other words, this practice of exposing people to their ignorance is not only difficult to accomplish in adulthood because of the many ways in which people have committed themselves to their lifestyle, but also because of the humiliation one would typically feel when confronting the implication of that exposure, that is, that all of one's life had been lived pursuing the wrong things. In light of this, part of what makes educating adults about their ignorance more difficult is that they have had more time to live according to falsehoods, and have therefore developed a way of living that is dependent upon a wide range of complicated interconnections predicated upon those falsehoods. Adults thus typically have much more *invested* in the worldview that they have adopted.

In the previous chapter, I discussed the fact that the infrastructure of the world—which is to say the domain of the world that is the product of human activity—is created and maintained primarily by adults. Indeed, it is a kind of rite of passage into adulthood for young people to involve themselves in the community through one vocation or another. One of the consequences of our involvement in the adult world is that we find ourselves participating in a complex set of interconnected relationships, both with people and with institutions. Those interrelations produce standards for us to live up to, reputations for us to uphold, and the desire to achieve ambitions set up within the context of those interrelations. To be immersed in this kind of situation—as middle-aged adults typically are—sets in motion a kind of momentum that we typically feel we must maintain, and indeed typically feel—correctly—lies to a significant extent beyond our control.[21]

One can reasonably imagine that Euthyphro is someone living according to the trajectory of his vocational choice and the various commitments surrounding it. It is presumably within this kind of situation that Euthyphro is unable to offer an account of the very kind of knowledge his practice would seem to depend upon, namely knowledge of what it is that pleases the gods. When Euthyphro has his own ignorance exposed to him, he cannot help taking that ignorance to be a threat to his complex set of interconnected relationships; at least, he would be right to feel that threat. Were people to learn that the person whose expertise is ostensibly concerned with which actions please the gods was in fact shown, over the course of a brief conversation, to know nothing about this at all, that person would no longer have the respect of the community, his meaningful role in Athenian society, or a way to make a living. In the face of the real circumstances of his vocation, Euthyphro leaves Socrates's company abruptly (*Euthyphro*, 15e4–5), without having allowed the conversation to achieve its natural end. It is probably the case that he is not interested in coming to a better understanding of piety. He had entered the conversation on the pretense that he would help Socrates understand piety. Once he had demonstrated himself not to be capable of accounting for piety, he likely wanted to put the humiliation behind him by pretending it never happened.

One of the possible consequences of having endured the undesirable encounter with Socrates is that Euthyphro is changed by that conversation for the worse. One could imagine someone in Euthyphro's situation being transformed by the conversation to the extent that he or she would now more rigorously guard against entering situations in which he or she would be challenged in his or her beliefs. Such a transformation would no doubt be counterproductive to the project of cultivating wisdom.

We have now seen that the typical characteristics of adulthood which obstruct the activity that Socrates wants most to pursue include immersion into a web of responsibilities, many of which implicitly commit the adult to opinions and attitudes—whether actually believed or merely adopted for convenience—that keep them from being willing to participate in open-ended questioning of the presuppositions that govern their lives. That is, merely living typically commits us to taking positions on important philosophical issues determined by the complex web of life, not our own rational inquiry.

Why, then, does Socrates prefer to ask questions of young men to asking those same questions of boys in adolescence? To answer this question, I will examine some important insights found in Plato's *Lysis*. The *Lysis* centers around Socrates's discussion of some of the puzzles associated with the concept of friendship; he engages in this discussion with Lysis and Menexenus, who are probably each between 12 and 14 years old. Socrates is initially invited to meet these young men by Hippothales, who is probably around

20 years old.[22] Hippothales is infatuated with Lysis, and is chastised by Socrates for writing love poems about him without having yet successfully courted him (*Lysis*, 204d1–3, 205d5–7). Socrates tells Hippothales that he will demonstrate to him how one ought to behave toward one's beloved. He eventually subjects Lysis and Menexenus to a complicated argument concerning the nature of friendship, but before doing so, Socrates raises the issue of development, claiming to Lysis that children are eased slowly into responsibility over their own lives as they become more knowledgeable (*Lysis*, 209c4–7). Certain details highlighted within the narrative of this dialogue shed light on why it is that the conversation offers Socrates less than what he would prefer in a philosophical conversation.

First of all, we should note that it appears that Socrates does not keep as close tabs on adolescents as he does on adults and young adults, since he is only able to identify the adolescents by who their parents are (*Lysis*, 204e1–205a1). Theaetetus, similarly, was not familiar to Socrates by name (*Theaetetus*, 144c5–8). However, once Socrates saw Theaetetus, he knew whose son he was. In other words, he could recognize Theaetetus as someone who participates in social life, just not someone that he knows. By contrast, Socrates does not know these boys, and does not recognize them. The only thread he has to draw a connection between himself and them is through their parents. This is most likely because of the fact that adolescents only participate in the social life of the city by way of their parents or guardians. Socrates would not necessarily have had occasion to converse with them directly. Indeed, the only reason he does so here is as a result of having been invited by young men more likely to converse with him.[23]

Throughout the dialogue, we are provided with even more evidence of the dependent mode of their participation in public life. Near the end of Socrates's discussion with Lysis, the children are picked up from the new wrestling school by the slaves in charge of looking after them. Socrates only briefly considers protesting this, realizing that he has no way of deliberating with the slaves, since they themselves have no direct authority over the children (or themselves) (*Lysis*, 223a1–9). The children are not only dependently participating in public life—which is to say, participating in public life on conditions set by others, and for durations set by others; they are also dependent upon people who are not themselves in charge of their own lives.

This ending to the dialogue, in which the external force of the slaves stops the conversation Socrates is having with the adolescents, is made especially conspicuous by the fact that earlier in the discussion Socrates had pointed out to Lysis that he, Lysis, did not have control over his own life. Lysis argued (correctly, from the standpoint presented here) that he did not have control over his life because he was still young. Socrates responded that, though it is true that Lysis does not have control over many things in his life, he does have control over some things, namely, those things about which he has become competent (*Lysis*, 207d4–210d4). While it is certainly true that wise parents take authority over those matters about which their children are not yet knowledgeable, it is also true that many of those children will grow up not having ever become knowledgeable about those same things. Thus, while the parents of Lysis may wish him to develop knowledge of, say, chariot-racing before being given responsibility over it, he will probably one day inherit that chariot whether he has demonstrated competence or not; it is his *childhood* primarily that gives his parents the ability to withhold control.

Because of these attributes of childhood, Socrates is very limited in what he is able to do. He cannot find children to discuss things with him in public places, since those public places are only made available to children through their caregivers. Thus, when Socrates tries to engage in a discussion with an adolescent he is able to get to know, that conversation is limited not only by the subject matter and the unpredictable nature of the argument but also by the rules and regulations independently set down by parents and enforced by slaves.

In addition to this issue of the limited agency of children, there is, perhaps more importantly, the issue of the limited agency of children in maintaining the level of concentration necessary to participate in philosophical dialogue. After having conversed with the boys about friendship, and having perhaps been impressed by the enthusiasm and thoughtfulness of Lysis in particular, Socrates notes that they should take a break since he and they "are a little groggy from this discussion" (*Lysis*, 222c2–4). Shortly after this, he "had a mind to get something going with one of the older men there" (*Lysis*, 223a1–2), which was interrupted by the arrival of the guardians. Socrates probably did sense that the young boys were beginning to lose their ability to focus on the discussion. He, however, had not lost that ability. To participate in a discussion with adolescents means to participate with people who have not fully developed their own capacity to focus their attention on complex matters. While Socrates is willing to work around those limited capacities, he does not share those limitations. To participate in conversation with young people one has to work on their terms, and on the terms of the limits of their social agency, both of which would typically inhibit the success of the process.

What is most important about these examples of the character of different stages in life, for our purposes, is that they illustrate very powerful natural forces operative against engagement in philosophy. First, philosophical conversation depends on having matured into an independent agent in the world who is mentally and physically capable of the demands associated with such conversation. Second, it requires a willingness to commit one's own life to the force of the argument—one must be willing to submit to the transformational character of the discussion. It is in the nature of adolescence that one is not in a position to have the agency required for such commitment. It is in the nature of adulthood to be committed to other things holding sway over such commitment. Philosophical education is thus most effectively begun at the transition between adolescence and adulthood. It is likely at least for this reason that Socrates cares most of all about talking to the young men of Athens that are equipped with great talent in philosophy.

It is, however, also likely that Socrates cares most of all about the young men of Athens because of the characteristics of young adulthood discussed in chapter 1, the characteristic that makes young adults both so attractive to people wishing to enact change, and dangerous to the existing social institutions. Young men are on the verge of taking on a role in Athenian society; they are equipped with sufficient maturity to begin to engage in adult conversation; they have yet to become entrenched in vocations that would impose upon them standards of behavior specific to that vocation; they have lived long enough to demonstrate the extent of their potential, though have yet to realize it; finally, they are at an age most likely to be informed by a fixation on the excitement of creating and being exposed to new possibilities, rather than upon addressing themselves to the determinate facts of actuality. Socrates gravitates toward the young in general because they are at the natural stage of human development where they are primed for philosophical education and old enough for him to determine whether they are capable of it. They are at an age in which openness to the truth, openness to being compelled by reason, by creative thought, is not only possible without the threat of public shame, it is not only a prospect whose consequences are not perceived to be damaging to long-standing worldview, but it is also potentially desirable.

There is, however, a counterpoint to the desirability of transformation that typically comes in young adulthood. With young men of great potential comes great risk. This, too, connects to the discussion of the previous chapter concerning the revolutionary potential of youth. Young men with less at stake in existing social and political institutions are much more likely to be willing to transform or even destroy those institutions without understanding their meaning to the people living within them. This creates the possibility, no doubt, to produce great changes to the social landscape; it also, however, holds the potential to be needlessly and carelessly destructive.[24] In other words, not only are the young at a natural age at which to be philosophically educated, they are also at an age where they most need that education.

It is worth noting that, though young men of this specific age have typically not yet cluttered their lives with the kind of social and interpersonal connections that would for the most part render them reluctant to participate in serious philosophical discourse, they will—if indeed they have acquired the necessary skills to engage in philosophical discourse—have had teachers or mentors. It is therefore the case that Socrates must engage with those mentors on occasion, too, in order to avail himself of the company of the talented young men. We must now turn to examine one such mentor, Theodorus, who is not only someone around whom the young congregate and is likely an effective instructor in his specialized area, but also someone whose teaching can become a hindrance to educational development if taken beyond its proper course.

2. How Socrates Teaches (143e5–149e9)

The initial interaction Socrates has with Theaetetus can be organized into two distinct phases, each of which has further articulated steps: First, Socrates compels Theaetetus to consider subject matter he had not considered before, and then to consider it questionable. In this phase, Theaetetus must consider the authority of his teacher, and the relationship between disciplinary expertise and wisdom. Second, Socrates interrogates Theaetetus concerning those questions that he had previously never considered. He does so, first, by interrogating Theaetetus in a way that requires him to be responsible for taking ownership over his claims, second, by compelling Theaetetus to experience estrangement from his own positions by drawing his attention to ideas he had had without having consciously chosen them, and, third, by encouraging Theaetetus to use the resources of the ideas he had consciously adopted as a means to construct conscious opinions. This last step then leads Theaetetus back into the initial step of giving an account of that position to once again be scrutinized. Let us examine each of these phases in turn, as they constitute an important aspect of Socrates's unique way of teaching. To begin the discussion of calling into question Theaetetus's relationship to authority, let us consider Theodorus.

a. Initiation into Questioning

(1) Distinguishing Authority from Expertise. Theodorus is a popular geometry teacher around whom the young congregate. In the opening moments of his conversation with Theodorus, Socrates praises him as deserving the crowd around him, doing so immediately before asking Theodorus to introduce him to his best students (143e1–3). As was established above, it seems clear that Theodorus has something that Socrates wants, and Socrates is content to compliment Theodorus in order to endear himself to him. The evidence that appears as the dialogue unfolds suggests that Socrates at the very least believes that Theodorus's methods and subject matter have served their purpose in the education of Theaetetus, and perhaps considers Theodorus to be limited in what he is able to offer.[25] We must therefore approach this opening account with some caution.

When Socrates asks Theodorus to tell him who his best student is, Theodorus says that it is Theaetetus, and then brags about how gifted he is (144a2–3), even claiming that he would be worried others would think that he was in love with him, were it not for the fact that Theaetetus resembles Socrates in that he is physically unattractive (though not as ugly as Socrates).[26] It is this strikingly rude claim that provides Socrates with his first topic of conversation.

The explicit topic of Socrates's opening discussion with Theaetetus is an evaluation of Theodorus's ability to judge similarity, and to judge what is good and beautiful. It is predicated on questioning Theodorus's authority as a judge, and thus implicitly on undermining his authority as a teacher. After Theodorus calls Theaetetus over to them, Socrates, without yet formally introducing himself, tells Theaetetus to look at him so that Socrates can see what he himself looks like (144d8–e2). He then explains that Theodorus told him that they resembled each other, and asks Theaetetus if Theodorus's judgment should be trusted. The first words Theaetetus hears from his new teacher constitute a challenge to the judgment of the old teacher.

In performing this opening inquiry, Socrates asks if one should seek the counsel of others only concerning those things about which they are experts, or about anything at all, thereby challenging the unwitting tendency people often have, and Theaetetus appears to have, to assume that one who has proven to have expertise in one area presumably has expertise in all other areas.[27] Socrates also draws attention to the corresponding tendency of experts to presume their expertise transcends the narrow field concerning which they have cultivated actual knowledge. People give advice and opinions concerning any number of things; the fact that Theodorus is presumably a good geometry teacher, and is certainly esteemed as one by Theaetetus, should not necessarily give Theaetetus reason to assume that Theodorus is expert in other things too. Though the explicit issue of their likeness to one another is a relatively trivial one, and perhaps at first reads simply as a pretext for Socrates to begin talking to Theaetetus, the fact that Socrates brings it up draws attention to the mistaken presumptions that Theodorus's expertise in geometry has any bearing on his opinions about other things about which he is ignorant.

Theaetetus agrees with Socrates immediately that, were they tuning their lyres, they ought to find out first whether or not Theodorus was a musician before asking him advice, and that therefore, since Theodorus is not a skilled painter as far as Theaetetus knows, and painters are the experts of the human face, they need not concern themselves with his opinion of their likeness to one another.[28] Socrates then asks if Theodorus is an expert geometer, which Theaetetus agrees he is. He asks if Theaetetus thinks Theodorus is equally well skilled in the various other aspects of "everything connected to education," to which Theaetetus responds, "That's my opinion at least" (145a10). Based on this considerably less certain answer, Socrates claims that Theodorus's opinion of Theaetetus ought to provoke their enthusiastic scrutiny.

Either Socrates is claiming here that, since Theodorus is supposed to be an excellent educator, they (he and Theaetetus) ought to take his judgment seriously and subject the skill and character of Theaetetus to serious scrutiny, or Socrates is claiming that the uncertainty with which Theaetetus endorsed his teacher's ability across the spectrum of concerns in education means that they should examine his character in order to discover the quality of Theodorus's judgment. In either case, it turns out that both Theaetetus and Theodorus are under scrutiny. Also in either case, Socrates has subjected each of them to this scrutiny in a way that the person was not prepared for.[29] In the case of Theodorus, he no doubt *should* have been conscious of the fact that, in providing his own judgment about his student, he is putting himself on display; his praise of Theaetetus would inevitably have reflected on his judgment. In the case of Theaetetus, however, we are provided with an opportunity to notice an interesting aspect of Socrates's method. By asking Theaetetus to answer questions concerning something as small as the resemblance in appearance between the two of them, Socrates had forced Theaetetus into a series of implicit claims regarding the merits of his teacher, his perhaps excessive and youthful credulity regarding that teacher, and his general attitude toward authority. Socrates, having forced Theaetetus into a situation in which he has unwittingly demonstrated attributes of his character (and, by implication, Theodorus's, too), now explicitly creates for Theaetetus the obligation to show himself, in order to prove not only his own merits, and not only the merits of his teacher's judgment of him, but also his teacher's merits as both a judge and a teacher.

As was said above, Socrates forces Theaetetus, at least, to question his own pre-reflective certainty concerning the extent of Theodorus's authority. He took Theodorus's remark about the unfavorable resemblance between Theaetetus and himself and turned it into a means to question Theodorus's reliability as a teacher. By simply questioning Theodorus's authority on a wide range of topics, he explicitly opens Theaetetus up to the notion that he is now at an age where he ought not to confuse authority with expertise. Perhaps more importantly, he implicitly opens Theaetetus up to the possibility that he ought to question seriously Theodorus's continued value to his education. The fact that Theaetetus is probably not yet prepared to abandon Theodorus as an instructor, and perhaps continues to hold an unwarranted high opinion of Theodorus once the conversation ends, does nothing to undermine what has happened. It merely draws our attention to the need both for time to pass and for persistent repetition in order for this lesson to sink in.

Consider how this might be experienced by Theaetetus. He has been asked over to talk to his teacher, whom it seems clear he holds in very high esteem, and to the famous Socrates. Theaetetus probably has heard a great deal about Socrates, and, depending on the people with whom his family consorts, may well have heard some unfavorable information. In the *Apology*, which takes place only several days or a couple of weeks later, Socrates describes the "old charges" against him, which essentially consist in the reputation that has built up around him as a result of rumors, that he makes the weaker argument the stronger and is a student of all things under the stars (*Apology* 18b6–c2).[30] It is quite possible that Theaetetus approaches Socrates having heard a version of these "charges," and therefore approaches him aware to some degree that over the course of the conversation he is about to have, he will be confused and disoriented, may be compelled to adopt rationally derived commitments he would not otherwise hold, and will have the way that he lives scrutinized. Almost immediately Theaetetus is put in a situation where he is forced to evaluate the judgment of his teacher—in his teacher's presence—in a range of areas, in particular, as an educator. It is also strongly implied that he ought to begin to question authority. Finally, he is told that he is to display his abilities for Socrates, and Socrates is to examine him (145b6–9). We can safely assume that Theaetetus experiences this line of questioning with considerably greater intensity than his two elders.

We should also note, regarding how the situation appears to Theaetetus, that Socrates has forced him into a conversation somewhat dishonestly by cloaking it in the language of contractual obligation. Socrates declares that, because of the fact that Theodorus has praised him more than he has ever praised anyone to Socrates's knowledge, they must now go on to examine Theaetetus (145b6). When Theaetetus responds that Theodorus might be joking, perhaps to signal that he would rather not be put on display before an audience, Socrates instructs him not to "back out of what has been agreed upon by pretending that he was speaking in jest" (145c4–5). Nothing was ever "agreed upon," though. Either Theaetetus has been tricked into believing there had been an agreement or he is understandably too shy to protest what he knows was not an agreement. In any case, this is the second situation—along with Socrates's apparent flattery of Theodorus—in which Socrates appears to be both manipulative and dishonest in order to initiate the activity about which he "cares most." Caring most of all about this kind of activity seems to imply treating it as more important than honest, transparent communication.

In response to this characterization of Socrates as behaving dishonestly, one might suggest that he is simply engaging in playfulness. According to this interpretation, one could imagine that his elevation of the terminology to the level of legal contract is intended to poke fun at the pressure he is exerting on Theaetetus. It could no doubt be the case that Socrates is being playful, but insofar as Socrates is in a position of power in relation to Theaetetus, it is less likely—and it at least certainly does not imply—that Theaetetus takes himself to be capable of treating such playfulness as playfulness. The latter continues to find himself in a situation in which older and more authoritative people are making jokes about what he is required to do. Further, Socrates's levity—if that is indeed what it is—remains directed at satisfying his curiosity about the talents of Theaetetus, and at directing Theaetetus toward philosophy. It remains, in other words, that Socrates has an agenda, and is using various means to pursue it that involve the imposition of his will on someone who probably does not feel he has any option besides compliance.

(2) Distinguishing Disciplinary Knowledge from Wisdom. Immediately following the questions concerning Theodorus's expertise, Socrates cryptically implies the limited (though no doubt real and high) value of the subject matter Theaetetus is learning from Theodorus. As these cryptic remarks both launch the conversation into the discussion that will preoccupy them for the duration of the dialogue, and also provide an interpretive key concerning the distinction between knowledge and wisdom, we should examine them carefully.

Socrates first lists the various things Theaetetus *is* learning from Theodorus, including geometry, and "that which pertains to astronomy, harmony, and calculations" (145d1–2). Socrates then claims that he is competently conversant in "everything else" about these areas of study except a "small point about which [he is] perplexed" (145d6–8), that is, whether learning consists in becoming wiser (*sophōteron*) in whatever one learns (*manthanei*). Socrates claims that he has gotten down virtually everything about these areas of study with one exception. But the exception—whether learning is to be become wiser in what one learns—does not appear to be a last remaining part of any of these specific disciplines—geometry, astronomy, harmony, and calculation—but rather appears to be a general issue applicable to all dimensions of learning. It appears that Socrates is implying—though not exactly saying explicitly—that he can do geometry and those other disciplines more or less as effectively as a person can, but that if this were the extent of his understanding of those disciplines, it is not obviously the case that he would be wise in those disciplines. To become wise in what one learns requires not only the capability of performing the functions associated with that discipline; it requires an attitude toward the active engagement in that discipline. To be "wise in" what we learn requires understanding and contextualizing the activity itself. It requires one to stand outside of the activity at the same time as one engages in it, to be knowledgeable concerning the systematic demands of that discipline and wise concerning what are, by contrast, nonsystematic occasions for its application. The question—presented by Socrates to Theaetetus as something obvious and assumed (145d8–9)—is whether one can take for granted that disciplinary knowledge logically entails, or at least naturally brings with it, wisdom concerning one's active engagement in that discipline.

When framed in this way, it is easy to see that it is not the case that to learn is "to become wiser in whatever one learns." A person can certainly cultivate disciplinary knowledge without ever having given any consideration to it within a wider context, be it the context of the person's own life or that of the world in which that discipline participates. Theaetetus, however, automatically answers that "of course" to learn is to become wise in what one is learning. In the series of questions that immediately follows, Theaetetus demonstrates that he is not thinking about how he answers, with the result that he misses the distinction between knowledge and wisdom, and therefore misses on his first chance to grasp how the kind of thing Socrates's questioning seeks to accomplish differs in important ways from forms of disciplinary knowledge.[31]

While Theaetetus misses his chance, we should not do the same. As has been suggested already, the cultivation of highly developed knowledge within a given field has the tendency to provide the knower with a lens through which to see the world. While this in itself has the potential to enhance a person's understanding of the world, it need not have that effect. Indeed, for many, being provided with a lens through which to see the world ends up meaning being provided with something that they can—erroneously, it should be emphasized—take that "lens" as a universal set of terms through which to judge reality. Due to the developmental nature of the soul, and our tendency to becoming increasingly invested in the world, fields of learning bear with them the danger that they might take the form of modes of indoctrination. For example, a medical doctor's expertise in human anatomy bears the possibility of developing the habit to think of people primarily in terms of the mechanics of their bodies, and to treat her work as involved with fixing those bodies. Nothing about expertise in anatomy requires that the doctor identify that expertise as subordinate to the restoration of the well-being of the person as a whole.[32] The terms of medicine themselves teach nothing about the means of deployment of knowledge concerning medicine, but the ways of the soul in cultivating expertise *do* have the potential to "teach" the careless person perniciously about the universal deployment of that knowledge.

This structure applies to any field of knowledge available to us. To know something is not the same as to actively apply that knowledge;[33] the application of knowledge on the world always depends upon a wide range of skills and resources not inherent to the field itself. The fact that Theaetetus did not point this out when given the opportunity to do so ended up depriving us of the opportunity to hear Socrates give consideration to that distinction. Having pointed it out now, however, we are able to see that, though the discussion of this distinction never directly plays a role in the explicit content of the remaining conversation, it does play a tacit role in Socrates's project of cultivating transformation in Theaetetus. Further, it helps shed light on the interpretation of the speech in which he compares his questioning of people to psychological midwifery, as we shall see at the end of this chapter.

(3) What These Questions Accomplish. Note here that Socrates is not explicitly trying to convince Theaetetus either that Theodorus is a teacher of questionable judgment, or that the mathematical education he is receiving is ultimately inadequate to the attainment of wisdom. All Socrates has done is ask whether either of these is the case. It is very likely that it did not ever occur to Theaetetus to wonder whether or not Theodorus was a good educator, and it is even more likely that Theaetetus has yet to entertain the notion that mathematics could not provide as much education as he needs. Indeed, regarding this latter point, it seems likely that it is not merely the case that Theaetetus took for granted that his education into technical expertise in various forms of calculation would culminate in wisdom; rather, the matter of the relationship of his mathematical education to wisdom and to the shaping of his soul has probably never occurred to him yet. Therefore, for Socrates to ask such questions is to introduce to Theaetetus the very notion that these things too are questionable.

Having said that Socrates has opened up a line of questioning previously concealed from Theaetetus, we can nonetheless see that it seems that Theaetetus already had the potential to be made aware of both Theodorus's quality as an educator and the subordinate value of mathematical education to the fullness of his life. As we will see below, Theaetetus's mathematical discoveries had already shown evidence of his potential to go beyond what Theodorus was capable of teaching. Likewise, Theaetetus mentions to Socrates that he has puzzled over questions of the nature of knowledge, having heard people describe Socrates's style of questioning (148e1–6). These pieces of evidence concerning Theaetetus's character demonstrate, first, that Theodorus was right to the extent that his praise of Theaetetus was praise of the *potential* in his character, and second, that Theaetetus is, so to speak, ripe for Socrates's "plucking" and that Socrates is increasingly aware of this fact. Theaetetus's mathematical demonstration, which we will discuss in a moment, makes Socrates declare that "Theodorus will not be found guilty of false evidence" (148b4–5); Theaetetus's frank admission of his persistent and interested puzzlement with these matters provokes Socrates both to describe Theaetetus as pregnant and to present himself as a midwife willing to aid in Theaetetus's labor process. In each of these cases, Theaetetus has acted in a way which indicates to us that he has the germ of insight regarding the importance of his education. Nonetheless, if the question were never put to him to reflect on the two things that perhaps govern his post-adolescent daily activities—studying mathematics and doing so with Theodorus—he might not take a conscious role in the decisions that usher in his adulthood. Socrates's questions, in other words, are not merely a part of Theaetetus's education; they announce to him the considerations he ought to entertain to cultivate wisdom. Socrates is introducing to Theaetetus the notion that his soul is, and is always, in the process of being shaped, and that he ought to take responsibility for his interests, and to take responsibility for the people with whom he chooses to cultivate them.

b. The Mechanics of Inquiry: Interrogation, Estrangement, Adoption

(1) Interrogation: Making Words Matter. As I discussed already, Socrates asks Theaetetus whether knowledge of the mathematical sciences (including geometry, astronomy, harmony, and calculation) constitutes wisdom. By asking this question he introduces to Theaetetus, perhaps for the first time, the notion that mathematical knowledge might *not* constitute wisdom. He does so by asking leading questions, which compel Theaetetus to answers that are both representative of intuitively plausible common sense positions and are also either false or at least true only in a sense requiring greater discussion and much qualification. Socrates asks—in the following order—whether to learn something is to become wise concerning that precise thing, whether those that are wise are wise by wisdom, whether wisdom differs at all from knowledge, whether those things about which one is knowledgeable are the same things about which one is wise, and finally whether knowledge and wisdom are the same thing (145e7). To all but the middle question, Theaetetus answers with brief and certain affirmation. To the middle question, whether "this sort of thing" (i.e., wisdom) differs at all from knowledge, Theaetetus has to ask again what "sort of thing" is being carried over from the previous question (145e3). While he was clearly not paying close attention in that case, it would be wrong to think that he was following sufficiently in the other cases, as the momentum of his answers seems to have overridden attention to the questions themselves. Theaetetus seems to be anticipating a purpose to which Socrates is ultimately moving, and appears to wish not to impede him in that purpose.

It is worth briefly dwelling on this familiar phenomenon of answering questions in anticipation of an expected point, rather than seriously considering one's answers, because it is common both in conversations generally, and more particularly in the way Socrates's interlocutors choose to answer him. Socrates asked Theaetetus a series of questions that in other circumstances would have produced a lengthy discussion. The very same questions that could, if asked of the right person, elicit complex and profound discussion, when asked of the wrong person, produce a poor answer. What is precisely lacking in the person unable to hear the seriousness of the question is wisdom. At this early stage in the conversation, in which Theaetetus is undoubtedly worried about the impression he is giving to Socrates, he has yet to entertain the notion that words like knowledge and wisdom—words he probably uses frequently—are worthy of questioning.

It is not surprising that Theaetetus would answer in this way, and we ought to imagine that Socrates was well aware of this fact. As was mentioned above, Theaetetus is presumably anxious while under scrutiny from the famous Socrates. Thus, when Socrates puts a leading question to him—"To learn, *isn't it* to become wiser in whatever one learns?" (145d8–9)—we can imagine that Theaetetus feels compelled to agree, and to put up the fewest obstructions to Socrates's point, which, he would think, no doubt builds on agreement with that statement. In other words, it is possible that Theaetetus identifies Socrates as having control of the conversation, and identifies himself as a listener whose responsibility it is to provide agreement, and acknowledge confusion where appropriate. If he does identify his role this way, he does so erroneously, as he would have noticed had he attended more seriously to the way in which Socrates framed the discussion as it began, namely, as an opportunity for Theaetetus to display himself, and for Socrates to assess him through his answers.

Since it was predictable that Theaetetus would answer without thinking carefully, we should ask why Socrates leads him in the "wrong" direction. It would be a mistake to assume that Socrates is more interested in provoking agreement so that he can continue his speeches than in the answers provided by Theaetetus. It would also be a mistake to assume that he does not intend his leading questions to put pressure on Theaetetus to answer too hastily, and specifically to agree to claims without thinking about them. We must always remember—especially given that the *Theaetetus* takes place so late in Socrates's life—that this is someone whose preferred activity is talking to people, asking them questions, and finding out about their character; Socrates is someone whose primary interest is in consideration of and care for the soul. He spends his life in dialogue, and thus would have sensitivity to the dynamics of interpersonal relations, and would be familiar with the variety of characters he can interact with. In other words, Theaetetus is not the first young man to answer Socrates's questions unthinkingly; it is useful for Socrates to know that this is the level at which he is operating in choosing how to proceed further. We should therefore expect that Socrates is not surprised by Theaetetus's answers. We should also assume that his concern is not primarily with whether or not Theaetetus provides the right answer.

Indeed, let us highlight two very important lessons to learn from this approach of Socrates's: first, it is useful to Socrates to establish for himself the level of engagement of the person with whom he is speaking. He must learn if Theaetetus's thoughts are directed at the question he is being asked, if they are directed at where he anticipates it is leading, or if he is too caught up in his own anxiety, or in the strangeness of the situation. Socrates must assess Theaetetus's maturity, in other words, because gauging what kind of person he is dealing with will help him communicate better with that person by allowing him to tailor his words to that person's unique needs. Second, in leading Theaetetus in what is arguably the wrong direction, Socrates creates a situation where, if Theaetetus proves himself to be a little hasty and a little immature, then he will learn much more by having to develop that erroneously grounded answer. This exchange provides a glimpse into what are for Socrates two great tools of education: his tendency to dissemble or at least not to be transparent regarding the motivations behind his decisions throughout the conversation, and his tendency to compel his students to make explicit their mistaken impressions, regardless of how silly or wrong-headed.

Another key point to note here is that Socrates is developing a relationship with Theaetetus. Since the relationship depends primarily upon the character and potential of Theaetetus, he must get Theaetetus talking, so that they have something to talk about that is intimately relevant to his own life. If their discussion is built on the consideration of the words and ideas of Theaetetus, then he is more likely to be interested in that discussion. The relationship, at this early stage, needs a plane on which to operate, and forcing Theaetetus to stake a claim on a given opinion invests him in the future of the conversation, and ultimately the relationship.

While it is essential for Socrates to allow Theaetetus to make the mistake that he does, *we* do not make that same mistake; one of the distinctions between the pedagogical craft that is dramatized for us through Socrates and Theaetetus, and that in which we are participants through Plato's text, is that the latter not only considers it important to dramatize the educational virtue of allowing students to commit errors in their thinking, but also considers it important to record those errors to allow readers independent of the discussion to consider the trajectory of the conversation, as well as the trajectory that has been closed off by those errors. His readers will perhaps first follow along with the text, as though it were even more binding than the leading questions asked by Socrates, which is to say, as though the fact that Socrates allows the answers Theaetetus has given to stand implies his tacit consent to those answers. Readers will, however, have the occasion to revisit it. In rereading, the reader has the opportunity (should she take it) to perform what might be called a forensic analysis of the errors along the way, something that is lost to Socrates and Theaetetus by virtue of the ephemeral nature of conversation.[34] We, the readers, are in this sense Plato's students. We must therefore examine the mistakes that were made in the important discussion of knowledge and wisdom that precedes Theaetetus's first definition of knowledge.

As we discussed at the end of section 1 of this chapter, it seems clear that Theaetetus is not correct in agreeing that knowledge and wisdom are the same. Socrates, at least, has a personal relationship to the *distinction* between knowledge and wisdom. A few days after this conversation, in the *Apology*, he will relate the story of how Chaerophon heard from the oracle that nobody was wiser than Socrates (*Apology*, 20e3–21a7). He later explains that he interprets the idea of the wisdom that he possesses to come from his knowledge of his own ignorance, his knowledge that he knows nothing (*Apology*, 21d3–9). It is not merely the fact that he knows this about himself, but the way of life that grows out of that knowledge, which constitutes his wisdom. Wisdom is, in this characterization, importantly related to a very specific kind of knowledge, that is, knowledge that the inclination to presume to know is both deeply ingrained in human beings, and typically misleading. Socrates's practice is responsive to that reality.

In this particular case, Socrates's responsiveness takes the form of using his own reputation to undermine his interlocutor's certainty, both of the trajectory of the conversation and of the answers to his questions. After Theaetetus hastily agrees that knowledge and wisdom are the same, Socrates demonstrates that his leading questions were in fact misleading, since Socrates now admits that he does not himself know for certain what knowledge is. Indeed, he is "perplexed" and is "incapable of grasping" by himself what knowledge is (145e9–146a1). Therefore, to say that this thing about which he is at least perplexed and which he is incapable of grasping is the same as wisdom cannot have been a sincere claim. To know that one thing is like something else requires that one knows that first thing, at least to the extent of identifying attributes shared with the second thing. Since Socrates is not able to grasp what knowledge is, he surely does not know—at least not in the way he had implied by his leading question—that knowledge and wisdom are the same. Having noted this, Socrates then asks if someone—anyone—is willing to speak up and explain what it is (146a). He is met with silence. Had we been given a description of this moment, perhaps we would have a clearer idea of the atmosphere this claim created. We can speculate, though. Socrates had built some momentum behind the notion that the question of knowledge (and, implicitly, though unmentioned, of wisdom) was an essentially settled issue. After having trapped Theaetetus in agreement with this erroneous trajectory, Socrates suddenly claims that the issue is unsettled in his mind. We can imagine that Socrates's company (whatever their number) experienced a mixture of, on the one hand, shock at realizing that they had been rather blindly assenting to positions the basic atomic elements about which they turn out to know nothing, and perhaps, on the other hand, anxious anticipation of the difficult conversation that will inevitably follow. In any case, we can certainly imagine that this is a moment in which Socrates is taking advantage of his own reputation to undermine the presuppositions of both his interlocutor and their audience: If *Socrates* remains ignorant of the nature of knowledge, perhaps those who thought they knew will now proceed more cautiously. This illustrates another aspect of Socratic interrogation: it not only challenges one to stand by a position while it is subjected to open examination, it also brings with it the imperative that one must answer seriously, carefully, and for oneself.

Whatever his audience might be thinking, Socrates is compelled to wonder aloud whether or not he is being boorish by asking them such a question, especially when his only motivation is to converse and make friends (146a6–8). Perhaps he too feels discomfort at the atmosphere he is largely responsible for having created. It is only at this point that Theodorus finally responds. His response is to place responsibility for answering the question concerning knowledge on one of his students, as he is unaccustomed to this sort of conversation, and is too old to change his ways sufficiently that he would be able to participate effectively (146b2–4). This line of questioning had been predicated on demonstrating both the qualities of Theaetetus and the judgment of Theodorus. Socrates has, however, ostensibly opened up the discussion to be an inquiry into the nature of knowledge, and one in which anyone present is invited to participate. It is only when Theodorus eventually encourages Theaetetus to speak up and provide an answer, and Socrates adds to the pressure—arguing first, that since Theaetetus has such admiration for Theodorus, he has an obligation to, and also that he has an obligation merely insofar as Theodorus is his elder—that Theaetetus finally speaks. Theaetetus speaks on the condition that if he gets anything wrong, they will simply have to correct him (146c5–6). Socrates reminds him that, while they will try to, they might not be able to. In other words, the question is sufficiently opaque that there is no certainty that the answer will be available to anyone. This observation by Socrates is perhaps intended to encourage Theaetetus that the question is sufficiently difficult that anyone would struggle with it.

(2) Estrangement: Theaetetus's First Definition. Having alerted Theaetetus (as well as Theodorus and anyone else present) that he must take seriously the positions he advocates, and having challenged him to present a definition of knowledge, Socrates next uses a technique that estranges Theaetetus from himself. That is, he forces Theaetetus to recognize the ways in which he has failed—all his life—to give consideration to his own opinion about the nature of something as fundamental as knowledge, and has therefore been operating with presumptions about the world of which he was never aware. Let us examine this process.

In his first definition of knowledge, Theaetetus makes a mistake familiar from other dialogues, but also familiar from what might be called an everyday misunderstanding of what a definition is.[35] That is, Theaetetus provides Socrates with several examples of what he takes to be knowledge rather than any single definition. Each of the sciences and crafts mentioned by Theaetetus *presumes* knowledge of that craft, but simply to list various fields whose practitioners must have a form of knowledge in fact gets us nowhere in our understanding of what it is to know. Note that here Socrates points Theaetetus in the direction of what kind of thing knowledge would have to be if the list does indeed provide examples of knowledge; whatever it is that the examples hold in common—whatever makes them identifiable as examples of knowledge—is knowledge. It is implied that knowledge will involve a form of identification through unification. To name instances is to assume that which is held in common without articulating it. Theaetetus must therefore try again, this time articulating what had been implicitly used to perform the identification he has just performed.

Already, a theme that will become so important toward the end of the dialogue—giving an account—is showing its relevance. Giving an account is the most important aspect of Socrates's method of educating Theaetetus. We will have occasion in chapter 6 to talk at length about the importance of giving an account, both to the nature of knowledge and to the cultivation of wisdom. For now, let us highlight characteristics of giving an account relevant to the immediate dramatic circumstances.

Theaetetus, like any human being, has ideas about the world that he has tacitly taken up, and that are directly relevant to his everyday life. One of these happens to be what the nature of knowledge is. To live and act is to operate with an implicit notion of knowledge.[36] However, one can function more or less adequately within one's life without having it made explicit to oneself what one takes knowledge to be. Making Theaetetus try to articulate concepts that are essential to his daily life means making him aware of presumptions that he has not consciously addressed himself to, and yet that are intimately at work in his actions. That is the first accomplishment of forcing him to give account; it is to compel him to show to himself his own presumptions. The second accomplishment is to make him recognize that—as with many tacit thoughts—what he had thought to be true was demonstrably false. Theaetetus had operated under a misapprehension of which he was not even aware. The third accomplishment of forcing him to give account is to demonstrate to him—or anyone who does so—that even to articulate successfully one's implicit notion is very difficult, and requires practice; indeed, what one typically finds—and what Theaetetus finds in his first attempt to define knowledge—is that one has failed to articulate one's own tacit notions. Not only did Theaetetus fail to provide a proper definition of knowledge, he demonstrated a tacit notion—one which is implied by the fact that he named several diverse phenomena "knowledge," and thus was able to identify each as such without saying in what *way* each was identifiable as such—that he failed to present *despite consciously trying to do so.*

This last point is crucial and requires careful emphasis from another angle. Theaetetus is not able to articulate the implicit notions he has taken for granted throughout his life. When he tries to do so, he discovers that there are in fact deeper implicit notions governing those he has just made explicit. It might be that those deeper notions are in fact empty—that he in fact has no notion at all of what knowledge is, for example—or he might find what many of us find when we seriously think about something otherwise familiar for the first time, that is, that our tacit notions do not make any sense. Despite the fact, though, that Theaetetus might discover that there were no grounds for his presumptions, it remains the case that he is not able in his first attempt to identify even that. In other words, in failing to identify the tacit notion of knowledge that made possible his ability to identify examples of knowledge, he failed to make it available—by giving account of it—so that he or Socrates could see that it was true, fraught with contradictions, totally false, or nonexistent. As long as he fails to articulate it, it will remain unknown to him.[37] This phenomenon of tacit notions is significant for at least two reasons that should be highlighted. First of all, the fact that we retain tacitly presumed notions about the world of which we have either little or no awareness demonstrates at least one sense in which we are alien to ourselves. The fact that we cannot easily give an account of *why* we believe the nature of knowledge to be this or that, and yet take ourselves to be capable of identifying instances of it indicates that part of the process of Socratic education consists in trying to uncover one's own thoughts for oneself, potentially for the first time.[38] The very activities one likely took to be most intimately one's own, the activities that together constituted one's character, were, many of them, predicated upon notions one never consciously and thoughtfully chose. Most alarmingly, one cannot without struggle identify those predicative notions. One can respond to this fact by taking flight from it, as Euthyphro does, or one can experience it as an imperative, that is, as demanding of us that we, as much as possible, cultivate the ability and the desire to articulate our thoughts, and in making them explicit, examine them.

Second, the recognition that we accumulate tacit presumptions about the world without reflecting on them allows us to play a more active role in our own lives. If one successfully identifies the fact that tacitly held notions to some extent govern one's actions, and that it is worthwhile though difficult to articulate those notions, one can take on the project of unearthing and criticizing them such that one less commonly acts unconsciously according to what are potentially misapprehensions and falsehoods. It is also possible, under the right circumstances, for one to improve progressively at giving account of one's thoughts, with the result that one is, in fact, both aware of the reality of one's self-estrangement, and perpetually courting self-knowledge. This has the curious effect of producing a great sense of freedom from the increased recognition of the extent to which we are not free in our own psychological space.

I should emphasize that what I have presented is the *possibility* of consciousness of one's estrangement from oneself that exists in Socrates's method of interrogation. Creating that possibility is the limit of Socrates's role. His interlocutor is the one who must experience that sense of estrangement, and the imperative to continue to give account that results from it. Theaetetus surely has only the germ of such an imperative—the imperative to give account—in such a brief discussion thus far. He *does* however express the kind of perplexity that is needed to cultivate it. To anticipate where we will go in this chapter for a moment, this is how I interpret what Socrates calls Theaetetus's pregnancy.

(3) Adoption: Making Ideas One's Own. As I said, Theaetetus failed to articulate his own tacit notion of what knowledge is when he gave his attempt at a first definition. He did not feel consciously estranged from himself; he did, however, feel perplexed. The way in which he responded to Socrates's explanation concerning the failure of that definition shows us another side of the process of learning, one whose necessity is equal to the disorientation of estrangement that I have outlined above. That is, the process of making ideas derived from others one's own. To explain this, I will first briefly restate Socrates's criticism, summarize Theaetetus's response concerning his geometric proof, and then present what I take to be significant about that response, namely, that Theaetetus presents something familiar to him but different from what Socrates had said, calling these two things the same, with the result that he is able to adopt the foreign idea comfortably into the fabric of his thinking, and to use it to *change* that thinking.[39] This, I will show, demonstrates the poetic dimension of learning.

We have already seen that Socrates criticized Theaetetus's first definition on the grounds that he had presented mere examples of knowledge, when a definition was on order. To give examples as one's answer presumes that the questioner already knows what knowledge is, and can therefore identify the continuity through each instance provided. But if the person cannot, or if the person is trying to determine whether the answerer knows the concept to be defined, one has to give an answer identifying what the thing is, independent of its instances, so that, in those instances, one knows what one is referring to in using the word.

Theaetetus responds by saying that this notion that identifying instances does not adequately demonstrate knowledge of a concept seems clear to him now. The clarity of it arises, not merely from what Socrates has said—which, indeed, is not exactly clear, since much of his meaning is left unarticulated—but from how what he has *inferred* from what Socrates has said relates to a geometric problem he had apparently been engaged with recently (147c8–d1). By comparing Socrates's point to his own experience he makes it his own. Let us look at the problem (147d3–148b3), with attention both to what his discovery accomplished, and to how it relates to Socrates's point.[40]

Theodorus had been, at an unspecified though presumably recent time, demonstrating a series of lines that were incommensurable to a one-foot line. Incommensurability in this case means that two lines cannot have a third line of different length shared in common. Theodorus demonstrated this on a three-foot, a five-foot and a seventeen-foot line (and this presumably is taken to apply to all prime numbers). Theaetetus and his friend who shares Socrates's name tried to unify all of these numbers, in order to be able to comprehend why this is the case. They took all numbers that can be divided into square roots and put them into one category, called Square Numbers.[41] They then took those that can only be divided by two different numbers (e.g., seventeen would be by seventeen and one, five by five and one, etc.) and called them Oblong Numbers. They further put those that *did* have a commensurable divisor, but only when it was multiplied three times (e.g., nine is three by three) and called them cubed numbers, and so on.

As a result of having performed this method of organization, Theaetetus and Socrates the Younger accomplished an explanation for the fact about numbers that was shown to them by Theodorus. In other words, it was not enough for Theodorus to show Theaetetus that prime numbers had the character of not having a commensurable divisor. This bare fact was not all that Theaetetus saw in having it shown to him. What Theaetetus saw is that those facts *point* beyond themselves to something deeper, and that that deeper thing was drawing him to it. Theaetetus was compelled to strive to know.[42] One need not have been so compelled, but Theaetetus was. He therefore organized the facts he had been given in such a way that he was able to explain the reason for them. There are different kinds of number, each of which is constituted in such a way that its examples have characteristics unique to them. These characteristics produce what is revealed to us as the oddity that some numbers have commensurable roots, others do not, and indeed, among those that do not, there are different ways in which they do not. Further, Theaetetus found a way to represent this explanation visually in the form of the geometric figures of square, rectangle, and cube. This insightful activity is what compelled Socrates to declare that Theodorus did not speak falsely in complimenting Theaetetus, which is to say that Socrates now sees the quality he was looking for in him (148b3–4).[43]

Theaetetus accomplished an explanation of what lies behind what presents itself in prime numbers. In addition to this, Theaetetus accomplished two other things that we should take note of. First, he went beyond the numbers that were initially made available to him in order to generate a new approach to those same numbers. He translated them into different types of number by expressing them as geometric forms. Once he had expressed four as a square, seventeen as a rectangle and nine as a cube, he was able to return to the domain of number with a way of reading it not initially immediately clear to him. This was a creative act; while the explanation given by Theaetetus was true, he had to articulate it for it to become apparent as true. The truth of that insight was hidden from him (and, indeed, from anyone prior to its demonstration by him, if indeed he is the first figure in mathematics to make this discovery) until he made it clear to himself by articulating it.[44] Second, in conversation with Socrates, Theaetetus used similar creative thinking to try to understand what was problematic with his initial definition of knowledge. Theaetetus, in listing geometry and all the other arts as instances of knowledge, was doing as Theodorus had done in listing three, five, and seventeen. For Theaetetus to understand this, he had to draw the connection between the two activities, allowing the geometry exercise to provide him with directions he could apply to this new, unfamiliar inquiry. He was able to begin the process of *making* the idea his own, and consequently transforming the reality as he experiences it of what knowledge is, as much as the reality of the structure of those numbers was transformed for him.

Taken together, these aspects of Socrates's interrogation have extracted from Theaetetus his own patterns of thought, and have shown those patterns of thought to him. This further provided him with the resources to make the subject matter about which they were concerned—the underlying material that is *ultimately* being extracted from him—his own. This is rendered analogous to the birthing process by Socrates.

3. Socrates as Midwife (149a1–151d3)

When Socrates compliments Theaetetus for the latter's demonstration of having appropriated Socrates's criticism and applied it to his own experience—specifically saying that it turns out that Theodorus was not speaking falsely in praising him—he does so to encourage him to try again. Theaetetus either misconstrues that compliment or tries to evade the persistent demand to give an account, arguing that he does not deserve Theodorus's and now Socrates's praise due to the fact that he would not be able to achieve the same accomplishment with the question of knowledge that he had with his own geometric proof (148b5–8). Theaetetus expects himself to be measured against an absolute standard. Socrates points out that he is like a young and talented runner whose potential cannot be justly measured against the fastest runner at his peak (148c1–4). It so happens that discussing the nature of knowledge constitutes one of the most difficult tasks one can undertake; Socrates, himself presumably analogous to the fastest runner at his peak, struggles with this very question. Therefore, Theaetetus should engage in the project with confidence, knowing, as he momentarily demonstrates that he does, that the subject matter is important and worthy of the effort. Note here that Socrates is claiming that in spite of the fact that he surely will fail to define knowledge adequately, Theaetetus must strive to do so confidently (148c9–d2). In other words, Socrates is here suggesting that Theaetetus consciously adopt an orientation toward knowledge that is at first glance rather puzzling, that is, coincidently to strive boldly to know while at the same time becoming increasingly aware that one cannot achieve that knowledge.

When Socrates is given Theaetetus's consent, he picks up where he has left off, asking him to imitate or reenact the performance with numbers, this time with knowledge as his object, which is to say, to make the question of knowledge his own, so that he might better discover what he is able to come up with. Theaetetus once again does not consider himself up to the task. He claims that he has heard of Socrates's interest in this kind of question, and has tried to give consideration to it on his own (148e1–3). Those efforts have failed because he found himself unable either to persuade himself that he says anything adequately or to hear someone else speaking in the way that Socrates urges; but he has nonetheless also been unable to rid himself of his concern with it.

Theaetetus claims that he is persistently unconvinced that he is even able to engage in this sort of discussion, and he cannot find anyone who will do so in a way that helps him (148e3–7). It is in this statement that Theaetetus articulates one of the great obstacles to philosophical education, and implicitly makes the argument for the necessity of good teachers. He finds these issues intrinsically interesting, yet doubts he is even able to talk about them and cannot find anyone who can. Philosophical questioning cannot be answered alone. One requires a guide, and there is no reason to assume that a person who is interested will be able to find such a guide. This is perhaps part of the reason for Socrates's compulsion to seek out talented young men. If they do not know where to find him, he has to find them. Theaetetus is, in Socrates's view, pregnant and in need of a midwife. Socrates is that midwife (*maia*).

Socrates tells Theaetetus that his mother was a "noble and farouche" midwife, and that he is, too (149a2). Theaetetus has heard about Socrates's mother's vocation, but not about Socrates's own. Socrates tells him that others are not aware that he has this art and that as a result they say that he is strange and that he makes human beings perplexed. Others do not understand Socrates because they do not know what his art (*technē*) is (149a6–10).

Here we are given another example of a set of characteristics which, on their own, cannot be understood. What is required is for us to identify the organizing principle underlying those characteristics. Socrates's seemingly strange behavior can only be understood if we learn its organizing structure. Fortunately, this is what he provides us with. Socrates warns Theaetetus that he must reflect on what characterizes midwifery "in its entirety" if he wants to understand (149b4–7). A mere list of attributes will not provide understanding, and may, it is implied, create a distorted sense of the art.

First, midwives are at a stage in life at which they are themselves no longer conceiving, but they did conceive when they were younger. Those who have always been barren cannot be midwives because human beings are too weak to act as guides concerning things about which they are inexperienced (149b10–c3). A midwife has been fertile and has given birth, but is now at a stage in life where she no longer is able to do so. One of the advantages of having had this experience is that midwives are able to identify who is pregnant and who is not (presumably at an early enough stage that her condition is not obvious even to the pregnant woman, but one at which it would surely be useful to know, in order to make any necessary health and lifestyle adjustments). Second, midwives are able to encourage and stimulate labor, to aid in making it less painful, to make those who would seem unable to bear, and to induce miscarriage if it seems necessary or desirable. Third, midwives are excellent matchmakers; which is to say that they find people that together would be fertile, and productive of healthy babies.

This attribute is perhaps the one Socrates had in mind when he warned Theaetetus against misunderstanding the craft by not thinking of it in its entirety, first because it is an aspect of that craft with which Theaetetus is not familiar, and second because of the superficial similarity this craft bears to pimping (*proagōgia*) (150a1–6). This latter reason explains the former one. Midwives are masters at finding matches appropriate to the production of good pregnancies. This art they regard with greater esteem than all others associated with pregnancy. However, because midwives are people of dignity and worth, they engage in matchmaking rarely and cautiously, since there is a wrongful form of matchmaking—called pimping—that is not honorable. They do not wish to develop a reputation wrongfully for performing a dishonorable activity when they are in fact performing one of the most honorable and noble ones. It is nonetheless the case that the only kind of person who can truly perform the craft of matchmaking is the midwife. We should, as we shall now discuss, have Socrates and his trial in mind when thinking about this, as Socrates will essentially claim that *his* craft is misunderstood by those who would not consider it in its entirety.

Though Socrates will explicitly draw an analogy between his craft and that of the midwives, he begins that analogy by pointing out a distinction between them. The midwives perform an enormously important, poorly understood, and insufficiently respected craft. His craft, however, is even more important, more poorly understood, and less sufficiently respected. The reason for this is that, while the patients of midwives bring forth only real children, the offspring of Socrates's patients can be either real or false (150a8–b4). His job therefore has the added feature of having to scrutinize whether or not the offspring is real. His task is more difficult than that of the other midwives because his preoccupation is with the soul rather than with the body. All manifestations of a body will be real, and the midwives will respond to real circumstances in inducing the child's birth. The possibilities of the soul—which is to say mental or spiritual possibilities—are immaterial and indeterminate, and therefore not of necessity tethered to reality.[45] When Socrates induces an idea from the young men of Athens, he has the added responsibility of assessing its relation to reality. This distinction is not intended to denigrate the responsibilities of midwifery, or those of any craft focused on the treatment of bodies, or to denigrate bodies as such; rather, it is to acknowledge that there exist a far greater range of variables associated with psychic possibilities, and therefore far greater risk of corruption. This attribute—or at least Socrates's conviction concerning it—should enrich our understanding of why he cares about this particular craft most of all. Its responsibilities are the greatest of all for the ethical and political life of human beings, insofar as they give shape not only to the kinds of ideas one has, but, in consequence, to the kind of person one is.

Having said that, however, Socrates continues to draw what is otherwise a mostly direct parallel to "somatic" midwifery. Socrates induces the thoughts of young men to come forth. While it is the young men who are pregnant, meaning that they come to him fertile and ready to realize mental creativity, it is he, Socrates, who delivers them of their ideas. He, like the midwives, is barren—although unlike the midwives, he strongly insinuates that he has been barren his whole life (150c3–d2).[46] His barrenness is barrenness of wisdom. Those who have mistakenly decided that they did not need Socrates during their pregnancy have miscarried, insofar as they have produced false images rather than true ones. One such student is Aristeides, son of Lysimachus. In such cases, the young men typically stumble upon their own ignorance much later, and return to him. Some he takes back, others he does not, according to his daemon (151a1–5). Those that do come back begin to make progress again. Those with whom he decides not to associate turn out not to be pregnant; he therefore matches them with others with whom ideas can be conceived, for example, he has paired many with the Sophist, Prodicus (151b2–10). Socrates describes this immediately before encouraging Theaetetus to continue to try to produce a definition of knowledge while at the same time warning him against being angry in the event that Socrates finds that he was pregnant with nothing at all, as others have been. Following from this warning, Theaetetus expresses his willingness to go on (151d7–e1).

One could hastily interpret this speech as presenting Socrates as someone who compels people to show him what they think they know, so that he might assess the legitimacy of their claims through rational inquiry. This is no doubt true insofar as it describes the activity that Socrates engages in with the young men (and is engaged in here with Theaetetus). But to leave the interpretation at this level is equivalent to interpreting the activity of teaching to be merely the transmission of information from one person who knows to another who does not know. While those events are manifest in the result of teaching, there is much more beneath the surface; good teaching must involve the production of a relationship with people at an appropriate stage of development, and ideally without the kinds of commitments that accumulate throughout adult life to inhibit free and open inquiry. It involves catering to the needs of the particular student, to allow them the opportunity to begin serious inquiry concerning their ideas about matters essential to their lives. In thinking about this speech, as in thinking about teaching, we need to dig beneath the surface of the basic actions that Socrates describes, which we now have the resources to do.

Socrates's midwifery is not only like teaching as it has been characterized so far. Socrates is attempting to unearth in his "students" the ideas with which they operate in their daily lives. In so doing, he will tend to provoke them to become angry, or to flee from further inquiry. When Socrates warns Theaetetus not to leave angrily, it is not because he has dealt with young men that are unusually temperamental about pedantic rational arguments; rather, it is because the conversation will rapidly become personal. It will become personal because, in articulating the definitions of concepts with which he has been unknowingly operating, Theaetetus will be shown who he is, and will be shown who he is in the presence of others.[47] Socrates here, and we can assume in other such circumstances too, does what he can to frame the discussion in such a way that Theaetetus will not be made to feel more vulnerable than he must, but, in drawing Theaetetus's attention to the tendencies people have during the process of delivering themselves of their ideas, he does not deny that Theaetetus will be made to feel vulnerable.

Socrates's psychological midwifery is more than just a mere academic exercise. It is a kind of personal interaction that is transformational and somewhat traumatic—we should remember that Socrates describes the process of giving birth to the ideas as painful, and should remember that he explicitly drew an analogy to the pains of childbirth. As was discussed above, Theaetetus struggled with philosophical questions on his own in a fashion that produced great frustration. The frustration grew out of being gripped by intimately relevant philosophical questions, yet lacking the conceptual equipment and the experience necessary to sort through them. His frustration came from simultaneously believing something was important, and believing that he could not adequately address its importance. This is psychological pregnancy. It is Socrates's job, as a midwife and as a teacher of wisdom, to equip Theaetetus with the means to address the importance of his questions.

We should note, finally, regarding this speech, the significance of Socrates's claim to have been barren of wisdom all of his life (150c3–7). This, too, contrasts with his claim that the midwives had to have had experience giving birth, because human beings are too weak to act as guides concerning things about which they are inexperienced. Socrates does not have experience with wisdom, and yet he engages in psychological midwifery. Indeed, he appears to be the only person so engaged. What would it mean to have experience with wisdom, and why does Socrates of all people not have that experience? Who can secure wisdom?[48] As I have characterized it thus far, wisdom consists in the confrontation with a contradictory pair of imperatives. On the one hand, we must strive better to know the nature of reality and the nature of the soul. On the other hand, and as a result of this process of striving, we must reconcile ourselves to the uncertainty that lies at the heart of our experience. Socrates is an inadequate midwife only if we were to hold him to a standard no human being could achieve.[49] Socrates, too, is a student of wisdom.[50] In fact, regarding philosophical education there are no teachers who are not also students, and there cannot be. This is due to the fact that it is in the nature of the soul that our pursuit of knowledge cannot achieve its accomplishment, yet we are called by that same nature to pursue it nonetheless.[51]

Conclusion

This chapter has addressed the question, how can wisdom be taught? The common sense answer to this question is that it cannot, insofar as it is characterized by an attitude toward the world and toward one's experiences of it. In other words, the subject matter of such lessons—the activity of the soul—is inaccessible to any teacher. However, in this chapter I have argued that one can teach wisdom, provided that one modifies one's conception of teaching to accord with the characteristics of the soul discussed in chapter 1—the salient characteristics of which being the essential passivity of the soul in relation to its knowledge of the world, and the fact that the soul is essentially a temporal development. I presented Socrates in the *Theaetetus* as a paradigmatic demonstration of this kind of teacher. He is a psychological midwife who seeks out young men at a stage in life where they are able most of all to benefit from serious philosophical discussion of a sort that implicates the whole of their character, and therefore compels them to undergo a turning of their soul toward further philosophical inquiry, and toward the recognition that they must care for their own soul, and must do so by giving account of themselves in dialogue with others. In shifting our attention to the student, I will claim that it is characteristic of Socrates's kind of teacher always to continue to be a student, due to the fact that the project of wisdom is never complete, yet is nevertheless experienced as perpetually worthy of pursuit.

CHAPTER 3

The Delivery of an Idea (151d4–160e6)

> Though one perceives the particular, perception is of the universal.
>
> —Aristotle, *Posterior Analytics*, II.19 100a16–17

Introduction

In the previous chapter, our attention was directed to Socrates's maieutic craft, and its application to Theaetetus. I claimed that cultivating in a person the pursuit of wisdom begins with the process of training one to question one's own presumptions, and implicitly to cultivate recognition of the intrinsically desirable nature of such a process. Teaching one to pursue wisdom consists in developing an understanding of the contrasting insights that one's understanding of reality is always incomplete, and that striving better to understand is intrinsically valuable. While the previous chapter was directed at what it is to teach a person to be philosophical, this chapter is, in part, directed at what it is to learn to be philosophical. Our attention shifts from the teacher to the student. In that context, Socrates uses the examination of Theaetetus's first definition of knowledge as an example of how to think through the implications of an idea. To begin thinking about what it is to be a student, then, I would like to think about thinking.

We do not automatically think well. Thinking well requires training. Let us not mistake training for activity. We are always involved in the activity of thinking. We are always thinking—indeed, we think, so to speak, without even thinking about it. Our immediate impressions do not give us everything there is to know about reality; by means of something manifestly true of reality that we are compelled to think about, we can at times be totally misled in our thinking to false conclusions. For example, from birth, we are typically given the impression that food, shelter, clothing, and emotional comfort are automatically provided for us. It takes a long time—perhaps a lifetime—for us to be reconciled to the fact that, on the contrary, this manifest reality (one hopes) of the early years of our lives that our essential needs are provided for us is false when generally applied to the whole of life. We sometimes suffer psychologically from our unwillingness to reject this initial impression.[1]

In our experience, it might not be made apparent to us that thinking requires training. The immediate impressions we have do not necessarily explicitly indicate to us that we must reflect on them. We clearly should, though, because, as indicated above, sometimes they are wrong, and these wrong impressions can be difficult to shed. This was one of the implicit messages in Socrates's description of himself as a midwife. Theaetetus was not marked by Socrates to be special for having an idea; we all, in the everyday sense of the word, have ideas. Rather, Theaetetus was marked to be someone puzzled and compelled to wonder by the seeming incommensurability of various manifest attributes of reality. I argued in the previous chapter that this indicated, first, that Theaetetus was someone for whom the essential, initial childhood training for a predisposition to do philosophy was already accomplished, and second, that Theaetetus harbored implicit claims about the world that he was not able to articulate, but felt he needed to. This was his "intellectual pregnancy."

Indeed, one of the attributes of "intellectual pregnancy" that distinguishes it from the bodily pregnancy to which it is metaphorically related is that intellectual pregnancy does not *necessarily* make itself apparent to us. To recognize one's intellectual pregnancy is to have the groundwork for creative thought and active participation in one's own education, which Theaetetus to a large extent had. The failure to recognize one's intellectual pregnancy, by contrast, occasions the retention of intellectual offspring. What does this mean, if we step outside of the analogy? We accumulate implicit presumptions about reality. Throughout life, however, we have experiences that do not cohere with those presumptions. The incoherence of conflicting presumptions provokes wonder, which is to say that it provokes a sense in us that reality is not comprehensible according to the terms we already have for grasping it. Thus reality continually calls for our reflection. If we fail to acknowledge this lack of coherence—if we fail to dwell with the wonder provoked by our recognizably incomplete understanding—and thus to challenge our presumptions, we retain those presumptions without diagnosing their responsibility in provoking that initial incoherence. We therefore further entrench ideas worthy of questioning.

By aiding in the birth of the idea, Socrates is not only bringing to the attention of Theaetetus the presumptions that governed his thinking; he is also helping Theaetetus experience the process of thinking an idea through to completion. This provides him with the important experience of seeing the way in which an idea has implications that stretch beyond terrain immediately apparent at his current level of understanding. It is worth dwelling for a moment on this notion of thinking through an idea. When we make a claim, that claim is not isolated. Claims carry with them implications, whether we acknowledge them or not. It is sometimes the case that the claims seem to be manifestly true, and that they will continue to appear to be true until we make the effort to consider the implications of what appeared obviously true to begin with. On occasion it will turn out to be the case that what we thought was true was not true, and our only way of discovering this is through deeper reflection on the effects of the presumed truth elsewhere.

This idea, too—that ideas carry with them implications that may or may not be immediately apparent—has implications. First, it means that, insofar as our experience of the world is constantly generating ideas, our experience does not immediately give us the whole of reality. There is, so to speak, a creative bottleneck in experience, each new idea demanding to be worked out in its implications but typically being superseded by others. This perhaps accounts for the need to think through the most fundamental ideas, insofar as their implications have the greatest reach. Second, the fact that ideas carry potentially concealed implications means that we ought to adopt an attitude toward our experience of reality that is very different from the attitude we are typically inclined to adopt. We are typically inclined simply to take for granted that what is immediately apparent is exhaustive of what is there to be apprehended. The very different attitude that we ought to adopt is to be at one and the same time hesitant to commit to certainty about particular ideas, and eagerly curious to reflect on the impressions we are immediately compelled to adopt. If our immediate impressions about reality carry with them claims about which we do not have immediate certainty, yet which we harbor without being aware that we do so, then we ought to strive to know better, and simultaneously ought not to be committed to certainty. This attitude that we ought to adopt is the philosophical attitude.

The philosophical attitude bears the structural characteristics of *erōs*.[2] When I use the term *erōs*, I take it to mean the experience of simultaneously wanting to be one with something, and wanting to hold it admiringly at a distance.[3] Indeed, as we shall see in the discussion of this chapter, as well as in subsequent chapters, Socrates characterizes our experience, from its rudimentary level of immediate apprehension all the way up to the highest philosophical apprehension, in terms of erotic, procreative coupling.[4]

Due to the fact that such a substantial quantity of the dialogue is devoted to the discussion of the first definition of knowledge, I will devote two chapters to its analysis. In this chapter, I focus on the "delivery" of the first definition of knowledge provided by Theaetetus—that knowledge (*epistēmē*) is perception (*aisthēsis*) (151e2–3). In chapter 4, I focus on the analysis of this definition, articulating its implications both for the concept of knowledge and for the educational experience of Theaetetus. The orienting theme of the current chapter is that an important part of philosophical education is being compelled to express for oneself the implications of one's commitments. I frame the discussion according to specific lessons Socrates hopes Theaetetus will learn. Section 1 consists in the initial discussion of the delivery of Theaetetus's "offspring." Here, I emphasize the significance of the fact that considerable discussion is necessary to move from a bare definition to an idea. I claim that Socrates here demonstrates to Theaetetus that he had not previously known the meaning of his own idea, and provides him with a lesson in the importance of working through implications. Specifically, Socrates shows Theaetetus that in at least a certain version of the claim that knowledge is perception one is required to commit to the claims, first, that each perceiver is independently the arbiter of truth, and, second, that we erroneously attribute to what is perceived that it *is*, when in fact it merely *becomes*. In section 2, I discuss Socrates's examination of Theaetetus's definition of knowledge. I orient the discussion around his demonstration to Theaetetus that there could be no knowledge without a commitment to the fact that nothing can both be and not be at the same time, in the same place, and in the same way. In other words, this section is a lesson concerning what has to be taken for granted in the structure of reality. Section 2 of this chapter is in important ways the centerpiece of my entire analysis of the dialogue, insofar as it most explicitly develops the analogy between erotic coupling and perception, which is essential to our understanding of the implicit claim being made concerning the actual relationship between knowledge and perception.[5]

This chapter is thus concerned with two forms of initiation: the initiation into the activity of reflection on thinking, and the initiation into what we take to be our immediate apprehension of things. In both cases, the object of discussion is an activity intimate to everyday life, and therefore an activity resistant to reflection. Moreover, each activity—reflection and sensuous apprehension—is dependent upon the other in a manner that is hidden when it is examined independently of that other.

1. The Labor of Articulation (151d4–152a10)

Socrates's "intellectual midwifery" occurs in two stages resulting from the distinction between delivering an idea and delivering a baby. Socrates distinguished his practice of intellectual midwifery from bodily midwifery by noting that it involved not only the delivery of the idea, but also evaluating the idea to discover whether it is true or merely imaginary (150a8–c3). In bodily labor the birth of the baby leaves no possibility for mistaking that it is real; after birth in intellectual labor, by contrast, there is additional work required, this time shared by the patient and the midwife. The fact that the idea is "born" does not entail its "reality." What Socrates did not say, though subsequently demonstrated, is that the labor process itself is divided into two stages, the first consisting in the pregnant person presenting a definition, the second consisting in the midwife and patient together articulating the implications to the definition. This second phase of the labor essentially consists in revealing what the idea *actually* is, a revelation one might erroneously assume is entailed in the first utterance of the definition.[6] Only as a result of the additional process of drawing out its implications can the idea effectively be subjected to examination, because only after the implications have been drawn can it be known what is being evaluated. Thus, Theaetetus gives his definition of knowledge, and only much later—after the implications are drawn—does Socrates declare that the idea has been delivered, and is therefore ready for scrutiny.[7]

a. Preparation for Labor and the Proper Conditions for Conversation

Theaetetus claims to be sufficiently encouraged to provide a definition of knowledge of his own immediately following Socrates's midwife speech (151d7–e1). What Theaetetus says indicates a change in his attitude toward the explicit purpose of the conversation. Socrates has just implied that Theaetetus is someone pregnant with an idea that it would be best for them to examine together. Socrates's speech shifts the emphasis from asking Theaetetus to provide a definition of knowledge, to the task of helping Theaetetus with an idea that may or may not be one he wishes to identify as his own. In other words, Socrates's speech indicates that he is not merely interested in examining Theaetetus's quality as a young philosopher, but also in contributing to Theaetetus's philosophical development. The pressure is not on Theaetetus to provide a complete and nuanced account of knowledge, but rather to provide, as best he can, what his immediate impression of knowledge is, so that he can be educated by that process.

Socrates surely did not expect Theaetetus to accomplish an adequate account of knowledge. If we imagine how we would generally expect a person to behave in a situation like this, we might expect that Theaetetus, when asked to provide a definition of knowledge, gave little thought to what Socrates's expectations of him were. Having been put on the spot, he was probably mostly preoccupied with how to answer. If Theaetetus is particularly self-conscious in this moment, he is not in an adequate position to recognize that Socrates is initiating a process of working through the idea rather than determining whether Theaetetus could give the best answer. When one is exclusively preoccupied with how well one is answering rather than with trying to express the relevant subject matter, one has implicitly adopted a defensive attitude, an attitude in which one presumes to be under scrutiny rather than to be involved in a shared investigation.[8] In contrast to this attitude, when Socrates compares himself to a midwife, making explicit (part of) what he wants of Theaetetus, the latter is able to answer without anticipating what is being expected and unfavorably comparing what he is capable of uttering with that anticipated expectation. He is able, in other words, more freely to think of an answer.

Though Socrates's speech apparently was encouraging, insofar as Theaetetus characterizes it as such (151d7), we should not forget the terms of the analogy to childbirth, and therefore should emphasize not only the importance of encouragement to this project but also the importance of recognizing its seriousness and difficulty. A midwife treats a woman who *will* have a child, assuming it comes to term. The process of childbirth has very specific and serious demands that must be addressed in order for it to go smoothly. When a woman is experiencing pregnancy for the first time, it is only reasonable for her to be frightened of the risks to her life and to her child's life, as well as to the unanticipated changes to her life that result from that birth.[9] While it would surely be an important responsibility of the midwife to reassure the pregnant woman that she is capable of successfully giving birth, it would be unwise for the midwife to assuage the woman's fears by underemphasizing the importance of the labor that she must perform.

We ought to think of Socrates and Theaetetus in terms of this relationship, insofar as Socrates sets the relationship up in that way. Socrates is the guide, and Theaetetus ought to assume, if he trusts Socrates (and whether he understands or not) that that guidance will lead to the goal of delivering him of his ideas. Theaetetus's encouragement ought to come from the fact that Socrates is there to look after the development of his soul, and, more specifically, the fact that Socrates is trying to teach him how to think more deeply about the things that fill him with wonder. By contrast, he ought to recognize that the issues that he is thinking about are serious, and that to deal with them seriously is not merely to present a few interesting or exciting ideas, but rather to work through the ideas thoroughly.

Note that I say Theaetetus "ought" to adopt this view. We, or any third party looking on, might well recognize that Socrates has Theaetetus's interest in mind, and that he will in fact benefit Theaetetus if the latter allows him to. This does not mean that Theaetetus recognizes this. Socrates probably will not be able to establish fully in one long conversation the kind of trust in him required for this process to be successful. Indeed, though Theaetetus frequently demonstrates in words and in behavior that he trusts Socrates, he nonetheless on several occasions behaves in ways that betray a lack of trust on his part. For example, at one point Theaetetus chooses not to give his opinion of an argument that Socrates presents, on the grounds that he does not know whether Socrates himself agrees with the argument he has given (157c4–6). It seems clear that Theaetetus wants to know if Socrates believes it in order to avoid agreeing with something Socrates will later refute, or disagreeing with something Socrates will prove to be true. Theaetetus does not trust that—whatever Socrates's opinions might be—the purpose of asking Theaetetus to give *his* opinion concerning the argument is to get him to think independently. Were Theaetetus actually to trust Socrates, he would not be concerned with Socrates's opinions, or with saving face in Socrates's presence, but would be only concerned with allowing Socrates to help him in his delivery.

The fact that, despite explicitly *believing* otherwise, Theaetetus *demonstrates* a lack of trust in Socrates demonstrates to us an important aspect of the process of learning from a guide. It takes trust, but that trust takes time to establish. Even if Socrates in fact merits Theaetetus's trust, he must earn it. This means not only making Theaetetus willing to trust him, but also making Theaetetus *actually* trust him. The latter can only be achieved over considerable time, cannot be realized by Socrates's efforts alone, and does not obviously lie within the conscious control of Theaetetus. Theaetetus must develop a sense of security in his ability to explore, and this sense of security must be tempered by a sense of responsibility to respect the ideas he is exploring. It is not yet clear to Theaetetus, though, that he must develop these attributes. We will see that his sense of security wavers, as does his sense of responsibility. Socrates can only begin to educate Theaetetus in serious philosophical conversation by having such a conversation, and must therefore expect that the basic criteria of serious conversation—that is, liberty to follow the ideas where they lead tempered by respect for the seriousness of the topic—will not be consistently met. He will have to do most of the work, and the motivations behind that work will not always be understood.

b. Why Socrates Does Not Take Theaetetus's Definition on Its Own Terms

Sufficiently encouraged by Socrates, Theaetetus provides his first definition of knowledge: knowledge (*epistēmē*) is perception (*aisthēsis*)[10] (151e2–3).[11]

He reasons that, because of the fact that when someone knows, they perceive what they know, knowledge must be perception. Socrates claims that this is a splendid example of what he is looking for in a definition (151e4–8), not, let us emphasize, that this is a good definition. We should further note that Socrates does not respond to this definition disputatively. He does not, for example, go on to ask how Theaetetus knew that people perceive when they know, given that he has yet to establish what knowledge is. He does not ask why the simultaneity of knowledge and perception entails their identity, even though Theaetetus appears merely to assume this. He does not provide examples of what might typically be called knowledge that do not occur simultaneously with what we typically call perceptions. Socrates does not begin by disputing Theaetetus's definition because he is trying primarily to educate Theaetetus, and his method of education begins with getting Theaetetus to commit to a definition, so that his investment in that definition will lead him in the process of thinking through its implications.[12] For Theaetetus to commit requires that Theaetetus trust Socrates. It would shatter the fragile nascent trust between them if Socrates were to criticize immediately the idea that is to be worked through. It would also undermine the purpose of the project if Socrates were to put him on the defensive immediately. It is very important that Theaetetus be committed to the position for the analysis to have its most powerful effect, and that he understand that he is not being evaluated based on his answers, but rather is being prepared for the process of working through those answers.

Instead of disputing Theaetetus's definition, Socrates associates it with an idea already established and worked out. He claims that Theaetetus is giving a speech that is not trivial, and one given previously by the famous sophist Protagoras, namely, that "of all things (a) human being is the measure, of the things which are, that they are, and of the things which are not, that they are not" (152a3–5). Theaetetus indicates that he is quite familiar with this speech. When Socrates describes what is meant by this speech—that as things *appear* for each of us, so they *are* for each of us—Theaetetus agrees with this characterization (152a7–10). Thereafter, the conversation is grounded in Socrates's account of Protagoras's version of Theaetetus's definition, that is, "the same things" said "in a somewhat different way" (152a2). Before examining the metaphysics of this claim, let us consider the method of connecting two apparently distinct claims.

What is the relationship between Theaetetus's claim that knowledge is perception and Protagoras's claim that man is the measure of all things? We will have occasion to outline them in great detail below. For now it will be sufficient simply to anticipate some of those connections in broad strokes, for the purpose of demonstrating some of the implications that will be drawn for Theaetetus by Socrates. Theaetetus's claim that knowledge is perception and Protagoras's claim that man is the measure of all things are certainly not the same when considered from the standpoint of the question that they seek to address. Theaetetus's claim seeks to answer the question "What is knowledge?" while Protagoras's claim—though it is surely relevant to this first question—is explicitly addressing the ontological status of things.[13] Protagoras's claim is that all things have their being or non-being, only to the extent that they are measured by human beings, and only according to that human measurement. Though Protagoras's claim is ontological rather than epistemological, his claim does nonetheless have an epistemological implication that makes it a pertinent parallel to Theaetetus's definition. For Protagoras (as characterized here by Socrates), each of us is the arbiter of the truth of anything we experience; each of us is a site of truth.[14] Further, each of us is such a site discretely, which is to say that each person's "truth" is unaffected by the "truths" of others. How I experience the world dictates the truth of that world for me; it is likewise the case for you and for everyone else.

As I mentioned above, this begins as an explicitly ontological claim. Protagoras is essentially rejecting the subsistent reality of objects independent of experience, and, further, rejecting the continuity of the objects between subjects. Whether the object is or is not depends on me. Moreover, the fact that I am the sole arbiter of the being of the object means that the being of the object for anyone else has no bearing on the being of that same object for me. Yet despite the fact that it is an explicitly ontological claim, it is only a *small* further step to see how what Protagoras says is relevant to the claim that knowledge is perception, and it is here that we are given a glimpse of the unexpected reach—at least for Theaetetus or perhaps anyone new to philosophy—of his initial definition. If each of us is the discrete arbiter of the being of each object of experience, as Protagoras claims, then it is how each of us perceives the object that dictates for each of us what that object is. The purchase the object has on reality is dictated *for* each perceiver *by* each perceiver. It is then only a further step to elevate the status of our perception of the object to *knowledge* of the object. If I am the measure of all things, to describe how I perceive those things is the same as to describe what those things are. I am unerring in my perception, since perception is equivalent to the apprehension of being. If I am unerring in my apprehension of all things, and if knowledge is the correspondence of the being of the object with my apprehension of it, then my perception of the object is also knowledge of it.[15]

Though it takes only a few steps for us to see the connection between an ontological and an epistemological claim, it was *Socrates* who enriched

Theaetetus's epistemological claim by presenting Protagoras's ontological claim in response, and Socrates did so before the conversation about Theaetetus's definition even began. Because of Socrates's interpolation of Protagoras's definition at the outset, the stage was already set for the discussion of knowledge as perception to implicate the issue of the ontological status of objects. Socrates initiates a shift in the conversation by demonstrating that by talking about knowledge one is always talking about objects of knowledge, and by demonstrating what the relationship is between the being of objects of knowledge, and the nature of knowledge.

In the discussion that immediately follows from this initial interpolation, Socrates guides Theaetetus through an account of perception. I have just noted that, in part as a result of Socrates having tethered the Protagorean claim to the initial definition, the question of the being of objects of perception underlies that discussion. While, in our analysis of it, we should pay careful attention to the way in which the definition of knowledge invokes the being of objects of knowledge, we should also attend to the account of perception on its own merits, independent of the question of being. In what follows, I will argue that Socrates simultaneously demonstrates that knowledge and perception cannot be the same, and does so by giving an account of perception that is true, and therefore not without qualification equivalent to knowledge.

2. Perception as Erotic Coupling (152b1–160e6)

The outer sphere of Socrates's project in relation to Theaetetus is to cultivate his conspicuous potential for philosophy, and to do so by engaging him in philosophical dialogue. The first step in getting Theaetetus to develop his thinking is to have him invest himself in an idea, and to see that idea drawn out to make evident to him its implications. This step has the virtue of demonstrating that one's ideas have implications one need not have been aware of, but that one ought to become aware of, and as a consequence of this, to demonstrate the need for dialogue as a means to aid in the demonstration of those implications. The result of this step would ideally be that Theaetetus would be better able to think through his ideas in the future, and more willing to subject them to the scrutiny of others. The explicit idea Theaetetus is to be invested in is his claim that knowledge is perception. Socrates must therefore help him to work through this incredibly rich topic so that he can learn the virtues of working through his ideas, and engaging in dialogue as the principle method of working through them. It is with this aim that Socrates leads Theaetetus into the complex, digressive, varied discussion that follows, and we should keep this in mind, so that we can better understand several otherwise seemingly bizarre conversational choices that Socrates makes.

a. Perception as Initiation

Theaetetus's claim that knowledge is perception initially makes sense, as does the claim attributed to Protagoras that man is the measure of all things. More than that, each is in a certain sense true. Of course, we are trying to move from what is "in a certain sense true" to what is true without qualification. But let us spend a moment defending the initial plausibility of these claims, and let us do so with emphasis on the idea of initiation. Knowledge is initiated within us. There is no point in talking about knowledge without invoking ourselves as knowers. This is perhaps best illustrated in comparison to other things that are not knowers. Water, like a human being, interacts with the world around it. It undergoes change in its material constitution, and does so as a result of its interaction with other things. But, despite the fact that the rocks or fire or air with which the water interacts have an effect on the water, they make no impression on the water. The water has no stance toward the rocks; it is *merely* altered by them.

By contrast, human beings have attitudes toward other things. For us, things are not just things; they are *objects*, and they are *our* objects. We do more than just cause material reconfiguration of ourselves and other objects as a result of our interaction with them. We experience, we measure, other things. Things, understood as objects, are *of* our experience. In other words, insofar as the things in the world are, for us, experienced things, they are measured in terms of our experience. We may talk about them as though they are independent things sharing space with us, but the fact that we can talk about them in this way is made possible because they appear for us primarily as objects of our experience.

Considered from this standpoint, it certainly makes sense to begin an account of knowledge with perception, and, with that in mind, to think of knowledge as something characteristically human, because we are the kind of beings that measure things. To be the kind of thing that can know means to be something that can make contact with the things in the world in such a way that those things are objects for it. Perception is the name for that kind of contact, that kind of power. To be a knower is essentially to be the kind of thing that measures things; that is, to turn things into objects—to have things matter to one—is to be something that measures.

This initial stance of intuitive plausibility does not make quite as sharp a claim as does Theaetetus. It is perhaps evidence of his lack of experience that he speaks in absolute terms about something that requires subtle distinctions. Theaetetus does not say that knowledge begins with perception, but rather that it *is* perception.[16] Nor, in his characterization of Protagoras, does Socrates interpret the claim that man is the measure of all things to mean that human beings constitute the sphere in which the being of things is opened up. Rather, Socrates interprets Protagoras—perhaps justly—as being more radical, and it is from this standpoint that his evaluation begins.

b. Relational Identity and the Denial of Independent Being

As I mentioned above, to interpret the claim that human beings are the measure of all things that they are or are not in the most radical sense is to say that we are, each of us severally and discretely, the arbiters of the being of all things. The first example Socrates gives to illustrate this impression is that, when the wind blows, one person will get a chill from the draft, while another will not (152b1–4).[17] For the first person, it *is* cold, for the second it *is* not cold. In each case, something—for now we will say "the wind"—has its being designated, and in each case that designation is different. In presenting this example, Socrates characterizes the wind, in one case, appearing to be cold, while in the other appearing not to be cold. The appearance of the cold is the perception of the cold. In each case, then, it would seem uncontroversial to say that how the wind appears for each person is also how it *is* for each person. Put differently, each person is the arbiter of the being of the experience of the wind, and it would make no sense to deny to either person their experience that the wind was cold or not cold, as each is the measure of what it is for herself. From this example, that is, without further considering contrasting examples, it would seem that perception is one and the same as knowledge, and consequently a reflection of what is. For this person, the draft *is* cold because she perceives it in that way (152c2–3). The experience of perceiving the cold in this way is at the same time knowledge that the draft is cold.

Even before considering counter-examples, there are surely ways in which the conclusions drawn from this characterization of the experience of a cold draft can be criticized.[18] Socrates does not go on to perform that criticism, however. Instead, he wonders aloud whether Protagoras is all-wise, whether he has spoken in riddles (*ēnixato*), and if he has left them with truth "as if it were a forbidden secret to his pupils" (152c10–11). Socrates goes on to articulate what he implies is the deeper meaning to the claim Protagoras has made (a claim which, he alleges, Theaetetus has agreed to). He claims that what has so far appeared to be a description of the nature of knowledge of what *is* turns out to be a demonstration that what we typically take to be, *is not*. According to this speech—one, we should note, that is never attributed to anyone, and that is at least not obviously to be attributed to Socrates—we are wrong to think that anything is a discrete independent thing (a "one alone by itself"), and we address things erroneously when we do so (152d2–e1). Let us consider what this means.

We know the wind in terms of its attributes. It is a cold wind, a warm wind, a strong wind, or a gentle wind. Those attributes emerge for us because we experience them; they have relational identity. When we call the wind cold because it feels cold, we imply that it "is" cold, in the sense of having an identity one of whose characteristics is coldness, and that this is the case independent of our experience. But when we do so, says the speech, we do so falsely; the proof of this—though not the explanation—is found in hearing someone else call the wind warm. When she calls it warm, she does so no less falsely than we do when we call it cold, but not because her account differs from ours. Rather, her account is false, as ours is, because the identity of the wind cannot be given independent of the ones who experience it.

This claim implies a more general one about the being of objects of experience that Socrates presents as underlying the enigmatic claim of Protagoras, namely that they have no independent being.[19] Let us examine Socrates's presentation of Protagoras's claim:

> After all, nothing is one alone by itself, and you would not address anything correctly or of any sort whatsoever, but if you address it as big, it will also appear small, and if heavy, light, and all things in this way, on the grounds that nothing is one, neither something nor of any sort whatsoever. But all things—it's those we say are the things which are (not addressing them correctly)—come to be from locomotion and motion and mutual mixing; for nothing ever is, but (everything) always becomes. (152d2–e1)

We said before that an object is always *for* someone experiencing it. All objects have what we falsely call their "being," and ought actually to call their becoming, again, according to Socrates's version of Protagoras's speech, in each case through mixing with a subject. From the mixing of particular objects with particular subjects emerge attributes such as "cold" or "warm" and the like. Because the object is given different attributes depending on the character of the mix it produces in tandem with its corresponding subjects, it is as its relational identity, ever-changing, or perpetually in motion. If perpetual motion and intermixing is constant, that which we typically construe as a thing turns out always to be undergoing transformation, which makes it impossible for us to designate accurately what it is that we are referring to over any given time span of intermixing, and, importantly, independent of its intermixing. What we call a "being" in fact perpetually always "becomes" (152e1). "It" is becoming cold for me while simultaneously becoming warm for her. Though Socrates does not designate any specific thinker as the source of this doctrine, he claims that all the wise in succession converge on this point, with the exception of Parmenides. Protagoras, Heraclitus, Empedocles, Epicharmus, and Homer all reject the notion that we can speak of being, due to the fact that all that we can say is that there is the activity of intermixing that can, at best, be called "becoming." What we *call* a thing, everything that "is," is "the offspring of flowing and motion" (152e6–7).[20]

This notion of offspring—which recurs throughout the discussion—is important; though Socrates neither asserts it as his own nor repudiates it, there is nonetheless a significant insight that one can derive by thinking of perception as the offspring of contact between perceiver and perceptible object. One might typically assume the everyday view that we experience things in the world because the sense organs of our bodies come into contact with independent objects. According to the broad near-consensus of the wise (with the exception of Parmenides), though, says Socrates, what we call independent objects *emerge* from the contact between motions (152e2–3). If this is the case, then what we would typically have assumed to be the "world," that is, whatever lies beyond our senses awaiting our sensuous contact, would not resemble what emerges from our perception of the world. If the objects emerge from contact with the world as the "offspring" of that contact, we can no longer make reference to that constituted world—that is, to that "offspring"—to find the objects that are the presumptive source of its constitution. We make contact with "becomings," rather than beings, that develop what we take to be their complete identities only as a result of contact with subjects. We name the object that emerges from our contact, our procreation with becomings "wind" or "table," and, in so doing, erroneously presume that what we have just named, along with all of its attributes, precedes the circumstances of its contact with us, when in fact it was that contact that gave it its identity. The identity of the wind or the table—its being—is tenuously contingent upon its being perceived in this particular way at this particular moment by us. The emergent "being" of the object will change in a way that corresponds to the subject that perceives it. It has no independent being. Nothing about which we can speak, in fact, has independent being.[21]

c. Motions: Corporeal and Incorporeal, Generating and Managing

This idea that the objects of experience are all offspring that "become" through the interaction between perceiver and thing is Socrates's initial account of the truth of reality according to all the wise with the exception of Parmenides. We will return to it shortly because Socrates reformulates this vision several times. Before he restates it, though, Socrates presents several justifications for adopting the positions that motion is primary, that being is illusory, and that what we think "is" in fact "becomes." In other words, Socrates lists evidence one might readily appeal to in order to demonstrate this initial counterintuitive account (153a5–8). First, locomotion and rubbing is the cause of fire and heat, which are the forces that manage and generate all things, and therefore motion is primary (153a8–b1). Second, motion and rubbing are the causes of the procreation of animals through sexual intercourse (153b2–3). Third, motion and exercise are required for the maintenance of living bodies, whereas stillness and idleness are causes of the corruption of bodies (153b5–7). Fourth, the improvement of souls is provided by the stimulation of learning, which is a kind of intellectual motion, while, by contrast, the deterioration of souls occurs when they are not stimulated to change (153b9–c2). Fifth, without the motion of the sun, the world as a whole would fall into corruption and decay (153c7–d5). In each of these cases, so the argument goes, essential things are utterly dependent upon motion for their maintenance, and, we should add, in at least all but the fourth case (that of learning), for their generation. Socrates asks if these together are to be taken as sufficient demonstration that the good is "motion both in terms of soul and in terms of body" (153c4–5).[22]

Socrates presents this list in order to add evidence to his claim that it is immensely difficult to refute the consensus of so many wise men (153a4–6). It is as if to say, "not only would we look foolish to refute such venerated figures as these, we would also look foolish because they are providing accounts of reality that are responsive to what is manifestly obvious if we spend a moment thinking about it." We should, however, pay attention to the examples themselves, and ask ourselves the question: what are the kinds of motion Socrates provides here, and what do they tell us about motion in general? Some of the motions described are presumed to generate while others to manage. Further, most of the motions described are corporeal, while at least one appears to be strictly intelligible. Let us examine each, bearing these two distinctions in mind.

The locomotion and rubbing that generate fire are presented as being responsible for creating "that which both generates [*genna*] and manages [*epitropeuei*] everything" (153a9).[23] Perhaps this is saying that fire is primary among the elements, in the sense that fire is the source from which the other elements emerge; yet it nonetheless appears that locomotion and rubbing precede even fire. It is appropriate that this is the first example Socrates gives. In a certain sense—specifically, if indeed fire generates and manages everything—he need not provide further examples, since he has reached the foundation. If he has reached the foundation, though, the account of the conditions required for the generation of fire (those being whatever it is that rubs together to produce the friction and thus the heat needed to generate fire) would be unnecessary. What is in locomotion if the primary element (fire) has yet to be generated? Nothing is to be generated or managed without fire and heat, yet fire and heat are said to be generated by locomotion and rubbing. It seems, on reflection, that fire (or something else if a better candidate emerges) must either be primary or conditioned, but cannot be both. If locomotion and rubbing are necessary for the generation of the given substance, then that substance, it would seem, must be the result of the activity of some other that is engaged in the locomotion and rubbing.

Perhaps Socrates—who is, we should remember, presenting a case for the idea that reality provides "adequate signs for the speech that says that motion supplies that which seems to be" (153a6–7), and not himself endorsing the claims made by that speech—means only that fire is the source of generation in the sense meant in the second example (sexual intercourse). Here, where locomotion and rubbing during sexual intercourse is said to be the cause of the generation of all of the kinds of animals, generation is said differently than we might have imagined it in the first case. The individual members of each species of animal are generated in sexual intercourse, whereas the species as a whole is managed by it. It would be impossible—in a sense, as it turns out, similar to the case of fire—for one to claim that animals as such came to be out of the locomotion and rubbing of sexual intercourse, insofar as the procreative sexual intercourse needed to generate particular animals depends on their being particular animals of that species already engaging in that intercourse.[24] In this example of sexual intercourse, motion is necessary for the management of the species and for the generation of individual members of the species. However, it is *neither* sufficient for the generation of the species, *nor* even possible for the generation of the species. Likewise, assuming that fire is the primary substance, motion would be necessary for the management of fire, and for the generation of particular instances of fire, but not sufficient for the generation of fire as such. Rather, if there is a sense in which fire is primary, it would appear that it must have co-emerged with motion.[25]

The third and fourth examples (bodily exercise and learning, respectively) present cases that have explicitly to do with management rather than with generation. We exercise the body and the mind—the former through bodily motion, the latter through the activity of the mind—for the purpose of managing their respective kinds of health.[26] In each case, motion is presented as necessary for health, and, insofar as health perpetuates life and illness causes life to deteriorate, necessary for life. Because these examples make no claims about generation, they do not fall into the problem of having to deal with the metaphysical puzzles associated with generation and primary substances that the first and second do. What makes the examples of bodily exercise and learning interesting is that they introduce the distinction between the corporeal and the incorporeal.

The first example Socrates presented, that of fire, had purported to be that which generated and managed everything that is. We already discussed the problem of identifying as a primary substance and a primary cause something that is itself generated by locomotion and rubbing. However, even if it were to make sense to talk about fire as being both something generated and the cause of the generation of all things, it is said to be both caused and a cause in strictly material terms. Let us assume that fire is necessary for the generation of all material things (perhaps insofar as it is fire that increases density of matter, out of which all bodies are constituted). How can something that generates through motion that consists in friction generated by rubbing two material things together generate something that has no material form? How does fire generate thoughts? Or, to use Socrates's example of learning, how does the rubbing of material things generate educational development?

Putting aside for the moment the rather substantial questions of the interaction between corporeal and incorporeal entities and of the cause of the generation of life, let us turn to the fifth example. It is said that the motion of the sun is a necessary condition for life. The sun is here presented as the generating source of all of life in the world, as well as the necessary condition for the maintenance of that life. Unlike in the case of fire, no attempt is made to account for the source of the being of the sun. Its motion is simply recognized as a necessary cause of the order of all earthly reality.

Socrates presented this list to Theaetetus in order to demonstrate that there is considerable immediately available evidence to support the notion that motion is primary, and that those things that are taken to be beings are in fact themselves always in motion and therefore undergoing change. However, on closer examination, what his examples demonstrate is that, while it seems clear that motion is essential to the maintenance of everything in our experience, and is responsible for the generation of particulars—particular fires through friction, particular animals through sexual intercourse—it cannot be used to account for the origin of the primary substances it posits. Nor does it seem to be capable of accounting for the reality of intelligible things that have no material content to engage in motion.

Theaetetus does not yet notice that questions ought to be raised regarding the metaphysical claims to which he has (presumably unwittingly) committed himself. Though the examples that Socrates has presented here might provide immediate evidence to reinforce the presumption that all is primarily motion, these examples ought to be countered with the serious metaphysical questions that I have merely pointed to—specifically, the problem of presuming primary substances, the problem of absolute generation, and the problem of accounting for all of reality in strictly material terms. None of these issues are explicitly addressed in the discussion, at least in part because Theaetetus neither raises them himself, nor even offers the slightest resistance to the examples, the latter of which would at least give Socrates cause to voice resistance himself. These remarks therefore announce, on the one hand, problems with the unqualified claim that all is motion, and on the other hand, what is more relevant to the education of Theaetetus, problems with Theaetetus's attention to that claim. This latter problem is especially serious, because Theaetetus has agreed to everything that has been said despite the fact that, on reflection, some of what has been said is deeply problematic, while some requires more detailed discussion. Theaetetus's inattentiveness is a symptom of the fact that he is unable to apprehend immediately that there is a problem to be discussed.

d. The Principle of Non-Contradiction and the Necessity of Independent Being

Having failed to engage Theaetetus's attention to the puzzling implications of unqualified, absolute motion, Socrates chooses to draw out a different implication. He follows the speech to its most radical limits, it seems, in order to elicit a questioning or at least uncertain response from Theaetetus, so that Theaetetus can be shown the unexpected claims to which he would be committed were he to adopt the speech as his own. Specifically, Socrates will challenge Theaetetus by pointing out that if he agrees to the claims that motion is primary and that being is a fiction, he will have to deny any metaphysical commitment to the idea that something can both be and not be in the same way at the same time and in the same place, that is, what we know to be the principle of non-contradiction. Let us examine how this is so. In order to do so, we will present the speech in favor of the primacy of motion, presuming its account to be true.

Let us assume that nothing is fixed, but all is in motion.[27] Continuing to "follow the speech of the moment" (153e5), Socrates characterizes those things that erroneously appear to us as independent things, as in fact being emergent results of the interaction of motion with our perceiving organs.

Socrates takes the example of color (153d9).[28] We would be mistaken to consider color to be something that exists independent of vision. Color is not in the objects themselves, but is rather the product of the eye being applied to them. It is something "having come to be" (*gegenēmenon*) (153e7–8). Though Socrates does not use this term, we might describe color as an event, since it is not intrinsic to the surface with which our eyes make contact, but is rather the result of the aggregate of perceiver and perceptible object. In other words, color does not subsist when subject and object are no longer in contact with each other, because it is intrinsic only to the interaction between them; it is the name given to what is seen. Further, because the object—that is, the manifold of reality waiting to be perceived by me—is in constant motion, contact between subject and object will always generate new colors. In our everyday understanding, we may construe this table as brown today and brown tomorrow, but we will do so despite the fact that during that time what I am calling the table will have continued to undergo change. What I take to be the second occurrence of seeing the table as brown is, rather, according to this account, a completely distinct event of contact between my eyes and their object, out of which emerges something that I construe as a brown table.

There are three points that must be emphasized about the details of this in many ways intuitively plausible account of perception. When we rigorously follow out the implications of this interpretation of the event of perception, we see that some untenable conclusions are implied in it. First, since the event of the emergence of color depends upon the contact of my eye with an object (or, in keeping with this account, a motion) whose objectivity is impossible to fix, the color that emerges is never to be found independent of the contact of eye to motion; there is no objective attribute to anything outside the event of contact, since attribution only occurs within the event of contact. Second, since the event of contact is between *my* eye and the motion, the experience of color is shared neither between different species of perceiving beings nor even within a species; each contact is an experience unique to each individual because no perceiver shares his or her specific perceiving organ with any other perceiver. My experience of the object sets up strict borders around itself that no other person can cross. Third, since the motion that makes contact with the eye is constantly undergoing change, it is novel in each moment of contact, and there is thus not even shared experience of color within the individual perceiver. The parts which, in contact with each other, generate the color are both constantly changing. There is therefore not only no subsistence to the object. There is also no subsistence to the subject: therefore, in addition to there being no shared experience within the species, there is no shared experience within an individual. For perception to be possible, the perceiver must rely upon the sense she has of continuous experience as a subsisting perceiver. On this account, however, there is no continuous experience whatsoever, insofar as the "being" that emerges from the perpetually changing motion that the subject perceives cannot in fact be shared by the subject with her future self, from moment to moment. Since there is nothing subsisting from moment to moment, there are no grounds on which to base comparison. There is therefore no more a fixed unchanging being called "subject" than there is one called "object." Both emerge only from the coupling of motions.[29]

The consistency of this formulation, when taken to its conclusion, comes into direct conflict with fundamental experiences we have. The problem with this formulation seems to be that the speech quarrels with something deeply ingrained in us, something that is at least not obviously false, namely, that things are identical with themselves, and that they are altered not simply by how they are in relation to other things, but only according to changes they themselves undergo. In order for the perceptions to be unique to each of us, and *not* to refer to objective attributes, but, rather, to be something whose existence only occurs in the contact between the perceiver and the perceptible, this would have to presume the stability of the perceiver and the perceptible, and the implication of the stability of the perceiver and the perceptible would seem to indicate that even the perceptions that emerge from this coupling would have to have a kind of stability. Socrates illustrates this point with an example, though an example that is not taken from the apparently unstable domain of perception. Let us first present the example, and then make note of the effect it has on Theaetetus.

Socrates proposes that Theaetetus think of the relationship between certain quantities of dice (154c1–5). If I put six dice next to four dice, I say "the six dice *are* one and a half times the four." If I put the same six dice next to twelve, I say "the six dice *are* half the twelve." The ratios of 3:2 and 1:2 respectively occur between the two, which is to say that those ratios are the product of the contact between the two sets of dice—just as the perceptions were said to be the product of contact between the perceiver and perceptible object. For the contact to produce that which lies between them they must remain self-same, that is, the six must remain six, and so on. Further, the resulting ratio is accountable only as a reflection of particular attributes of each number. In other words, the number six does not become something different by mere virtue of the fact that it is put in relation to the number twelve in comparison to the number four. Six can only change if six itself becomes a different number, and can only relate differently to four and to twelve if it remains the number it currently is.

What does this have to do with perception, or with Protagoras? To answer this, let us apply the insights of the analogy to number to the original account. When the object perceived is placed into contact with this perceiver as opposed to that one, it is perhaps the case that the perceptual result differs—indeed, it seems that this is necessarily so, insofar as each brings to bear on the contact with the object a unique perspective. However, one cannot exactly make the same claim about the perceived object. Placing six in front of four as opposed to putting it in front of twelve produces the result "one and a half greater" as opposed to "less by half." This placement, however, not only does not alter the character of six, but also in fact depends upon six's self-identity in order to produce this specific ratio. Correspondingly, though my perception of the object will differ from yours, not only will those perceptions not themselves produce changes in the object—though the object appears differently to each of us—but those perceptions are made by attributes belonging to the object itself.[30]

This illustration depends upon an analogy to number, whose rhetorical power lies with the fact that relations between things are presented in terms that depend upon numerical fixity. In the case of the dice example, it is impossible—if we accept basic axioms about the nature of numbers—to deny fixed value.[31] Since we know by definition that six did not stop being six as a result of being measured in relation to different objects, if the analogy stands, we know that the perceiver and the perceptible are not changed by their being measured in relation to their objects, either. Socrates presents this analogy to Theaetetus to force him to stand back and examine what they have thus far claimed, and so that they avoid letting themselves get carried away making further claims they would not, on reflection, hold.

According to Socrates, whenever we entertain such ideas as these—that is, that all is flux, that therefore all knowledge of things depends only upon the particular subject-object relationship, and that therefore nothing can properly be said to "be," but can rather only properly be said to "become"—we are confronted with ideas we must reconcile ourselves to, those being that (1) nothing becomes greater or less in bulk or in number as long as it is equal to itself; (2) nothing that has not had addition or subtraction applied to it becomes greater or less, but on the contrary remains equal to itself; (3) nothing that was not before can ever be later without coming to be and becoming (155a3–b2).[32] Though we may consciously avoid articulating these notions to ourselves, we will nonetheless unavoidably have to face them in our own thoughts. Indeed, we would not be capable of thinking about any of these issues—including thinking about the account of flux that challenges these three ideas—if we did not at a deeper level appeal to them.[33] Whatever we might choose to say, whatever we consciously identify to be true, in thought, we insist on the truth of these claims.

This distinction between thought and speech is brought up by Theaetetus, and is worth close consideration in relation to the principle of non-contradiction. In response to Socrates's analogy to number, Theaetetus claimed that if he wanted to maintain consistency with what he had said previously, he would be compelled to deny the point that is illustrated there. In other words, to be consistent with his agreement to the notion that all is flux, he must deny that objects can undergo change only if they change in themselves in relation to themselves. On the other hand, if he did so, he would be denying the actual content of his thought. The analogy to number effectively denied to Theaetetus the ability to claim *in thought* that a change in a given entity's relative position alone implied a change in the entity itself. That the six is half relative to one number and one and a half times relative to another does nothing to affect the six in itself (though it certainly does affect its relational identity); as was stated above, because it is the nature of six (or any number) to be a quantity, if it were the case that change in relation, and the resulting change in ratio, were to have an effect on six, it would be made evident by six's no longer being six. Theaetetus, like anyone else, could continue to insist otherwise in words spoken to others. Socrates's choice of number as the example establishes the clarity of a certain kind of idea, one whose self-evidence imposes itself on thought. This is certainly no arbitrary example, since it provides us with something that appears to be shared between anyone capable of thinking. If we share in the recognition that six is unchanged in itself by its being put in relation to different numbers, then it would seem that when we conceive of that idea, it is not *we* that are the measure, but rather the bare facts themselves about the constitution of number and ratio. These facts of number and ratio impose themselves on anyone who thinks them.

There is an important consequence of this phenomenon of facts imposing themselves on one who thinks them, one that is illustrated by Theaetetus's response to the example. He can choose either to acknowledge that six in itself does not change through its relative status, but rather only through increase or decrease, or he can lie to Socrates, and claim otherwise for the purpose of maintaining consistency to the radical version of the speech about motion. It is as a result of the imposition of facts that error and deceit emerge as possibilities for Theaetetus or anyone. That is, because of the fact that there are things the measure of which does *not* depend on the perceiver, but rather on the object perceived, we can make mistakes about what is, and can consciously choose to deny what is. The availability of facts both to be perceived, and to set standards of measure independent of us, opens up the domain within which people can deceive others and make mistakes.

These standards of measure and the consequent possibilities of error and deceit together open up yet another domain. That domain is philosophy. Theaetetus can choose to deny the fact which Socrates has pointed out to him, despite being, in thought, persuaded by it, or he can choose to acknowledge in words his own thoughts, with the result that there is a contradiction in the speech concerning motion and the non-being of independent objects which Socrates just gave, and with the resulting imperative that they ought to continue to discuss it until they figure out what exactly is wrong. What I call here "the imperative that they continue" could also be given the name "wonder" when it is described from the standpoint of experience. Wonder is precisely what Theaetetus claims to have in the face of these very problems. It is also the starting point of philosophy (155d3).

e. The Myth of Infinite Motions

Socrates listed three versions of dogmatic commitments that obstruct us from accepting the motion speech, each of which is a version of the principle of non-contradiction.[34] He claims that we are faced with these whenever we are forced to grapple with problems emerging from talking about changes to attributes of one being that do not result from a change intrinsic to that being, which is to say from talking about the ontological status of relational attributes. Socrates does not want to deny that there is reality to his being "taller than Theaetetus" when the latter is young and "smaller than Theaetetus" when the latter is grown up, all without himself undergoing change. Nor, indeed, does Socrates want to deny that the fact that there is reality to relational being is significant.[35] It is with this in mind that Socrates attempts to restate the account of absolute motion that appeared previously to have been refuted. It is important that we bear in mind the difference between this account and the former less detailed one, and why Socrates chooses to maintain a version of the account, despite the fact that the example of the six dice appeared to have refuted what was said.

The first account claimed that there was no independent reality—except an ill-defined perpetual motion—to objects of perception, but rather that all attributes of objects, as well as distinct objecthood itself, are generated only through perception (153e6–154a2). This time, Socrates aims only to account for the generation of perceptions, and to distinguish them from the object with which our senses make contact to provoke perceptions. He does not claim that what emerge as distinct entities have no identity prior to their coming into relation. Rather, he seeks to account for the relations that do emerge. That is, no matter how dogmatically we wish to assert the independent reality of objects of perception, we cannot deny that they have attributes that only make sense when characterized in terms of their relation to others, and these therefore must be taken into account.

Before moving on to discuss in what way these dogmas confront the speech about motion, though, Socrates warns against "ferreting out the hidden away truth of a renowned man, or rather, renowned men" in the presence of the uninitiated (155e1–2). These uninitiated people consist in those who believe that "nothing else is except whatever they are capable of getting a tight grip on with their hands, but actions, becomings, and everything invisible they don't accept as in the class (part) of being" (155e6–10). Included among those things that are not visible are the relational identities that have caused such confusion. The uninitiated who wish to deny the reality of such things are, according to Socrates, "without the Muses to a large degree" (156a3–4).[36] Socrates does not explain why it is important that the uninitiated be excluded from their conversation. Instead, he goes on to provide a long and difficult speech that provides a more sophisticated account of the primordial activity of motion. This speech initially takes the form of a myth. Perhaps it is the case that those he designates as unmusical, insofar as they are unwilling to recognize the being of "actions, becomings, and everything invisible" (155e8–9), are incapable of experiencing wonder, if by wonder we mean the impression that there is something unaccounted-for by our immediate experience of things, though it is by no means obvious that this is what Socrates had in mind.

Let us assume that Socrates wants to exclude those incapable of experiencing wonder, because they are committed to the notion that experience exhaustively accounts for the nature of reality, and are therefore resistant to the experience of wonder that generates an interest in philosophical dialogue. At the very least, then, what is being acknowledged by Socrates here is that the conversation depends upon the character of its members. Were he and Theaetetus to be stuck in that conversation with someone insisting dogmatically on a kind of brute materialism, and being unable to see the purpose of what is under discussion, then the conversation would be compromised. That is, an unmusical participant in the conversation would not only fail to add anything useful to the conversation; they would also detract from it. This idea that the conversation between Socrates and Theaetetus would deteriorate as a result of the involvement of people who were not personally committed to philosophical dialogue builds on a theme that has been prevalent throughout this section of the dialogue, that is, that placing things into contact with one another has generative power. The addition of the unmusical person to the conversation would generate an undesirable "ratio," one that would have the effect of ruining Socrates's implementation of his maieutic art. In turning to Socrates's speech, we should imagine how it would be met by the presence of the unmusical person, and if, as indeed I intend to show, this speech proves to contain profound insight, we should imagine the extent to which the presence of the unmusical person would have denied it to us as participants.

Socrates presents the myth in two stages. The first stage is the myth proper (156a4–c4), the second, the explanation of what the myth *wants* (*bouletai*) to say (156c8–157c1). Let us first describe the myth, second, analyze it and summarize what its claims are, third, present what Socrates claims the myth wants to say, and, finally, examine this second speech.

Socrates begins by saying that the myth comes from the "mysteries" of "the rest" (namely, those who *are* musical) who are "far cleverer" (156a4–5). This is the extent of his attribution of authorship. He says that "their principle" "from which everything is attached" is that all that there is comes from motion, and that there is "nothing else beyond this" (156a7–9).[37] While all is motion, there are two species of motion, each of which is "infinite in multitude," but one of which has "power to affect" and one of which has "power to be affected" (156a10–12). The "association" and "rubbing" that occurs between these infinite powers produces offspring in the form of that which is perceived and that which is perception (156a12–b2).[38] The latter (perception) is always "falling out together with" and "getting generated with" that which is perceived (156b2–4). The perceptions take the names of "sights and hearings and smellings and freezings and burnings and, yes, pleasures certainly and pain and desires and fears" (156b5–7); in addition to these there are "very many" other named perceptions, as well as "the nameless" perceptions that are "without limit" (156b8–9). Corresponding to these perceptions are co-generated colors and various other things perceived. With this Socrates ends his presentation of the myth by asking Theaetetus if he can see what the myth wants to accomplish (156c4–5). Before considering the answer (provided, not by Theaetetus, but by Socrates), let us examine what we take from this initial presentation.

Socrates starts with the same premise with which he began when he first provided a schematic version of the idea of infinite motion (152d2–e1). All that is has its origin in motion. Motion is infinite; however, Socrates adds this time that infinite motion is primarily, or primordially, dual in nature. He does not explain why, but rather only says that the primary infinite motion is made up of the infinite power to affect and the infinite power to be affected. Why is motion primarily dual in nature? We cannot look to the text for an answer to this, because nobody provides such an answer. Nonetheless, it seems that if we are to accept that the primordial origin of being is infinite motion, we have to identify what its characteristics would be. It is perhaps possible for us to conceive of all of the things in reality being fundamentally *in* motion. But can we conceive of reality being fundamentally *motion*? We must think carefully about the ontological character of what Socrates is presenting as fundamental motion. If we do, it becomes clear that it must be dual. Following from this, by implication, relationality must be co-fundamental with motion, both logically and ontologically.

If all is motion, then this implies that there be at least an active element causing motion; for, if there were only a passively moved element, motion as such would never happen.[39] Whatever the material constitution of this "infinite motion" from the myth, if it is indeed primary, it would have activity as an attribute of its being. However, activity as such requires material on which to act;[40] that which acts *imposes* its action on some kind of context, otherwise it would have no opportunity to act. More generally, motion as such would be impossible unless it were relative to some context in relation to which it moves. This means that motion cannot be completely accounted for strictly in terms of activity. If all is motion, then all must simultaneously include the acting element of motion *and* the domain on which the action occurs, that is, the passive recipient of the action. Motion must *be* relative to a domain it is *being* moved *through*. This is what the constitution of a reality of absolute flux would necessarily consist in. Thus, absolute or infinite motion must consist in that which moves and that which is moved; more generally, to posit motion at all is to implicitly presume a dual aspect to reality.

We must further be clear on what is implied and what is not implied by this claim that if reality consists of infinite motion, then it must be dual in nature (i.e., must consist in both absolute activity and absolute passivity). This claim about reality implies that activity and passivity are co-fundamental attributes of infinite motion. Indeed, Socrates reports that the myth claims they are two species (156a8). It cannot mean, however, that there are two species of motion in the sense that, say gorillas and chimpanzees are two species of primate or pens and pencils are two species of writing utensil; at least, it cannot do so and remain consistent. That would be impossible, because if these were two metaphysically discrete species of motion, it would mean that neither absolute activity nor absolute passivity would be *absolutely* in motion; each would be unmoving with respect to activity or to passivity (i.e., to its identity as a species of activity or a species of passivity), and in a way analogous to the motionlessness (i.e., changelessness) of the gorilla or the chimpanzee with regard to its species identity. Put differently, if absolute active motion were to remain distinct from absolute passive motion—because it were a species distinct from the other—it would be motionless with regard to its identity as absolute active motion. Though Socrates characterizes the duality of absolute motion loosely as consisting of two species, were he to be rigorous about it, it would have to be the case that absolute motion is and must be at all times qualified in the following sense: it must be at one and the same time activity and passivity, which is to say, understood according to both terms, and perpetually oscillating between the two, in order for it to be at all.[41] Though neither the activity nor the passivity of motion can be coherently understood without its corresponding other, this mutual interdependence has to take the form of perpetually changing between passivity and activity with respect to its internal self-relation. What *emerges* from this oscillating internal self-differentiation—perceivers and perceptibles—would appear not to oscillate in precisely the same way (which, we will see, Socrates refers to as the "slower motion" in his presentation of what the myth wants to say), but rather to maintain some kind of identity as what we would call subjects and objects.

The interaction between active and passive motion, according to the myth, is procreative and is strongly implied to be analogous to sexual intercourse. This procreative aspect of dual infinite motion is rather obscure. The interaction between active and passive motion generates, as its offspring, twins, that is, the perception and the perceived. It is not clear in what sense it is meant to do so, but there are a few possibilities it suggests. While in the account of active and passive motion Socrates does not explicitly state that each is mutually dependent on the reality of the other, or that each implies the other, he does explicitly state this regarding the perceiver and the perceived, that is, perceiver and perceived have their being only insofar as they are in relation to each other.[42] This latter case can at least be understood as the offspring of the active and passive motions insofar as the logical interdependence between perceiver and perceived is a species of active and passive motion. Their interdependence, as it were, calls upon the logical interdependence of activity and passivity.

The infinite motions generate perceivers and perceived objects. Each of the twins takes a variety of forms. The perceiving side takes the form of sight, hearing, freezing and burning, pleasure and pain, desires and fears, among many others that we have names for, and an infinite number more that we have no name for (156b4–7). There is no limit, in other words, to the possible manifestations of perception as such. The side of the perceived has a corresponding set of perceptibles that is therefore likewise without limit. Thus is the basic myth accounting for all that there is, as well as all that is and could possibly be perceived of what there is.

Let us briefly recall what Socrates's description of the myth was responding to. Theaetetus's sense of wonder had been provoked because it appeared that what we think of as entities possessed of attributes—for example, Socrates possessed of tallness—turn out not to possess those attributes themselves, since Socrates had possessed tallness in relation to the younger Theaetetus, and now possesses shortness in relation to the older Theaetetus, without himself having undergone any change (155b4–c1). If the attributes of a thing do not belong to it, but rather belong only to the activity of perception, then it would seem that the being of the thing does not belong to it, and is always fluctuating according to its relations; if Socrates is now tall, now short, now hot, now cold, and so on, it would appear that what Socrates *is* undergoes changes according to the relations that characterize his attributes. In response to this wonder, Socrates had presented the myth.

How can it be that the being of a given thing does not belong to it, when we are committed to thinking otherwise? It can, by virtue of the fact that what always appears to be one is in fact necessarily two, and it is out of those two that its oneness, its being, emerges. Moving backwards through Socrates's myth, we begin with the color white (though we could begin with the object that is hot or the sound that is loud).[43] Though it certainly appears that the color white is the attribute of the surface of the thing I encounter with sight, and that my encountering of that thing is a passive reception of its whiteness, this is a poor account of what has happened because it offers no distinction between the thing and my perception of the thing. If the account were to do so, it would change. To name "whiteness" is to name, not the surface of the thing, but rather the perception of its surface. Already implied in this improved account is an activity shared by two entities (perceiver and perceptible) the result of which activity is whiteness. White is the result of the contact between perceiver and perceptible. The power the perception of whiteness *has*, to be what it *is*, stems from the fact that precisely the same activity of perception can be described from two standpoints, namely, one in which the perceived object is described, and one in which the perceiving subject is described. Whichever one we describe, we nonetheless presume the other. An important implication of the fact that a perception is in fact what emerges from the inextricable contact of subject and object is that we ought not to confuse the event of perception with the object, and should not forget the extent to which we are actively implicated in the generation of the event of perception.

Before moving on to discuss Socrates's elaboration on this myth, we should consider some other examples Socrates gives of perceptions that are generated in the interaction of infinite motions, because they are more obviously examples of relational identities. He claims not only that what we would call sensations are generated, but also that more elaborate experiences and emotional states, such as pleasure and pain and desire and fear, are generated by the primordial coupling (156b5–9). Since nothing is said by way of explanation for these examples, we must once again merely speculate regarding Socrates's meaning, which is certainly not clear. At the very least, it appears that these emotional states analogously emerge from the interaction of perceiver and perceptible. It seems clear that the object perceived does not contain within it fearsomeness, desirability, pleasurableness or painfulness. For example, we experience the tiger as fearful to us, because it wants to kill us, yet its cubs experience it as desirable as a mother. Though we may want to say that its quality as a fearsome killer somehow belongs to the tiger, this attribute is not something that the tiger in itself can enact. On the contrary, this attribute emerges only as a result of its relationship to something else, and is therefore highly changeable and not a necessarily intrinsic attribute of the tiger.

If it is the case that perceptibles on their own do not contain the attributes we typically assume that they have—insofar as those attributes exist in the perception that emerges out of the coupling of perceiver and perceptible (which themselves are said to have emerged from the coupling of infinite motions)—then it must be correspondingly the case that perceivers on their own do not contain the attributes we typically assume that *they* have. Fearfulness, desire, pleasure, and pain as much as sight and hearing must always be *of* something. A perceptible object is implied. Indeed, this structure of mutual interdependence is presumed by the very naming of them as perceiver and perceptible. Perceivers always, by definition, perceive objects. Perceptible objects are always *for* subjects. Among the implications of the dualistic account of motion was that it demonstrated that when we make the attempt to name what is fundamental in terms of flux—as Socrates alleges all great thinkers with the exception of Parmenides have done—we will fail to do so coherently unless we present it as a relationship.[44]

There are several points to take away from our study of the original presentation of the myth, and I will briefly summarize them in the order in which they appeared for us.

First, we have seen that if reality emerges from perpetual flux, what is required is that that flux be primordially self-differentiated into activity and passivity, albeit an activity and passivity that itself perpetually oscillates between the two.

Second, we have seen that it is the coupling of activity and passivity that produces perceptible reality. This returns us to what I suggested was the erotic dimension of perception.[45] I had defined *erōs* as the simultaneous desire to be one with something and to hold it admiringly at a distance. The characterization of (what I have suggested must be self-oscillating) activity and passivity has this dimension to it, to the extent that the active motion acts *on* what is passive for the purpose of bringing it into activity, while at the same time acts on it because it is passivity; thus, activity has its being in acting on "the passive," while at the same time seeking to transform it into "the active." In the contact between perceiver and perceptible object, too, we have the experience of the perceiver striving both to "have" the perceptible object and to identify that object as distinct.[46] From out of this coupling is conceived the perception. Though this section explicitly demonstrates the erotic dimension of perception, it only gently pushes us in the direction of considering the erotic dimension of knowledge, which we will discuss later.

Third, we have seen that the myth helps us to draw a clear distinction between what we would think was the identity of an object and the relational identity produced in the perceptual coupling that produces perceptions. This is important because it articulates in the domain of perception what Socrates had previously only shown in a mathematical example, namely, that relational attributes of objects—though they have a reality that cannot reasonably be denied—are not to be presumed inextricable from the object itself. We must therefore acknowledge that we have a role to play in the production of the perception of the object. Indeed, the domain of perception appears to be one that results from and announces a reality that is constituted by relationships. This does not mean—as Socrates's Protagoras had indicated—that what I have just called a "reality" is in fact an illusion. Rather, it indicates that there is an emergent world created by interactions. What is to be done with this insight we do not yet know, but it will surely be an important component of the proper account of knowledge.

Let us now move on to what Socrates takes the myth to want to accomplish.

f. Reformulating the Myth

Socrates's first formulation of the myth does not satisfy Theaetetus; on the contrary, it appears only to confuse him further (156c4–6). Though, unlike Theaetetus (and from the advantageous standpoint of the reader), we have a solid grasp of that first formulation, we were nonetheless left with the problematic lack of any account of the generation of incorporeal entities, as well as the lack of an adequate explanation of corporeal entities as such. So it is as much in our interest as in the interest of the disoriented Theaetetus for Socrates to reformulate the myth in an explanatory manner, as he does:

> Now everything slow conceives its motion in the same and relative to the things consorting with it and precisely in this way generates,

> and the things precisely so generated are faster, for they are born(e) and their motion is by nature in bearing (moving locally). Whenever, then, an eye and something else of the things commensurate with it consort and generate the whiteness and perception cognate with it, which would never have come to be if each of the two of them had come to anything else, it's precisely at that time when they are being born(e) between—the sight from the side of the eyes and the whiteness from the side of that which (is) giving birth along with sight to the color—that the eye, and behold, becomes full of sight and precisely at that time sees and becomes not sight but an eye seeing. And that which cogenerated the color gets filled all round with whiteness and becomes in turn not whiteness but white, whether it (is) wood or stone or whatever thing *(khrema)* turns out to get colored with a color *(khroma)* of this sort. (156c10–e8)

Note that the terms used in the explanation of the myth are not directly analogous to those used in the myth proper; they, rather, introduce different kinds of metaphysical categories, and so must be dealt with independently and then compared with the first. Here, instead of claiming that reality begins with, or *is* primarily, the active and passive motions, Socrates claims that what the myth *wants* to say is that there are slow and fast motions. The slower motions keep themselves in the same place and consort with one another, thereby begetting the faster motions.[47] Again, note that the slow and the fast are almost certainly not intended to be analogous to the active and passive, insofar as—unlike the active and passive—Socrates explicitly introduces a metaphysical order to the slow and the fast, with the slow being primary, and the fast begotten of the slow (156c10–d4). It seems that the slower motions refer to the perceivers and perceptible objects, insofar as they are that from which the perceptions are begotten.[48] Socrates does not explain in what way he means to say that the slower motions (perceivers and perceptible objects) move, though it does appear to be a reference not to the obvious fact that perceivers and objects move through space, but rather to the alteration each undergoes as a result of the perceptual contact it makes with a given distinct perceiver or perceptible. The faster motions that are begotten are those of perceptions; they are fast, it seems, because it is their nature to be begotten (156d3–4), which is to say that the being of perceptions is not fixed. This is the case insofar as perceptions are relational identities, derived from perceivers and perceptibles, and are thus dependent for their being on the contact between these two more primary beings. The alterability of perceivers and perceptibles is less and slower than that of perceptions because the latter have their nature in being derived from the contact between the former. The becoming of each of these orders of motion—the slow changes undergone by perceivers and perceptibles and the fast changes undergone by perceptions resulting from the interactions of perceivers and perceptibles—is always dependent on relations with other things. Nothing is itself by itself, and all is becoming, though some becomings—specifically, perceptions, whose existence is exclusively relational—are more fleeting than others—specifically perceivers and perceptibles, each of whose existence is deeply *informed* by relationality, but not constituted exclusively by it. Let us develop this metaphysical distinction further.

While all is becoming, the kinds of becoming admit of difference, and it is those different sorts of becoming that are referred to in the distinction between slow and fast. While both the slow and the fast becomings are generated in the coupling of perceiver and perceptible, the faster kind—the perceptions themselves, for example, the color "white"—are dependent upon this or that particular coupling, whereas the slower becomings—the perceiver and perceptible as perceiver and perceptible, for example, the eye seeing and white object being seen—depend only on *any* correspondent to couple with. That is, the eye undergoes the slow and less variable change from eye-with-sight to eye-seeing, and the object correspondingly goes from being visible object to being object-seen when each is in contact with any given other. By contrast, perceptions themselves are much more volatile, having their natures dependent upon so many more, and such transient, contingent factors. Thus, not only is the claim that all is flux fundamentally dependent upon the fixity of the differentiation of active and passive elements, and upon the metaphysically dependent differentiation of perceiver and perceived, it also depends upon the necessary differentiation of motion according to degrees of rapidity. Flux, too, must be fundamentally broken down into kinds or species.

Though Socrates, Theaetetus, and Theodorus will later be led by the argument to reject the first definition of knowledge, and to reject Socrates's characterization of the Protagorean-Heraclitean metaphysical account, they do not explicitly reject this myth.[49] This myth was presented and worked through for the purpose of improving the consistency of the metaphysics of flux. In improving it, Socrates made it impossible for them to maintain the commitment to the idea that all is motion in an unqualified sense. We shall see that Theaetetus was not able to draw from this that there is a weakness in his initial claim, because he is unable to draw together all the implications into a coherent whole. We shall also see that this leads Socrates to attempt the tactic of disputation or cross-examination.

g. Testing Theaetetus by Testing the Argument

Socrates asks whether this speech is pleasing and appetizing to Theaetetus (157c1–3). Theaetetus claims that he is unable to say what he thinks of the speech because he cannot tell whether Socrates is sincerely advocating this position or presenting it as a test of Theaetetus's response. It matters to Theaetetus—as it does to us, perhaps—whether Socrates believes what is being said or not. In fact, Theaetetus speaks as though establishing whether Socrates presents this speech having been already persuaded by it is a necessary precondition for his having an opinion (157c4–6). Socrates, however, is barren, as he immediately reminds Theaetetus. Though he surely does have an opinion on the matter, Socrates refuses to make explicit what it is, perhaps, as I have been arguing, precisely because it would have too much influence on Theaetetus, thereby undermining the project of compelling him to commit to a position so that, by being invested in it, he can experience the subjection of his own ideas to scrutiny.[50]

From this moment of indecision on Theaetetus's part, they move on to Socrates asking questions related to the theme of becoming and flux, though no longer directly connected to the myth and to the specific claims presented in the myth. The myth itself is neither refuted nor accepted.

In confessing to Socrates that he is uncertain whether he is giving his own opinion or not, Theaetetus implicitly demonstrates that he is not able to handle thinking for himself about these issues. He wants to know where Socrates stands so that he will know where he himself should stand. Of course, one of the basic points implicit in Socrates's maieutic art is that the topic itself, along with the details of the account one gives, should be the governing force of one's ideas. That Theaetetus continues to miss the point means that he is ill-prepared to move carefully through the consideration of the various parts of the myth. Instead, Socrates pulls back to the much more general question, whether or not Theaetetus agrees now that all is becoming and that nothing, properly speaking "is" in the fullest sense (157d6–8). This more general discussion loses the complication and nuance of the myth and its explanation. Since Theaetetus was unable to offer an opinion when the complexity of the metaphysics of flux was on display, since he was unable to follow the discussion at that point, he is surely even less properly situated to answer, in an informed way, the much more general question he is now faced with. The much more general question is nonetheless the one he does answer. It does not seem as though it is possible for him to be giving more than an opinion, and that is what he gives, responding by claiming that based on what they have recently said (which he demonstrated he did not understand), it seems that this is the case.

Immediately, as though having been holding it back waiting for the trap to be set, Socrates responds to Theaetetus's rather tentative commitment by providing what he characterizes as the most common critical response of the view that they have been developing about perception, the response widely regarded as having refuted that view (157e1–158a3). He claims that Theaetetus's definition has failed to account for verifiable error, most conspicuously demonstrated in dreams and madness. Specifically, the madman making claims obviously at odds with reality cannot be said to be a real measure of reality, since how he measures is clearly delusional. Likewise, what we take to be true in dreams cannot be taken as a measure of reality.

Theaetetus is quick to concede that Socrates has damaged the credibility of the position to which he had assented (158a9–b5). In response Socrates reminds him that there is a well-rehearsed counter-refutation to this as well, namely that there is no immediately available evidence to prove conclusively that we are dreaming. Indeed, in dreaming as in waking, we are certain of the opinions we hold; this epistemic limit appears to present itself in madness and illness as well. According to the counter-refutation the dreamer and the madman are as licensed to their views of reality as anyone else; thus there could never be information available in immediate experience to provide evidence against that experience (158b6–d10). Each experience is self-justifying, on this view. There is no error.[51] But in denying error, this view is denying the effectiveness of the very means by which it claims knowledge is derived, that is, denying the effectiveness of perception: because of the fact that each of us perceives uniquely—insofar as our unique character as a perceiver is always necessarily a factor in the perceptions we have—each of us has unique knowledge. Each of us is, for ourselves, the absolute measure of all things, both that they are and that they are not. But, another person might suggest, there are states of mind or ways of experiencing in which the unique factor—that is, the character of the individual perceiver—is in some way corrupted by madness or unchecked fantasy, and is therefore an inadequate measure. If we are able to claim that there is such a thing as a corrupted perceiver then we must also say that the reality that is perceived is the measure, and that those perceiving inadequately fail to live up to this measure. To this, one might respond that because of the commitments made in the original argument, there could be no arbitration of the inadequacy of the corrupted perceiver. On the contrary, at the time of the perception, the opinions of (what would thus be erroneously called) the corrupted perceiver would appear perfectly coherent to that perceiver, which is to say that if they are the sole arbiters of the being or non-being of things, they are the sole arbiters, *simpliciter*. What the first person has achieved in this radicalization of the original point, though, is a Pyrrhic victory. To claim that experience is inadequate to provide evidence of the inadequacy of the perceiver's perception of reality is to say that that with which each person measures reality is inadequate to measure reality. It is to say that no knowledge is available from experience. To say that knowledge is perception, on this model, is to say that knowledge is not perception.

Socrates does not move through this line of thought. Instead, he takes a bewildered Theaetetus through a response that he imagines a Protagorean would provide, a response that provides a more concrete version of the claim that each is uniquely a measure of all things. This argument is built on the foundation of recognizing the sharp distinction between things that are different. What is absolutely other shares in no attributes with that to which it is absolutely other (158e8–12). What is other is dissimilar (159a4–5). Things that are becoming similar to each other are becoming the same with respect to the specific things that make them similar. Likewise, things that are becoming dissimilar to each other are becoming other to each other with respect to those specific things that are making them dissimilar. Thus, for example, Healthy Socrates is dissimilar to Ill Socrates. Healthy Socrates is other than Ill Socrates with respect to health or illness. The result of this dissimilarity emerges in the perception that is generated when Healthy Socrates consumes wine and when Ill Socrates does so. What is generated in the first instance is the perception "sweetness," and in the second case, the perception "bitterness." This familiar phenomenon, the argument goes, is usually clumsily interpreted to mean that Socrates finds wine bitter when he is sick and sweet when he is healthy. The affirmation of the continuity of Socrates in this formulation obscures the important fact that a dissimilar perceiver is coupled with the same perceptible, or as Socrates says, from case to case "it does not take the same me" (159d9). If we were to eliminate the variable of Socrates from the wine, in order to eliminate the source of variance, we would be left with neither sweetness nor bitterness, nor any perception at all.

The implication of this demonstration that particular and changeable attributes of the perceiver are directly involved in the generation of perceptions, according to the position Socrates is now characterizing on behalf of those responding to the dream-criticism, is that the domain of knowledge is the domain of perceptions, and that that domain is subject to contingencies found in each discrete individual act of perceiving. It does not matter whether we want to use the term "being" or the term "becoming" to describe what we perceive, as long as we always add the caveat "for so and so" (160b5–c2). Thus, the wine is sweet *for* the Healthy Socrates, not sweet without qualification. If nothing can be what it is without qualification, and must on the contrary always be for something and must always be coupled with that with which it co-generates perceptions, then objects on their own cannot be a measure of reality. Each of us is that measure, and in no way is anyone ever capable of being in error because of what has been said. This final clarification of the original claim and its verification with Theaetetus leads Socrates to declare that they have conceived the idea, and that it is now ready for their assessment (160d5–e4).

Conclusion

Before moving on to present and to analyze their assessment, let us stand back from our discussion of this massively complex and occasionally repetitive process by which Socrates has "delivered" Theaetetus of the idea that knowledge is perception. In this chapter, we began by reflecting on the truth of the notion that perception is the event that initiates our thinking and our experience, and by reflecting on the fact that we are each, individually, sites of experience, in order to give credit to the intuitive plausibility of the first definition. We then discussed the fact that Socrates took Theaetetus's initial definition to the limits of its credibility, by turning it into a version of what one might call Protagoras's radical relativism. In so doing, they were led temporarily to the claims that all is flux and that consequently there is no independent being, and, rather, that being must be said to emerge only as an illusory product of the coupling of perceiver and perceptible object (which is to say that there is no reality independent of the act of perception). By drawing out this implication, Socrates was able to get Theaetetus to commit to (and hopefully actually recognize, though this is not certain) the notion that in fact our experience commits us to the recognition of the reality of independent beings, due to our permanent reliance upon various versions of the principle of non-contradiction. Having said this, though, we were further shown an insight that adds nuance to this commitment.[52] That is, through our presentation and analysis of the myth of infinite motions, we saw that though there are independent beings for which change cannot be caused strictly by the attributes they have as a result of their relationships to other beings, there is nonetheless substantial reality to the relational identity of those attributes. We saw this in the account of perception as that which emerges from the erotic coupling that occurs between perceivers and perceptible objects. Finally, we saw that though these insights I have mentioned were at work in Socrates's presentation, they did not seem to be understood by Theaetetus, with the result that the level of the conversation remained in the more general terrain of whether or not all was motion, terrain which the preceding discussion demonstrated to be far too conceptually limited.

We are thus in a situation where Socrates can know better the work he has to do to awaken Theaetetus to the demands that the discussion has for him, and where we must be careful not to rely too much on what is explicitly said at the expense of the work we must do to extract from this discussion the underlying philosophical richness. With these insights in mind, let us now move on to the examination of the product of Theaetetus's "labor."

CHAPTER 4

Learning to Think through Perception (160e7–186e11)

It seemed to me that I should take refuge in accounts and look in them for the truth of beings.

—*Phaedo*, 99e5–6

Introduction

In the previous chapter, we examined how Socrates attempted to demonstrate to Theaetetus that we are held accountable to standards beyond our own desires, both in engaging in philosophical dialogue and in our immediate apprehension of objects. We also dealt with the rich, complex discussion of perception, specifically, that perception is the product of the coupling of perceiver and perceptible object and that it is generative of relational attributes.

In this chapter, I claim that the lessons presented in the previous chapter—the formal lesson concerning ideas and implication and the more concrete lesson concerning the quality of Theaetetus's first definition of knowledge—end up converging on an account of the soul as the place of perception, and as the site of reflection on our perceptions. In this new lesson, Socrates demonstrates something that Theaetetus may or may not be prepared to understand, namely, that as a subject of knowledge and a site of perception, his own soul is always undergoing changes, and is as much the object of concern as whatever is being discussed in whatever particular kind of knowledge he pursues.

I claim that there are simultaneous but related themes through the analysis of this first definition: first, that while perception appears to be an immediate apprehension preceding and providing material for thought, it in fact requires the process of thought; second, that because thought is a mediating force in our immediate apprehension through perception—that is, because thought is involved in what we would presume to be "pre-cognitive" activity and therefore involved in our immediate access to the world—this structure has built into it the normatively charged demand that we reflect upon the implications of that thinking we always pre-reflectively undergo;[1] third, that this activity of reflection requires or involves us in existential or personal transformation; and fourth, that this personal transformation is best undergone through dialogue. Theaetetus's education into the process of thinking philosophically is therefore not merely personally but also theoretically invested in his consideration of the nuances of perception. I will now briefly elaborate on the interconnection of these themes before outlining the sections of the chapter.

As was discussed in chapters 2 and 3, opinions have implications that we typically fail to recognize, with the result that we hold those opinions with the false self-confidence that we know what we opine. We must therefore think about and question what exceeds our understanding in order to understand what we are, in fact, already invested in by holding those opinions in the first place. Moreover, those opinions are always in the process of mediating our perception. For this reason, perception, too, requires reflection. We act as if we can "just perceive" something and have it fully disclosed for our reflection, but, on reflection, we find that this is not true. Perception is immediate only in the sense of being the result of direct engagement with the world outside of us. While this is so, perception is nonetheless a structure that is undergone and developed—a structure that can mature and that can apprehend with greater subtlety—and that is therefore deeply mediated. While it is perhaps clear that reflection is a process of working through what one has encountered in one's experience, it will be shown that perception is, too.

In essence, what I emphasize in this chapter is that what is to be recognized in one's experience cannot force itself upon one. It is in the nature of the objects one apprehends that they have the capacity to demonstrate in what way one is misapprehending them. The question is whether or not one sees the error that one is being shown. This is essential to perception as much as it is to philosophical reflection. Socrates is attempting to educate Theaetetus into a new approach to his experience, one that treats his experience as questionable, and an approach that requires of him that he change how he perceives.

The relationship between the integration of the implications of one's ideas into one's thinking, and the integration of one's perceptions into one's reflection is connected to the powerful observation made by Aristotle—and presented as an epigraph to chapter 1—that we begin by what is most evident to us, and move to what is most evident in itself. Socrates provides both a lesson in the meaning of such an insight and, with Theaetetus, who is learning that lesson, a demonstration of it. The idea which this lesson disproves is that knowledge is constituted by what is immediate. Further, the discussion between Socrates and Theaetetus consists in learning both to take what is implied by the manifest reality of perception as a starting point for inquiry, and to identify it as a starting point. In so doing, what subsequently appears as immediate will be apprehended with greater depth. Thus the activity of reflection that they are undergoing together will later lead to the enrichment of future perception. What is claimed here, in essence, is that it is in the nature of perception to be something that is necessarily integrated with the activity of reflection, and to undergo transformation as a result of that activity. These themes get developed through the lengthy drama that unfolds between the three interlocutors, as they scrutinize Theaetetus's claim that knowledge is perception.

Section 1 focuses on Socrates's lesson concerning the articulation of an idea. Continuing the analogy to childbirth, I show that Socrates treats newly articulated ideas delicately, and with the care appropriate to them, and struggles (and fails) to compel both interlocutors, though especially Theodorus, to do likewise. Section 2 returns to the discussion of perception, this time through an analysis of Socrates's account of the philosopher. I argue that this account in fact argues that knowledge *is* perception, but on an account different from the one initially presumed by Theaetetus, an account of perception in which it is not abstracted from the other capacities of the soul; such an improved account of perception makes possible the recognition that perceptual apprehension is perpetually undergoing change, and perpetually integrated with the activity of reflection. Because the discussion of the relationship between perception and soul has not yet occurred at this point in the conversation (despite efforts by Socrates to elicit it from Theaetetus), neither Theaetetus nor Theodorus is able to notice that the philosopher has a transformed, cultivated perception. Finally, in section 3, I will present the previously lacking account of the soul as the coherent whole for which perceptions are tools in the process of thinking through.

1. Treating One's Claims with Care (160e7–172c2)

Theaetetus's conversational comportment should be recognizable to most of us. Though we are trained, if we read a lot of Plato, to find Socrates's manner of speaking familiar, it is likely that for most people, Theaetetus is the better representative of how they speak and how they think, and Socrates's manner the more alien one. Theaetetus is certainly both intellectually curious and willing to make the effort to converse at the level Socrates sets for him. He is also, however, hasty in his responses to Socrates's questions, preoccupied with anticipating the kind of answer expected of him at the expense of not giving his own actual opinion, and unwilling to stand by what are presented as his opinions once they have been criticized. He is, in other words, not a serious participant in the conversation. He is *willing* to be and in fact *wants* to be serious, but is nonetheless ignorant of what it means to be serious and consequently is unable to be serious.

By contrast to this, Theodorus neither is a serious participant nor particularly wants to be one. If we do not recognize ourselves in the character of Theaetetus, perhaps we see ourselves in Theodorus, who is not intellectually curious and is not willing to make the effort to cultivate curiosity. He does not share with Theaetetus a tendency to give hasty responses, choosing rather to agree or disagree according to the particulate preferences and loyalties he brought to the conversation. Probably as a result of his more or less consistently dogmatic support of positions advocated by people he likes, instead of folding in the face of criticism of opinions he has expressed as Theaetetus does, Theodorus gets defensive, and occasionally falls silent, simply refusing to respond to critical remarks against his opinion.[2]

At this point in the dialogue, the discussion shifts from consistent and direct engagement with accounts of perception and its implications toward a more meta-conversational discussion. They discuss the extent to which Theaetetus is committed to the position that he has presented; whether or not Theodorus is living up to his obligations, both (implicitly) as a teacher to Theaetetus and (explicitly) as an advocate for Protagoras; whether Socrates is living up to the obligation of justly representing the views of the dead; and, most generally, how to talk about ideas well and why they, Socrates, Theaetetus, and Theodorus are failing to do so. This meta-conversational turn will be the theme of this section.

We have seen that Socrates is trying to teach Theaetetus to engage in the practice of thinking about his ideas through their implications, by making Theaetetus commit to an idea and have it worked out. We have seen Socrates demonstrate this using Theaetetus's definition of knowledge as perception. Socrates worked out a version of this definition to imply that man is the measure of all things, that all is flux, that there is in fact no being prior to its emergence in perception, that there is therefore no being at all, but rather only becoming from motion, and that these implications contradict the dogmas of thought (i.e., the principle of non-contradiction). We have seen that thus far Socrates has failed to make Theaetetus commit in a way that compels him to be invested in his own purported opinions, and that Theaetetus is rather satisfied to be led around by Socrates's speeches. Socrates must therefore make the conversation itself the issue. In this section, I am therefore going to focus on the question of how to converse about an idea seriously, how to care for an idea.

a. What One Is and Is Not Responsible For

As was pointed out at the end of the previous chapter, Theaetetus now appears to have an idea that is adequately worked out for evaluation. Moreover, as was just sketched out above, Theaetetus now knows some intricate and radical implications associated with his commitment to the idea that knowledge is perception. His idea, therefore, has turned out to be much more elaborate than he would have initially expected. We can imagine it coming as a surprise to him to have Socrates persistently say of these additional claims that they are also his own. This fact that he "owns" the implications Socrates has drawn from the initial claim is the first part of an important lesson. It is his idea. The second part of the lesson—the more difficult part that relies on the first—is that he must now take responsibility for it. The kind of responsibility that Theaetetus takes for his idea is not yet settled, however. Declaring that Theaetetus's idea is delivered, Socrates presents him with a list of different degrees to which he can claim responsibility for the idea.

> Well this, it seems, we have at last generated with difficulty, whatever in fact it is. But after its birth, on its name-day, it truly has to be run around in a circle by the speech, as we examine it, lest, without our being aware of it, that which is coming to be be unworthy of rearing but be a wind-egg and a falsehood. Or do you believe that in any case, regardless, you must rear that which is your own just because it is yours and you must not expose it, or will you in fact put up with seeing its being tested, and will you not be vehemently distressed if someone slips it away from you though you are giving birth for the first time? (160e7–161a6)

First, Theaetetus must establish whether or not his pregnancy was real; he must test whether his idea in fact has any purchase on reality, or if it is merely a fantasy. He must then establish whether it is his *legitimate* offspring; when the idea is examined, Theaetetus might discover that claims were embedded in the idea on his behalf that are in fact not ones he would himself ever consciously endorse. Third, assuming he has established it to be real and legitimately his own, he must choose whether he wants to claim or reject it; were he even to decide that it did indeed accurately represent what he wanted it to, this mere fact need not require of Theaetetus that he be responsible for it. Theaetetus may have no idea at all, that is, one that was never coherent in the first place; an idea that turns out to have come from someone else, that is, one he recognizes as something he unwittingly adopted from the prevailing opinions of his upbringing or education; or an idea that is his own, but that under scrutiny he chooses to reject. This flexibility of his commitment to the idea ought to give Theaetetus a greater sense of security in his comportment in the conversation, and a greater willingness to take thoughtful risks.

The fact that one's opinions are always qualified by the fact that they are subject to revision might appear straightforward. After all, what could be more obvious than to say that when we have an erroneous idea, an idea we did not consciously adopt, or an idea we consciously adopted but later did not affirm, we are free to reject it? Most of us probably consider ourselves to be ultimately uncoerced in our beliefs. This fact about us is sharply put into focus at the moments when we make the conscious decision not to affirm a given idea. When it occurs to me that a commonly held belief is false, and when I declare that I choose not to endorse that belief despite the ease with which I could have done so, I draw to my own attention the fact that in principle I am capable of opinions regardless of the force I might perceive to be exerted on me to think otherwise. By telling Theaetetus he is now in a position to make a decision concerning his own opinion about the idea, Socrates is telling Theaetetus that he is free to think about it what he will, and, now with the added advantage of a better standpoint from which to evaluate whether or not it is true. Socrates is further telling Theaetetus that, insofar as it is his idea that is being presented as ready for potential rejection on various grounds, holding an opinion never implies the foreclosure of its revision.

If it is straightforward to us from an epistemological and a logical standpoint that opinion is always revisable, it is less straightforward to us from a moral, psychological, or existential standpoint. It is here that Socrates's skill and sensitivity toward Theaetetus is demonstrated. It is commonly the case that when people present their opinions, and when those opinions are subjected to scrutiny and proved either false or dubious, they feel invested in the idea to the extent that they believe themselves obligated to defend it. People commonly do not like to have their ideas criticized. One reason one might feel defensive is that one thinks that to prove the falsehood of one's idea is to prove the poverty of one's intelligence. Another reason one might feel defensive is that one is typically invested in an interpretive framework that constrains one's willingness to realize the freedom to be compelled by the better argument. One might be defensive because, whether the idea is true or not, one is unwilling—because of some pathological tendencies one has developed—to reject the idea, and one is therefore threatened by the idea being proved false, insofar as being proved false means one must live according to a framework whose flaws one is in some sense conscious of. For a young person in the midst of having her opinions shaped, while it is in an important sense easier than it is in adulthood to let go of one's commitments, the experience of critical intervention is also likely to generate a sense of insecurity; the fact that this particular idea is shown to be a bad one might be taken to mean that all of one's ideas are silly and misguided. As though in anticipation of this, Socrates presents to Theaetetus various ways in which one can, so to speak, "opt out" of the definition he has given. This appears to be done to diminish the significance of Theaetetus's having been previously committed to a definition that stands to be refuted. Socrates is saying to him, through the use of the indirect method of metaphorical childbirth, that the fact that Theaetetus came up with the idea does not tether him to it, and that while he is now in a position to take responsibility for it, previously—prior to the "birth"—he had not merely been unable to perform the evaluation for which he will be responsible; he could not reasonably be expected to be responsible for it. The only thing one can reasonably be held responsible for, prior to the evaluation of one's own ideas, is a willingness to engage in such an evaluation, which amounts to a willingness to subject oneself to the possibility of conscious transformation of one's views. In asking him whether or not he would be willing to reject the idea even when he identifies it as his own, Socrates is once again asking if he is willing to subject himself to such conscious transformation. By framing it in this way, he further diminishes the significance of Theaetetus's investment in that particular answer.

Unfortunately for both Theaetetus and Socrates, Theodorus interrupts this important moment by assuring Socrates that Theaetetus is up for the challenge of scrutinizing the idea, and that Socrates should go ahead and refute it for them. Theodorus does here what he does elsewhere, which is to treat the discussion as though it were an intellectual game, and not a process of education.[3] Socrates tells Theodorus that he, Socrates, is being treated as though he were a "sack of speeches" (161b1). Socrates goes on to tell Theodorus that, while he is in fact capable of presenting counterarguments quite easily, he will not, and that Theodorus does not "understand that which is happening" (161b3). While the fact that Socrates can easily give the speeches of wise men would seem to indicate that he is a "sack of speeches," Theodorus takes for granted that Socrates utilizes those speeches only for the end of perpetually providing counterpoints to whatever the given claim happens to be. That is, Theodorus is not able to perceive the purpose to which these speeches are directed. The present purpose is the creation of appropriate conditions for Theaetetus to be capable of evaluating the beliefs that he holds regarding the nature of knowledge. Insofar as it concerns encouraging a person to engage in a difficult activity with which he is at present inexperienced, the process is rather delicate.

After Theodorus's clumsy interruption, Socrates does not insist on returning to asking Theaetetus to either claim or reject the idea as his own. Nor does he do as Theodorus asked—not exactly, that is—which was to produce a speech demonstrating why everything that had been said about motions and becomings was wrong. Instead, Socrates explicitly claims that he will not at all speak himself, implying that he will speak the views and opinions of others only (161b8). In what follows, Socrates presents versions of arguments refuting Protagoras, followed by rebukes given by Socrates as though from Protagoras himself, interrupted periodically by admonishment of Theodorus for not participating in the defense of his friend. Let us briefly sketch this section of the dialogue, keeping in mind that Socrates is engaging in this activity, not merely to demonstrate complexities in disputation, but also, and more importantly, to demonstrate how not to engage in philosophical discussion.

b. Socrates's Performance of Disputation

Socrates begins by presenting a sophistical form of counterargument in the voice of an anonymous antagonist, but an argument that contains important insights. In this voice he indicates that while he likes most of what Protagoras says, the claim that "man is the measure of all things" is not radical enough (161c2–162a4). Why are animals not equally the measure? If nobody can correctly act as an arbiter of the truth of what anyone else says, then why must we confine ourselves to human beings? Why not dog-faced baboons as the measure of all things? If it is the case that the being of things is to be measured by the perceiver, then anything that perceives has license to claim legitimate authority. One could be even more radical than this. Protagoras wrote a book making this claim. Why should any of us give any regard to what is said there if each of us is innately sufficiently qualified to be the measure of the truth, even if that is precisely the claim made in his book? If we are by our very nature, insofar as we can perceive, sole arbiters of truth, then regardless of what we perceive—even if it contradicts Protagoras's claim—each of us sufficiently fulfills the only basic criterion of truth, and therefore has no need to be interested in his argument.

On the surface, the point here is that Protagoras is explicitly providing a universal rule—that man is the measure of all things—whose form, as universal, belies its content; there cannot be a rule that applies in a way that transcends the perceptions of individual consciousness if individual consciousness is circumscribed as the limit to the measurement of truth. More deeply, however, if we have indeed accurately characterized Protagoras—which Socrates will later somewhat ambivalently insinuate we have not—his actions betray his claim.[4] Protagoras aims at persuading people that his claim is correct. But, says Socrates, it would appear to have been more consistent were he to have said that "dog-faced baboon" is the measure of all things, in order to demonstrate immediately that his opinion was as worthless to anyone else as a tadpole's; if each of us is a measure, we are complete, with respect to knowledge, within ourselves. In fact, though, the writing of a book to express a universal claim about reality that one has extracted from one's particular experience, and the taking up of that claim by others, demonstrates that the domain of dialogue is the domain of supra-individual, or intersubjective meaning. The notion that man is the measure of all things cannot apply as radically as it would seem to insist it must, otherwise the entire motivation to communicate even this very point would be compromised.

The question Socrates points to here is the following: Why do we communicate? What is the purpose of talking to one another if not to express what we have gathered through our perceptions, and consequently to compel the other to subject her own internal arbitration of what she perceives to the enrichment of another's perceptions? Communication implies the presumption that we, as perceiving consciousnesses, can articulate for others our experience of objects that are shared in common.[5] When Protagoras advocates the view that man is the measure of all things, and distributes written accounts of this view, he does so at least for the purpose of persuading others that what he is saying is true. Doing this *means* claiming that there is a set of circumstances (i.e., a reality) that is available equally to all. It also means that he, Protagoras, claims to know extra-sensible structures implied by those available circumstances that can be inferred from them, articulated by us, and communicated between us. Drawing out what is implied by his claims, though, would undermine the purpose of, and thus render ridiculous, any form of conversation.[6] The form of conversation would consist in the exchange of opinions with others whose opinions are already each, regardless of the possibility that they contradict one another, in principle true, and whose truths, moreover, have their character defined by non-communicability.

Theodorus, who wishes to be loyal to his friend Protagoras, is unable to agree with Socrates despite feeling compelled by the argument, on the grounds that he would be refuting a friend (162a5–9).[7] He therefore chooses to remain silent. Theodorus's behavior dramatizes Socrates's point about the Protagorean attitude: in order for one to maintain the illusion that the truth is something defined exclusively by one's own private experience, what one must do is remain silent. From Theodorus's standpoint, if he does not give *voice* to the fact that he agrees with Socrates's criticism of Protagoras, it will mean he has not declared that he disagrees with his friend. We saw before that Theaetetus confessed that he found himself in a position where loyalty to the claim he had made, and agreement with what appeared true, were at odds with one another (154d1–4). Socrates applauded him for being honest, since, while he could make his lips speak falsely, he could not maintain the lie in his mind; acknowledging that fact means recognizing one is capable of delusions, and is an important step in preventing them. Here, Theodorus—who was present for that exchange, but appears not to have absorbed its insights—demonstrates his desire not to enter into that contradiction with himself, but instead of making his speech coincide with his unspoken thoughts, he gives no speech at all. Further, Theodorus demonstrates that he believes commitments to particular positions are more important than commitments to truth. He demonstrates this in the way that is most pernicious of all, by an unwillingness to speak. This unwillingness to speak is a version of the failure to recognize the primary basic responsibility a person actually has with regard to serious discussion, that is, to subject one's views to scrutiny.

Socrates does not attack Theodorus directly on these grounds, rather choosing to criticize him for presuming he can participate without making commitments. Socrates tells Theodorus that he is like a Spartan wanting to watch the naked wrestlers without getting naked himself (162b1–4). At the level of the conversation itself, this means that Theodorus wants to be entertained by the conversation without having to make a contribution. But perhaps more pointedly, Theodorus does not want the terms of reality to apply to himself as they do to others. He wants to receive the insights of others, to hear the likes of Protagoras criticized, without himself having to acknowledge being compelled by those same insights.[8]

Because of this silence on Theodorus's part, Socrates is forced to turn to Theaetetus. Theaetetus contrasts sharply with Theodorus, now admitting that he has been immediately convinced by the success of Socrates's critical attack on Protagoras (162c8–d3). Theaetetus utterly subjects himself to the persuasive power of the argument. Socrates is struggling here to gather each of his interlocutors into the kind of mindset required for dialogue, and they are failing in exactly opposing ways. They are supposed to take each idea seriously and to respond to what is presented thoughtfully (and, one would presume, independently). However, Theodorus at first mostly acts as a spectator, and later, when he is asked not to behave as a spectator, allows his loyalties to keep him silent. Theaetetus, who is new to all of the various positions available to be taken, demonstrates himself to be excessively credulous in the face of each particular counterargument.

Perhaps reacting to this problem, Socrates immediately adopts Protagoras's voice, claiming that he, Socrates, was being unfair with him (162d7–163a4).[9] If we were to read this exchange without considering the context, it would appear to be a fine example of Socrates making the weaker argument the stronger; he knows he has convinced Theodorus despite the latter's silence, and knows Theaetetus is convinced, and he therefore changes sides. One might erroneously assume that Socrates is playing a game, and infer from this that Socrates either does not care about the truth, or that his argumentative techniques are an illustration of the Protagorean point that rhetoric and persuasion somehow have ontological priority over what is called only later, at a more superficial level, the truth. In fact, though, we know that Socrates is trying to get Theaetetus to make his views explicit, which is to say that Socrates is trying to make Theaetetus display his soul for examination. In order to do this, he needs Theaetetus to commit to claims, and needs him to do so in earnest. He also needs Theodorus to treat the discussion with seriousness, especially since the latter is a committed partisan of both Protagoras, and, seemingly to a lesser extent, Socrates. Theodorus would therefore usefully demonstrate the struggle of working through ideas that do not correspond. Neither Theaetetus nor Theodorus successfully accomplishes the task Socrates needs them to (though in the case of Theaetetus it is more a matter of inexperience, while in the case of Theodorus, it appears to be a matter of the cumulative effect of too many bad intellectual and interpersonal habits). Socrates must therefore, essentially on his own, perform the manipulative tactics of sophistical argumentation, using his two floundering interlocutors as props.

Socrates's Protagoras chastises Socrates for persuading people with likelihood and semblance, rather than with serious argument. More precisely, Socrates argued from plausibility when he ought to have been arguing from necessity. Socrates is accusing himself of being sophistical. They must find a better way to make their arguments, and, implicitly, Theaetetus and Theodorus ought not to be so easily convinced by those worse arguments. In the face of this criticism, Socrates presents a more nuanced example of what it means to perceive (163b1–7). Socrates asks Theaetetus what we perceive when we hear a foreign language. Theaetetus says that we *do* perceive and therefore *know* the sounds that are made, and the various attributes belonging to the sounds of the language. We do not, however, either perceive or know the meaning of the words. What we perceive is true, it is just not completely true. Socrates claims to like this answer given by Theaetetus, though he does suggestively say that he will not dispute the point in order that Theaetetus "may grow" (163c4–5).[10] In paying attention to the example, and to this suggestive response, we must remember that Socrates-as-antagonist-of-Protagoras is a performance being utilized by Socrates-as-teacher, and that therefore his examples have been chosen as much for that larger project as for the debate with Protagoras. We must think about what he is trying to do in the grander project as well as in the immediate one. What is Socrates choosing not to dispute, and why? We are not given an explicit answer, but we are invited, by Socrates's suggestive comment, to speculate for ourselves.

One of the curious phenomena about language is the way in which it demonstrates ambiguities in our perception. While listening to the speaker of a language unknown to us, we perceive sounds, but not the meaning those sounds convey. A reversal occurs when we come to understand the language, one that occurs gradually, but one whose result ends up producing perceptions strikingly at odds with those we began with; we can no longer hear the sound of the language. The sounds made in speaking words withdraw for our perception in favor of the meaning they convey. The fact that English is my native language obstructs my ability to hear it as a series of sounds. It would therefore be misleading to talk about our experience of learning a language as one of moving from what is imperceptible to what is perceptible. Though this is true, it is only partially true. Coming to perceive the meaning behind the sounds is partially made possible by our having inhibited the perception of the sounds themselves.[11] Language therefore depends as much on an inhibition of hearing as upon hearing itself, which is to say that it depends on one both perceiving and not perceiving the same thing at the same time. This issue will come up again shortly.

Rather than complicate matters on this particular issue though, Socrates chooses instead to present the as-yet-unmentioned dimension of memory (163d1–7). Notice that Socrates is not allowing any of the issues that come to bear on the problem of knowledge to be developed here, as he was earlier. Rather, he is merely adding more layers of undeveloped complexity. The treatment of memory is merely cursory, suggestive, and—when treated as providing complete refutations—sophistical. Socrates uses the phenomenon of memory to raise the question concerning whether or not memory counts as knowing if knowledge is perception (164a1–b7). After all, when we no longer perceive the object but are only recalling what we had perceived, it would seem that this is something different from perception of the object. It would be "dreadful" (163d8–9), and "a monster" (163e15), according to Theaetetus, to have to claim that we no longer know what we have perceived when we shut our eyes and merely remember it. And, indeed, as a consequence of this problem, it would appear that we simply must recognize that to know and to perceive cannot be the same. If we do not want to claim that when we close our eyes we no longer know what we thought we knew, which is to say that if we do not want to claim that memory is somehow excluded from knowledge, we must plainly acknowledge that knowledge and perception are two distinct things.

After initially claiming that this would appear to undermine the definition of knowledge offered by Theaetetus, Socrates claims that though they say they are "not competitors but philosophers," they are unwittingly "doing the same things as those dreadful men" (164d2–4). He claims that this is not how he would proceed with such a discussion were he in the presence of Protagoras himself. Indeed, he claims that Protagoras has become like an orphan, since he has been abandoned by his presumptive defenders, particularly by Theodorus (164e2–7).[12] The latter claims that he chose long ago to pursue the path of geometry as opposed to that of speeches, and that for this reason he should not be regarded as Protagoras's defender (164e8–165a4).

Socrates does not explain in greater detail what exactly is wrong with pointing out that the phenomenon of memory indicates that knowledge and perception cannot be exactly equivalent. We might think that this phenomenon does compel such a conclusion. Indeed, it points in the direction of an insight that Theaetetus comes to later in the discussion, namely, that the perceptions themselves lack the capacity to perceive each other, and that there must be a certain something that synthesizes distinct perceptions into coherent, knowable objects of knowledge, that is, the soul "itself through itself" (185e1). We will discuss the details of this observation by Theaetetus later. For now, I make note of it for two reasons. First, here as there, there is evidence of a mediating force independent of perception whose reality strongly implies something to which both perceptions and memories belong. Second, here, unlike in the later discussion, Theaetetus fails to make note of anything significant about the phenomenon of memory, other than to agree with Socrates that it undermines the equation of knowledge with perception. Socrates needs Theaetetus to learn this for himself. It would be a waste of insights that could be derived from Theaetetus's first definition to simply refute the argument.

The fact that Socrates would be concerned with how the argument unfolds for Theaetetus and with what precisely it can offer him tells us something critical that distinguishes Socrates's activity from mere disputation. If we hold claims accountable only to the potential they have to withstand criticism, we carry with us a deeply impoverished conception of knowledge. Using this specific case as an example, Socrates appears to consider it as preferable *not* to have Theaetetus be satisfied with having his definition of knowledge as perception refuted, choosing instead to strive for Theaetetus to use the ultimate refutation of this definition of knowledge as a means for the achievement of recognizing powerful insights into the nature of the soul. When the moment arrives that Theaetetus does bring up the soul, Socrates expresses his gratitude for Theaetetus having saved Socrates a long speech (185e5–8). At that point, Socrates will have extracted from Theaetetus insights he would not have derived had they decided the definition was refuted here. This is a strategic benefit in continuing to labor through the argument as though Protagoras were present.

Socrates, wanting to engage in the discussion in a way that he would were Protagoras's defenders present, asks whether one can both know and not know the same thing at the same time (165b3–5). We already know that the example of language indicates to us that the answer to this question is clearly "yes." In order to know language we must also not know it, as long as we make the allowance that a more precise formulation would diminish the oddity of the claim, that is, "in order to be capable of knowing a language from the standpoint of understanding the meaning conveyed, one must simultaneously not know the language from the standpoint of the sounds its utterance produces." Formulated in this way, we would be in a good position to solve one of the puzzles we encountered earlier, for example, when Socrates is at the same time and in the same place being-taller and being-shorter (155b4–8). It is not the case that the same thing can be at the same time and in the same way both known and not known. Rather, the point is that the same thing can be known or not known from different standpoints, and that, in at least some cases, these standpoints are mutually exclusive, which is to say that in order to know it from one standpoint, one must foreclose knowing it from the other.

Theaetetus does not immediately allow himself to entertain this idea that we can both know and not know the same thing at the same time. He claims that simultaneously both knowing and not knowing the same thing would appear to be of necessity impossible (165b7). In order to discourage Theaetetus's haste, Socrates uses the trivial example of having one eye open and one closed, and consequently simultaneously seeing and not seeing what is in front of one's eyes (165b8–c1). When Theaetetus is reluctantly forced to acknowledge that, were he to remain consistent, he would be forced to claim that this person is both seeing and not seeing at the same time insofar as he both sees and does not see, he further acknowledges that saying this is absurd means abandoning his definition. This is an example of an argument that Socrates claims "the mercenary in speeches" would use against him (165d8). It works only because proving it wrong requires more patience than Theaetetus is capable of giving it. In the much more compelling example of language, we have just seen that while it is true that a person both knows and does not know what one perceives whether one knows the language or not, this is not mystifying if we recognize that it is because it can be taken up *as* two distinct kinds of thing (as meaning-signifying and as bare sound), it no longer appears to threaten the dogmas that persist in our thinking, that is, the three iterations of the principle of non-contradiction. In the much more basic case of one eye being open and the other being shut, we can see that *I* am seeing the object, but am not using one of my eyes to do so. Theaetetus, having just hastily denied something both true and salient to the point being made—that is, that we do in fact both know and not know the object we perceive—is being pressured to slow down his thinking.

Socrates notes that this mercenary argumentative tactic will typically have the effect of making the listener admire the skilled disputant, and to be forced to submit to him (165e1–5). As though in response to the injustice of this method, Socrates speaks again on behalf of Protagoras (166a2–168c2). The latter (i.e., Socrates-as-Protagoras) claims Socrates is winning the argument against Protagoras's position by frightening a boy, and one who is not able to anticipate where the argument is going. In order really to refute Protagoras, Socrates-as-Protagoras claims, Socrates would have to refute claims Theaetetus was making on his behalf *in the way that he, Protagoras*, would claim them (166a7–b2). In other words, it proves only that Socrates is able to refute versions of his position that Theaetetus is capable of articulating. This claim Socrates makes on behalf of Protagoras returns us to the point that it is the idea, not the person, one is dealing with. There is no victory being aimed at, rather, only understanding. It is for this reason that—even if it seems clear that Theaetetus's or Protagoras's point (again, as it is presented here) is wrong—we must imagine ourselves arguing about it with its best advocate.

c. The True versus the Better

In this spirit, Socrates takes it upon himself, speaking on behalf of Protagoras, to present a more consistent version of his position. He claims that Protagoras does reject the true-false distinction, insofar as one's personal experiences provide unique circumstances for apprehension and evaluation, thereby making truth or falsehood beyond those unique experiences irrelevant. However, Protagoras does not reject the distinction between better and worse perception. There are those who know better than others, Protagoras himself being one of them. It is the responsibility of the wise to make the perception of those who "opine by a poor condition of the soul" improved, so that they opine out of a healthier condition (167b1–3). The wise person, for Socrates's Protagoras, is like a physician, whose duty is to improve the perceptions of the patient so that she perceives better, and consequently improve the condition of her soul. It is, therefore, not the case that any person opines falsely. Their opinion reflects the condition of their soul; if the soul is healthy, it will opine in a way that is good, if the soul is sick, it opines poorly. Thus, in advocating his own position, Protagoras does not claim he knows the truth, rather only that his opinion is better, which is to say that it is healthier.

Human beings agree in practice, if not in argument, that there are degrees of wisdom, at least relative to specific spheres of expertise, a point that Socrates's Protagoras acknowledges. When a person is sick, she turns to her doctor to save her, implicitly evaluating that doctor as more wise with regard to sickness than, say, her music teacher. Each of us may have expertise, but each also seeks expertise from those who have specialized knowledge we do not have. This is indisputable. Further, most—though not, apparently, Protagoras—would say that this distinction between levels of expertise also counts as a distinction between degrees of knowledge, and at the extremes of the continuum, between intelligence and folly.

For Protagoras, truth belongs in its entirety to each person individually, while good and bad can be evaluated objectively. Earlier, we saw that for the claim in Protagoras's book that "man is the measure" to be consistent, it would have no justification for being persuasive. If each were equally the measure, Protagoras's claim would contradict itself by claiming generally something that, according to its very doctrine, must be discretely individuated. We return once again to this point: if Protagoras's book is true, it is true only for him, and therefore is written for nobody but himself, since each person has her own opinion validated as true in principle. It is more complicated than this though. Protagoras's book is true for him, because he declares it so. It is also false for those who are unconvinced by his claim. That it would be so vindicates the truth of the book, because the claims of the book must be both true for him and false for others, for them to be true. Those claims must be false for others and true for him to be true at the register where it makes claims about the truth or falsehood of truth and falsehood. Why, though, do the rules concerning truth not apply at this second order? If I say "What Protagoras says—that man is the measure of all things—is true in general, because it is true for him and not true for me" I am simultaneously agreeing that it applies universally and denying that it does so. If I say "What Protagoras says is false in general, because I agree that his claim applies equally to me as to him" I am simultaneously denying that it applies generally because it does so and affirming that it applies generally because it does not.

Making this logical paradox more explicit, Socrates's shift of emphasis to the affirmation of better and worse or good and bad counts as a slight withdrawal for Protagoras, albeit one that leaves more room for him to remain consistent (171e4–10). There are some issues about which the individual is the measure, and some about which it is not. The health of a person is not to be placed in the domain of her opinion, but should, rather, be placed in the domain of the opinion of the expert. A person's perceptions are infallible and thus always true; the value of what is done with those perceptions is best evaluated by the expert.[13]

Satisfied with this presentation of what Socrates imagines Protagoras might say, Theodorus congratulates Socrates on justly defending the honor of Protagoras (168c7–8). Socrates's Protagoras had been criticizing them for using a child to answer for Protagoras. Socrates points out that it was in part to Theodorus that the admonishment was directed (168d8–e3). The only other adult present (and thus the only person mature enough to stand against Socrates's attacks) was Theodorus, who did nothing. Theodorus responds by trying to defuse the attention directed at him, noting that Socrates is not like the Spartans—who demand that one strips if one wishes either to take part in, or to be a spectator at, their matches—because he offers his interlocutors no choice but to strip *and* participate (169a7–b5). Socrates once again tries to clarify his practice. He is not either aiming at harming them or forcing them to follow stifling rules. Rather, his aim is to improve their health, and indeed he has suffered at the hands of many before who have given him a hard time, and does not identify the practice as an abuse (169b7–c3). It is Socrates's point that one *is* morally required to participate, not by Socrates's personal law, but by the very nature of one's human existence. One must participate in the evaluation of one's own thoughts, and this means treating those thoughts, when they are under analysis, with care.

Regarding this issue of the imperative to treat one's ideas and arguments with care, it is clear from this exchange between Socrates and Theodorus that the mere intellectual recognition of problems in one's thinking is insufficient to produce practical changes in one's behavior. This is the case because the imperative is associated with pleasure and pain.[14] Socrates knows that the practice is good and, to improve the life of Theodorus, as that of anyone else, he must convince him that the practice is good. While it would be wrong to claim that Theodorus's experience of pain when scrutinizing his own ideas and arguments is false, it is nonetheless the case that he will never be able really to recognize that that process is good until he no longer considers the pain of that practice to provide sufficient justification to stop it.

To drive the point home regarding the objectivity of what is good Socrates draws an analogy to the political domain (172a1–c2). There are those who will go some distance with Protagoras, but not all the way, who will say that in the political domain, whatever laws a city lays down for itself, as well as whatever norms a city has for itself in identifying what it counts as beautiful and fine, will belong to it according to its opinion, and whatever its opinion is, it is true for it. However, no city could seriously consider that whatever it sets down for itself as its own advantage is guaranteed to be to its own advantage. If the city is falling apart or is overtaken by conquerors, it is not adequately serving its own advantage, regardless of whether the actions it took that precipitated the city's downfall were deemed to be to its advantage. It is, in this domain, beholden to standards it does not set for itself.

This analogy to the city as a means of illustrating the reality of external objective standards, along with the general discussion of normative value replacing truth value as the sole objective criterion for judgment, should lead into a difficult discussion of what counts as the measure of normative value. If man is the measure of all things with regard to their ontological status, who or what is the measure of all things with regard to whether or not they are good, or healthy, or better? A superficial answer has already been given, namely, that it is the wise person or the expert; but this is a poor answer, because it says nothing regarding the sense in which the person is wise, or in what way one qualifies as an expert. One of the virtues of discussing these issues in terms of political questions is that it addresses concrete circumstances where (certain) objective measures are clear. However, the discussion of the political question does not happen. Having gotten himself absorbed in a discussion of the political domain, Socrates stops his train of thought and in the process halts the discussion of expertise. The political discussion, Socrates reasons, would prove to be a new and more complicated topic to introduce, and would lead them off course (172c1–2). When Socrates has his own words thrown back at him by Theodorus—that they are at their leisure after all, and should therefore proceed with whatever discussion they want (172c3)—Socrates is compelled to focus on the very fact that he and they take the attitude that, since they are at their leisure they may speak at the length they see fit concerning the topic they see fit. It is with this in mind that he is compelled to lead them into a discussion about philosophers.

2. The Philosopher and the Everyday World (172c3–177c7)

The digression to the distinction between philosophers and the public speakers (*rhētores*) has been taken in a variety of ways by scholars. It has been taken to be interesting but unimportant to the dialogue as a whole,[15] a caricature that fits Theodorus's naive image of a philosopher better than a real philosopher,[16] to be philosophically unimportant,[17] to be a "tirade" possibly motivated by Plato's need to vent his frustrations from his experience at Syracuse,[18] to be admittedly indirect to the question of knowledge, yet nonetheless to be asking the reader to reflect on what it is actually worthwhile to strive to know, thereby to be an issue of tremendous importance conspicuously occurring in the middle of the dialogue,[19] or to be important for tying the discussion of perception to the cultivation of practical knowledge (*phronēsis*).[20] In this section I will essentially agree with the last version, claiming that Socrates's account is extremely relevant to the education of Theaetetus, as he is trying to present a version of perception that is a part of knowledge. I will also criticize various aspects of the other interpretations. In essence, I will argue that the digression concerning the philosopher displays the mutually determinative interplay between perception and thought, and that it further displays the sharp divergence in the way that the world appears for people whose lives have been cultivated in better and worse ways.[21]

a. Leisure and Self-Constraint

The immediate context of Socrates's transition to the discussion of the philosopher is Theodorus's misunderstanding of Socrates's use of the term "leisure." Socrates had described leisure to Theaetetus as being the context from which they could sit and think about such things as the nature of knowledge (154e8–155a3). The periods that constitute a break from everyday demands on one's life were presented as providing the chance to reflect on ideas that are undoubtedly important, but that one does not otherwise have the time to think about. One reason for the importance of occupying one's leisure time in this sort of reflection is that the time during which we face our everyday demands and responsibilities requires us to make use of such terms as "knowledge," "being," "justice," "courage," and so on, and we make use of them without typically recognizing that we do not really know what they mean. Socrates's leisure, as it is presented in Plato's dialogues, consists in engaging in conversation with people about ideas that they live with without really understanding. This is what Socrates has in mind when he indicates that he and Theaetetus have the advantage of leisure.

Theodorus might, on the surface, appear to be similarly inclined to think that leisure ought to be spent questioning people concerning implicit presumptions that they have, when he says that they ought to allow the conversation to stray into a discussion of the just and unjust and the holy and unholy (172b5–c3). He might on the surface be described as wanting to follow the *logos*. However, Theodorus thinks of leisure as providing the opportunity to allow their minds to wander toward whatever idea interests them at the given moment. It implies for him absolute conversational license.

When Socrates begins to be caught up in the discussion of political notions of truth and falsehood and good and bad, he realizes that initiating such a discussion would essentially foreclose the completion of the discussion to which they are currently directed. That they are at their leisure, for Theodorus, means that it does not matter if they lose that thread. For Socrates, however, the whole context of the discussion was the examination of the soul of Theaetetus, and the initiation of Theaetetus into the kind of activity Socrates believes to be most important, that is, self-examination, the very activity Theodorus unwittingly threatens to undermine. Socrates certainly allows the conversation to flow freely and unpredictably—into myth, into outrageous examples, into discussion of the way in which they are engaging in the discussion, into stories from history or from tragedy—but, for Socrates, that free flow must be oriented by its purpose.

Because the organizing principle of the conversation makes allowances for a great deal of free movement, it is easily mistaken by the uninitiated, and apparently is mistaken by Theodorus, for a conversation driven only by license and whim. It is therefore not surprising that Socrates is led by Theodorus's remark to reflect on the way the philosopher is perceived in the law courts (172c4–177b9). The law courts provide a context in which discussion is layered with *conspicuous* organizing principles, principles that are in fact hostile to those that govern the philosopher's mode of discussion. The people who spend their time making arguments there ridicule the philosopher as a bumbler unable to follow rules, when in fact the philosopher is unaccustomed to following rules that pay insufficient regard for the topic under discussion, which is to say unaccustomed to following rules that prefer instead to be preoccupied with giving the more persuasive argument and therefore winning.[22] Though Theodorus speaks as though he does not approve of this, and speaks strongly in favor of the philosopher, the things he says here indicate that he conceives of the philosopher according to the same terms as those in the courts.

This issue of how the philosopher is perceived in public institutions must be on Socrates's mind, for reasons not merely having to do with improving Theaetetus's ability to engage in self-reflection. Though Socrates is in a certain sense at his leisure, if his thought is directed at what he will say when he meets the charges against him, he is probably aware that leisure is a luxury he may not have for long, due to the fact that Socrates is awaiting the trial that, in fact, will lead to his death. Socrates suggestively says that "it appears" that they have leisure, and that he is struck, not for the first time, by the idea that philosophers appear ridiculous in the eyes of those who spend time in public institutions, due to the fact that philosophers are unpracticed in the arts associated with concision and rhetoric (172c4–8). Socrates must be anticipating the ridicule he will probably face when forced to speak in an environment not accustomed to (and perhaps not likely persuaded by) the leisurely style.

b. Freedom versus Domestication

According to Socrates, those who participate in public life at the law courts are in comparison to the philosophers as domestics in comparison to those that are free (172c10–d1). Let us consider specifically in what sense those reared in philosophy are free. Being at their leisure means, most basically, that Socrates and Theodorus can discuss whatever they wish and for as long as they wish. This freedom, for Socrates, means taking the time, when it is available, to discuss matters according to the requirements of the matters themselves. He will follow the argument, follow the matter under discussion, where it must go. It is a freedom that is realized in taking responsibility for the real terms of the world, and devoting one's time to sorting them out as they come up. Note that the leisure itself is only a part of this freedom. The leisure makes possible the opportunity to be concerned, not with the length or shortness of the speech, but the "that which is" of the topic under discussion. We have seen, over the discussion so far, that discussing "that which is" not only has the effect of increasing one's understanding of reality; it also has the effect of transforming how one lives such that one is constrained only by the terms of reality. This transformation, though, requires labor. Leisure and reflection concerning the being of "that which is" together are what characterize the philosophers as free.

By contrast to the transformation one undergoes in being constrained only by the terms of reality, those in the law courts are always beholden to the instrumental concerns of institutions. They therefore tailor speeches to meet the demands of those institutions. In doing so, they are compelled to adopt techniques of persuasion and manipulation, and this practice has the further effect of making them become manipulative and corrupt. The pressure of living up to the demands of the court requires them to appeal not to the truth but to forms of manipulation and lies. If they succeed in their practices, they believe that their techniques of manipulation demonstrate their wisdom (173b3). This makes them believe that what in fact are the very acts that are corrupting them are the source of their psychic health and well-being.

In his response to the description of the public speaker being corrupted by the behavior he is most proud of (i.e., lying and manipulating), Theodorus demonstrates a singular misunderstanding of this point, and of the true value of philosophy. Theodorus responds that, while the public speaker is a slave to the speeches, for the philosophers at leisure, speech is like a domestic servant (173c3–4). Presumably, what Theodorus means here is that the institutional demands imposed on public speakers make them slaves, while the lack of such demands make the philosophers free. The institutional demands require of public speakers that they behave as though the speeches are *their* domestic servants, in order to make speeches tools of manipulation, rather than media of truth. By contrast, the liberation from institutions gives the philosophers the opportunity to allow themselves properly to be *beholden* to the speeches. Though Theodorus intended to valorize philosophy here, what he in fact has done is demonstrate that he views it as entertainment.

c. The Perception of the Philosopher

To begin with, Socrates characterizes the circumstances under which the philosopher is cultivated (173c7–174a3). The young philosopher does not know where public institutions are located, does not know either the intricacies of the social order or the place of particular people within it, and does not know any of the customary leisure activities of his fellow citizens. The young philosopher is not even aware of his ignorance of these things; they fall outside of his field of perception. He has made no conscious choice to abstain, but is rather simply unaware of them. He lives in this way because he is only a part of the city in body, not in spirit. His spirit sees these things as trivial and remote. The things that interest the philosopher are universal underlying structures.

The philosopher is here characterized as more or less directed to things not as particulars, but as instances of what is universal.[23] Though Socrates at first claims that the philosopher is both ignorant of political matters and ignorant of this ignorance, he subsequently claims these things appear trivial and remote to him. It seems that it is not the case that the philosopher's attention is directed elsewhere, but rather that his perception of the things of politics has been transformed. The philosopher perceives political activities in a manner strikingly different from his fellow citizens. This contrast between the cultivated perception of the philosopher and the perception of his fellow citizens provides a powerful demonstration of the fact that the same perceptible objects not only can generate different meanings, but also cannot be perceived completely, because any standpoint excludes others. Let us examine this further.

The perception of the philosopher in comparison to his fellow citizens can be illustrated using the example of the foreign language. The philosopher's fellow citizens are like the person hearing a language foreign to them. That foreign language is perceived and even "known" in a qualified sense.

The foreign language is a real part of the sensory fabric of the world of the person hearing it, and the sounds that person hears are real sounds. But the person does not really know what the sounds mean. If the person is particularly foolish, he will think the sounds are a kind of amusing gibberish that does not have any meaning. A less foolish person might recognize that it means something, but would find that what it means is mysterious to her. This person might resign herself to the mystery and make no effort to understand. In either case, the foreign language would probably for the most part withdraw to the background of the person's perception. By contrast to this, to the person who understands the foreign language, the idea that it is gibberish, or unknowably mysterious would be quite alien. If such a person tried to perceive the language in this way, she would find it impossible. Embedded in her very perception would be sounds immediately, meaningfully signifying.[24]

Likewise, the universal patterns that the philosopher finds in particular instances appear to him as immediately as the assortment of disbursed, unrelated things do for the non-philosophical person. We should consider for ourselves the different ways in which one might apprehend the situation of the law court. The public speaker, prosecutor, or "sykophant" immediately apprehends two sides of the issue and, knowing which side is his own, conceives of ways in which he can most effectively defend that side according to the standard practices of the courts.[25] By contrast, the philosopher immediately apprehends those same circumstances as a corrupted manifestation of an institution whose purpose should be the peaceful adjudication of grievances. He sees people engaging in competition to improve their reputations, and using the public institution as an instrument for that end. While public speakers take the institution of the court for granted, and master its conventions for the sake of thriving according to the standards it has set for the measure of success, the philosopher questions the institution itself, as well as its conventions and standards. In perceiving all aspects of the institution as questionable, the philosopher denies to himself the ability to thrive according to its standards. Just as the fluent speaker of the language is rendered essentially unable to hear it as foreign, the philosopher is unable to treat the conventions of the law court as to-be-taken-for-granted.

Socrates uses several examples to characterize further the seeming remoteness of the philosopher in relation to his city. In each case, the philosopher perceives the world from a remote standpoint. The philosopher is not familiar with his neighbor; indeed, he does not know who his neighbor is, and almost does not know whether his neighbor is even a human being (174b1–4). He is, rather, preoccupied with what it means to be a human being, and how one should live as a human being. Because of this interest, the philosopher behaves in a manner that appears ridiculous when he is compelled for whatever reason to speak in the context of public institutions.[26] He knows nothing of bad behavior and evil, having had no experience practicing it (174d7–c3). Tyrants and kings appear to him equivalent to herdsmen, though in fact worse, because their job is to milk people, and people are animals "more peevish and conspiratorial" than swine or cattle (174d8). Tyrants appear not to have acquired great power over many people, but, on the contrary, to have enslaved themselves within the boundaries of their own walls. Their concerns with power appear, to the philosopher, trivial. People who brag about either the wealth they have generated, or the prestige of their family lineage, appear laughable because that wealth is so little, and the lineage so short from the universal standpoint (174e2–175b6). The philosopher laughs at all of these things, because in each case the people misconstrue petty issues as though they were important.

The philosopher's perspective of indifference to typical human concerns is illustrated as well in the things that *do* interest him. In watching people deliberate about some dispute, he is compelled to consider what justice is (175b10–c3). In discussions about whether this or that king is happy, he is compelled to consider what the nature of kingship is, and what happiness is (175c5–8). He adopts a perspective that sees the concepts that account for instances, not because he wishes to remove himself from this world, but because the matters of this world direct him to the concepts.[27] Public speakers see only the reality that is created by the rules and customs governing behavior in the courts, and respond only to these. Rules and customs, though, draw attention to themselves, which is apparent to those capable of noticing. They draw attention to themselves as decisions that have already been made; like all decisions, those that govern the courts had justifications, and we can ask what those justifications might be. The philosopher sees the same rules and customs, but has cause to ask the question, "for what reason were these instituted?" Correspondingly, when people call this or that action "just," the philosopher experiences it as a decision that appeals to some reason, and follows the justificatory reason back to its source of appeal. The philosopher does indeed withdraw from the world, but only insofar as he is directed at the conditioning reason for particular circumstances of this world. The philosopher, on this model, operates in the indeterminate and free space opened up by the recognition of contingency in actuality.

Let us not, however, draw the wrong conclusion from this language of withdrawal, of indifference to typical human affairs and of appeals to sources. According to the characterization given by Socrates, the philosopher and the non-philosopher alike are responsive to the particularity of their immediate circumstances; they are both responsive to reality and they both perceive. The activity of each in relation to that shared reality is to *do* something with it according to their respective capacities to understand it. What distinguishes them is that one is directed to the demands created by that reality—that is, to working within the rules created by the terms that emerge from them—while the other is directed to the demands that went into its creation—that is, to the way in which that reality is constituted. What is important to recognize is that each kind of person cares about the reality to which she is responding. While it might appear to us that the typical attitude is one that cares, while the philosophical attitude is one that is withdrawn and is therefore one that does not care, it is in fact the case that both care, but that only the latter is consciously invested in what that reality is, which is to say under what terms that reality emerged as it did.

Let us return to the question concerning whether the philosopher obstructs himself from a certain kind of knowledge of reality by withdrawing in this way. I presented that question in the context of an analogy to language. The sounds made in speaking a given language withdraw for the person who has become conversant in that language. Earlier, I presented this example as a situation in which one can both know and not know the same thing at the same time. In learning the language, I go from hearing a foreign series of sounds to hearing the meaning behind them, and so go from knowing strange sounds and not knowing what they mean to knowing meaningful words and losing the strangeness of the sounds that they make. What is lost in this case? When someone is speaking a language foreign to me, it can become part of the auditory background of my experience—that is, something to which I am indifferent, though it informs my aesthetic apprehension of the world around me—or it can become a puzzling curiosity for my conscious attention. As background, I take it up in much the same way that one might unthinkingly take up those parts of reality that influence one's experience but that one chooses to ignore. As curiosity, I take it up as something whose reality I simply inadequately apprehend. What is lost in the philosophical reflection that is perceived by others as a kind of withdrawal is something like what is lost in learning a language, in that it brings to the foreground what is otherwise unnoticed, and makes of it something not a cause of curiosity, but a cause of wonder. Unlike curiosity, wonder is purposive; it compels one to strive to know.

d. Is Socrates a Philosopher?

This characterization of the philosopher's activity helps to explain what might initially appear to some—and what surely would appear to those whom Socrates had characterized as the "uninitiated" (155e6) who are "without the muses" (156a3)—to be someone remote from his humanity, as well as someone standing in odd contrast to Socrates. We might think that Socrates is someone who stands out for his tremendous humanity, insofar as he has chosen to devote his life not only to inquiring into the nature of reality and into the question of how to live, but also to challenging others to do the same, and to examining their souls for the purpose of trying to improve them. Socrates stands out, in other words, as someone for whom human concerns seem to subordinate all others.[28] In contrast to this, the philosopher, who is unable to identify the humanity of his neighbor, appears to be someone so preoccupied with his own intellectual gratification that he is compelled to treat the world of his experience and the others within that world with contempt. This characterization, though, is incorrect.[29]

As we saw, the philosopher is not so much contemptuous of the world and of his neighbor; he is, rather, inclined to apprehend the world and everything in that world in terms of its being. He is therefore oriented in such a way that the world has become something worthy of his efforts to understand. This orientation directs the philosopher away from the terms that the world has set for him, and toward conclusions that are not directly communicable to anyone not likewise disposed to the world in this way. When Socrates speaks of the philosopher not seeing the humanity of his neighbor, he is saying that insofar as the neighbor is someone directed merely at responding to the terms set up by the world—that is, responding in a slavish fashion, just as the person trained in the law courts does—the humanity of the neighbor is obscured for the philosopher, which is to say that the philosopher has had his understanding of humanity, as much as his understanding of the world, transformed in such a way that the humanity of his neighbors appears remote to him. The philosopher is not indifferent to other human beings; he is, on the contrary, better able to understand humanity such that he can evaluate its cultivated presence in others.

To be reared in philosophy is to be reared in a way that alters how one perceives reality, and in a very specific sense: the philosopher perceives the world as welcoming one to question it. This is not how we for the most part perceive the world. We perceive it as given to us in exactly the way that we take it up. We perceive what things are for, how they relate to each other, how we live, what is good and what is bad, not as questions, but as answers already provided. We all experience moments of puzzlement or mystery or confusion, moments which fleetingly remind us that not everything is settled, that not all answers have been provided, and that the answers that have been provided are not exhaustive of those that can be. We then quickly produce the first answer that comes to mind to account for this puzzlement, and, relieved, return to the world that is already accounted for.[30] From the standpoint inclined to revert to open acceptance of the terms of reality, the philosopher seems alien, because the philosopher is free.

Theaetetus was not entirely wrong to suggest that knowledge is perception. He erred only in failing to recognize that it is a specific kind of perception, and a kind integrated into the whole of the human capacities to apprehend the world, one that takes time and effort to develop well.

3. Soul as the Place of Perception (177c8–186e11)

Thus far, I have presented the long discussion concerning Theaetetus's first definition as a lesson taught by Socrates, namely, that ideas have implications beyond what is immediately apparent, and that working out those implications is the only method available to us for evaluating whether we should continue to believe them. I have claimed that part of the reason for the need to teach this lesson is that it is very difficult to maintain such a practice; indeed, our tendency is either simply to ignore the implications of our ideas or to believe them unwittingly. Socrates uses the discussion of knowledge as perception to make his point. The first major implication of this definition was that each perceiver is correspondingly a knower and is in some sense therefore infallible. The second implication was that no object of perception *is*, but rather all such objects only *become*. This would have to be the case because the only thing that would qualify as knowledge according to this definition would be what appears before our perceptions; if the only thing that can be known is something that is altered at each turn by how it is perceived, then this object cannot be said to have a fixed identity. It is always changing. Indeed, its nature is change. Therefore the object *is* only *as* that which undergoes change, what is becoming now this and now that. Theaetetus is only able to evaluate his first definition when these implications are equally taken into account.

In working through these implications, Socrates has been led to make claims about the activity in which they are engaged, characterizing the person who engages in reflection on the structures underlying immediate experience—the philosopher—as one whose soul becomes shaped to apprehend those structures in immediate experience. Socrates, therefore, without having taken the time to make it explicit, addressed the theme of the transformation of the soul.

When Socrates returns the discussion to the issue of perception, he continues the process of directing Theaetetus—first as an observer of the discussion with Theodorus, and then as a participant—back to the implications of the concept of knowledge as perception. This time, Socrates is more explicitly focused on thinking about perception on its own terms, and, we eventually find out, on eliciting from Theaetetus the recognition that for there to be perception at all, it must occur for the soul. In directing Theaetetus to the recognition of the soul as what might be called the place of perception (though this is not what they call it), Socrates is not merely trying to refute the claim that knowledge is perception. Rather, it turns out that Socrates is trying to direct Theaetetus to an understanding of what the subject of knowledge is, which is to say, what he, Theaetetus, is.

a. Knowledge Concerning the Future

Socrates's discussion of the philosopher reaches its end when he points out that any person willing to deceive consciously and publicly will nonetheless likely experience moments when, in private communion with themselves, they are forced to reckon with themselves and with their public deceptions (177b1–9). He then interrupts himself to return to the original discussion of knowledge, once again, on the second of three occasions, warning against allowing a larger discussion to overtake the matter of the examination of Theaetetus.

The point of reentry into the discussion concerns the future. One of the characteristics of the future is that it provides a standpoint of evaluation of predictive claims (178b2–179b5). Lawmakers claim that their policies will improve the city. Farmers claim that the current climate and soil conditions will yield such-and-such quantity of their crop. Protagoras claims hiring him as a teacher will make students wiser. Each of these cases demonstrates that we must reject at least a certain interpretation of Protagoras's claim that man is the measure of all things, and, by consequence, a certain version of the claim that knowledge is perception. First, if we have reliable memories or documentation, we can evaluate after the fact whether the specific policies of the lawmaker have brought about the anticipated improvements to the city, whether the predicted yield of the farmer was realized, and whether Protagoras's teaching techniques indeed cultivated wisdom in his student. If they do not, the purported expert in public policy, farming, or moral education was in fact not an adequate measure. We have seen already that Protagoras's claim suffers under the reality of error, insofar as the bare fact of error implies something sufficiently static to be evaluated as inadequately apprehended by its perceiver. The second illustration of the need to reject Protagoras's claim is that regardless of the accuracy of the experts' predictions, no person would seriously claim that a non-expert would be better at giving those predictions.

We would not trust the violin tuner over the farmer to evaluate future crop yields, for example. On these grounds, it seems impossible to claim without qualification that each perceiver is the sole arbiter of the truth.[31]

Though Theodorus now finds these remarks sufficiently impressive for him to vocalize his disagreement with his friend Protagoras, Socrates remains unimpressed. He claims that there are many ways in which one can demonstrate that not every opinion is true (179c1–3), which implies what we have said all along: Socrates is not especially interested in refuting the claim or in finding its weaknesses. That would be easy and more importantly would not accomplish his goal. The more difficult notion to prove false, and therefore the notion to which they ought to direct their thought, is that immediate impressions are, for each person, true. More precisely, Socrates says, perhaps the claim that perception is always true cannot be refuted (179c4–d1). Socrates presents the notion that perceptions are irrefutable as "not a trivial one" and one involving "not a few," whom Theodorus goes on to identify as the Ionians under the influence of Heraclitus (179d4–8).

Theodorus complains that the followers of Heraclitus are impossible to talk to, because they will never let anything be still, but will always allow the meaning of words to slip away from one's grasp (179e4–8).[32] Theodorus compares the experience of talking to the Ephesian Circle to the experience of having been driven to madness by the gadfly. This, of course, is a metaphor Socrates uses to refer to himself in the *Apology* (*Apology*, 30e6).[33] Socrates suggests that the Ionians do not talk in this maddening way with their students (180b5–9). In other words, while disputing with a hostile interlocutor, Heraclitus (or, it seems, Socrates) might decide to withdraw from the act of making positive claims, while instead criticizing the claims being made by those that do make positive claims, insofar as those claims are made carelessly. By contrast, both might find themselves in situations where it is appropriate to acknowledge the things that are by speaking in a more explicit fashion than they would publicly.

b. Challenging Heraclitus

In order to examine the position of Heraclitus fairly, Socrates provides a brief account of the history of the view that all is change (180c9–d10). The ancients first presented the doctrine of change in the form of poetry, in order that its meaning might be concealed. They claimed that all that changes comes from two streams, Oceanus and Tethys, and that nothing is at rest. Those who followed the ancients were wiser to the extent that they tried to make explicit in plain language the fact that everything is in motion. It was their virtue to make things explicit because it could serve to convince regular people of the falsity of their thoughtless convictions that some things were in motion and some at rest.

In contrast to both the obscure and the explicit believers in the theory that all is flux, Socrates realizes that he nearly forgot those others who, unlike this first group, believe that everything is one and at rest (180d10–e6). These others—Melissus and Parmenides—agree with Heraclitus and the rest that there is no variety to the law of nature; if there is motion, all must be in motion and multiple, while if there is rest, all must be at rest and be one. Socrates proposes that he and Theaetetus are trapped in the middle of a tug-of-war between the believers that all is motion and the believers that all is rest, and that they ought first to examine one set of believers (i.e., the believers that all is motion) to discover if it is true (180e6–181b1). If it is, they need not look at the other. If it is false, they will then be compelled to examine the other. Socrates suggests that they begin with the advocates of perpetual motion.

Socrates begins by describing the claim that motion is of two kinds, alteration and locomotion (181b8–d7). Note that in the two previous speeches about motion—neither of which was refuted by Socrates—we had heard versions of the idea that motion was divided into two. First, we heard that motion was at one and the same time constituted by the power (*dunamin*) of absolute activity—that is, to affect (*poiein*)—and absolute passivity—that is, to be affected (*paschein*) (156a3–7). Second, we heard that there were the slower motions of the perceiver and the perceptible and the faster motions of the perception resulting from the combination of the slower ones (156c7–d4). We now have the division of motions into types. This third distinction is a kind of taxonomy of motions, and one which applies both to the slower and faster motions of the second myth, and to the ontologically primary active and passive motion of the first myth. The primordial motion that must be simultaneously active and passive must also manifest itself as both locomotion and alteration. In contact with one another, the active and the passive motions are endowed with potential. The passive motion—which is to say, the perceiver, the subject, the one-experiencing—in receiving the active motion, becomes capable of perceiving. Correspondingly, the active motion—the perceptible object of experience—becomes capable of being perceived, which is to say that it becomes a certain sort or a certain quality (182a4–b8). Out of these comes the perception itself *that* the thing is white or hot or whatever the attribute might be.

Let us examine what this account Socrates has reported implies. What we would typically call subjects and objects or perceivers and perceptibles are now characterized as merely abstractions from a constant motion. We perform that abstraction due to the fact that our assessment of subjects and objects typically occurs through the lens of our own reality as subjects. In fact, though, both the objecthood of the object and the subjecthood of the subject are given *in* the contact with its contrary; they co-emerge. I am not merely a subject who, in making contact with a given thing, apprehends the thing. Rather, contact with the thing enacts my power to be a perceiver, as well; both the ability to perceive and the perception of the specific object are given by the contact with the object. The point is that my being a perceiver is made possible only by the fact that there is a perceptible object for me. This fact is made invisible to me because there is always a perceptible for me to perceive. This is not merely an empirical claim. More precisely, the fact that I, as a subject, co-emerge with the object is concealed from me because the "I" for which my subjectivity could ever be visible is always generated in contact with the perceptible object. I cannot evaluate the event of generation of my subjectivity using *only* resources made available in the perceptions that are made possible by that generation.[34] It is likewise true that the object is given the possibility to be a perceptible only by the contact it makes with the perceiver. There is, in this activity, a simultaneous gift of the power necessary to produce the perception and the perception itself.

Following the establishment of this point, Socrates questions Theodorus concerning the idea that things are perpetually changing, both locally (locomotion) and internally (alteration) (182d1–9). Since what we call "the hot" or "the white" is always in both locomotion and alteration we do wrong to name it; naming implies a kind of being rather than an activity of becoming. To maintain this claim, though, it would appear also to follow that there can be no perceiver and no perceptible, since each of these would likewise have to be in constant motion. The activity of seeing is no more seeing than not-seeing, since it must change from seeing, because it cannot abide in a single state and still undergo alteration.[35] This undermines the constancy of any act of perceiving or of any object perceived. Socrates is, indeed, led to conclude that in defining knowledge as perception we no more defined knowledge than non-knowledge (182e10–11).

Let us make a note of what has, and what has not, been refuted in this line of reasoning. In addressing the constant alteration of the perceiver and perceptible, Socrates does not directly address the previous account of the interdependence of perceiver and perceptible. In fact, he does nothing to refute any of the accounts of how perception emerges, but rather only points out that this account of perception cannot provide enough to account for knowledge, or even to account for the phenomenon of our experience of things, and of names of things. While in this account and in the previous myths about motion Socrates was addressing the nature of perception, in the subsequent criticism, he addresses only the inadequacy of perception to account for knowledge. We should bear this in mind, and not make the mistake of assuming that Socrates rejects all that was said, but rather consider the possibility that he has given us a rich account of perception that we must build on ourselves in trying further to account for knowledge.

We should note that when Socrates makes declarations of what has been accomplished—that is, that not all is in motion, that man is not the measure of all things, that knowledge is not perception—when he arrives at the definition given by Theaetetus, he adds the qualification that knowledge is not perception "at least in terms of the quest for all things to be in motion" (183c3–4). In other words, an account of knowledge as perception that does not insist on claiming that all things are in motion, a differently qualified account of knowledge as perception, is not ruled out. We will return to this.

Theaetetus is finally invited back into the conversation, and Theodorus is happy to cede the spot to him (183d5–6). The way in which Theaetetus reemerges is by asking Socrates to turn next to the discussion of Parmenides and the others who claim that all is at rest and all is one. Though Theodorus claims that asking Socrates to give a speech is like taking a horse to the plains—that is, that it is Socrates's natural place and that he would happily indulge—Socrates unexpectedly refuses. He does not want to talk about these people, and in particular Parmenides. To Socrates, Parmenides is "awesome" and "uncanny," and a man of "grand and noble depth," and he would be embarrassed to talk about him in this way (183e6–184a2).

Why does Socrates not want to talk about Parmenides? In referring to Parmenides as "awesome" and "uncanny" Socrates refers to a passage from Homer. That passage is spoken by Helen of Troy to Priam, her new father-in-law.[36] She had initiated a war between the Greeks and the Trojans, and now standing before the leader of one army, finds him awesome and uncanny. Socrates, too, has initiated a war, between those advocating motion, and those advocating rest, and perhaps now regrets it.[37] He claims that to engage in this discussion would be essentially to take leave of the question of knowledge for much greater questions. For Socrates, what is most urgent at the moment is in the soul of young Theaetetus, not the grandest questions of the philosopher. It is the pregnancy that is most urgent.[38]

Socrates is here concerned with doing justice to the subject matter, not merely with the possibility that the question of knowledge will be overtaken by the question of being, nor with the possibility that reflecting on Parmenides will distract from focus on Theaetetus. If they were to talk seriously about Parmenides, they would have to talk at great length. If they were to give it only the time available, without overtaking the maieutic art, they would be doing it an injustice. For Socrates, freedom does indeed require leisure, but it does not—as Theodorus wrongly claimed—mean subordinating the speeches to oneself. On the contrary, they must subordinate themselves to the speeches to such an extent that those speeches should not begin unless there is a reasonable chance they will be discussed through to their natural end.

Socrates resumes his questioning of Theaetetus by drawing attention to that for which perception occurs. Thus far we have only talked about the perceiver insofar as she is engaged in the act of perceiving. It turns out that we were, in essence, talking only about the sense organ itself. Socrates offers two alternatives. Either the sense organ is that *by* which we perceive, or it is that *through* which we perceive (184c1–8). If it were the case that the sense organs are that by which we perceive, then we would be a mere arbitrary accumulation of sensations, each being absorbed independent of the others, none of which being related, or even relatable, to the others. It is clearly *through* the senses that *we* perceive. The senses through which we perceive are all parts, and each sense perceives only those things appropriate to its part. For example, to smell is to perceive only odors and nothing else, and nowhere else but through smelling do we perceive odor. So it is with each of the senses. The fact that each sense is unique in relation to the others and has its own discrete domain means, however, that none of the organs by themselves is able to account for the other organs. Yet we are able to identify and compare our perceptions despite this. We must therefore ask by what we are able to know and to compare each of these. Nothing in the perception of a smell can provide us with the ability to compare smell to taste. Nothing in any of the discrete perceptions can provide us with the ability to compare. Further, we must be able to account for the fact that we are able to take an assortment of sensations—each of which is discretely absorbed through distinct sense organs—and turn them into things that have a taste, a shape, a color, a smell, a sound, and a feel. This would have to be the organ that predicates of things, too, being and non-being, identity and difference, likeness and unlikeness, and unity and plurality. It turns out that this is none other than the soul, and it is Theaetetus who suggests soul as the site of perception.

What Theaetetus says is that the soul itself through itself examines what is common to things. This makes Socrates very happy. Socrates says that this is the evidence that Theaetetus is beautiful and not ugly as Theodorus had said. Those who say what is beautiful are beautiful (185e3–6). Not only is Theaetetus beautiful, he arrived at the idea that the soul through itself examines what is common without Socrates explicitly suggesting it to him. Socrates believed the claims about the soul to be true, and wanted Theaetetus to believe the same thing.

We must examine this more closely. The problem comes up as a result of the fact that in our experience there are things, and—as was entailed in what I just said—those things *are*. Putting aside for the moment the distinction between what actually is and what appears to be and taking for granted only the fact that things appear to be, something other than the senses must account for this appearance of things. Each of the senses is capable of apprehending only a restricted kind of object. The ear cannot see, for example. Yet we are able to recognize this fact about each sense. We know that there are sensations other than those heard, and the ear cannot give them to us, and likewise with all the other senses. If each sense is able only to do what it does then the senses cannot be a source of knowledge; knowing the senses does not happen in the senses. The fact that we are able to differentiate between senses means that something other than the senses experiences and makes use of them. Further, that we are able to say of objects that they "are" implies an activity distinct from sensation. Sensation alone cannot account for assessments about sensation.[39]

This account of the soul need not depend upon knowledge claims about the being of objects. All that it depends upon is the activity that constitutes our experience of objects. It might be, therefore, that perception emerges from contact of ensouled bodies with material flux. Nonetheless, what comes to be as a result of that process is the experience of things, and, in addition to and implied by those things, the evidence of the being of something which is able to know them. With the evidence of our experience of objects taken into account, let us further consider Theaetetus's and Socrates's discussion of the soul.

Theaetetus says of the soul that it is not a tool (*organon*). Each individual sense organ is a tool.[40] I use my eyes to navigate the field of colors, shapes, and (with the help of other sense organs) depths. But were I to lose my eyes, or were they to deteriorate to the point of not functioning anymore, I would continue to experience with the privation of vision. I would be deprived of an immensely powerful and important tool for experiencing the world, but my being and my ability to know would not cease. Unlike these, the soul is not a tool. It is not an additional thing alongside the sense organs that does the organizing of the perceptions. It is those perceptions as well. It is the whole of the being that knows.[41]

Conclusion

Though we are witnessing a conversation about the nature of knowledge, this conversation is primarily a lesson. It is a lesson in how to think and particularly how to think with other people. Theaetetus was evidently not previously aware either that his ideas had implications he did not know, or that it was important and problematic that he did not know of those implications. Thus, to have it demonstrated to him that counterintuitive, and in some cases impossible, implications are to be drawn from his definition of knowledge not only gives Theaetetus insights into the nature of knowledge and perception, but also insights into the process of thinking through ideas generally.

In addition to the lesson, we have also learned that the fact that subject and object are interdependently determinative of the appearance of things, and thus determinative of relational identities attributed to objects, implies the erotic nature of perception. This is something that the philosopher, as characterized by Socrates, understands in a way that intimately informs that philosopher's own perceptions. The philosopher identifies that his apprehension of objects of experience directs him to what lies both within and beyond those objects. The philosopher's perception of the object is procreative in the sense of generating deeper understanding of reality, by pointing to the account (*logos*) that underlies and gives the object meaning.

In identifying soul as that for which there is perception, as the site at which perceptions can be compared and thought about, Theaetetus directed himself at something capable of undergoing change of the kind that can move from generating wind-eggs to generating true ideas. He has had it demonstrated to him that the soul can be shaped to perceive more meaning from reality than it does, but that this requires time and a great deal of work to accomplish. The content of the discussion of the first definition therefore moved from immediate apprehension to that which apprehends, and also to that which is transformed in the form of the discussion itself. We, too, have moved, in our treatment of the dialogue, to the soul of Theaetetus, and to the ways of the human soul in general. In moving on to the second definition of knowledge in the next chapter, we will begin with a discussion of opinion, which is to say a discussion of one of the principle activities that both informs and is informed by perception.

CHAPTER 5

The Shortcomings of Abstraction (187a1–201c7)

> Evidently even of the things that are thought to be substances, most are only potentialities—e.g., the parts of animals (for none of them exists separately; and when they are separated, then they too exist, all of them, merely as matter) . . . for none of them is one, but they are like a heap before it is fused by heat and some one thing is made out of the bits. One might suppose especially that the parts of living things and the corresponding parts of the soul are both . . . Yet all the parts must exist only potentially.
>
> —Aristotle, *Metaphysics*, VII.16 1040b5–13

Introduction

The analysis of the first definition of knowledge culminated in the recognition that perceptions do not occur for themselves, but rather occur for persons. Perception therefore could not be the site of knowledge, because perception itself does nothing with perceptible objects; rather, it is the person, using perception, who knows; perception is a tool, an organ, of the knowing person. The analysis of perception as mere brute, discrete sense-information abstracts from the reality of how it is that we perceive, and therefore presents perception in a context foreign to us. Perception is always woven into the activity of being a person, which means that it is woven into a fabric that includes many other powers, included among which are several others discussed in this dialogue, such as reflection, memory, imagination, speech and opinion, (and among which we ought also to include emotion, which is acknowledged though never explicitly thematically analyzed in the *Theaetetus*). To examine perception, therefore, strictly in terms of its "internal" characteristics, comes at the expense of excluding its relational attributes.[1] We saw in the previous chapter that the analysis of the first definition of knowledge demonstrated that, though relational attributes are highly changeable, especially compared to the comparatively slow-changing entities whose interaction with one another generates those attributes, relational attributes nonetheless do have genuine purchase on reality. Indeed, failing to acknowledge relational identities diminishes one's understanding of the objects under examination, insofar as objects at no time exist in a vacuum and, on the contrary, have as part of their essential character relations to others, and consequently resulting from those relations, relational attributes. To reduce entities to their non-relational character is therefore to ignore something belonging to the nature of reality.

It is, moreover, impossible to analyze entities accurately without regard for the attributes that emerge from their interaction with others. This is due to the fact that discussing entities discrete from one another requires that one discuss the intra-relational attributes of the entities themselves, that is, how a given entity functions as an organism, as a whole, consists of the emergent relational identities of its parts. One is therefore acknowledging the need to attend to relational attributes within the entity under discussion even when one abstracts that entity from its attributes in relation to others. One must take the attributes that emerge from the relationship between entities into account; otherwise one is being inconsistent in one's analysis.

The point of this chapter is, in essence, to claim that taking into account the emergent relational attributes between parts within a given entity is essential to providing a true account of that entity. The failure to give a successful account of knowledge rests on the failure to recognize this fact. More specifically, the way in which Theaetetus allows Socrates to proceed fails to recognize that knowledge is something that emerges from the integration of powers, and therefore cannot be found in the abstract analysis of a particular one. Let us now take a moment to flesh out how this is so, before summarizing what will follow in the chapter.

It is strikingly the case with the various powers associated with living human beings that ignoring the way in which they relate to each other gives a poor account of how we experience the world, and as a consequence of this, gives a poor account of knowledge. We saw in Chapter 4 that the abstraction of perception from the powers with which it is interrelated makes possible an account of perception that exists nowhere in a person's experience. Socrates described well the poverty of the way that they had been characterizing perception when he said "it's surely dreadful, my boy, if many kinds of perceptions sit in us as if in wooden horses, but all these do not strain together toward some single look" (184d1–3). There, Socrates was drawing attention to the poverty of a concept of perception that assumes each organ of perception is itself performing the action, rather than all perception being done *by* the person *using* them as tools. Here, though, we might add that to situate perception correctly within the context of a living person's activity is to be forced to situate it within the interrelation of the various organs constitutive of the intra-relational identity that *is* the person as a whole.[2]

From this one ought to assume that the examination of any of the other characteristics informing one's experience of the world in abstraction from the whole of experience—that is, the abstract analysis of other individual candidates for knowledge—will produce a similarly distortive account of experience, in each case producing a uniquely distortive account, insofar as each organ of the soul has its own unique character. We ought to have this in mind when we consider the examination of opinion given by Socrates and Theaetetus, which treats it independent of its integration into the whole of experience, and ought to understand that it will not, consequently, successfully account for knowledge.

In the previous chapter, I argued that the primary lesson to be derived from the analysis of the first definition of knowledge was that because it turns out that perception is deeply informed by the mediating force of thought, we ought to engage in reflection on the manner in which our thinking mediates our presumptively immediate apprehension of the world. I argued that this kind of reflection takes the form of working through implications of our own ideas, particularly in dialogue with others. In this chapter, I will present the analysis of the second definitions of knowledge, presenting it as providing more distinct lessons for Theaetetus and for us. Specifically, the primary lessons to be found in the analysis of the second definition are that abstraction of human capacities from one another, and abstraction of active human agency from passive receptivity, will always fail to derive an adequate understanding of knowledge.

In addition to the presentation of these primary lessons, I will continue to focus attention on the progression of Theaetetus's participation in the conversation. In the analysis of the second definition—that is, that knowledge is true opinion—Theaetetus repeatedly provides what appear to be unhesitating opinions on issues about which it is highly unlikely he is sufficiently equipped to provide a thoughtful answer. First, prior to its explicit demonstration in argument, this exemplifies that opinion and knowledge cannot be the same, insofar as Theaetetus's easy adoption of those opinions is not only evidently grounded in a misunderstanding of the question, but also obstructs the question from being answered. Second, and more importantly, the *persistent* statement of unlearned opinion on Theaetetus's part causes the discussion to deteriorate.

This last point about Theaetetus's behavior causing the discussion to deteriorate brings up an issue already addressed, but worth repeating with slightly different emphasis. Theaetetus's hasty answers require Socrates to take for granted for argument's sake ideas that are highly questionable, and that would presumably not be entertained in other contexts. This leads them down a conversational path that is not as fruitful as it might otherwise have been. Despite the shortcomings of the conversation, *we* ought to pay attention to what underlies the purpose of Socrates's otherwise seemingly odd behavior. [3] Specifically, we ought to recognize the implicit acknowledgment of the reality of relational attributes as supplying positive claims to supplement the aporetic results of the explicit content of the conversation. With this in mind, I will draw attention to those moments where the conversation is led astray, and to the ways in which the conversation might have been more fruitfully developed.

In this chapter, I will discuss in detail the second definition of knowledge, that true opinion (*alēthēs doxa*) is knowledge (*epistēmē*) (187b6). In section 1, I demonstrate the interrelation between thinking, as reflection and deliberation, and opining. I argue that the false start to the discussion of the second definition results from the failure to attend to the fact that thinking and opining must be understood in connection to one another. In section 2, I present the two images of knowledge provided by Socrates, namely, first, the wax slab within the soul that makes memory possible, therefore both allowing us to think and providing the variable accounting for error, and second, the bird-enclosure that provides the distinction between the habituated enactment of knowledge (*hexis*) and the mere possession of it (*ktēsis*), as though in storage. I argue that each of these images provides a great deal of insight, though each is framed in such a way that it fails to account for (and in fact obscures) the passive dimension of the cultivation of knowledge. It is for this reason, I argue, that Socrates ends the discussion with both a metaphor of passivity for their quest (i.e., the "river-guide" [200e7]) and an example (i.e., of the power of oratory [201a8–9]) that demonstrates the powerful and dangerous exploitation of the insufficiently acknowledged passive element of opinion, each of which illustrates the poverty of opinion (true or otherwise) as a candidate for knowledge when treated on its own, abstracted from the rest of what constitutes the person.

1. Opining and Thinking (187a1–191a8)

It is Socrates who initiates the discussion that culminates in Theaetetus's second definition of knowledge (187b5–6). That is, continuing with the pattern of the dialogue so far, Socrates is setting the agenda for what will be discussed, taking seriously and examining claims made by Theaetetus that the latter neither himself examined, nor seemed fully to understand. Because we know that Socrates is primarily trying to provoke specific reactions from Theaetetus, we have to proceed carefully when we read claims Socrates makes that appear to be representative of his own views. It is true generally that in Plato's dialogues, one ought to attend to the context of the conversation before making interpretive claims about the words used; in this particular case, Theaetetus engages in a dialectically immature habit of automatically agreeing to propositions put forward by Socrates, with the result that the conversation is led toward attempting to justify claims that cannot be justified. As will become clear in this section, Socrates seems to frame this particular discussion in such a way that it is set up to produce unsatisfying results, with those unsatisfying results highlighting the significance of what has been omitted.

Put plainly, Socrates wants Theaetetus to challenge the claims that Socrates puts before him. As we have already discussed, though it is Theaetetus that gives the initial definition, it is always Socrates who provides the propositions that elaborate that initial definition. If Theaetetus merely agrees to what is said—and, indeed, to what typically is presented for the purpose of verifying that it is consistent with *what Theaetetus would say*—without thinking about it, then the conversation is made to move in directions to which Theaetetus is oblivious, and in which he is not truly invested. It seems that it is for this reason that Socrates suggests ideas that ought to be challenged, and, when those ideas are not challenged, allows the implications to be drawn, such that the ideas end up having to be rejected. That both the definitions and the dialogue as a whole end in impasses appears to be harmonious with Socrates's intentions and pedagogical motivations.

There is, in consequence to these conversational demands on Socrates, opportunity to misread things Socrates says as though Socrates is himself advocating them. This way of interpreting Socrates's behavior may make it seem like it is impossible to know one way or another which ideas Socrates is himself committed to. But, first of all, just like Theaetetus, we must invest our own thinking in the discussion, and must therefore sort through the arguments, as well as the dynamics of the discussion, for ourselves. Second, there are indeed moments at which Socrates phrases his statements in such a way that he either appears tentatively committed to them,[4] or appears more invested in the claim he is making than merely to offer a paraphrase of what he expects Theaetetus has meant. Thus, though we must tread carefully, compelling evidence can be found for how to differentiate between one kind of statement and another.

Let us begin by examining how the second definition comes about. Following Theaetetus's agreement that perception cannot be the same as knowledge, Socrates points out that they had not begun by trying to find out what knowledge is not, and that, therefore, they ought to move away from perception to something that, apparently unlike perception, *could* be a candidate for knowledge. Socrates strongly encourages the consideration of mental activity as an alternative candidate: "But still and all, we've advanced so far at least, so altogether not to seek it in perception but in that name, whatever the soul has, whenever it alone by itself deals with the things which are" (187a3–6). This reformulation of the discussion implies that they must abstract the account of knowledge from what occurs in perception.[5] This should strike us as odd, since Socrates's characterization of the philosopher (172c3–177c7) championed the fact that the philosopher had cultivated an ability to apprehend immediately the deeper structures at work in the objects he perceived. It was the philosopher's cultivated *perception* that made him so remarkably astute at identifying underlying structures that were in fact on display but nonetheless not seen by other people. In our discussion of this in chapter 4, we drew the conclusion that the account of perception with which they were working had abstracted sensation illicitly from the other aspects of experience that contribute to our immediate apprehension of objects, and that therefore an adequate account of perception would have to include consideration of the conceptual element in immediate apprehension. We also noted that the fact that perception was said always to be for the person and in the soul, and that it could only make sense when analyzed taking into account such conditions, reinforced this point. Therefore, to then go on to reformulate the discussion in a way that dismisses the perceptual apprehension of objects is a mistake. Indeed, it is a repetition of the kind of mistake they had made previously.

The most important insight from the previous definition had been that the activity of perceiving carries with it an intellectual dimension, and that as such a person's perception can be cultivated to "see" more or less of what is present, as well as to "see" different aspects of what is present. Thus it is the development of the person's soul that is at issue in trying to cultivate her knowledge, because what is being cultivated is how that person immediately experiences things prior to reflection; moreover, to cultivate how a person immediately experiences things prior to reflection is to cultivate the terms from which, and through the use of which, reflection occurs. It is essential both to the explicit discussion of the question of knowledge *and* to the implicit project of educating Theaetetus, that we emphasize the relationship between the reflective activity of thinking and immediate apprehension. One's immediate apprehensions set the terms for the reflection and discussion that is to follow. Those apprehensions are the resources with which one builds one's understanding of the world. This is why it is essential that one attend to the cultivation of one's immediate apprehensions. One is at their behest, in a sense, and one can never immediately "get behind" them in order to correct them. It is therefore precisely *not* the right way to proceed to abstract either perception or the mind's activity when it is alone by itself, if one wants to discover anything that actually happens in our experience of knowledge. This is nonetheless what Socrates and Theaetetus do.

To summarize what we have so far established, there are two activities that appear to be central to the philosophical orientation that Socrates is trying to cultivate in Theaetetus. The first consists in an activity—engaging in dialogue, either with oneself or with another (though probably, as will also be discussed below, both are essential)—that happens to be essential to the development of the second—immediate apprehension of the world—a second which happens always to be occurring and which therefore deeply informs the first. There is a circular relationship between thinking and conversing on the one hand, and immediate apprehension on the other. While thinking and conversing shape immediate apprehension, it is in response to immediate apprehension that thinking occurs at all. During the discussion of perception, Socrates directed Theaetetus to the consideration of highly cultivated perception. During the following discussion, another activity is examined whose immediacy gives shape to how we go about deliberating, namely opinion. Once again, the examination of this activity is performed without attending to its integration with other aspects of our experience.

Let us look at how this abstraction fails; in doing so, we will pay particular attention to Theaetetus's habit of casually adopting opinions he has no justification for adopting without further inquiry.

a. Theaetetus's Hastily Adopted Opinions

While Theaetetus has begun the process of learning how to think ideas through their implications, he continues to allow Socrates to provide all of the propositions, and, perhaps to Socrates's frustration, continues to assume simply that these propositions given by Socrates are true until Socrates shows him otherwise. As we will see below, Socrates characterizes opinion as the "determination" at which one arrives where one no longer entertains doubt (190a1–5). It is a state one reaches when one stops deliberating. There is no need that one be justified in reaching such a determination.[6] In the stage-setting of the second definition, Theaetetus repeatedly adopts opinions suggested by Socrates about which he could not possibly rationally justify certainty. Theaetetus's unwillingness to entertain doubt, his excessive credulity, is a problem; not only is Theaetetus's hasty adoption of opinions a problem because it gives him a sense of certainty with the potential to conceal from him the lack of sufficient grounds for opinion, it also demonstrates to us—well in advance of its explicit articulation in the conversation—the problem with the second definition of knowledge, that is, that one can easily adopt an opinion that is true, but one might do so for the wrong reasons. In this particular case, the reasons for Theaetetus's adoption of his opinion probably include the confused demonstration of deference to a venerable interlocutor, the indirect expression of self-doubt (i.e., fear of asking questions that might put himself under more scrutiny), and perhaps laziness.

This habit of quick agreement is slow to break, and we surely could not reasonably expect it to be broken an hour or so into one conversation. Socrates has, at best, the chance to draw Theaetetus's attention to this bad habit. He tries to do so by persistently putting forward claims that Theaetetus would have no reason to adopt prior to discussing them. Socrates provides Theaetetus with the opportunity to open up his thinking, through the conversation, by giving him provocative claims to question. As a result, by working through the inadequacies of the second definition of knowledge, they work through inadequacies that Theaetetus's own thinking too readily draws upon. We must have this in mind as we examine the framing of this second definition.

b. The Statement of the Second Definition

As was already mentioned, Socrates grounds the new start to the conversation by claiming that they are beginning with what the soul does when it communes alone with itself about the things which are.[7] This Theaetetus calls opinion (*doxa*).[8] Theaetetus then cautiously claims that "true opinion [*alēthēs doxa*] is probably [*kinduneuei*] knowledge [*epistēmē*]" (187b5–6).[9] We already know that because perceptions alone do not account for our ability to compare and to deliberate about what is, perceptions cannot be equivalent to knowledge. For Theaetetus, opinion in general cannot be knowledge, because there is such a thing as false opinion. On the other hand, true opinion does appear to be what knowledge is, insofar as it is a correspondence between what one presumes to be true and the world to which it refers. Theaetetus acknowledges that it is possible that this is wrong, but that he need not worry about that, since they can simply revise what they are saying in that case (187b7–8).

Socrates applauds this sentiment. Despite the lack of attentiveness we are in the midst of illustrating, Theaetetus's attitude has at least improved from the much more tentative one with which he began (187c1). The important lesson he has begun to learn is to present ideas with conviction, to commit to them, for the purpose of having them scrutinized, with the result that he is transformed by that scrutiny. Theaetetus seems to have come to recognize that he is not being explicitly, personally evaluated by the claims he makes, and that, on the contrary, making claims shamelessly—as long as it is for the purpose of their being scrutinized—is precisely the means by which he will learn. While Theaetetus has learned this, he has not learned to challenge the claims that Socrates presents to him.

In response to Theaetetus's second definition, Socrates asks whether Theaetetus means that, when there is a pair of appearances, one true and one false, the true opinion is knowledge (187c6–8). This is a striking and odd formulation, and one which Theaetetus should not simply accept. Theaetetus had plainly suggested that when we have an opinion that is true, this would appear to be knowledge, and that this qualification must be added to the equation of knowledge and opinion because of the reality of false opinion. Socrates's strict isolation of "simply" true opinion and false opinion is odd because he limits the inquiry to exclude the phenomena of learning and forgetting (188a1–4). As a result of this exclusion, any notion of how an opinion comes to be or is discarded is lost. What is odd about Socrates's suggestion to abstract true and false opinion from the process by which they emerge is that it occurs shortly after Socrates expresses his puzzlement with the fact that false opinion *comes to be* in us (187d1–7). That is, Socrates expresses interest in discussing the *development* of false opinion, the *becoming* and *shaping* of how we opine. Socrates then asks Theaetetus if he thinks they ought to reflect further on this thing that puzzles Socrates—the becoming of false opinions—or if they are "to go on to examine it in a somewhat different way than a little while ago" (187d9–10). In light of what we have seen concerning the importance of how opinions come to be, it is certainly the case that how opinions come to be in us is precisely what they ought to be focusing their attention on. Nor is it at all clear what a "somewhat different way" of examining might be, or why an as yet unarticulated alternative would be more desirable as a line of inquiry than the one Socrates claims to be interested in. Even if Theaetetus were stirred to shift the focus of the discussion by this "somewhat different way," which he apparently is, he ought to be asking questions about what that might involve. Instead, Theaetetus reminds Socrates that Theodorus had said they were at their leisure and suggests that they follow this "somewhat different" approach, and does so without asking questions and without explaining his reasoning for making this suggestion.[10]

Using Theaetetus's agreement as his prompt, Socrates asks if they are to say that there are false opinions and true opinions and that it is this way by nature (187e4–7). Theaetetus agrees. The language used by Socrates here is so vague that it is not at all clear what he means, and, unless Theaetetus in fact understands something about what Socrates has said that we do not, he should not be agreeing without asking questions. The way in which Socrates is speaking demands clarification, and this is a demand that is never made during the conversation. Moreover, as a result of this agreement, Socrates makes the suggestion that about all things there is only either to know or not to know, and that, for this claim to be so, he is dismissing both learning and forgetting from consideration, "on the grounds that they [learning and forgetting] are between them [i.e., knowing and not knowing], for nothing is pertinent there for our speech" (188a3–4). We might wonder what Socrates means here by "our speech." Is he acknowledging that they are not concerned with reality, but rather with the unjustifiably constrained domain that this discussion now occupies (one in which all of our experience is reduced to states of true opinion or false opinion)? How might he be justified in excluding the dimension of becoming—the dimension that includes learning and forgetting—from the discussion? This, too, goes unquestioned by Theaetetus, who merely agrees that the domain Socrates has set up includes only "to know [*eidenai*] and not to know [*mē eidenai*]" (188a6).[11]

On what grounds might Socrates be justified in excluding learning and forgetting from "all things and each individually" (*panta kai kath' hekaston*) (188a1)? We must remember that the context of the discussion that Socrates has allowed Theaetetus's agreement (i.e., Theaetetus's unexamined opinion) to lead them to is the idea that opinion is knowledge. To isolate the opinionated orientation toward the world from all other kinds (for example, one could relate to the world questioningly, confusedly, perhaps indifferently) does not adequately reflect how we actually experience the world. Putting aside reality, though, if one does abstract and focus exclusively on opining, one must exclude both learning and forgetting. First, learning involves, at some point in the process, at least the temporary forfeiture of opinion. The aporetic moment, the moment at which one comes to identify that one's opinions fail to guide one adequately in one's thinking, is the moment at which one is learning. Learning can be neither knowledge nor ignorance in this sense. It is, rather, a release of one's hold on either the whole of or, more likely, an aspect of, one's interpretive framework. Learning is in this sense submissive to an aspect of reality. Second, forgetting, too, cannot be made a part of the sphere of opinion. In forgetting, we are required to forfeit opinion, not because we recognize that what we had previously thought was false, but because we realize that what we expected to think, we cannot. We are unable to have an opinion, though we think we ought to have one. In each case, the exclusion of the topic from discussion is the result of the fact that Theaetetus and Socrates are speculating within an abstract sphere informed exclusively by true and false opinion. They must speculate within that sphere because Socrates needs Theaetetus to recognize that opinion on its own is a poor candidate for knowledge. It is, in this sense, a reductio ad absurdum argument either elaborately set up by Socrates, or, more likely, improvised for the purpose of drawing attention to Theaetetus's dialectical immaturity. It is a tactic that must continue until Theaetetus notices that they have taken an illicit step from the start.

Continuing to elaborate this abstracted, false account of reality, Socrates suggests that one opines either about the things one knows or about the things one does not know (188a8). In putting it this way, Socrates makes opinion sound like a *relationship* to one's knowledge or one's ignorance. If this definition is sustained, it essentially denies the definition they are trying to articulate. If opinion is an orientation either to one's own knowledge or to one's own ignorance, then knowledge will be merely *about* true opinion. True opinion would presume knowledge from the outset. With this as a starting point, Socrates returns to the notion that it is impossible both to know and not to know the same thing (188a10–b1). As we saw in chapter 3, though it is impossible for the same thing both to be and not to be at the same time, in the same place and in the same way, the removal of any of these qualifiers simultaneously removes the impossibility. It is possible both to know and not to know the same thing; indeed, as we saw with the example of language—where knowledge of the meaning obscures the brute sounds the language makes, while knowledge of the alien sounds of the foreign language implies ignorance of its meaning—in some cases it is *necessary* both to know and not to know the same thing in order to know it in any way at all. Thus, on the basis of what we've already seen in the dialogue, we can recognize that Socrates's claim about both knowing and not knowing is in fact false.

Socrates provides one possibility of what it might mean to hold a false opinion: perhaps it is possible that the object about which a person holds a false opinion is an object that person knows, but simply the *wrong* object (188b3–6). In other words, the person holding a false opinion would have as her resource for opinion only objects she knows. In such a case, the occurrence of her erring happens only when she opines about the wrong object. This example is at first jarringly obscure. We should remember how jarring it was when Socrates began the examination of the claim that knowledge is perception by saying Protagoras said the same thing when he said "man is the measure of all things" (151e9–152a5). In each case, Socrates anticipates a problem with the definition, but a problem that he chooses not to reveal immediately. Further, in each case, the problem Socrates chooses not to reveal is an ontological problem. In the first definition, the problem was that equating knowledge with perception (when perception is conceived strictly in terms of sense-experience) meant erasing the being of the object of knowledge altogether by denying that anything that is has anything other than relational identity.[12] In this case, the ontological problem Socrates anticipates is that, if knowledge is equated with true opinion, false opinion will depend for its reality upon non-being *being* an object of opinion. In each case, finally, the vocabulary with which they are operating is inadequate to consider the problem the definition produces. The discussion of the first definition was only able to articulate that relational identities could not be absolutely dependent upon the perceivers if the provisional ontological claim implicit in the definition were sustained, because the being of the perceivers themselves would have to dissolve as much as that of the objects, leaving no way of accounting for our actual experience of knowledge. Because of the fact that Socrates and Theaetetus were unable to preserve the account of perception with the more nuanced ontology that Socrates presented in his myth, they were left with the less productive activity of rejecting the more general version of the first definition. In the case of this initial discussion of the second definition, because Socrates and Theaetetus have excluded the process by which one comes to an opinion, they are forced to use fewer conceptual tools than the actual conditions demand. Again, in both cases Socrates adopts the strategy of allowing the discussion to reach an impasse by explicitly excluding the conceptual tool to which Theaetetus pays insufficient attention. Likewise, in both cases, Socrates has the task of forcing Theaetetus to notice and work through to its conclusion the mistaken line of thinking.[13]

Within the restricted confines of their discussion of opinion, Socrates asks Theaetetus whether one holding a false opinion is confusing one thing he does not know with another thing he does not know (188c2–4). Socrates gives the example of a person who knows nothing about Socrates and Theaetetus presuming that he knows both, and yet confusing the two of them. This seems to Theaetetus obviously impossible. How could one have an opinion of any kind about something without first having encountered it? More specifically, how could someone who knows nothing of Socrates or Theaetetus think Socrates is Theaetetus and vice versa. We can now see how Socrates is beginning to produce a problem for Theaetetus. The person with a false opinion cannot know the thing about which he has a false opinion. How could he have a false opinion of it if he does not know it? Well, if that is the case, then how could he have any opinion about it at all? The person who knows nothing of Socrates and Theaetetus cannot have them confused with each other, because he cannot even name either of them in the first place. If he can, if he knows them, then it would appear that we are back to the previous claim that false opinion is the confusion of two known things.

Socrates clarifies his point. If we either know or do not know those things about which we opine either falsely or truly then no other options seem to be available to us (188c5–7). We must remember that Socrates has explicitly excluded both forgetting and learning from this account. We should also remember that he has formulated the account in a way that is not faithful to what Theaetetus said, that is, that opinion is a relationship to knowledge, rather than knowledge itself. To get out of this predicament, Socrates suggests that they think, not about knowing and not knowing, but about being and not being (188c9–d1). That is, perhaps it must be the case that those who opine falsely are opining about things which are not at all, and therefore, when anyone thinks anything that is not true, they are thinking only of non-being (188d2–7). The problem with this formulation is that, if we consider perception, for example seeing, it is impossible that a person sees nothing at all. That is, if one is seeing, one is seeing at least something.[14] This is surely how it is with all the senses. Does the same apply to opinion? If we opine about what is not, are we not opining about nothing at all? It seems that this is so (189a11). It seems, further, that to opine what is not (which appears to be impossible) is not the same as to opine falsely. The latter seems like it must take as its object what is, and that it is an inadequate relation to what is that is at issue.

Having established that they cannot talk about false opinion as though it were of nothing, Socrates essentially returns to the definition he gave at the start. He began by saying true opinion must be opinion about what is, and false opinion is mistaking one thing one knows and which therefore is for another thing one knows and which therefore is. Now, however, the attention is shifted to the act of misidentification of the person opining. One opines about something, but misses the thing one intends to opine about, rather opining about another thing that is; Socrates calls this "else-opining" or "mistaking one thing for another" (*allodoxian*) (189b12–c6).

Theaetetus claims that this is what is truly false: it is to confuse one thing that is with another that is. Thus, for example, to say of what is beautiful that it is ugly is to say what is truly false.[15] Socrates scolds Theaetetus for this, pointing out that he is inadvertently speaking as though a contrary can become its contrary through being what it is (189d1–5). What is false would seem to be unable to become truly false. Socrates returns to the point, asking Theaetetus if it is his contention that one can opine something to be other than it is (189d7–8). If this is so, as Theaetetus contends, then one must be thinking either of both of the beings (the one that one is trying to opine and the one that one mistakenly opines), or at least one of the two. One must be invoking the mistaken thing, and the thing for which it is mistaken.

c. What Socrates Calls Thinking and Opining

Socrates has established agreement from Theaetetus, first, that it is possible for one to opine something to be something other than what it is, and, second, that when one does this one must either think both of the things one has confused at the same time, or each of them in turn (189d10–e3). Having established such an agreement, Socrates is compelled to provide an account of what he calls thinking. Specifically, Socrates calls thinking a "speech which the soul by itself goes through before itself about whatever it is examining" (189e6–7).[16] Thinking, as Socrates characterizes it, is dialogue with oneself. When the dialogue stops, when the soul decides it is no longer going to converse with itself and rests with what it has, this is opinion. This account of opinion interprets opinion as a kind of rest.[17] We should remember from chapter 3 that idleness or inactivity within the soul (as well as within the body) was characterized by Socrates as being a kind of corruption (153b4–c2). Is opinion really a kind of corruption of the soul, or is it merely like a kind of corruption of the soul? It seems that it is merely like a kind of corruption. Rather, as was noted in chapter 3, just as we saw that, despite Socrates's characterization of rest as a kind of corruption of the soul, we can conceive of circumstances in which rest is actually beneficial to one's thinking; we should thus also think about the ambiguity in putting the soul's dialogue to rest. Put plainly, just as rest, which is otherwise a condition that causes the deterioration of the body and soul, when integrated into the rhythms and demands of motion, is a source of health and regeneration, perhaps likewise opinion, when integrated into the demands of thinking, is also regenerative. Perhaps it is the case that there is a natural rhythm to thinking, and that it must rest periodically in order to take up anew what has been settled in rest (i.e., opinion). Let us consider further what the relationship between thinking and opinion is, noting both the inadequacy of opinion as a candidate for knowledge, and its necessary place in the becoming of knowledge.

An opinion is a foreclosure, if a temporary one, of further deliberation. To have adopted an opinion is, in a certain sense, to have decided that one has been given adequate justification not to continue to deliberate. I use the term "decided" here somewhat loosely, as it is not necessarily the case that one need have consciously arrived at the conclusion that no deliberation is necessary. In fact, it is probably often the case that one does not consciously arrive at an opinion.[18] These latter cases—that is, those in which one has adopted an opinion that implicitly presumes to be based on adequate justification, but without any explicit recognition of this presumption—are essentially those that we discussed in chapter 2, that is, the presumptions Socrates seeks to compel his interlocutor to articulate for the purpose of examination. What this new account of opinion offers to enrich that discussion of presumptions is that such opinions constitute an end to dialogue.[19] For example, if one has the presumption that government is intrinsically untrustworthy and therefore something one would be foolish to invest financial resources in, this presumption sets a limit on what is to be open for future discussion in such a way that one is closed off from potentially wise proposals—that is, until discussion has been reopened to make this presumption questionable.

This last point about opinion—that it constitutes the end of dialogue (or, in Socrates's way of formulating it, the end of thinking) until dialogue is reopened—indicates that opinion is not, and could not be, merely an end. That is, based on what has been said here, and based on the contrast Socrates presented at 189e–190a between thinking and opining, one might be given the impression that opinion is simply what one reaches when one gives up thinking, and that, therefore, opinion is somehow "inferior" to thinking. One might suggest the radically skeptical position that opinion is the illegitimate conclusion to thought, and that we ought to avoid opinion for the purpose of keeping dialogue open, because this would allow us to prevent the cultivation of illegitimately grounded presumptions about the world. We would, however, be wrong to draw such a conclusion. What the point about opinion should draw our attention to is that one of the primary resources with which thinking operates *is* opinion. This is precisely what we do in everyday conversation. We bring to the activity of thinking opinions that are presented for the purpose of being subjected to revision (either consciously so or, as is often the case in conversations with Socrates, unwittingly). Further, in engaging in discussion with others, we imitate the activity of thinking as Socrates characterizes it. That is, we bring to the discussion with someone else ideas that are open to scrutiny.

The analogy that exists between conversation and thinking is striking. One striking area of similarity between conversations one has with oneself and conversations one has with others is the potential for an analogous kind of pathology. In thinking, one can cultivate the tendency to suppress deliberation; one can convince oneself that one's thought is uncontestable. Indeed, the ability to convince oneself in this way is essential to the possibility of embedding presumptions; in order for us to be able to hold an opinion *not* motivated by the force of reason or of manifest reality, we must be capable of suspending disputation freely. In conversation, one can suppress deliberation equally, by selecting "like-minded" people with whom one is willing to converse. In each of these cases, one can protect one's own prejudices, but one cannot completely eliminate the possibility of exposure to change. Thoughts can have the effect of convincing us against our will, and others around us can provide unanticipated challenges to our prejudices, no matter how careful we are.[20] Interestingly, therefore, one is vulnerable to being subject to transformation in conversation and in one's private thoughts.

Let us further consider this vulnerability to which our entrenched opinions are subject. Transformation even against one's will is a virtue to Socrates's process of *elenchus* that is not made evident in the explicit language of the text: When one leaves Socrates's company, the critical insights he used against one's opinions linger. One can, whether one wants to or not, adopt as one of the interlocutors in one's own private thinking, the voice of Socrates. This fact about Socrates's effect on one's opinions is insinuated by his repeated mention of the experience one has when one is left alone with one's thoughts: Socrates on multiple occasions, refers to the experience one has of being forced to reckon with oneself regardless of being explicitly steadfast in one's opinion (155a1–2; 177b1–9; 190c1–4).[21] When one holds false opinions, and has these challenged in conversation with someone else, one might be unwilling to concede one's error to that other person, but one will nonetheless be faced with oneself privately. In other words, one will be forced to reckon with the changes that conversation has wrought in one's own thinking. In this very important sense of thinking as a conversation one has with oneself, one can adopt the voices of others, and thus the border between oneself and others is shown to be remarkably porous.

d. The Integrated Whole of Thinking and Opinion

Socrates has offered an account of thinking as conversation, and of opinion as the point at which one has decided to stop thinking. I have suggested that opinion constitutes the material with which we begin the "conversation" of thinking. If we remove from consideration the "conversation" one has with oneself, we remove the resource with which opinions are generated. The image of thinking without opinion seems superficially to match nothing more than Theodorus's vision of the philosopher at leisure—someone who can pursue any particular topic of interest until a new one comes along, without concern for or even consideration of the demands internal to the topic.[22] Though Socrates has Theaetetus quickly reject both the notion that false opinions are about true things (and therefore about things that we know) and that false opinions are of false things (which neither exist nor, consequently, could be thought), he claims that, if they continue this rejection, they will be led "to agree to many strange things" (190e7). Socrates does not tell Theaetetus what those strange things are, but it is clear already that the problem with their rejection of the above formulations of the structure of false opinion rests on the exclusion of becoming. It is this to which Socrates now turns, using two images of the emergence of opinion.

2. Two Images of the Becoming of Opinion (191a9–201c7)

The first interrogation of opinion went poorly because Socrates excluded from consideration the process of learning, and therefore the process by which opinions are formulated. Having reached an impasse with the exclusion of learning, Socrates says that they went wrong by rejecting the idea that one can opine what one does not know to be what one knows (191a10–b1). He then goes on to ask Theaetetus if there is such a thing as not knowing something and then coming to know it (191c4–5). Though Socrates himself does not emphasize the fact that the discussion that follows is altered by the addition of the experiences of mistaking false opinion for knowledge and of coming-to-know as possibilities, we can formulate the combination of these two claims to present a very different picture of the topic of knowledge that has been discussed so far: we typically take our world to consist of things we know, in some sense. We also come to know about things we previously did not know. Among the things we previously did not know, though, were things we opined about as though we knew, but did not know. With these two conceptual additions, therefore, Socrates transforms the conversation into one about the way in which our understanding takes shape. It made no sense to talk about true and false opinion independent of learning and forgetting, because in such a context true and false opinion never would occur. On the contrary, learning and forgetting are essential to the shaping of our opinions, and of our knowledge of things. Taking into account the fact that things become apparent to us to varying degrees of depth and in varying ways, we ought to entertain doubts about the lack of nuance in the strict categories of knowledge and non-knowledge, and in the strict categories of true and false opinion.

Socrates takes concern for the becoming of opinion, and more specifically, of false opinion, as the primary focus of the conversation now, as he shifts into the first of two images of opinion, that is, of a wax block existing within the soul. I will now present the image of the wax block, and will then move on to discuss its virtues and shortcomings, as well as what it tells us about Socrates's pedagogical project.

a. The Wax Image: The Reintroduction of a Developmental Model

Socrates suggests that, for the sake of argument, they imagine the soul to be a wax block (191c9–d1). The constitution of the wax block varies according to the character of the person in whose soul it lies. Socrates does not immediately explain in what way this is so, though he will very shortly (194c5–195b1). For some, the wax is larger, for others smaller, for some more pure, for others more mixed with other material, for some soft and pliable, for others hard. Socrates asks Theaetetus to imagine that the wax is a gift from Memory, who is the mother of the muses. Whatever in our perceptions that is impressed on this piece of wax is remembered, whatever fails to be impressed on the wax, or gets wiped off the wax, is forgotten.[23]

This gift from memory, the mother of all muses, acts as a receptacle for the perceptions that we have.[24] The block receives the imprint of those perceptible objects, such that the imprint can be consulted later, and thus can revive for us the initial perceptual experience to the extent it was imprinted. The wax slab is the place within the soul that receives perception; it receives the imprint of perceptions, and sets the limit to what we retain from the perception. It gives to us, from the object, the subject matter of deliberative thinking.

This wax slab receives the imprint of our perception (*aisthēsis*), providing us with the ability to revisit those imprints later, and is thus akin to written characters on a wax tablet or in a notebook. We must, though, be careful in articulating the process being characterized in this image, insofar as it allocates the roles that must be played in actually generating knowledge in a somewhat puzzling way. Socrates characterizes the wax slab as something we use to remember "whatever we want to [*boulēthōmen*]" by "submitting it to our perceptions [*aisthēsesi*] and thoughts [*ennoiais*]" (191d4–7). The sequence would appear to involve, first, the inscription of perceived objects onto the wax slab, and second, the examination—performed by an additional power in us—of the inscriptions according to what we want.[25]

The way in which Socrates presents the process of remembering according to the image of the wax slab involves an underdeveloped account of precisely this "whatever we want." On his formulation, choosing to remember whatever we want to among the things that have been imprinted upon the wax slab comes across as though it were independent of what has been imprinted, as though it were an independent actor within the process of remembering. It seems that he is saying that we receive imprints, and then some part of us scrutinizes those imprints for those that are worthy of retention. But we do not perceive only or even mostly things we choose to perceive. Further, we retain from among those unchosen experiences in a manner that is not entirely within our conscious control. Those unchosen perceptions deeply inform the kind of people we are, and thus the kinds of memories we tend to recall and reflect upon. To talk about the wax slab that stands for memory as though it were something we freely and unproblematically manipulate is to make it strongly resemble an organ of some other conscious actor. As we discussed in chapter 4, the soul was said to be that which perceived *through* the sense organs, and was therefore not itself an organ (185d7–e2). Socrates's odd formulation of the act of imprinting onto the wax slab neglects to attend to the unified soul as a site of reception of imprints whose form—whose character—mediates the imprinting both consciously and unconsciously. These issues of the extent of one's agency and the hyperbolic attribution of control over one's own thoughts do not get developed immediately, though they will become central to the discussion when Socrates and Theaetetus analyze the second image of knowledge as true opinion, that is, the bird cage.

This issue of the relationship between the reception of memorables—which is to say, perceptions that make an imprint on the wax slab—and the examination of those memorables deserves further emphasis on our part. It would be false to assume that the wax slab receives the imprint of any and every perceptually encountered object indifferently and with equal receptivity. At the basic level of sensations, among the myriad things a person tastes, touches, sees, hears, and smells, some will leave a stronger, some a weaker mark on us. We are more or less interested in, more or less disturbed by, in general more or less affected by some perceived objects in comparison to others. Further, we are more or less affected by objects in the seemingly immediate and constant stream of perception, in other words, prior to the process of deliberation about which objects we would be more or less interested in examining. This fact that the stream of experience always includes a selective dimension of perception indicates that perception is already informed by intellect, and that memory, too, is already informed by intellect. The character of the person is at play even in the seemingly passive reception and retention of objects of perception. Correspondingly, the process by which we engage in the examination of the wax imprints of perception is informed by the passive element of receptivity.[26] Reflection leaves its imprint, so to speak, on perception, just as perception does on reflection. To characterize these as the active and the passive, the intelligent and unintelligent elements of the soul, respectively, is to obscure their co-determination, and therefore to insinuate that one or the other ought to be the better candidate for the locus of knowledge.

Putting aside for a moment in what way we actually relate to the wax slabs in our souls (i.e., to what extent we freely examine our memories of perceptions, and to what extent that examination is shaped by the imprint of those perceptions), we should note the importance of this capacity of memory. As the foundation for any intellectual relationship to perception, the wax slab is something whose constitution will be a matter of significance. We can imagine a number of ways in which the wax might fail to receive imprints well. It may not receive the imprint in as much detail or in a way that can withstand other, later imprints. The wax might be full of material that obstructs the imprint. It might be too small to receive enough of the imprint, and so on. If we follow my interpretation of the phenomenon of remembering objects of perception as one inherently informed by intellect and character, we ought to anticipate that the variability of these attributes of the wax slab, that is, the varying quality of its receptivity to perceptual imprints, is associated with the varying degrees of psychic health. We will return to the issue of psychic health in a moment. In the meantime, Socrates and Theaetetus are preoccupied with accounting for the reality of error; Socrates therefore attempts to isolate the kind of situation in which error is possible within the context of the wax image.

Socrates attempts to find error through a thought experiment in which he isolates two objects of perception, and imagines them being perceived and not perceived and opined about truly and falsely.[27] Socrates then lists the possible combinations, finally eliminating all but those in which error does occur (192a1–d1). After Socrates presents the formal structure of all combinations, Theaetetus expresses confusion with them. Socrates therefore takes as his examples of the two objects Theaetetus and Theodorus. I will translate the formal possibilities enumerated by Socrates into the example in each case where it would serve to clarify.[28] The first four cases Socrates presents involve only the memory of the two objects (i.e., for our purposes, Theaetetus and Theodorus), and are cases in which one does not err. (1) When one knows two objects, and is not in the midst of perceiving either of the two objects, and when the imprint of the objects is such that one is able to remember each of them accurately, one does not err. Thus when I know both Theaetetus and Theodorus well, and do not confuse them in memory, I do not err. (2) When one knows only one object, neither knows nor has perceived the other object and is therefore unable to confuse the one known with the other, is not perceiving the known object, and is able to remember it accurately, one does not err. If I know Theaetetus but neither know nor have ever perceived Theodorus, I do not confuse Theaetetus with Theodorus when I am remembering Theaetetus. (3) When one has never perceived either object—that is, when one has no imprint of any quality of either object—one does not err about either of them. If I neither know nor have perceived Theaetetus or Theodorus, I do not err about either of them. (4) When one does not know and has not perceived one of the objects, it is impossible that one erroneously thinks one does not know the other object one is currently perceiving and has an accurate imprint of, confusing it with the object one does not know. If I neither know nor have perceived Theaetetus, I will never err by thinking I am remembering Theaetetus when I am in fact remembering Theodorus (this being the logical reverse of the second combination).

While in each of these cases, it is impossible that one not know what one knows, and know what one does not know, Socrates adds other combinations, this time concerning what one perceives but what has not yet made a lasting imprint. (5) When one perceives both objects at the same time, it is impossible that one should believe one of the objects is the other. Perceiving both Theaetetus and Theodorus, I will never think the perceptible object Theaetetus is the perceptible object Theodorus (regardless of whether I get their identities confused). The remainder of these perceptual examples (i.e., those I have numbered 6–8) correspond directly to the memory examples 1–4 above. (6) When one perceives an object, one cannot think it is some object one has never perceived. (7) When one perceives neither object, one cannot think an object one has never perceived is another object one has never perceived. (8) When one has not perceived an object, one cannot think it is an object one has perceived.

These latter four cases (5–8) all correspond in the immediate act of perception with what, in accurate memory, was described in the previous four. While 1–4 dealt strictly with what has been remembered and 5–8 dealt with immediate perception, the following six cases (9–14) combine the perceiving and the remembering, and are likewise cases in which error is impossible. (9) When one both has the accurate imprint of two objects and one is in the midst of perceiving those same two objects, one cannot believe one of the objects one both perceives and knows is the other. If I know both Theaetetus and Theodorus and perceive both, I cannot, for example, confuse Theaetetus for Theodorus. (10) When one perceives and knows one object, and has the accurate imprint of the other but does not perceive that other, one does not mistake the one perceived and known with the one known but not perceived. If I know both Theaetetus and Theodorus, accurately remember Theodorus, and perceive Theaetetus, I will not confuse them with each other. (11) When one both knows and perceives one object, and perceives another, one does not confuse the perceived and known with the perceived. If I know and perceive Theaetetus and meet Theodorus for the first time, I do not confuse Theodorus with Theaetetus. (12) When one neither knows nor perceives, one does not confuse this with what one likewise neither knows nor perceives. Having neither seen nor heard of either Theaetetus or Theodorus, I could never get them confused with each other. (13) When one neither perceives nor knows one object, one does not confuse this with what one does not perceive. When I neither know nor perceive Theaetetus I cannot confuse him with Theodorus, whom I do not perceive. (14) When one neither perceives nor knows one object, one does not confuse this with what one does not know. Neither knowing nor perceiving Theaetetus, I cannot confuse him with Theodorus, whom I do not know.

These fourteen examples all present situations in which error does not occur according to the wax model Socrates has still yet to elaborate fully. There are, however, other combinations in which error does occur, according to Socrates (192c9–d1). (15) In the case where one knows something but does not perceive it, it is possible to mistake it for something which one knows and perceives. That is, the fact that I know both Theaetetus and Theodorus does not *of necessity* mean that I will never confuse them with one another. If Theodorus is not around, I might mistake Theaetetus for Theodorus, due to either the inadequate imprint of Theodorus on my memory, or the inadequate perception of Theaetetus in the moment. (16) When one knows one object but does not perceive it, one can think that it is another object one perceives but does not know. If I know Theaetetus but do not know Theodorus, I can certainly think Theodorus is Theaetetus if Theaetetus is not around. (17) Or (the reverse of 15) one can mistake what one knows and perceives for something one knows but does not perceive. These three are the forms of falsity Socrates identifies. The only situations in which Socrates might opine false things are the following: if, for example, Socrates sees Theaetetus and Theodorus at a distance, knows them both, but reverses who he's seeing (thinking Theaetetus is Theodorus and the reverse), or if Socrates sees only one, claims to see Theodorus when in fact he is seeing Theaetetus, or, seeing neither Theodorus nor Theaetetus, thinks he is seeing one of them. This means that the only circumstances in which one is in a position to err, to opine falsely, is when one knows something. It is thus, they conclude, in the cases of things about which we know and perceive that error of all kinds occur (194b1–7).

How is it, though, that these things that we presume to know—which is to say these things that leave an imprint in our souls and thus make us capable of remembering them—can be erroneously understood? Here, we return to the material constitution of the wax or the character of the person's soul. The wax in the soul can vary in shape, size, depth, and solidity. The character of the wax is intimately connected with how one receives the imprints of perception. Socrates claims this about the constitution of the wax: "Whenever the wax in someone's soul is deep, extensive, smooth, and kneaded in a measured way, the things that are proceeding through perceptions, in putting their seals into that feature of the soul which Homer, in hinting at its similarity to wax [*kēros*], said was heart [*kear*], it's then that the seals for them come to be pure in the wax and with adequate depth prove to be long lasting" (194c6–d1). In such ideal conditions, the soul's wax is ready to receive imprints that last a long time and in great detail, which is to say that the person is able to remember long after and accurately. Further, people of this sort learn easily, as they pick up in great detail what it is that they perceive, and are able therefore to take from those imprints into their memories many and varied experiences, and because of the strong integrity of the wax, have the opportunity to reflect on them at length.

By contrast to this ideal, others are lacking in various ways in relation to the quality of their wax. Those whose wax is too liquid receive imprints quickly and deeply, but forget very easily. Those whose wax is too hard learn very poorly, and the little they do learn they hold only rigidly. Those whose wax is too mixed with other materials—of which Socrates suggests earth and dung (194e2–195a2)—receive imprints either shallowly or deeply depending on the consistency, but, regardless, receive them without clarity. These imprints are incomplete and inaccurate, whatever their duration. In this case of imprints distorted by impurities, the person also learns poorly, this time insofar as she misapprehends what she learns. Though Socrates does not go into detail about it, the different kinds of impurity demonstrate pathologies of character that would impair a person's ability to learn.[29] Indeed, though we will soon go on to consider the obvious limitations of this image, we should nonetheless notice first how appropriate this image of the wax is for identifying the quite real differences that characterize different souls in their capacities to remember, and consequently, to learn and to think.

One particular virtue of emphasizing the real differences characterizing different capacities to remember is that it directs our attention to the importance that we ought to place in the process of remembering. As embodied human beings we are always in the midst of the activity of perceiving. We, therefore, must make the "wax" more substantial, more pure, neither too hard nor too soft, and of an even consistency; that is, we *must* do what we can to create a soul possessed of these attributes, because it is in the nature of our experience that we are required—for the sake of living intelligently in the world—to be capable of remembering widely and accurately.

How might it be possible to "shape the wax in one's soul"? Socrates does not discuss this issue because he is interrupted by the discovery of a problem with this first image (195b9–10). However, we can imagine that the very activity he is engaged in with Theaetetus is one among the many activities that shape the soul. Socrates is beginning the process of cultivating in Theaetetus the ability to perceive the world as made up of objects provocative of wonder, objects that "ask" of him that he strive to know them, and, *as* objects that perpetually provoke wonder, objects that cannot be known exhaustively. I have claimed that the philosophical orientation consists in adopting this attitude, the erotic attitude, the result of which attitude being the cumulative shaping of an increasingly acute perception of reality, and one that desires an increased understanding of that reality. How might this translate into the analogy of wax in one's soul? To cultivate an attitude that is able to identify an increasing number and variety of objects as "wonderful"—which is to say to cultivate the desire to know about a given topic—would be to grow the size of the wax in one's soul, such that one is able to receive more from the world. To engage in dialectical analysis of one's presumptions would be to make the consistency of the wax more receptive to imprinting. To train oneself to be answerable to the principles that make thinking possible (such as the principle of non-contradiction) and to the implication of one's ideas, would be to make the consistency of the wax sufficiently solid that it can receive imprints without falling apart. Finally, to produce a psychological space for oneself where one does not cultivate a range of neuroses, too, is essential, and amounts to the elimination of impurities from one's wax. Though it is impossible to guarantee for oneself the avoidance of the cultivation of neuroses—insofar as one will always emerge from a childhood that produced behavior, and possibly neuroses, prior to one's being in a position to make choices about how to behave well and cultivate habits well—the process of subjecting oneself to questioning through dialogue with others would better shape one's understanding of the distinction between reality and one's own capricious, idiosyncratic attitude toward it.[30] From this it seems clear, on the one hand, that the wax image draws our attention to the need to give consideration to the extent of our ability to retain what we perceive—which would seem to insinuate that we ought to put conscious effort into the shaping of our capacity to retain information received in our experience—but, on the other hand, that the image provides us with the tools to identify why it is that we are not obviously in control of the shaping of memory.

The wax image, thus, has a number of virtues. It provides an account of the shaping of opinion insinuating that the character of one's soul plays a role in one's ability to know. It is the first account that suggests the interrelation of perceiving and thinking in generating opinion, an integrated approach that was implicitly demanded in response to the account Socrates gave of the contrast between the philosopher and the public orator (172c3–177c7). As we have already discussed, that speech presented someone able to see immediately the conditioning structures of political institutions where others saw only the demands that those political institutions made on their behavior. What is found in the objects of perception already involves the interpretive framework of the character of the person perceiving. The wax image shows this by presenting the mediating role of memory in informing what is retained from perception.[31]

In addition to this fact about the role played by character in determining what is retained from perception, the wax image also demonstrates the way in which error can emerge from knowledge: the person who knows both Theaetetus and Theodorus has many more possibilities opened up to her by knowing them, including the possibility of error. The only situations in which error is even possible (numbers 15–17 from the list above) are those that are grounded in knowledge. The wax image is therefore answerable to much more about our experience of the world than the initial account of true and false opinion.[32] It has, however, important shortcomings.

Socrates identifies the major shortcoming of the wax image, but only after accusing himself of merely chattering; he has been, so he says, moving the speeches (*tous logous*) up and down, not being convinced by anything, and not getting free of any of the speeches (195c1–5). What Socrates means by this is never made explicit. However, "not getting free of any of the speeches" seems to refer to having one's thought ordered strictly by the parameters set for the discussion by the selected guiding image. Socrates explicitly suggests that the image itself is flawed because it isolates memory as the site of error, due to the fact that memory is the site of the relation between perception and intellect (195e8–196d2). It turns out, according to Socrates's explicit suggestion that, in fact, error occurs not only in the relation between intellect and perception, but also within intellect itself. *We* will see that this formulation on Socrates's part is built on the premise that the perceptual dimension of experience excludes intellect, which we will reject. Indeed, we will see that the real problem with the wax image is its unnatural separation of perception from intellect. Let us sort through Socrates's self-criticism, carefully distinguishing it from our own criticism.

Socrates began the wax analogy, whether intentionally or not, by limiting that which makes an impression on the soul to perceptions. Perceptions, in this case, were taken to exclude thoughts that were not explicitly derived from perceptual experience but provoked by another perceptual experience. For example, if we imagine seeing three apples in a bowl and two apples on a nearby plate, his exclusion of non-perceptual impressions would imply the exclusion of, in this particular case, the thought of the equation $3 + 2 = 5$. Therefore, according to the critical voice Socrates subsequently uses against himself, he had (erroneously, he now thinks) implied that error neither occurs in perception alone (which cannot err because it makes no claim either way about the being of what is perceived) nor in thinking alone, but rather in the conjunction of the two (195d1). That is, the wax image is taken now to have been an account of how perception makes an imprint on intellect. This imprint introduces the variable of memory, whose quality is taken to be precisely the variable that opens up the possibility of error. Memory, as the site of the translation of perceptual experience into intellect, the wax image suggested, is also the site of the possibility of error. Socrates is now critical of this formulation, which had been mostly assumed and not made explicit.

Criticizing himself, Socrates argues that the problem with claiming that error emerges from the translation of perceptual imprints into thoughts is that there are certainly purely intellectual errors, and therefore that there are errors outside of the domain of perception.[33] Socrates proposes that the fact that mathematical errors occur demonstrates this problem. Moreover, knowing the character of the number five and of the number seven does not sufficiently guarantee that one will correctly identify their sum, and this is, agrees Theaetetus, even more likely to be the case with larger numbers (196b2–4). In the case of mathematical error, they suggest, there is no need to appeal to perception to find error because people are deceived in the thoughts themselves (196c6–10). If people are deceived in the thoughts themselves, then, whatever the merits might be of the wax image, it cannot effectively account for error to say that it occurs in the conjunction of perception and thought. Socrates ostensibly is compelled to reject this image on these grounds. We, the readers, ought to be mindful of the role Socrates is playing in educating Theaetetus, and ought therefore to assess the problems with the wax image for ourselves.

The shortcoming of the wax image that is proposed here by Socrates—that intellectual error independent of perception demonstrates that the relationship between perception and intellect is not the cause of error—is not the most significant one. It seems as though the wax example is poor because it cannot explain errors that require no appeal to perception. In fact, the mistake was to conceive of the wax image in the first place as strictly dealing with imprints from perceptions. The example could very easily account for intellectual error, were Socrates and Theaetetus willing to expand the terrain to which the image referred to include the way in which we actually experience perception, rather than in the illicit isolation of perception from intellect. The fact that one gets the sum of two numbers wrong has to do, not with how well one grasps the individual numbers, however large or small. Rather, the error has to do with one having poorly executed the process of addition. This poor execution may be the result of one having failed to receive the imprint of one's arithmetic lessons adequately, or one having not taken the time (for whatever reason) to do carefully what one can do when one has the time. Assuming the error has to do with incapacity of some kind on the part of the person performing the equation, the training process which cultivated the skill to handle the addition of numbers is what is implicated, which is to say that learning is implicated, as well as the character of the soul of the person, that is (at least in part) the shape of the wax. The intellectual error associated with basic arithmetic is not an error of pure thought, because it is an error having to do with the poor execution of an intellectual activity developed through training and experience. The reality of what is abstractly called intellectual error that I have just described is to be contrasted with errors that we might typically call perceptual errors, which we erroneously assume are errors that exclude thinking. The argument against the wax image is convincing, for *us*, only of the fact that there is no clear-cut division of these two realms within the context of a human being learning how to think and how to perceive.

Because Socrates and Theaetetus abandon the wax image for the wrong reasons, that abandonment confuses the discussion rather than clarifying it. They should be attending to the integration of human capacities to generate the process by which an understanding of the world emerges. Instead, they are preoccupied with the need to account for the source of error. It is preoccupation with this problem that motivates the generation of an alternative image, namely the image of the bird cage. We must keep in mind the distinction between what problems and what insights are revealed by the introduction of this new image, and the misleading purpose of its introduction. As we will now see, immediately prior to working through the second image of knowledge as true opinion, Socrates and Theaetetus are led into a digression that initially appears to render the dialectical method problematic, the discussion of which draws our attention directly to the notion of philosophical discourse as a learning process cultivating understanding from ignorance. This digression serves to remind us, in the discussion that follows, of the misleading focus on the problem of error.

b. The Chatterbox Is Who He Is—Socrates's Second Sailing

Socrates claims that, not only can they not accept the wax image; they must also, according to what has been said so far in criticizing the account, either claim that no error is possible or that one can both know and not know the same thing at the same time.[34] When Theaetetus says that this would force them to choose between two impossible alternatives, Socrates quietly reminds him that the *speech* will not allow for anything other than these alternatives (196d1–2), and that they must thus be shameless in answering. Socrates encouraged Theaetetus to give answers boldly earlier, when he was at first at a loss to provide a definition of knowledge (148c11–d3; 151d3–e5). In what sense is he asking Theaetetus to be shameless now? The whole discussion was initially predicated on the difficulty to account for what knowledge is. What else, then, could it be but shameless to go around giving definitions of something one does not know? Further, they not only endeavored to account for some concept that they do not know; they also made use of that very concept during their discussion, talking about knowing and not knowing and so on as though they knew what they were talking about (196d10–e8). Even in describing the transgression itself, Socrates is forced to invoke, as though he *knew* it, the concept he does not *know*. They have been, in Socrates's wry way of putting it, "conversing impurely" (196e2). In response to this, Theaetetus rightly asks Socrates how else he would converse. Socrates's answer to this question is that he would converse in no other way, because he is who he is (197a1).

Socrates is presuming to teach Theaetetus, yet he is doing so while simultaneously acknowledging that he does not know what knowledge is. That Socrates proposes as a criticism of himself and Theaetetus that they are guilty of this in their inquiry ought not to be taken as an actual condemnation of either Theaetetus or himself. That, it seems to me, is the point of his bold assertion that he would search in no other way because "he is who he is." He would not change the method by which he inquires, despite having explicitly conceded that he is making use of resources he does not really understand. The message Socrates is communicating, whether or not Theaetetus understands it, is, first, that the only way available to proceed is one in which we use concepts we do not fully comprehend, and second, that by this way of proceeding, we have to test our concepts against those who would challenge them. These are the skills in which they are now training themselves. Further, for Socrates, this is the only acceptable way to proceed.

This situation of having to proceed for oneself is explicitly articulated by Socrates only a few days or weeks later (within the dramatic narrative of the dialogues) in the *Phaedo*. There, Socrates describes himself as a younger man having enthusiastically begun reading Anaxagoras's work entitled "Mind" in the hopes of finding an account of how the mind puts the world in order and makes it meaningful, because he believed this to be so, and thought a wise account of this would make better sense of it for him (*Phaedo*, 97b9–98b5). He then discovered to his disappointment that Anaxagoras was providing a strictly material account of the conditions of mind, and was therefore not dealing with the activity of mind at all (*Phaedo*, 97b6–c2). Having grown weary of the persistent presence and poverty of such accounts, as well as his own inability to find, in his examination of the things in the world, an adequate explanation of their cause, he decided to pursue a "second sailing" (*Phaedo*, 99c9–d2), which is to say to get out the oars and row when there was no wind to keep the ship moving. Socrates decided to take it upon himself to pursue in speech accounts of the world, when the world did not make itself plain to him on its own, and when others' attempts to do so failed to carry him over to the understanding he sought. Socrates presents this need to perform a "second sailing" in the specific context of his own search for the intelligible causes of things. Theaetetus must do likewise in his search for the nature of knowledge; despite the fact that his inquiry presumes understanding of the concept he is trying to understand, he must use those inadequate resources because there is nothing else that will accomplish his goal for him. The circumstances which motivated Socrates, and which he believes ought to motivate Theaetetus, are those circumstances that ought to motivate us.

Socrates and Theaetetus are in a sense liberated. Socrates has pointed out that they could not avoid invoking as a conceptual tool the very concept they are trying to define. They are aware of this inevitability now, and so, since they "are no good" as Socrates puts it (197a4), they have nothing to do but to be bold and continue. This is not the first time that this message has been communicated by Socrates in this dialogue.[35] We are indeed seeing a pattern emerge between the two. Socrates takes a basic definition of Theaetetus's and enhances it either by connecting it to its possible implications or by "discovering" problems associated with a concept on which the definition depends. Theaetetus is then discouraged. This discouragement is then offset by Socrates characterizing them, together, as being in a situation where they must each, singly though in dialogue together, sort things out for themselves. Moreover, since it has already been established that they will be unable to sort through things for themselves in a way that will satisfy their desire to know—because the process will require of them that they use a working understanding of the concept being striven for to inform their inquiry, which has, by virtue of the circumstances in which that working understanding emerges, no justification—they appear to have nothing to lose in trying, since the project is according to its initial terms doomed to fail. If indeed there is something to be lost, perhaps that is merely the initial construction of knowledge which appears from the start to be impossible. It is possible, in other words, that what this process is teaching Theaetetus is not what knowledge is, but rather what pretensions to knowledge he must reject.[36]

Socrates and Theaetetus must be shameless in their pursuit of the definition of knowledge. To be ashamed—not to pursue—is to accept the unacceptable, because it is to accept the idea that, because we do not begin with knowledge of that which we pursue, we cannot know what it is that we pursue. This is a predicament identified by Socrates in the *Meno*, which he calls a "debater's paradox," according to which "a man . . . cannot search either for what he knows—since he knows it, there is no need to search—nor for what he does not know, for he does not know what to look for" (*Meno*, 80e1–5). To accept this appraisal of the situation without examination is to give up on the possibility of knowledge, to foreclose inquiry of any kind. It is also, however, a question-begging attitude: to interpret Meno's paradox as an a priori foreclosure of the pursuit of knowledge of this or that object is to take for granted that knowledge has no beginning. It is also akin to being ignorant of one's own intellectual pregnancy, as we characterized it in chapter 2. This attitude merely assumes that one cannot come to know, because it defines knowledge in advance as something that is not conditioned by its context of emergence.

What, then, is the alternative to the attitude that abandons the pursuit? What is Socrates's shamelessness, his second sailing, promoting? To perform the second sailing is to recognize that the accomplishment of their project will be the initiation into a *process* rather than the perfect *accomplishment* of some specific goal. Socrates has chosen for them to take knowledge itself as the topic. To make knowledge the subject of inquiry has the unique effect of having the content of one's inquiry, as much as the form, illustrate the points, both that one must reject a conception of knowledge that it is impossible for us to have, and that our attention must be turned toward the understanding that we are in fact able to develop. Because "I am who I am," and once I recognize "who I am," I must take the goal of inquiry to be the cultivation of an attitude toward inquiry that sustains itself, and therefore must understand knowledge to be in this respect a subordinate goal.

c. Two Ways of Having Knowledge

In the shameless spirit he has just outlined, Socrates produces a new image of knowledge as true opinion. He says that "they" (i.e., those mysterious people that are never mentioned) now say that knowledge is something we *have* (*hexis*). Socrates suggests that he and Theaetetus amend knowledge to be something we *possess* (*ktēsis*). Knowledge, construed as *hexis*, is something immediately at one's disposal. It is, as we shall see, an active disposition. By contrast, knowledge as *ktēsis* means something one has obtained, a possession or property in one's holding. On the surface, the distinction between the two is obscure. *Hexis* is a cognate of the verb "to have" (*echein*), which sounds similar to possession. When Theaetetus asks Socrates if there even is a distinction between the two, Socrates responds that there may or may not be, but they are going to find out by examining it (197b5–7). Perhaps Socrates does not know, perhaps he does. In either case, though, Theaetetus will not find an answer to the question by assuming that there is no difference. Theaetetus presumes knowledge of the similarity of these terms in advance; Socrates suggests that they examine them to find out.

Let us consider the difference that Socrates finds between active use and mere possession. Socrates introduces an example of a person who owns a cloak to clarify the difference (197b9–11). In the sense intended by Socrates, one possesses a cloak if one has purchased it and has housed it (*ktēsis*), regardless of whether one ever wears it or uses it in any way (*hexis*). This appears to be introduced to set up a contrast with the kind of "having knowledge" that occurs when one is, so to speak, wearing the cloak. In other words, it appears that Socrates is using *hexis* to mean having knowledge as one is making use of it.[37]

Let us now examine Socrates's account of *ktēsis*. It is on the one hand quite intuitively plausible to think of knowledge as a possession one has, but a possession one need not have on one's mind at all times. In the discussion of the wax image, Socrates described the imprint of perceptions as being available for reflection because of memory. If the soul's wax is both pure and of the proper consistency then it can be used for the purpose of recalling previous experiences for the sake of reflection. We might identify this as an excellent example of knowledge as a possession. Further, this "knowledge as possession" is exactly what is represented in Euclides's documentation of the conversation that we now grapple with as the *Theaetetus*. Knowledge as possession is knowledge stored away for unanticipated future use. We can see, then, that there are certain respects in which it is appropriate to characterize knowledge as *ktēsis*.

The difference between *hexis* and *ktēsis* is between knowledge in its immediate application to a given activity, and knowledge as something available to be accessed yet currently unused. The relationship between the two, though, is one of mutual dependency. Having knowledge, on this formulation, depends upon the possession of it, while the possession of knowledge that is not yet in use is only manifestly demonstrated to be possessed when activated. On this account, *ktēsis* and *hexis* are distinct though interdependent aspects of knowledge.

Having established the relationship between having and possessing knowledge, let us remind ourselves of Socrates's immediate motivation for making such a distinction. Socrates uses the characterization of knowledge as *ktēsis* for the purpose of better accounting for error. Having put themselves in a position where they had to acknowledge that error is something that somehow emerges from a situation of knowledge, Socrates is here imagining that, while one might possess a certain knowledge, one might not be capable of consciously making use of it, that is, one might still have it "stored away" when one tries to call upon it. One, in a certain sense, "knows" on this model but is not disposed to actualize that knowledge, and one is therefore capable of error.

Again, we have to maintain critical perspective on the discourse concerning the bird cage image, and must do so bearing in mind the purpose of this discussion. In particular, we ought to note at the outset a problematic aspect of the conceptual underpinning of the bird cage image—namely the distinction between having and possessing knowledge—that we will return to over the course of the discussion. Specifically, the problem is that, while it is true that we appear to know about many things without making use of them as a resource at any given moment, the analogy that Socrates makes to possession, at least in its initial presentation through the analogy to the stored-away cloak, implies that knowledge is discrete to each individual person. That is, if it is like the cloak that I store away in my closet, it is something that I am excluding from others. Indeed, I exclude that knowledge both when I merely possess it and when I make use of it. Though there are surely examples of knowledge that can be *contingently* excluded from other people—for example, one might have secrets about oneself that one never volunteers to anyone else, or might choose to deprive others of information one has come to possess—one's possession of particular knowledge cannot in principle exclude others from access to it. This character of knowledge as non-exclusive in principle will emerge as a problem in the second image of knowledge, to which we will now turn.

d. The Bird Cage Image

Socrates asks Theaetetus to imagine bird collecting. A person who collects birds does not have the birds that he possesses—the birds remain flying around in an enclosure. The birds are, however, detectable due to the restrictions that have been set around the space within which they can move; having apprehended the birds, the collector has new power. She is able to access the birds more easily than previously. She knows what they are and can gain access to them. She is not *guaranteed* to be able to apprehend them—they might avoid her within the enclosure long enough to frustrate her into giving up—but she has dramatically increased the likelihood of apprehending them. This is an effective image of our experience because it attends nicely to the fact that our conscious engagement with the world does not put us entirely in control of our memories, and thus of our accumulated experiences. Acknowledgment of the passive element of our relationship to our own memories provides a correction to Socrates's characterization, in the wax image, of our actively choosing to impress on memory the perceptions and thoughts we wanted to retain. Let us look further at Socrates's elaboration of the image.

The soul contains an enclosure in which many birds of different types dwell. Some stay together in large groups, some in smaller groups, and many fly off on their own. We begin with no birds in the enclosure,[38] and over the course of life accumulate whatever quantities of them we are able to.[39] Whatever one has collected and brought into the enclosure, one knows to be there, and one can access it. To have knowledge in the enclosure is to have knowledge as a possession (*ktēsis*) that is not necessarily being used at the given moment, but that provides a capacity to acquire that knowledge when one needs it (197d1–2). Acquiring possessed knowledge from the enclosure is having an active disposition (*hexis*) toward one's knowledge, which is to say using that knowledge at the given moment.

Socrates begins their discussion of this image by appealing to Theaetetus's area of expertise, mathematics (198a4). Socrates suggests that the beginning of arithmetic is the collecting of the concepts of Even and Odd. Possessing these makes it possible for the one who does so both to know and to transmit that knowledge. Socrates suggests—it appears from what follows, disingenuously—that this means that the arithmetician who knows perfectly the concepts of Even and Odd is in possession of all numbers (198a8–11). However, when the arithmetician applies number—say, for example, by counting a room full of people, or by performing an arithmetical problem—he must still seek out number despite already possessing it. This is where the distinction between *hexis* and *ktēsis* is appropriate. The arithmetician possesses the conceptual structure of number, upon which he may later rely in generating numbers in each particular instance. Once having initially come to possess number in terms of odd and even, he can "enter the enclosure" to "grab" the appropriate number in counting people in a room and so on. Thus, on this account, collecting is "twofold" (198d1). According to the bird cage image, we seek out knowledge about the world first, and then, once we have that knowledge in our possession, must seek it out within our own soul, our own bird cage. This latter collecting is in a more controlled context insofar as it involves collecting what has already been collected. Let us consider what is said to have been accomplished by the twofold collecting, and then consider the problems that arise as a result of it.

The bird enclosure image was intended to address the problem of how it might be possible both to know and not to know at the same time. Socrates and Theaetetus can now point to the fact that one can know the object in the sense of possessing it, while at the same time failing to have it. One can, in other words, have had experience and understanding of the object, but at the same time be unable to recall the experience accurately. One can grab the wrong bird (199b4–5), and one presumably can also fail to grab a bird at all. Socrates asks Theaetetus if they have managed to solve their problems with this distinction. Theaetetus, as usual, agrees. Socrates responds, however, that, though they have gotten rid of the problem of one simultaneously knowing and not knowing the same object, by distinguishing between the possession of knowledge (*ktēsis*) and the active use of knowledge (*hexis*), this new formulation, in fact, introduces a much worse problem (199c9).[40]

What appears to be more dreadful to Socrates is that they might, once again, have eliminated the possibility of false opinion. If one errs only by mistaking one bird for another, then one is merely confusing one piece of knowledge with another (199c10–d9). Further, it seems that the possibility of erring at all only emerges with knowledge, and that this emergent possibility creates space for the possibility of *constant* error. It is, on this account, *by* knowledge that error occurs. One might say, though Socrates does not, that the conditions within the bird cage appear to consist only in a more limited version of the condition one faces with the outside world. One has to "hunt" within the enclosure, too. Indeed, the bird cage image seemingly requires that the more birds we accumulate, the more our enclosure appears to resemble the wild world of ignorance beyond it. This set of circumstances does not appear akin to knowledge.

In response to this problem, Theaetetus introduces the idea that there would be non-knowledge as well as knowledge in the enclosure (199e1–7). The collector, attempting to recall some piece of knowledge, erroneously grabs a piece of non-knowledge or falsehood that she presumes to have been knowledge. Theaetetus's account attempts to explain the fact that error seems to arise from acquired knowledge by sidestepping the problem; it is not acquired knowledge that one draws upon, but rather acquired non-knowledge, or acquired error. I am going to claim that Theaetetus's contribution here is more fruitful than the discussion will allow. Let us briefly develop his claim (which he does not do sufficiently), before presenting Socrates's criticism.

This contribution by Theaetetus—that the bird cage contains both birds of knowledge and birds of non-knowledge or error, and that it is the mistaken acquisition of the latter birds that generates error—has the potential to introduce the themes of fantasy and illusion to the discussion. Where he fails to develop the idea is with respect to the origin of the birds of non-knowledge.[41] It would appear to make no sense to imagine, within the context of the image of birds as bits of knowledge about reality, someone acquiring one that is *not* a bit of knowledge, but rather a distortion of knowledge. However, perhaps the birds of non-knowledge are generated in the procreation of birds of knowledge, in other words, perhaps error results from the interaction between bits of truth poorly mixed together.[42] Perhaps the false and the fictional are added to the enclosure as results of the improper breeding of truths within the enclosure. That is, in the enclosed space of one's own thinking, one's accumulated bits of knowledge, so to speak, "breed" with one another such that they produce "offspring" that are distortions of those bits of knowledge.[43] In other words, the interaction of one's various bits of accumulated knowledge results in the generation of fantasies, such that one grasps the wrong ideas when one is trying to recall.[44] Theaetetus does not develop the idea of the origin of the birds of non-knowledge, however. Because the idea is not developed in any specific direction, Socrates's criticism determines in what sense the birds of non-knowledge are said to originate, and does so in a sense that does not work properly. Let us examine his critical comments.

The problem that Socrates identifies—in the voice of a "skilled refuter"—with the account of birds of non-knowledge is that it must presume one of several notions, each of which is problematic.[45] He must presume: (1) that the bird-collector "knows" both knowledge and non-knowledge, insofar as everything in the bird cage is something that the collector knows in the sense of possession (*ktēsis*), in which case the acquisition of non-knowledge is puzzlingly characterized as a kind of knowledge (200a12–b2); (2) that the birds of non-knowledge represent things he possesses which he does *not* know, in which case, though the skilled refuter does not draw the implication, the assumption made in the bird cage image that the cage itself contains possessed knowledge is contradicted (200b2–4); (3) that some things in the cage are possessed-knowledge, while others are not (for no obvious reason, apparently, according to the skilled refuter), and therefore the collector errs when choosing poorly between them (200b4–7);[46] or (4) that this bird cage that somehow contains both knowledge and non-knowledge relies upon some further enclosure within which one must place the collected bits of knowledge in the larger cage to secure knowledge (200b7–c6). Each of these criticisms rests on the failure to explain the existence of non-knowledge within an enclosure that had been characterized as the place within which one housed only bits of knowledge to be drawn upon at a given moment when one needs to use them. This places Socrates and Theaetetus—if they commit to the image—in the situation of having to reject Theaetetus's suggestion or accepting it and dealing with these objections. Put most starkly, error must exist either in the enclosure itself as something attainable, or in the collector who fails to differentiate between bits of actual knowledge. If error exists in the enclosure, Socrates and Theaetetus must explain the mysterious presence of error in an enclosure presented as housing knowledge. If error exists in the collector, they must explain in what respect the enclosure counted in the first place as a site for housing knowledge.

This dilemma indicates to Socrates that their bird cage image had merely put off the discussion of how to apprehend knowledge one does not already possess. If one cannot account for how the collector can secure that she has adequately collected knowledge within the enclosure, then it would appear to be much more difficult to explain how the collector can apprehend knowledge beyond the enclosure. We are therefore left to consider another version of Meno's paradox: if the collector must know what she is collecting then she already has knowledge and has no need to collect. If this were to be the case, then the world outside the enclosure—filled as it is with birds of knowledge that the collector, when collecting them, already knows—is very difficult to differentiate from the space within the enclosure itself; in either case, the birds to be collected are already known and yet nonetheless need to be collected.[47] Even after Theaetetus tries to introduce error into the enclosure (birds of non-knowledge), and, indeed, even if one develops his account in the direction I indicated above (i.e., of error-birds being the "illegitimate" offspring of birds of knowledge) one is still left in the position of trying to account for the fact that the collector has in mind already what it is that she is trying to collect, yet nonetheless needs to collect it.

What is causing problems here is similar to what was causing problems in the discussion of the wax image, that is, the overemphasis on agency in the cultivation and accumulation of knowledge.[48] By characterizing knowledge strictly in terms of activity—either the activity of stamping perceptions and thoughts we wish to remember onto a wax slab or the activity of collecting this or that particular piece of knowledge we wish to possess—Socrates and Theaetetus are unable to account either for the acquisition of knowledge in the first place, or the reality of error. Neither image has been characterized in a way that pays sufficient attention to the fact that we passively accumulate experiences that act as resources to be applied (for better or worse) in cultivating the kind of knowledge that we actively pursue. Further, neither image, so characterized, pays attention to the fact that the resources derived from perception and thought—that is, from experience—form the opinions that are then deployed in the activity of reflection.

With this in mind, a return to the problem I have just characterized in the image of the bird cage will demonstrate itself not to be a problem at all. The bird collector would appear to have to know the bird she is collecting from the start in order to pursue it. This, in fact, only bears out the point I was making about our reliance upon a passively received conversance with the reality that contextualizes our knowledge pursuits. Our working understanding of the objects we seek better to understand is a condition for the experience of wonder (155d9–c6). The problem appeared to be that the world outside of our accumulated knowledge had to be virtually as graspable as our already-accumulated knowledge, insofar as, in each case, we would have to know in some sense the object we were seeking to know, and yet, insofar as we were seeking it, we would have not to know it. Taking into account our passive acquisition of a working understanding of the world, we would simply say that the relied-upon experiences create the conditions within which the world we strive to know emerges for us, and therefore create a context of comprehensibility. The world is our world, and one's soul stretches out to meet the world it experiences.

Neither image of knowledge presented by Socrates was entirely false. Each reflected something important about the nature of knowledge, but was formulated in such a way that it failed to emphasize how our experience of the world creates the context within which we seek to know. Though this passive aspect of knowing is not made part of the explicit thematic content of the discussion, Socrates does refer to it, appropriately, at the moment they reach their impasse. The second image having fallen apart, Theaetetus claims to feel pretty certain that they cannot improve on the idea that knowledge is true opinion—for what else could it be (200e1–6)? Socrates tells Theaetetus that they ought to follow the advice of the river-guide, who says "it will show up by itself" (200e7–201a2). One must travel the river and hope that it emerges. Control over our own acquisition of knowledge lies ultimately out of our grasp. What one cannot do is give up, because this is the only way to guarantee that we will not find what we seek. It is here that Socrates begins to direct Theaetetus to the passive element informing our understanding.

e. Passivity: The River-Guide and the Art of the Rhetorician

Socrates makes his remark about the river-guide because Theaetetus feels there is no better definition than the one he has, yet knows that definition to be inadequate. Theaetetus is now truly caught in *aporia* insofar as he knows that he cannot go back to discarded accounts of knowledge, but no longer feels he has the means to go forward. Socrates tells Theaetetus that the river-guide said "it will show up by itself," but means this showing up by itself to be something that must result from continued effort, even if that effort consists in groping in the dark: "So if we go and look for it, perhaps it too might turn up at our feet and show what is sought. But if we stay here, nothing will be plain" (200a1–a3).[49] This remark about the river-guide is not some offhand form of encouragement. It has a twofold purpose. First, it indicates that the method they must use necessarily takes the form of a search in terrain about which they have only a working grasp. Second, it is a caution against remaining certain under such conditions. Each of these points is very important and requires some discussion.

Regarding the method that Socrates and Theaetetus must use, the remark about the river-guide takes the paradoxical problems, first, of the collector's pursuit of birds of knowledge that she must of necessity in some sense know, and second, of Socrates's and Theaetetus's own predicament of invoking knowledge while being unable to say adequately what it is, and re-presents these not as problems to be solved, but as the proper conditions within which one engages in knowledge pursuit. It is not a "problem" in the sense of a conceptual flaw that must be overcome in order to improve one's grasp of the idea; it is, rather, the condition within which one engages in the pursuit at all. Specifically referring to the pursuit of knowledge as akin to moving down a river insinuates that while one has an inadequate (though "working") grasp of the object of one's pursuit, the path available for the pursuit is broadly determined, though within that context of determination it is both fraught with contingency and open to a variety of possibilities.[50] Further, the river has a momentum to it, a current, that one can either allow oneself to be pushed by, or that one can fight against, but that one cannot change.[51] Socrates is suggesting that they allow the current to move them, on the assumption that it is by recognizing that they are always moving and acting accordingly, by continuing to inquire, that they will derive any grasp at all of what they seek. They must be receptive to the unanticipated ideas that will emerge as they continue their pursuit.

The second purpose of Socrates's remark is to put a halt to Theaetetus's certainty regarding the correlation of true opinion and knowledge, or, more specifically, to cast doubt on the incautious claim that "to opine what is true surely is at any rate infallible, and everything that comes to be as a result of it becomes beautiful and good" (200e4–6). If they remain where they are, Theaetetus will be left continuing to believe this, without reflecting on how true opinion emerges, and on what is revealed by thinking about the sometimes dubious grounds for the emergence of true opinion. This is why the conversation shifts quickly to the *real* reason why Socrates does not believe that true opinion and knowledge are equivalent, that is, because of the power of rhetoric to generate opinions, true and false.

To demonstrate his reason for believing that true opinion and knowledge are not equivalent, Socrates points to the art of persuasion used by orators. This art allows them to make other people hold opinions with neither demonstration nor education (201a8–11). Expert orators have the skill to compel people to adopt opinions concerning a given issue without needing to provide adequate justification for adopting it. Socrates provides the example of the law court. In the same law courts that were previously characterized as domains of slavery when compared to the free domain occupied by the philosophers (175d-e), people operate under time constraints that essentially guarantee in advance that there would be no way to justify adequately to a jury that they ought to adopt this or that opinion. Yet, they surely must compel that jury to adopt the desired opinion. Some of the time, the opinion that the orator tries to persuade the jury to adopt must be the true one, which is to say that there are times when it is the appropriate thing to do to persuade those who could not possibly know to adopt the true opinion. Even in this context, when the jurors are persuaded to adopt the true opinion based on the convincing oratory skills of the advocate of the truth—even in circumstances, in other words, where people under duress to make a judgment in constrained condition *make the correct judgment*—it would be wrong to say that this counts as knowledge.[52]

Socrates's point here deserves more emphasis. It is easy enough for us to grasp that one can hold a true opinion without proper justification. One can construct scenarios in which a person believes something to be true that is *in fact* true, but does so for foolish reasons. For example, one might suffer from severe paranoia and consider all strangers to be a threat; this does not mean that when a particular stranger turns out to be a threat for whatever reason, that one had knowledge of that fact. This case straightforwardly presents a way in which true opinion is not knowledge. Socrates's claim points to the fact that true opinions we have not been educated, but merely persuaded, to adopt—whatever the motivation the orator has for persuading us, or whatever our own motivations for persuading ourselves—do not count as knowledge.[53]

This speech of Socrates draws a distinction—again, one not made explicit—between opinions into which we are educated, and opinions that we simply adopt. On the surface of our experience, it is probably more difficult than we think to draw a distinction between the two. We might think that those opinions about which we feel most strongly are those that are most justified. But, as we have seen repeatedly so far, we will not know this for certain unless we allow our opinions to be drawn for us through their full implications, and subjected to the scrutiny of inquiry by others. Opinions that are not articulated before others and generally accounted for cannot reveal to us their truth. That they are true is not the issue; rather, what their truth implies is the issue. This revelation of truth through an account before others is the project into which Socrates is initiating Theaetetus. It also points to the third definition of knowledge.

Conclusion

In this chapter, we have examined the second definition of knowledge—that true opinion (*alēthēs doxa*) is knowledge (*epistēmē*)—and have done so through a lens that diagnoses its inadequacy in terms of the tendency to abstraction, a tendency that we will see continues to hamper the progress of Socrates and Theaetetus in their discussion of *logos* at the end of the dialogue. We have further identified two different species of abstraction at work in this definition. First, in identifying true opinion as the new candidate for knowledge, they choose to discard perception completely, rather than integrating the capacity to perceive with the capacity to opine. In so doing, they abstract knowledge from perception completely, and indeed reintroduce perception only as a cause of error. Second, in presenting each of the images of knowledge (i.e., the wax slab and the bird cage), Socrates forces on Theaetetus a characterization of knowledge as something that is the product of conscious activity (either conscious imprinting of seals on the wax slab, or hunting birds to trap in the bird cage), one that abstracts knowledge from the essential passive element of our development of knowledge. The result of these abstractions is an impoverished characterization of knowledge.

In light of the importance of drawing attention to the theme of illicit abstraction, I began, in the first section, with an emphasis on the integrated (and circular) whole of thought and opinion. Thinking of these as bound to one another provides a model for thinking about how the other human capacities are integrated into the whole of a life. The integration of thinking and opinion also refers us back to the discussion of the integration of reflection and perception in the cultivation of the philosophical orientation. This opening section therefore repeats an approach that I argued one ought to keep in mind during the process of abstraction that occurs in the discussion that follows.

In section 2, we saw that the two images of knowledge provided what could have been, for Theaetetus, insights into the true nature of knowledge. These images failed to do so, I argued, because of the way in which they were presented. For Theaetetus, the wax image failed to account for false opinion because it could not account for purely intellectual error, and the bird cage failed to account for false opinion because it could not explain how falsehood could emerge for the bird collector in the first place. For us, though, the virtue of the wax image is its gesture to the role played by the character of the knower in her reception of the imprints. The failure of the image was caused, first by its focus strictly on perceptual imprints, second, by its construction of the fiction of a purely active agent manipulating memory, and third, by its failure to *exploit* the resource of its account of the role of character in explaining intellectual error. With respect to the bird cage, for us, its virtue was its insinuation that accumulated knowledge continues to exist, not necessarily tamed, within one's thinking (i.e., the cage). Its failure was its insistence on the activity of the collector both hunting within, and hunting outside of, the cage; this insistence provides no room for the passive experience of memory, or for the unanticipated ways in which our knowledge of the world shows itself to us in new experiences.

Having established that we must begin to think of knowledge as an integrated whole, we are prepared for the discussion of wholes that dominates our discussion of the third definition.

CHAPTER 6

Knowledge as a Whole (201c8–210d4)

> The states neither belong in us in a determinate form, nor come about from other states that are more cognitive; but they come about from perception—as in a battle when a rout occurs, if one man makes a stand another does and then another, until a position of strength is reached. And the soul is such as to be capable of undergoing this.
>
> —Aristotle, *Posterior Analytics*, II.19 100a10–14

Introduction

Our discussion of the second definition of knowledge demonstrated that the abstraction of particular capacities from the whole of the life of a human being makes a true account of knowledge impossible, and, indeed, makes an account of error impossible. We have also seen—in the cases of the wax and bird cage images—that failure to attend to the passive dimension of the process within which knowledge can occur produces accounts of knowledge which are not borne out in reality. If our analysis of the discussion of the second definition of knowledge functions primarily as a *reductio* argument concerning mistaken approaches to the question of knowledge, taking into account the insights that this *reductio* argument provides prepares us for the conceptual supplement to be found in the third definition of knowledge. Specifically, the primary lesson of the third definition is that the organization of various distinct powers results in something greater than the sum of its parts.

This lesson of the third definition provides the argument justifying the failure of the second definition, with the result, I will claim, that we must understand knowledge as something made manifest in the whole of a person's character in the activity of the soul. The consequence of this is that we are required to rethink the typical conception of knowledge (i.e., as a factual claim about which one has adequate justification to verify one's opinion), and are required to think of knowledge as something to be cultivated and improved, rather than something to be completely accomplished. As has been the case throughout the dialogue, parallel to, and related to, the explicit content of the discussion is the philosophical education that Theaetetus is undergoing. The account of knowledge that I have just announced in a preliminary fashion demonstrates the appropriateness of this parallel, because the process Theaetetus is undergoing with Socrates is an explicit and conscious version of this process of cultivation and improvement. We find, in the third definitions of knowledge, new issues that emerge during this process.

Whereas the implicit drama of the second definition consists in the meta-textual gesture to the reader that Theaetetus persistently adopts hasty unlearned opinion while discussing the claim that true opinion and knowledge are the same, in the analysis of the third definition, Theaetetus demonstrates two different, though related, limitations. His first limitation is that he cannot understand that the nature of this project is one of cultivation, and not one of solution. We are strongly reminded of the fact that Theaetetus is a mathematician by training, and appears to adopt a mathematical approach to philosophical problems; when he is asked by a highly ironic Socrates if they have managed to solve the problem of the nature of knowledge despite the fact that the wisest have for generations failed to do so, Theaetetus answers enthusiastically that they have (202d1–3). The point Socrates appears to be making is that they would be approaching the problem in the wrong way if they simply took it for granted that their inquiry was directed at a conclusion without remainder. The reason the wise had not previously "solved" the problem of knowledge was not because they were less up to the task, but rather because of something in the nature of the task itself resisting solution.

Theaetetus's second limitation is that he continues to be completely resistant to the possibility that knowledge could emerge from ignorance (203d4–7). Theaetetus's two limitations are in fact related; what relates the two limitations is that, while on the one hand, mathematical solutions build on certainties, on the other hand, it is the nature of cultivation to begin with mere potential—which is to say to begin with something that has not been actualized and is therefore decidedly uncertain—and to have a whole reality emerge from it. This indicates in Theaetetus an attitude about knowledge in general very likely shared by many people, that is, one grounded in an unexamined notion of objectively verifiable certainty analogous to mathematical certainty. This attitude about knowledge in general acts as an obstruction making it impossible to produce a satisfactory definition, when put under scrutiny. This is the case because of the fact that knowledge is built up and cultivated in one's experience, and one's experience has the persistent character of generating an understanding that emerges from out of already established states of affairs one has had to adjust to. Knowledge is, by nature, something emerging out of misapprehension. To understand it, therefore, one must adjust oneself not to apply the very particular, highly specialized knowledge, of which mathematics is a paradigmatic example, as a standard for the whole field of knowledge. This is a lesson that Theaetetus resists, and one that is probably common to most people.

This account of knowledge as an incomplete process of learning, which has been built up over the course of the dialogue by running under the surface of the discussion, is one to which we are often highly, and perhaps neurotically, resistant. We want knowledge always to take the form it does during the moments of satisfaction we derive from cleanly solving a mathematical problem. That knowledge is something emerging out of experience, and therefore always incomplete, strikes us not only as insufficient, but also, if true, as cause to reject its possibility completely. The impulse to reject knowledge as such on the grounds that it rests on uncertainty betrays a lingering commitment to knowledge as consisting of solutions, but a commitment one has found to be impossible to meet. Knowledge on this account that I am suggesting is being criticized—that is, knowledge as a form of objectively verifiable calculation—takes the form of something the accomplishment of which most of us abandon in adulthood as a realistic goal, but retain nonetheless as a measure of our failure or inadequacy. In fact, however, if knowledge rests on uncertain grounds, we ought to adjust our attitude and expectations, rather than dismiss the project as a whole. With this in mind, an examination of Socrates's characterization of the failure of his enterprise with Theaetetus proves to be highly compelling.

At the moment at which Socrates either chooses to announce or discovers a problem with their final attempt to salvage the third definition of knowledge, he describes himself as looking at a shadow-painting to which he has gotten too close, thereby shattering the illusion the image sought to provide (208e9–10). One might think that this is Socrates's characterization of their failure, which, in a certain sense, it is. They had been examining something that seemed real, but that Socrates can now identify in its artifice. But this is, from another standpoint, not a failure at all. In order properly to appreciate a work of art one must be capable of navigating between the "illusion" it creates and the reality of its having been crafted. Put more generally, any creative endeavor is made more successful if one can see both what results from the work and the work that went into creating that result. This is a version of the accomplishment of the philosopher as Socrates characterizes him: to be capable of seeing the various parts of reality both in their manifestation and in the causal structures that underlie them. If, in light of this notion of "apprehending the underlying structures," we consider what would be involved in "knowing" the shadow-painting, we can see that knowledge on this account begins with immediate apprehension of the shadow-painting, only to have the shadow-painting show how it has come to create the illusion of depth and shadow. Having come to see the image in terms of its cause, one might initially struggle to return to the naive view of the image.[1] However, when one eventually does, one need not think the image is somehow less real. On the contrary, the reality of the image is made clearer by understanding the context of its production. Understood in this way, knowledge is construed as something one cultivates using resources that initially appear in a form that is erroneously construed, yet nonetheless whose erroneous initial construal was *necessary* to the *process* of coming to know. What is perhaps most important for Theaetetus is to learn this, because it would change the way that he pursues knowledge for the better.

Indeed, as has been insinuated so far, while one *takes oneself* to be pursuing knowledge, what is *in fact* being pursued is not knowledge, but rather wisdom. In the shadow-painting analogy, one looks at the image hoping to see it as that of which it is an image, but if one observes carefully, one is eventually led to see the image, not *as* that of which it is an image, but *as* an image. This directs one out of the structure created by the image, and toward the activity in which, and through which, one views the image. We find a parallel in the pursuit that Socrates has initiated with Theaetetus. One pursues knowledge of knowledge itself. One is eventually compelled, however, to discard the conception of knowledge which motivated the pursuit in favor of the pursuit of an orientation toward one's experience, that is, toward wisdom. Knowledge turns out to be an image of wisdom, an image whose perceived beauty draws one toward a pursuit of which one was not initially aware, but which turns out to be more beautiful, because more true.

In this chapter, I will discuss the third definition of knowledge (*epistēmē*) as true opinion with an account (*hē meta logou alēthēs doxa*) (201c9–10). Section 1 is primarily focused on the idea that we cannot know what we cannot speak. Here, I discuss how the unspeakable can be used, and therefore can be relied upon, but cannot be spoken without obscuring the attribute most essential to them. In section 2, I develop this idea of the unspeakable being demonstrated, rather than articulated, in its relationship with the speakable. I present what is speakable—that is, what can be known—as something emerging from the coupling of unspeakable elements. This provides the theme of section 2, namely, the importance of the distinction between wholes and aggregates. This distinction between wholes and aggregates crystallizes the most important point to be derived from the final two definitions of knowledge: that wholes emerge from the gathering together of elements into an organized system. This insight can be understood to apply to knowledge as we experience it. Knowledge as we experience it is a constantly changing, dynamic, internally organized whole, rather than an aggregate of bits of factual information. As a whole, its constant interaction with external, transformational influence renders it as something constantly being shaped. It is in this sense, the sense of knowledge as something constantly shaped, that it has to be understood as something occurring within a vast sea of ignorance.[2] It is also in this sense that Theaetetus can be said to be learning in his discussion with Socrates.

This final chapter consists in the presentation of the powers human beings have that, when taken apart and separated from one another, would lead us to believe that knowledge is impossible, but when put together according to the way in which they are in fact organized in relation to one another, require that we reject the presumption that knowledge has its foundation in concrete facts that can be exhaustively established for us, and permanently so. We must reject such a conception of knowledge in favor of one in which it is understood as a dynamic and progressive cultivation of understanding within experience, a conception that has as its character incompleteness, but also potentially inexhaustible wonder.

With this in mind, let us consider for a moment how we have arrived at this interpretation of the nature of knowledge. In chapter 1, I presented what I take to be the themes Plato set before us for the consideration of the nature of knowledge, those being: that our beginnings are always concealed from us; that we die; that the people we become over time are part of continuous development with an uncertain though real trajectory; that all of this occurs within a context dependent upon the uncertainty and passivity associated with memory; and that these traits create circumstances in which reality does not disclose itself to us transparently, but, on the contrary, depends upon interpretations for which we are responsible. Chapter 1 thus dealt with the conditioning factors in the cultivation of knowledge. In light of these conditioning factors, chapter 2 dealt with the standpoint and the demands of the teacher, while chapters 3 and 4 dealt with the standpoint and demands of the student. Chapter 2 presented an account of what is called for in order for one to be a teacher of philosophy. It showed that the teacher calls one's attention to the fact that experience generates accumulated prejudices that must be subjected to questioning. This questioning is for the purpose of calling attention to the phenomenon of accumulated prejudice, and of instilling the desire to continue to undergo such a practice, by eliciting the recognition that one ought to do so in order to be capable of engaging more actively in one's own thinking. Chapter 3 considered how the student undergoes this process and experiences it as a call to articulate for himself the idea in its implications. Chapter 4 developed this notion in the direction of the need for the student to demonstrate to himself that his immediate impressions—and immediate perceptions—are in fact not immediate at all, but rather entail much more, and are dependent upon much more—than he initially recognized. In chapter 5, Socrates and Theaetetus discarded perception in favor of true opinion, thereby initiating the pernicious tendency to abstract parts of human activity from the whole, with the resulting insight—for *us*, though not for Theaetetus—that progress toward an account of knowledge would be accomplished only when the whole is taken into account. In this final chapter, we situate knowledge in the activity of living, in the whole generated through one's capacities to engage with the world, and therefore find knowledge to be an unfinished project, one most effectively undergone when one is aware of its character as a perpetually incomplete task perpetually worthy of pursuit.

1. Speech and the Unspeakable Elements (200e8–202c8)

a. The Metaphysics of Opinion and Deliberative Thought

Knowledge cannot simply be true opinion. If it were, then merely being persuaded to adopt the true opinion would be adequate to having knowledge. The fact that great orators are capable of making ignorant people adopt true opinions alone demonstrates that true opinion is not equivalent to knowledge. Much more than this, though, the fact that there are people expert in persuading others both to adopt a certain opinion without sufficient justification, and to do so convinced that they *do* have sufficient justification, ought to be taken by anyone capable of thinking as a call to cultivate the ability to engage in serious philosophical reflection. That there are orators capable of persuading people to adopt true opinions (or any opinions) without regard to whether they are able to understand what they opine leaves everyone vulnerable to manipulation, and, when successfully persuaded, to a tendency to adopt the presumption of knowledge where they have none. This vulnerability, when preyed upon effectively, closes one off to the kind of capacities Socrates seeks to cultivate. This vulnerability was described in chapter 2 as a fundamental part of the reality of human life, and as a motivation for Socrates's way of life; it also generally highlights the significance of dialectic as a tool to combat the adoption of opinions without reflection. As we saw in section 1 of chapter 5, Socrates called opinion the pause—whatever its cause might be—in thinking, and he characterizes thinking as the conversation one has with oneself (189e6–7). This pause is not inherently a problem; indeed, opinion as a pause in one's conversation with oneself is an important "stepping-stone" in dialectic. Rather, problems arise when the pause of opinion is taken to be permanent, or worse, when its relationship to conversation with oneself is completely obscured such that it is no longer recognizable for one *as* a pause, *as* an opinion.[3] This is the greatest threat of oratory: the orator is at his best when he is able to make one adopt an opinion without one being aware that one is doing so, and thus is able to make one take that opinion for granted as true.

Opinion must be placed within a context of dialogue if one is to dissolve this greatest threat of oratory, that is, the unwitting assent to opinions and the consequent foreclosure of further deliberation. Note how this reasoning appears rather odd or even question-begging. Opinion must be placed within the context of dialogue in order to ensure that it remains within a context of dialogue. Put more oddly still, we must continue to think about a given topic in order that we might continue to think about it. Rather than being truly question-begging, however, we would more properly recognize that thinking (understood in terms of dialogue, either with oneself or with another) is, on this formulation, taken to be a self-justifying ground, a primary good.

Indeed, as a primary good emerging from the nature of the human soul, thinking ought to be understood as having its own natural rhythm, one that involves it in moments of rest that we call opinion. We ought, as I claimed above, to consider opinion to be an important resource for thinking; but opinion is *for* thinking, *for* the process of continued deliberation. Let us further consider thinking and opinion, this time in terms that revisit the metaphysics of motion and rest discussed in chapter 3.

We saw in chapter 3 that, according to Socrates, we have an intuitive predisposition to think of motion as primary (153a8–c5). When he listed the five kinds of motion that incline us to think in this way, two of those had directly to do with the maintenance of our own personal health, the first having to do with the physical activity necessary to maintain bodily health, the second having to do with the studying necessary to maintain intellectual health. In each case, the moments of rest are essential to the maintenance of body and soul, too. The moments of rest, pleasurable in their own right though they may seem, have their pleasure insofar as they are required for the regenerating of one's capacity to engage in the activities one is actually directed to. As I noted there, one *can* lead a life dominated by rest, and it will cause the corruption of body and soul. One *cannot* lead a life dominated by activity, because rest will be forced on one by overexertion. Rest is thus a necessary part of the activity from which life is maintained, but a necessarily subordinate part.[4]

This structure of rest replenishing the reservoir of activity is analogous to the relationship between opinion and thinking. Opinion is a rest that gives pleasure through the temporary cessation of exertion, and a rest that can be taken mistakenly as an end. To maintain one's opinion untested and unarticulated, however, is to close off, to render inactive, the domain of thought to which that opinion belongs. One can have a false sense of security holding an opinion firmly and with certainty. Doing so can create the impression that one's life is made easier due to the fact that one has resolved the given issue for oneself. By contrast, to recognize that opinion is for the sake of thinking is to recognize that our primary relationship to the world is one of uncertainty, one of piecemeal constructions tested against the similarly uncertain constructions of others. To make opinion secondary to thinking is to recognize that, for human beings, what is primary is deliberative dialogue, which is to say that the foundation for our apprehension of the world is the uncertain, open discussion that occurs both within us and with others.

To be primarily so situated is to be placed in dialogue. It is therefore fortuitous and somewhat remarkable that Theaetetus is compelled to define knowledge on his third attempt as true opinion with an account. Let us briefly examine how he came to this third definition before examining both that definition and the way that it is examined by Theaetetus and Socrates.

b. Theaetetus's Memory of the Third Definition of Knowledge

In chapter 1, I mentioned that one of the attributes of memory is its passivity, a theme which has since emerged as central to the generation of opinions. I mentioned that that passivity is often the result of a very active, conscious effort at educating oneself. We, as we say, "commit ideas to memory," which is to say that we consciously choose information that we consider important, and study that information in the hopes that we will be capable of recalling it at a later time we cannot now anticipate.[5] We cannot, however, guarantee that this recalling will happen. The activity of committing to memory is an explicit demonstration of the passive dimension of intellect. We go to sometimes elaborate lengths to memorize, which is an admission on our part that, though we are consciously aware of the information at hand, we are not completely secure in the belief that we will later have access to it. Our efforts demonstrate that we know that the efficacy of the impression that we immediately have holds no guarantee regarding its recovery. Once we feel satisfied that we have sufficiently prepared ourselves to be capable of recalling, we forego conscious attention to the object we hope to recall. In fact, as soon as we feel confident, we let it go. Once we feel confident, we decide no longer to devote ourselves to thinking about it, and thus put our faith in the idea that it will reemerge when we need it. We submit it to the mysterious domain of accumulated experiences to which our conscious attention is not devoted.

It is from this mysterious domain that Theaetetus revives his third definition of knowledge. Having heard the refutation of his second definition in Socrates's example of the power of oratory, Theaetetus is compelled to remember that someone—he does not say (perhaps because he does not remember) who—told him once before that knowledge is true opinion with an account. Theaetetus then recalls that the person said that whatever admits of an account—whatever we are able to talk about—admits of knowledge, while those things about which we cannot give an account we cannot know (201c9–d5). The test, then, of what is knowable is whether or not it can be articulated. If it cannot, it cannot be known. With this definition of knowledge, we are implicitly introduced to the idea that some things *are*, yet cannot be known. It explicitly points us to the possibility that the limits to what we can know are not the same as the limits to what is, and to what is true.

This is certainly the most elaborate of Theaetetus's definitions, as well as the one containing the most suggestive and subtle claims. It is also a good sign that he is participating in the conversation somewhat more actively, here inserting himself appropriately without as much prompting as before. It is probably for this reason that Socrates enthusiastically tells Theaetetus that he is "really speaking beautifully" (201d6). Having said that this is an encouraging sign, though, we should nonetheless note that this third definition is the one that is least attributable to Theaetetus, as he himself makes explicit. He is recalling something said by someone else. According to the terms of the definition, therefore, he will have to display that he was educated into this definition, rather than merely having been persuaded to adopt it as an opinion. He must make it his own and the only way for him to do so—that is, both to demonstrate that it is his own and also to actually make it his own—is to give an account of it. This "making one's own" is what *having* knowledge, in the sense of *hexis*, means. This is also part of what philosophical discussion is supposed to cultivate. Socrates either has already made his own, or is in the midst of making his own, the various speeches that we have heard. As we have said several times already, though, while Theaetetus is being initiated into that practice—in the sense of being exposed to it and having minimally to participate in it—he is not yet himself engaging in the process of taking ownership of the ideas he is discussing.

In order to aid in the process of initiating him into the practice, Socrates asks Theaetetus to elaborate his definition on the specific point of the distinction between knowables and non-knowables (202d8–e1). What are those things about which there can be no account, and therefore no knowledge? This question Socrates asks goes directly to the essence of the definition. Are there really objects about which we can only be silent, and are these unknowable, and unknowable by virtue of the fact that they cannot be spoken of? Socrates asks, wondering if what Theaetetus is recalling is the same as something with which Socrates is familiar. Theaetetus, by way of acknowledgment that the idea is not his—and, if his definition holds true, acknowledgment that he does not know what he has just said—claims that he does not know if he could himself answer such questions, but that he could follow one who did.[6] Socrates will be forced to give the account, which means that Theaetetus continues to take a passive role.

Socrates's response is intriguing. He says that he will provide a dream in exchange for a dream (201e1).[7] Theaetetus gave him a definition whose author he does not mention and does not seem to remember, and one that he is not able to explain. Theaetetus, in other words, gave a minimal, and thus unsatisfying, account. In response, Socrates gives an answer even more remote from himself. He offers something he dreamt he heard some unspecified people say. If we knew the tone of this response, we might know if Socrates is teasing Theaetetus here, or if he is intentionally dissembling. At the very least we can say that Socrates has divested himself of authorship of what follows. He claims that the first things out of which everything is composed, including us, are like letters.

Socrates says that, in the dream, someone claimed that the first things were "just like elements [*stoicheia*], out of which we and everything else are composed, and they do not admit of speech" (201e2–4). One can only name such things, but cannot address them in any other way.[8] This banishment of predication includes banishing making claims about whether they are or are not (201e6–202a1). Even to use abstract pronouns such as "it," "each," or "alone" is to predicate of the sources more than the name, because it is to refer to each source using words referring equally to other things (202a2–5). Socrates explicitly draws a parallel between metaphysical elements and the elements of words, that is, letters. Just as the elements cannot themselves be predicated—because they are the building blocks necessary for making what is, and therefore cannot have being retroactively predicated of them—likewise, the letters that are necessary for making words cannot themselves be uttered, yet are the building blocks of utterance (202b1–9).[9] Whenever the soul has opinions about these elements, it "tells the truth about it but does not know, for whoever is incapable of giving and receiving an account [*logon*] is without knowledge of this very fact" (202c1–4). Though it is not entirely clear what one's soul telling the truth means, it is nonetheless the case that this truth-telling is (despite "telling" us) inarticulate. Whatever can be apprehended of the elements, it will never be articulated, and will therefore never be known. Let us further examine this puzzling discussion of the wonders of, and limits to, linguistic articulation.

Socrates's description here suggests to us many things, but it particularly suggests important things specifically about language. When I describe something, when I use language, I identify it and give it attributes, and do so in a way that is available to anyone who can hear or read. I obliterate its mystery to the extent that I speak about it. Language has the effect of equalizing anything to which it refers, in the sense that it makes everything it speaks equally available to be comprehended to all speakers of the language. Once something is spoken, anyone who can speak can speak it for themselves. To use language is to make what is spoken apparent. Thus, were we to speak the source of language, were we to bring into language what makes language possible, we would, in the process of speaking it, obscure the attribute that belongs to it most of all, that is most essential to it, that is, the fact that it precedes and makes possible linguistic expression. If Socrates's remembered dream has any purchase on reality, it demonstrates that reality contains insurmountable mystery. What first ushers in the ability to make-clear or to make-present, cannot itself be made present without first obliterating its characteristic attribute. Thus the speech Socrates remembers having dreamt of overhearing someone else give in fact appears to express the limit to speech, and—if the definition holds—appears to set the limit to knowledge.

We have already seen this sort of structure before in the discussion of what Socrates had called the three dogmas of thinking, dogmas upon which we insist whenever we try to entertain the consideration of ontology grounded in primordial flux (155a3–b2). I claimed in chapter 3 that each of the three dogmas was a version of the principle of non-contradiction, whose reality cannot be proven because it is itself the ground of proof. The principle of non-contradiction is, like this unnamed source (or these sources) of those things of which we can give account, something unaccountable. It can only be named and used; it is demonstrated or insinuated every time we use reason.

We might ask how it is that we are even speaking now of these things that cannot be known, but can only be named, if not for the fact that we *can* give account of them. The answer to this lies in the fact that the unspeakable elements are demonstrated in what they make possible. In the case of the example of letters in the analogy, the reality of the sounds these letters represent, which have no account of their own, is insinuated at all times by the words and meanings they make possible. The reality of the principle of noncontradiction is insinuated by our capacity to deliberate, to make anything at all rationally comprehensible. Each is known only through that which each makes possible. We know, Socrates says, continuing with the analogy, that there are letters only because of the words for which they are the necessary condition (202b7). We can perceive the letters in what they make us capable of.[10] Here, again, we return to perception, this time understood as a resource that, on its own, cannot possibly be equivalent to knowledge because it remains silent, but that is yet essential to it, and that is something to which we can be nothing other than grateful for its being given.[11]

Socrates ends this description of an overheard dream-speech with an interesting formulation of what one is to conclude from it. When we are inclined toward true opinion without speech, we opine correctly but do not *know* that we do so (202b9–c4). This formulation is important: if the difference between true opinion alone and true opinion with an account is that in the first case we opine correctly but do not know that we do, and in the second case we opine correctly and know that we do, and if the latter case in some sense counts as knowledge, then knowledge is both the demonstration of the justification of our opinion, and the demonstration we make to ourselves that we know what we know. The account simultaneously proves the opinion and makes us conscious of the grounds for our opinion. It essentially depends upon self-consciousness. Theaetetus will not have knowledge until he can show to himself that he does by giving an account. His reluctance to try to give an account forecloses in advance his ability to know what he knows and does not know. This is a lesson, again, that he cannot learn in one attempt. This last very important point—that self-consciousness takes time to come about—remains unarticulated in each of the definitions of knowledge.

c. What the Third Definition Provides

In this section of the *Theaetetus*, we have seen the most elaborate definition of knowledge yet. It has introduced three conceptual variables to improve on the inadequate second definition, variables we should briefly examine before moving on to the presentation of the examination performed by Socrates and Theaetetus. Those three conceptual resources include the account, the distinction between speakable and unspeakable, and the theme of self-consciousness. Let us briefly review each in turn.

Let us consider first the importance of the centrality of the account (*logos*) to this definition. As I have already suggested, to speak of something means in part to make it available, either to oneself or to others, for scrutiny. Whether explicitly acknowledged as such or not, to articulate one's opinions is to continue to leave them open for deliberation. If indeed the practice of giving an account is to have a share in knowledge, then to know will have to involve the knower in deliberation.

As compelling as it might be to suggest that openness to deliberation is intrinsic to knowledge, there are characteristics of our typical conception of knowledge that perhaps incline us to resist such a suggestion. We experience knowledge as in some important sense inherently private. In particular, we experience our immediate impressions of objects, that is, our direct contemplative apprehension of objects, in a way that seems particularly resistant to the openness of deliberation. The directness and immediacy of our impressions of things seems to precede discourse and to inform it fundamentally. This conception was central to our discussion of the philosopher in chapter 4. In that section of the dialogue (172c3–177c7), the philosopher is presented as immediately apprehending the truth, specifically, the actual, contingent structures that invisibly govern the way in which others live. For the third definition of knowledge to contribute conceptually to this presentation of the philosopher, we must ask about the status of our immediate experience of the object in relation to knowledge. In particular, we must ask what the highly cultivated apprehension of the object characteristic of the philosopher lacks, that the addition of an account will supplement. The account is what must be added to opinion to show that the opinion is properly grounded and not merely a result of effective persuasion, and to show to oneself the character of one's own impressions. On this characterization, the account seems to be merely the *proof* of knowledge. That is, the account demonstrates that the opinion one has is arrived at justifiably, and is therefore not mere opinion but in fact knowledge. If, though, the account is the test or the proof of knowledge and if what it is proving is mere opinion (which has been established not to be knowledge) it does not appear that any particular capacity is the source of knowledge.

The confusion produced by this formulation of the problem is the insistence on searching for a definition of knowledge as a fixed state where further deliberation is no longer necessary. Such a fixed state is one in which thinking is at an end, which is, according to Socrates, the state of opinion. If, on the other hand, as I have argued, the highest accomplishment of thinking is to become oriented philosophically—which is to say to be oriented in a way that is always reopened for dialogue, insofar as one experiences objects of knowledge never to be exhaustively articulated, but rather always directing one to further and deeper understanding—then knowledge can neither be some kind of opinion sanctioned by public scrutiny, nor the proof of such an opinion.

To continue to work through this puzzle of the locus of knowledge, as well as its reformulation outside of the narrow and inadequate parameters of the conversation between Socrates and Theaetetus, let us examine the second new conceptual variable introduced by the third definition, the distinction between the speakable and the unspeakable. It is this distinction that, in section 2 below, will introduce new difficulties to our discussion. Initially, however, they provide us with the conceptual resources to distinguish between what we can articulate and therefore know, and what we cannot articulate and cannot therefore know but must rely on as conditioning knowledge. The unspeakable elements remind us that language is something with a specific character, and as such is something whose way of revealing sets up the terms of revelation. Language is a clearing of reality, but is not a neutral clearing, that is, it is not one whose process transparently and unproblematically reveals anything and everything. If what Socrates, building on what Theaetetus says about the unspeakable, says about elements and letters is true, then to speak what is in principle unspeakable is to remove, in the speaking, its salient attribute.

The unspeakable, it seems, simply demands silence. To choose silence is a kind of appropriate orientation toward the unspeakable. This might indeed be the way in which one "knows" the elements necessary for the account one subsequently gives. We would, then, give account of the conditioning elements in our use of them. We perceive the elements only through what they make possible, and not through themselves. They are merely implied by the reality that they introduce. An account of knowledge that does not address this puzzling component is not sufficient.

The third important contribution made by Theaetetus's third definition is the introduction of the importance of self-consciousness. To give an account is to make plain to oneself one's own thinking, and is therefore to understand oneself better. Self-consciousness is necessarily inextricable from the account, insofar as it is in giving an account that we are able to express for ourselves what had previously acted as an unknown interpretive framework.[12] Self-consciousness had been an important component of Socrates's maieutics, as we discussed in chapter 2. Here it is made an important part of Theaetetus's definition. Self-consciousness is strongly linked to speech, because it is in speech that we are faced with the responses of others to our opinion, that our accounts are tested, and that we hear ourselves through thoughts projected onto the world. We know the value of what we have to say through speaking. We cannot know (but can only perceive), says Socrates (though not in his own voice), the unspeakables because of the fact that we cannot speak them.

Self-consciousness and knowledge take time to develop both in the literal, straightforward sense that they do so through the temporal medium of verbal articulation, and in the sense that it takes practice to be able to do so well. By defining knowledge in terms of something—that is, the account—that takes time to cash out, and that takes practice to cash out well, Theaetetus, with Socrates's guidance, has moved ever closer to articulating knowledge in terms that turn away from, and demonstrate the inadequacy of, defining it in abstraction from lived experience. Identifying the importance of giving an account, of suggesting limits around what *can* be given in an account, and by drawing on the important role played by giving an account in the cultivation of self-consciousness, they implicitly emphasize a turn toward the whole of lived experience.

2. Things, Alls, Parts, Wholes (202c9–210d4)

Socrates's addition of a "dream in exchange for a dream" persisted in drawing a clear distinction between perception and knowledge, claiming that the unspeakables are perceived (continuing with the analogy to letters and words) only as the "plaiting" that constitutes words (202b7–9), whereas the words themselves are knowable, because words, unlike letters, can be given account of.[13] Before getting into the discussion that is set up by this clear distinction, we should ask if it is right that it be so clear. We must admit that there is a difference between the immediate apprehension of something and the account that one gives about it, just as there is a difference between holding an opinion about something and deliberating about it. Perception and opinion both appear to provide a resource to be exploited by accounting and deliberating. Each case appears to be a version of the relationship between the ground for action and the action itself. Perception and opinion also appear, together, in their relationship to the reflective activity of thinking and giving account, to constitute something akin to the passive motion talked about in chapter 3, in its relationship to active motion. But does it seem correct to claim that the first (either perception or opinion) is the "plaiting" that constitutes knowledge, while the second (giving an account or deliberating) is the knowledge proper? The third definition of knowledge, we shall see, will ultimate fail because of its attempt to isolate a certain human capacity that contributes to the formation of one's understanding, and to take that isolated capacity to be knowledge. This is a recurrence of the discursive error in the second definition that was discussed in detail in chapter 5. It is therefore a deeply problematic distinction that Socrates draws between "perception as plaiting" and "giving an account as knowledge." Because they are reliant on such a problematic distinction, just as in the previous two definitions where a problematic distinction frames the discussion in such a way that it is doomed to lead to a dead end, likewise here the clean separation of one aspect of the process of learning from the others will produce an impasse.

As we have already discussed at length in this chapter, knowledge is going to have its place within the interactions between opinion, deliberation, and perception. In navigating Socrates's ensuing consideration of the relationships between, and the ontological status of, parts and wholes, as well as his consideration of the difference between aggregates and wholes, we will apply those insights to the question of the formation of knowledge from those three things (opinion, deliberation, and perception), and consider what knowledge is, among the candidates of aggregates, parts, and wholes.

a. Emergent Wholes

Socrates performs the now-familiar act of making Theaetetus officially commit to the claim that has now—rather more briefly than in the previous two definitions—been articulated (202c9–10). Socrates adds that in agreeing to it, Theaetetus appears to be claiming that he and Socrates had accomplished something that none of the great thinkers of the past had accounted for successfully. One might suspect that this remark made by Socrates is a prompt to Theaetetus that now would be an appropriate moment to exercise some humility, though if it is, Theaetetus misses it. Theaetetus claims that he agrees and thinks they have done beautifully (202d4–5). Perhaps Theaetetus imagines that Socrates was suggesting that nobody had managed to provide a complete account of knowledge, but that they—Socrates and Theaetetus—might have done so just now. The assumption that Theaetetus appears to be making, that is, that Socrates is announcing the significance of their accomplishment rather than the more plausible assumption that Socrates is gently suggesting that the project is likely not completed, could be the result of his mathematical background. The question "What is knowledge?" is perhaps for Theaetetus like a very difficult mathematical problem, one that requires a great deal of preparation and thoughtful consideration, but one that nonetheless admits of a solution. It appears more likely that Socrates was pointing out to Theaetetus that he ought not to misconstrue the discussion—or philosophical dialogue in general—in terms that would assume a permanent and absolute solution. On the contrary, their activity of dialectic gathers the available resources—that is, opinions, perceptions, the character and the ability of the interlocutors—and deliberates about them for the sake of the improvement of the quality of those very resources. Though Theaetetus has subjected himself to such educational development in this discussion, he is not aware that or why he has done so, as his inflated confidence here indicates. Having been told, in essence, that the smartest people have been preoccupied with this issue for generations and yet have not adequately answered the question, he responds by saying he believes that he and Socrates have managed to do so. Theaetetus fails to recognize that the issue they are dealing with is not to be taken as a solvable problem.

Socrates does agree that the speech is saying something that must be true. However, he is troubled by the point at the very heart of the speech, the point about which we have had much discussion, that is, that the elements of speech are not knowable because they cannot be accounted for. He therefore suggests that they examine a distinction in the elements of words between letters and syllables. Letters do not admit of speech; syllables do. We can say the syllable, but not the letter. Indeed, we can give an account of the syllable. The first syllable of Socrates's name "SO" *is* Sigma and Omega; this is its account (203a8–9). Were we asked what the first letter of Socrates's name is, we could name it—"Sigma"—but we could do no more with it, because it cannot be spoken.[14] We can say the sound of "Omega" as well as naming it. It would appear, then that the element is unknowable, but the syllable is knowable (203b10).

There is, nonetheless, a problem with this account, according to Socrates. To know the name "Socrates," one would have to know—that is, be capable of speaking—the syllables. To know the syllables, for example "SO," does one not have to know Sigma and Omega? Or, rather, does one know neither of them, but know both of them in knowing the syllable? This suggests that Socrates and Theaetetus must maintain that knowledge emerges from out of elements that are not known, if they want to maintain the premises of the third definition of knowledge as they have been elaborated by Socrates.[15] Theaetetus acknowledges that they have quickly and suddenly threatened the premises of their third definition, on the grounds that it would be dreadful for us to know neither letter, and, out of knowing neither letter, have their combination produce knowledge (203d6–7). It seems dreadful to Theaetetus, in other words, that knowledge should emerge from—and therefore be in some sense dependent upon—ignorance.

Here, yet again, Socrates approaches the idea that knowledge is built on a foundation of ignorance. This is something to which Theaetetus is so resistant that he "very suddenly" rejects the "beautiful speech" about the relationship between letters and syllables (203d11–e1). Socrates is reluctant to entertain this when Theaetetus rejects it, which is not the same as Socrates himself rejecting it. Indeed, elsewhere in Plato's corpus, Socrates characterizes himself and his own knowledge pursuits in precisely this way.[16] Thus, the way in which Socrates takes up Theaetetus's rejection of a claim he has himself elsewhere endorsed should be read carefully. In response to this hasty rejection, Socrates presents a conditional claim, one whose conditions are subsequently and problematically taken for granted by Theaetetus. Socrates claims that "if there's a necessity to know each of the two if one will know both, there's every necessity for whoever's going to know a syllable to know first its elements" (203d8–10). The condition that is to be assumed is that knowing both requires knowledge of each individually, or more generally, knowledge of a whole entails knowledge of the parts. This condition should not be so readily assumed, however, and indeed should be rejected. Its rejection would be easier to perform were they operating with a synthetic rather than an abstract account of knowledge, that is, if they operated with an account that characterized knowledge as a developmental process, as something developed through dialectic. The process of dialectic is what they themselves have been engaged in throughout the dialogue. We will now examine that process to demonstrate the difficulty in maintaining their interpretation of the relationship between wholes and parts.

As I mentioned in chapter 2, one of the remarkable things about Theaetetus's aborted first attempt at a definition of knowledge—that is, the one that amounted to a list of different kinds of knowledge—was that, despite demonstrating that he lacked the ability to give an account of knowledge, Theaetetus did harbor an idea of knowledge sufficient for him to be capable of identifying what he took to be instances of it. I characterized this as evidence of presumptions he harbored, as evidence, in other words, of his pregnancy. One might, as I did there, present these presumptions as the potential cause of the perpetuation of ignorance, which they are. However, one might also point to presumptions as evidence of knowledge. The discussion that follows—that is, the subsequent content of Plato's dialogue *Theaetetus*—does not consist in the utter rejection of the presumptions Theaetetus harbored; he very likely comes away, for example, thinking that geometry and shoe-making are kinds of knowledge. The whole in some sense remains what it was. Knowing the whole—that is, in Theaetetus' case at the outset of the discussion, being able to identify instances of knowledge—*makes possible* the process of learning the parts. This discussion enriches Theaetetus's understanding of knowledge by identifying problems and nuances in this thing the understanding of which one typically takes for granted.[17] The conversation itself, in other words, demonstrates that one uses one's working understanding of a whole when one inquires into its nature, which consists in understanding its parts and their interrelations. This is another way of articulating the relationship between opinion and the account, as well as between perception and reflection.

Despite the fact that this actual process of learning that Theaetetus is undergoing demonstrates that he should reject the strictures of the proposed condition that knowledge of the whole entails knowledge of the parts, Theaetetus accepts this condition without question. The problem they are therefore left with is how to explain the fact that we can know the syllables and cannot know the letters, when knowledge of the syllables implies knowledge of letters. Socrates notes, once again, that they are failing to live up to the obligations they have to the speech (203e2). Perhaps their first mistake was to identify the syllable as the sum of the letters. Instead, they should describe the syllable as a single, unitary whole emerging from the coupling of the elemental letters. In other words, what Socrates is suggesting is that they think of the result of the gathering together of elements not as an "all" but as a singular, indivisible "whole." The "all" is primarily an aggregate. The whole is something more than what has made it. The whole is akin to the offspring of the elemental letters, rather than the mere combination of the coupling "parents." In being the result of that initial coupling, the offspring displaces itself from its aggregate origins, and as a result is able to be seen and identified, to be accounted for.

b. That Which Reveals Itself through Others

Let us once again cash out the analogy to letters, as well as the idea that what is primary and unknowable displaces itself in favor of the wholes it "conceives," in terms of real knowledge of the world. I have repeatedly drawn attention to the principle of non-contradiction as a paradigmatic example of an idea that cannot be rationally justified, on the grounds that any justification would have to take it for granted in trying to justify it. Rather, the principle of non-contradiction shows itself in its "offspring"; we see the evidence of the reality of the principle of non-contradiction in the varied ways in which it is presumed. The logic of such an "account" of what cannot be accounted for is found elsewhere in the Platonic corpus, too. In Plato's *Timaeus*, the titular character describes the three fundamental kinds of being that have to be presumed for the reality that we experience. They include "form" (*eidos*), that which shares its name (*homōnumon*) and is similar (*homoion*) to form, being perceptible (*aisthēton*) and begotten (*gennēton*), and a "third kind," the space (*khora*) that must be presumed for these others to be. This space, this *khora*, is made available to us to understand only by a "bastard reasoning" that is "hardly to be trusted" (*Timaeus*, 51e8–52d1); while it *is* in the sense that it must be assumed to be in order for there to be anything to be given form, the *khora* can *only* be assumed.[18] Its presence is never able to be made manifest, due to the fact that that which occupies the *khora*—and thus displaces it as present—is what *proves* its presence. It shows itself only through other things that exploit it, and, in exploiting it, cause it to withdraw from presence. We will find that analogous characteristics are to be found in thinking itself. Let us examine thinking in terms of its character as an unspeakable cause.

Our ability to think about the world is made possible by the fact that our thinking takes on the character of what is thought. Aristotle astutely remarks that what is called "mind" has no form of its own, except the form of receptivity.[19] If the mind had an identifiable character independent of the character of the things it thought, this would set a limit to what could be thought. Not only, therefore, is mind something conformable to whatever it thinks, not only does mind have no independent form, but these attributes are the necessary conditions that make thinking possible. We are able to think because the mind has as its character receding in favor of whatever it receives. Mind cannot be spoken of, because to speak of it is to make it "hide" in favor of that which it allows one to think. Like the principle of non-contradiction, it is something that is to be used, to be exploited, yet never itself spoken of, never known. This account of "mind" given by Aristotle fits well with the analysis we are developing here in our reading of the *Theaetetus*. We are building a sense of the elements of human life that remain unspeakable in the sense of being unaccountable in discursive thinking. Understanding the sense in which elements are unspeakable contributes to our understanding of the nature of, and limits to, thinking, by presenting aspects of reality from which our experience emerges, and therefore by presenting aspects of reality which we cannot fully account for by turning back to them using the resources that they caused.[20]

With this in mind, let us move on to consider the distinction between aggregates and wholes, a distinction that demonstrates an analogous structure of emergence-from, and a structure that once again announces a limit to that of which we can give an account.

c. The Organizing Principle as the Distinction between Aggregates and Wholes

How does this account of the relationship between wholes and unspeakable elements play out in the conversation? Theaetetus characteristically provides a hasty assent to the idea that a whole is not the same as an all. This compels Socrates to return to a strategy he had previously used, namely to counter Theaetetus's hasty assent—to an account that, when properly thought through, would prove to contain valuable insight—with a counter-appeal to a less compelling account using Theaetetus's own mathematical background to render the counter-appeal persuasive. The power of number forcefully makes one point while obscuring another.[21] Socrates asks, if indeed the whole and the all are not the same, is it also true that the all and the things that make the all are different: "Whenever we say one, two, three, four, five, six, and we say twice three or thrice two, or four and two, or three and two and one—in all these cases are we saying the same or other?" (204b12–c2). Now, in saying all of these, we are surely always saying "six." However, the manner in which we say "six" differs in each case, and is motivated by different questions. This first example obscures the point that each distinct equation is asking a distinct question that happens to result in the answer, "six," and that each is therefore a distinct identification of equality.[22] If, however, we allow this fact to evade our attention, Socrates clearly gives us the chance in the following two examples to recognize the dubiousness of the claim he is making. Let us turn to each of them.

Socrates's second example consists of a list of units of measurement: When we say "plethron" we are always saying "one hundred feet." When we say "stadion" we are always saying "six hundred feet."[23] Taking this further, Socrates suggests that the number of the army is no different from the army and that this is the case in "all things of the sort" (204d10). Socrates is here suggesting that numeric equality implies equality without qualification, which he then makes explicit, saying: "For all the number is all that each of them is?" (204d10–11). It is important to note that this is framed as a question, and that Theaetetus agrees with this immediately. Let us examine, first, the examples of the units of measure, and second, the example of the army. Our consideration will show that neither of these is an adequate example of the sameness of wholes and alls.

To say that the stadion is six hundred feet is to state a definition. *As* units of measure, one stadion and six hundred feet are absolutely equivalent, and to combine six hundred of the one unit is precisely to produce one of the other. From this standpoint, the six hundred feet are simply the parts that, when combined to match the defined number, are neither more nor less than the stadion. However, this is not "all that each of them is." The foot is an empirical unit of measure, whose value is set differently according to different regional standards, which is to say that it is one with no "correct" value outside of the contingent circumstances under which it is set, which is to say that it has no intrinsic, a priori value to it. The stadion is a unit of measure, designed for a specific purpose, whose value was set according to the contingently derived value of the foot. One precedes the other in invention, and sets the terms by which the other is fixed. The Ionians, Olympians, and Miletans each had a slightly different version of the foot, with the result that each had a corresponding slightly different version of the stadion.[24] To claim that the stadion is completely said by its division into a number of units whose values are contingent upon the conventions of a given politically organized geographical region is false. It is a value that was set to meet the demand for a unit of measure of a certain size. It need never have existed had the demand been for a unit of measure that turned out to be eight hundred of our feet, or five hundred, and so on. To talk about the stadion is to invoke certain specific contingencies that arose in a certain specific cultural context, and is therefore to invoke much more than the mere numbers. Had Socrates hypothesized one otherwise indeterminate abstract unit of measure to be equal to ten of a likewise otherwise indeterminate abstract unit of measure (that was, by definition, one tenth the size)—that is, had Socrates used examples never leaving the terrain of pure number—and said that one is simply and completely the same as ten of the other, and that one has its being fully articulated as ten parts of the other, while the other is fully articulated as being the whole created by those ten, he would have been saying something true, but would have lost the power of having applied his point to reality.[25] Worse, with respect to Socrates's example of empirical units of measure, to point to the measure of each in relation to the other as exhaustively definitive of them is to obscure their other attributes, specifically the attributes that motivated their definition to begin with; it is to reduce them to pure quantity. He cannot legitimately do this with the stadion—or with any empirical unit of measure—because it is something more than the mere aggregate of smaller units.

The third example Socrates gives, that of the army, is even more obviously worthy of criticism. In fact, it is important that Socrates gives this example last. Units of measure might appear at first to be merely relations of number, the latter of which obscure the distinction between aggregates and wholes. An army, however, is clearly not the same as the aggregate of all of its members. That they are not simply equivalent is demonstrated first by the fact that one cannot make the claim in reverse order. Taking the army as one's starting point, one can say that that army "is" its thirty thousand members. However, having stripped those thirty thousand people of all attributes but their aggregate numeric value, one cannot say "this is an army." For it to be an army, it must have organization, arms, rank, articulated roles distinct from one another, and so on. It must, in other words, have characteristics relevant to, but by no means equivalent to, its number. If one takes these thirty thousand people and imposes on them all of the qualities listed and no doubt many others—that is, if one organizes them—it will have the effect of transforming an aggregate into a whole, which is to say that the coupling of the material resources and an organizing principle produces as its offspring a result that is more than the mere sum.[26]

Socrates, however, is not able to elicit this insight from Theaetetus. Theaetetus agrees to the idea that number is nothing other than parts of wholes, and wholes are nothing more than "alls" made up of those parts. This produces a new puzzle for them to address—a puzzle resulting from a highly questionable agreement. Let us briefly examine it. If it is the case that all of the parts are equal to the whole, then wholes turn out simply to be aggregates, and therefore not unitary indivisibles. Further, a whole, like an all, appears to be defined in terms of its completeness. What is whole leaves nothing out; what is all, likewise, leaves nothing out (205a1–5). The whole and the all must be all the parts together. But we had been saying that the whole, the syllable, could not be something that has parts, because if it had parts, that would imply that we could know the parts that make up the whole that is the syllable—for example, we have to know Sigma and Omega to know the syllable "SO"—and we were just saying that the elemental letters cannot be known. If the whole is to be known, on this formulation, it must not have parts, which means that it cannot be equivalent to an all.

The problem gets worse as we examine it further. In order not to have to know the letters, we would have to know the syllables as unitary wholes, not constituted by parts (though perhaps the offspring of parts). It turns out, though, that, either we now acknowledge that, insofar as a whole is defined by being all the parts, it *does* have parts (which returns us to the problem of having to know the parts) or we refuse to acknowledge this and say that it *does not* have parts, in which case it *too* is elemental, in which case we cannot know it according to this definition, because we cannot give an account of the fundamental elements (205e2).

Socrates now says that perhaps it is wrong to assume that we cannot know the elements. Perhaps we should say that in learning, we are trying to focus our attention on the elements. Socrates begins with letters, but moves on to talk briefly about learning to play the lyre as an example of what he means (206a5–c2). This is a useful transition, especially for our purposes, because it draws us back to perception. When one wants to play the lyre, one wants to produce individual sounds organized into a coherent and presumably beautiful whole. One wants to be capable of organizing those sounds. One begins by loving the sound as a whole. This *motivates* the project to begin with. But the project consists, to a great extent, in attention to the particular notes. To play the song properly one has to play the right notes, and to do so well one has to be preoccupied with the notes in a sense independent of their place in the song as a whole. As a result of this, one might have come to hear the song in a manner different from the one which motivated the project to begin with. What is curious about this example is that one might have the impression that the song was perfect when one heard it and thought "I want to play that!" because all one wanted to do was to do what had already been done, namely, realize that particular instance of beautiful music. The experience of trying to realize that project changes things, however. On the one hand, one's initial experiences of playing the desired piece turns it into something far less beautiful, into something clumsy and poorly put together. On the other hand, the experience turns the music into something much more complex, and perhaps even more beautiful, when one hears it played by skillful musicians. One hears the craftsmanship underlying another's expert playing of something one has struggled with oneself. One hears what individual notes are *doing* placed as they are here and there in the song. In other words, while the breaking down of the song into parts one has struggled to understand may indeed make the song sound worse coming from one's own hands, and while when one hears the song, one no longer hears it in the way one did when one first loved it, the song is now better appreciated for what it is. One has cultivated an ability to hear the song better. Moreover, one's experience of music generally is likely transformed, too, in the sense that one can experience all kinds of music as accomplishments of this learning process.

This account of learning to play music applies equally to the practice of learning to think. One's first encounter with a powerful idea—one's first sense that something in one's experience is a cause of wonder—motivates the inquiry. The work of inquiry simultaneously sharpens one's perception and renders one's own process of thinking more prosaic and frustrating. It does, however, give one a sense of the subtlety that underlies various concepts and claims, such that one can better see what is meant by the idea. Socrates has drawn the connection to the elements as the proper object of preoccupation not because he wants to suggest that we know them first and therefore can somehow give an account of them (despite what appears in the current account). Rather, they are the proper object of learning, out of which arises knowledge. He does not reject the notion that knowledge is built upon ignorance, nor does he reject the notion that one cannot give an account of the elements of knowledge. Rather, he suggests that knowledge takes a form, one among others, that does not involve speeches, though he never explicitly makes a speech about this (205c1–2). Similar to the case of learning to play and to appreciate music, the motivation to strive to know the elements generates the experience of the obscurity of those elements from discursive thought, while at the same time, or at least over time, generating a deeper appreciation of their significance, of what they mean.

d. What Is Added by the Account

Socrates changes the subject, or, more accurately, does not allow the conversation to continue in the direction of consideration of the non-discursive knowledge of elements.[27] Instead, he shifts the discussion to accounts, to *logoi*. What do we mean by the "account" when we say knowledge is true opinion with an account? Socrates suggests three possibilities. Let us examine each in turn:

1. According to the first answer, the account makes thought evident through the sounds of words and phrases (206d1–4). On this interpretation, everyone not dumb or mute is capable of such speech and any who opine rightly will know that they do so in speech. The initial problem with this account is that it appears not to say enough. True opinion made evident through words and phrases certainly does not guarantee knowledge, because one can have true opinion and give a ridiculous speech that does not adequately justify the true opinion one has. One can have a false justification for a true opinion.

2. The first version of an account, Socrates suggests, does not do justice to the dreamt-of person who presented it. Socrates suggests that they "not too readily issue a condemnation" (206e5). A more reasonable account of speech is to say that an account takes the form of answering the questioner concerning one's own opinion. That is, when someone challenges one to justify the opinion that one holds, one is answerable for one's opinion, and one is made answerable by way of the elements in that, when one answers, one must demonstrate one's knowledge of the constituent parts so that one can show that one's knowledge is built on the true foundation (206e7).

Socrates suggests as an example of an "account" that if he claimed to know something about wagons and a questioner were to challenge his claim to knowledge, he would say that wagons consist of wheels, axle, carriage-body, rails, and yoke (207a3). This would be true in a very general sense. However, the questioner—if she happened to be someone who *did* know about wagons—would respond that there are one hundred parts, say, and that therefore Socrates's "knowledge" was in fact merely superficial, and that as a result his opinion was hardly reliable. It would be akin, says Socrates, to them saying the name "Socrates" consists in three syllables. We would not admit this claim as knowledge of the spelling of his name (207a6). In each case, the poorer definition fails because it does not list the parts in sufficiently fine detail.

Is this second presentation of the account really any good? Can we properly be said to know if we can list all of the elements of the object that we claim to know, and about which we have a true opinion? When Socrates asks Theaetetus this, Theaetetus once again asks Socrates to give his opinion first (207c6).[28] Socrates will not allow him to get away with this, telling Theaetetus that he must give his own opinion. Theaetetus quickly agrees that this is a sufficient account of knowledge (207d2). Socrates then draws the consequence of this position. He asks Theaetetus if he is correspondingly convinced that one is a knower if one exchanges one element for another in accounting for the object. Theaetetus says no, he is not. The purpose of this question is made clear when Socrates reminds Theaetetus of his early experiences learning how to write. When one begins to learn to write, one makes mistakes. Perhaps when first spelling Theaetetus's name, one correctly uses a Theta, and one writing Theodorus's name mistakenly used a Tau (207e7–208a3). In a case where one demonstrates the misuse of the letter elsewhere, can one say that one knows the letter, even here? Theaetetus acknowledges that he certainly would not identify this as knowledge. Indeed, the same could occur for each syllable in the spelling of the name in its entirety. The person spelling the name "Theaetetus" could, at each step along the way, correctly use a letter she will elsewhere misuse. Thus it would seem that she would have no knowledge of the elements, even though she is able to provide an account of the elements. That is, she has true belief and can provide an account of her true belief, and yet does not know. It would, therefore, appear that—in this second account of speech in the third account of knowledge—they have failed.

In fact, I believe, the idea that the account necessary to demonstrate knowledge consists in listing the aggregate parts is a common one and Socrates's criticism of this version on the grounds that one can provide such an account yet can fail to transfer knowledge of the aggregate parts is important. It appears that knowledge is demonstrated when—strictly within the context of the topic one is discussing—one can master an understanding of its internal component parts. However, those internal component parts are also components of other things, and if one misuses those components elsewhere, one has demonstrated a lack of knowledge of them, and thus a lack of knowledge of the whole one appeared to have known.

This kind of demonstration of ignorance very likely occurs in many areas of life, but examples especially make themselves readily available in the moral sphere. One is often quite able to identify the self-destructive vices exercised by one's friends while failing to recognize similar vices in oneself. One might notice that a friend drinks too much, and might caution that friend that they ought to exercise better restraint. Perhaps one is correct in making such an assessment, and as a result, perhaps others identify one to be wise concerning indulgence and restraint. One can imagine this same person indulging in similar interventions with others concerning their excessive behavior, doing so sometimes ineptly, sometimes in a way that merely antagonizes the other person. The person demonstrates that, while he was able to identify indulgent behavior in a particular form, he nonetheless engages in a different kind of indulgent behavior (i.e., excessive acts of moral indignation or moral intervention) without detecting it in himself. Socrates's point here would be that one has not adequately accounted for one's knowledge of indulgent behavior if one demonstrates a failure to understand it when outside of the contexts where one has demonstrated what appeared to be knowledge.

Note that this fact, that one's misuse of the component parts elsewhere demonstrates one did not, in fact, sufficiently know the components, demonstrates that one is perpetually and indefinitely answerable to challenge, insofar as one could not possibly anticipate all of the ways in which component parts of the whole one claims to know could be used. Thus, if indeed the measure (or a measure) of one's knowledge of the whole one is addressing is giving an account of the parts that make up that whole, one will always be correctable according to ways in which those parts are elsewhere used.

This definition of the account makes it unrealistic, if not impossible, to define completely the parts that make up the whole. In addition to this weakness, though, the second definition of the account is also to be criticized for being incomplete. The whole is not merely made up of its parts; it is also the way in which those parts are organized.[29] Simply to list and define parts would not give one the whole of which one is striving to prove one's knowledge. Further, because the organizational structure of the parts has to be considered an essential aspect of the account, the way in which component parts are used elsewhere is less important than how they fit into the particular whole. Accounting for the organizing principle of the whole means knowing the way in which the parts function in this particular whole, independent of the way in which they participate in other wholes. Though knowing the organizational structure of the parts in the particular whole cannot provide complete knowledge (insofar as knowing how the given part is organized here does not occlude the possibility that one misuses it elsewhere), it is nonetheless a necessary component of the account insufficiently emphasized by its second definition.[30]

3. Having failed twice at the speech about speech, and in order to try to salvage the speech, Socrates calls upon a third account (208c10–11). Before Socrates gives the third account of speech, Theaetetus summarizes what he takes the previous two to have been. Let us look at Theaetetus's summary.

The first interpretation of the account presented it as an image of thought in sound. In this first example, the speech reflects back to us what we had in our own thoughts, so that we and others might be able to see what those thoughts are. The problem with the first definition of the account that was made explicit was that it was clear that we might continue to have a false speech, and merely making it available for us to see does not guarantee that we will be discerning in our examination of it. We might also add, though, that it is not obvious that one has knowledge prior to the expression of it in the account. Indeed, the whole interpretative framework of my analysis of the *Theaetetus* has been based on the idea that one cannot know without an account because one cannot know the nature of one's thoughts without making them explicit to oneself; expressing the thought transforms it into something knowable. This first account makes the account add far too little to the true opinion; it adds only a measure of true opinion. The second interpretation of the "account," as it is characterized by Theaetetus, consists in going to the whole through the elements. This interpretation was intended to improve on the first by providing a concrete test of the image. In the first, the image was the entirety of the addition to true opinion; in the second, true opinion is enhanced by an account that articulates the parts that together constitute the opinion. This, however, was shown wanting because it too proved unable to guarantee, to show or to justify, the truth of true opinion. One can be in error about the parts of the whole about which one has true opinion, as would be made evident by one's use of those parts elsewhere. Because the parts of a whole are not necessarily limited to the place they occupy in that particular whole, how they are used elsewhere might make evident that coincidence alone explained the truth of one's opinions. I added to this something that neither Socrates nor Theaetetus mentions, that this account pays insufficient attention to the organizing principle of the parts, and therefore overemphasizes the importance of recognizing the independent meaning of the parts. To these earlier, failed interpretations of the account, Socrates adds a third, one which he hopes will supplement true opinion sufficiently, or, put differently, one which will prove that that true opinion is adequately licensed. Socrates now claims that the speech that accounts for the truth of one's beliefs would be the one that effectively differentiates whatever one is accounting for from anything else (208c10–11). This, Socrates proposes, is the completion of the account of knowledge, and Theaetetus agrees.

Immediately after Theaetetus agrees to what Socrates has said, Socrates indicates that he now feels less like he knows than he did before, as though he has come too close to a shadow-painting, and in so doing has shattered the illusion that the image created (208e9–10). Before examining the rejection of the final account of speech, and thus the rejection of the third definition, let us take a moment to consider this rich characterization Socrates has given of himself at the end of the inquiry.

e. A Digression Concerning Shadow-Painting and the Ambiguity of Illusion

A shadow-painting (*skiagraphēma*) is a painting that uses shadows to give depth to whatever image is being drawn. If we look at it at the proper distance, it will give a greater semblance of reality to the image. If we look at it too closely, though, the artifice itself is noticeable, and therefore has the effect of distracting our attention and making us less able to maintain the illusion that what we are looking at is the object represented rather than the representation. The consequences of this depend, in part, on the purpose of the shadow-painting, and of our examination of it. One might look at the shadow-painting because one wants to see, for example, a pretty flower. Perhaps one even thinks the painting *is* a pretty flower. In either of these circumstances, to have one's attention drawn to the artifice might have the effect of undermining the purpose of one's desired activity. If looked at through this lens, Socrates's observation that he is standing too close to the shadows might appear to indicate that the problems he has identified with the third definition (and more precisely the third account of the account within the third definition) have destroyed the experience he, Socrates, had hoped for.

Knowing how Socrates is characterized in the *Theaetetus*, this scenario is unlikely, insofar as he would not seem to be someone who wants to maintain illusions if it means likewise maintaining his ignorance of them. In light of this, a more readily adoptable interpretation would have it that Socrates has discovered that their analysis has caused them to stand "too close" to the illusion for the *illusion's* sake, thereby allowing him and Theaetetus to discard it happily, since illusions distort reality and are to be rejected when possible. This way of reading the situation would fit comfortably into the generally accepted interpretation of Plato's thinking, and of the so-called Socratic Method. Might there be another way? I believe that the answer to this question is yes. I will demonstrate it by pointing to two examples we have already discussed so far, namely, the learning of music and the learning of a language.[31]

We discussed earlier the activity of learning to play music. At first the composition of the music has the effect of making one feel in some way good—that is, in some way emotionally or intellectually stimulated. When one begins to play, it is difficult and one finds oneself preoccupied with details that, on their own, fail to achieve the harmony that one expects it to (and the harmony that initially compelled one's interest).[32] One might find that the process here has caused the illusion of the music to be shattered. One sees the artifice when one attempts to craft something. Indeed, to be an artist is to develop a mature, sophisticated relationship to artifice: the artist foregoes the immediate experience of the work of art as something already completed. To appreciate the work of art, too, one must develop an attitude that is reconciled to the fact that it was crafted, which is to say that it is made up of constituent parts that, when isolated (i.e., stripped of the compositional context of the finished piece) do not share in the beauty of the work as a whole. One reconciles oneself to this, not for the sake of shattering illusion and seeing that works of art are not beautiful in parts as well as in wholes (and therefore, by implication, not beautiful at all), but rather so that one can better understand their beauty, in order that one can both appreciate them and strive to accomplish their beauty oneself.

One might also think of the learning of language in this regard. Just as it would be silly for someone to look at the painting too closely in order to "refute" its illusion, or to listen to a song carefully in order to demonstrate that its individual notes are not intrinsically beautiful to listen to, it would be equally silly to learn how to speak a language in order to shatter the illusion that its sounds are foreign. On the contrary, though the process of learning the language is often difficult, and one must speak poorly and in a way that can be embarrassing while one is learning, at the end, one is left with transparent access to meanings and to forms of expression. This example of language is useful in connection to the consideration of knowledge, I think, because, unlike the cases of paintings and music, one is less commonly satisfied to "enjoy" the foreign sounds of that language—that is, one is more explicitly directed at its needing to be understood.

What does this have to do with Socrates? Having completed what turns out to be the last account of knowledge as true opinion with an account, Socrates claims to have become too aware of the artifice of their shadow-painting. Like a painter, he is conscious of the ways in which they have tried to reenact what is real, and is no longer oriented to appreciate this particular instance of it. What he is well-oriented to, though, is a more highly cultivated ability to see the painting. Given the time to rest, he will be able better to appreciate what currently appears illusory.

To continue with this analogy, we must articulate what the illusion is that has been shattered. The answer to this question is knowledge. Drawn as they were by a conception of knowledge, they have approached too close to it, and have thus shattered the illusion. Having discovered that no account will be capable of providing the kind of guarantee that the illusion of knowledge indicated was necessary, they have discovered (or, more likely, Socrates has drawn attention to) the fact that they had generated the artifice themselves. In other words, the pursuit of knowledge led them—by way of an illusion—to the recognition that wisdom was the goal they were in fact accomplishing. What is generated out of the recognition of their illusory conception of knowledge is wisdom. Knowledge is the image of wisdom.

This notion that knowledge is an image of wisdom relates to a discussion about image-making that occurs the following day, as it is portrayed in the *Sophist*. There, Theaetetus is engaged in a conversation with an Eleatic Stranger, aiming at capturing an adequate account of the sophist in order that this figure can be distinguished from the philosopher. During that conversation, the Stranger draws a distinction between two kinds of image-making. One is concerned with imitating the proportions of an original, such that the original is replicated as accurately as possible. This practice the Stranger calls "eikastics" (235d1–236b2). The second form of image-making is concerned with shaping the proportions of the imitation, not according to its correct proportions, but rather according to the proportions that will best conform to the perspective of those who look at it. This practice the Stranger calls "phantastics" (236b4–c4). The phantastic art is less attentive to the truth of the original than the eikastic art is. Moreover, the phantastic art bears with it the danger of creating the impression that the falsely rendered image is an accurate presentation of the original.

In the context of our discussion, it would seem that the conception of knowledge with which Theaetetus and (ostensibly, for pedagogical purposes) Socrates were operating was a phantastic image of wisdom, but with an intriguing twist. While they had operated according to the assumption that knowledge was a kind of correspondence of language and reality, it was because of that inadequate account of knowledge that they were led to cultivate their dialectical practice. As a result of cultivating that practice, Theaetetus has begun a process, which Socrates has developed throughout his life, of cultivating wisdom. This notion will be made clearer to us as we discuss Theaetetus's wind-egg.

f. *Aporia*

Let us now return to the problem Socrates finds in his third interpretation of the account.[33] This third interpretation stated that the account adds to true opinion the demonstration of what differentiates it from everything else. In other words, giving an account consists in demonstrating the particular attributes of the object of one's speech, for the purpose of distinguishing it from all other objects. Thc account, on this third interpretation, is essentially classification. In reflecting on this third interpretation, though, Socrates has discovered that the differentiation would have had to be present in the true opinion already for that true opinion to be identifiable as such. This presents a difficulty for trying to distinguish the function of true opinion from the function of the account. Prior to the account, was one not touching on anything that differentiates the object from all others? It would appear not, if the account is to add anything to the initial true opinion. Otherwise, true opinion would already in advance contain the element the speech was to add, and we would be doing no more than defining true opinion plus an element of true opinion (i.e., differentiation). True opinion must already be about differentiation (209d1–2). Socrates begins to identify his own speech as exhortations given by a blind man (209e2–3). The dilemma is as follows: to add to what we already have in true opinion (a differentia) is utterly redundant. Making speeches, on the model with which they are operating, accomplishes nothing, unless there is something added by the speech. If the speech does indeed consist in providing the differentia, then in what way is it different in speech than it was in unvoiced true opinion? If it is moving from opinion of differentia to knowledge of differentia, then it would appear that the definition of knowledge we are now working with is true opinion with an account that is knowledge of differentia, or, we are saying that knowledge is true opinion with knowledge of differentia. Knowledge therefore appears to be true opinion with knowledge. The definition they are left with is question-begging.[34]

In response to this new disappointment, Theaetetus tells Socrates (when prompted by him) that he is no longer pregnant, that he has articulated not only all he had but more than that, because of Socrates (210b6–7). If Theaetetus continues to strive to articulate himself in the future, he will hopefully continue to do so until he reaches a point at which he has reached the limit of the adequacy of his account, with the result that he will therefore be inspired to proceed again to give a new account. Socrates tells Theaetetus that he suspects that whether or not Theaetetus is pregnant again, he will be better off for having talked about these matters with Socrates. They, together, will have made him better at delivering when he is next pregnant, and, even if he is never pregnant again, they will have made him tamer in his future discussions.[35] This, says Socrates, is all the god has made him able to do for anyone. Socrates then claims that he will go to the King Archon, and that they ought to meet the next day at dawn, to continue their discussion, which they do.

With this, the dialogue ends. To Theaetetus, who looks for a "solution" to the problem of knowledge, it appears, no doubt, that their conversation was unsuccessful. We, however, have already seen that that is an insufficient way to view the conversation.[36]

Conclusion

In this chapter we have completed and made explicit an account of the process that Socrates has sought to undertake with Theaetetus. I have claimed that Socrates wants to make Theaetetus see that the process of philosophical inquiry in which they are engaged is not for the purpose of deriving some end result, without remainder; this is how it would be if they were examining a mathematical problem, but they are not. On the contrary, Socrates repeatedly shows Theaetetus that they are engaging in an activity whose results will be either inconclusive or conclusively false. Motivated by a sense of wonder at the world—by a recognition that the world is more knowable than has as yet been made apparent to them, and that it is also intrinsically worth trying better to know—they inquire, only to discover that their inquiries fail to account completely for the wonder that they experience. They are left, thus (if the activity is undertaken seriously and if the impasses to which they are led are sufficiently recognized), with an increased and more subtle sense of wonder. Indeed, in keeping with Socrates's account of the perception of the philosopher, one might say they are cultivating a higher degree of sensitivity to wonder. The derivative accomplishment of such a practice—which is already of intrinsic value, insofar as recognizing that the world is good and worth striving to understand is of intrinsic value—is to produce a person capable of engaging patiently and thoughtfully in conversations of this sort with others. This is essentially the way in which Socrates characterizes the practice—though with muted acknowledgment of its importance—in the closing paragraph of the dialogue (210c1–5).

If cultivating the ability to engage in conversations of this sort patiently and thoughtfully is what Socrates hopes Theaetetus has accomplished as a result of the conversation, we might ask what we have learned about knowledge in the examination of Theaetetus's second and third definitions. I have argued that in each case the account of knowledge that is explicitly presented places emphasis on an attribute essential to the nature of knowledge, but that in each case the attribute is only a part of knowledge. If one examines each part individually—as Socrates and Theaetetus do in their examinations of perception (*aisthēsis*), opinion (*doxa*), and account (*logos*)—two important consequences resulting from such a method can lead one away from what one seeks. First, having identified that a particular candidate is not knowledge, one can mistakenly disregard it in further inquiry, as Socrates and Theaetetus do after having rejected perception (*aisthēsis*) as a candidate. This was a mistake, because *aisthēsis* is an essential part of knowledge. Not only does it provide resources about which one can deliberate, it is also an immediate apprehension whose character is capable of being cultivated, such that one can perceive more and more deeply, as a result of one's education and experience. Second, examining each candidate individually results in one being unable to see that those parts produce something greater than their sum.

What is this product that is greater than its sum? It is the integrated, organized activity of apprehending the world through the senses, producing attitudes and emotional responses to what is apprehended, retaining these for oneself, allowing them to remain within one such that one can revisit them, and applying the organization of this, accumulated over time, to one's further apprehensions, which is to say, to transform the character, the shape that each of these takes. I am, in short, talking about the integration of perception, opinion, memory, reflection, and deliberation into the activity of *living*, and living *as* a human being. The unity in principle of all these component activities and powers is the given condition of every person, and does not have to be accomplished; it is a unity, however, that can be cultivated, and this is the key to our education. This structural whole leaves open the possibility of subjecting each of the described attributes to questioning, and thus to self-conscious transformation, to transformation that strives better to use them. It is an erotic structure, insofar as the recognition of the incompleteness of knowledge is—in one who has been cultivated sufficiently to recognize it—a necessary condition for the recognition of the intrinsic beauty of that which is to be known. We must persist in holding it at a distance so that we can continue to pursue a deeper understanding of it. If the whole of these human capacities counts as knowledge in the generic sense available to us for the sake of cultivation, then this latter, self-conscious striving aimed at both the world and at the transformation of one's own soul is called wisdom.

CONCLUSION

The *Theaetetus* as a Whole

In this discussion, I have argued that the *Theaetetus* is both, on the one hand, a presentation of intuitively plausible approaches to understanding how we use our psychological resources to establish an accurate representation of the world and a demonstration of the problems these approaches run into, and, on the other hand, a dramatic presentation of philosophical education. I have argued that these two aspects of the dialogue are intimately related. Generally, I have done so by trying to solve the problems that emerge with each of these approaches by understanding knowledge not in terms of the possession of a result, but in terms of the changes one undergoes in the *process of learning*. I have ultimately argued that knowledge is not a matter of constructing a mental representation of the world but is much more a practical matter of establishing a meaningful way of living in the world. I focus especially on the way this meaningful relationship to the world is established through negotiating with the perspectives of others, and so my thesis ultimately argues that issues that initially look like simple matters of epistemology ultimately turn out to be inseparable from matters of ethics as well as matters of education, specifically, of concern for the education of the soul.[1]

I have performed this analysis by placing primary emphasis on Socrates's philosophical education of Theaetetus. I have argued that Socrates seeks to cultivate in Theaetetus an orientation toward the world that primarily values the process of dialectical inquiry. In order to accomplish that task he asks Theaetetus to give an account of knowledge. Over the course of their exploration of the nature of knowledge, Theaetetus must put his thoughts into words for Socrates to scrutinize, and is forced to think through the implications of his definitions. These practices constitute the essential components of the initiation into philosophical education. The first essential practice—that is, articulating one's thoughts for the purpose of being subjected to scrutiny—has the aim of generating knowledge of oneself, and in two related senses. First, it generates awareness of the particular unreflected-upon content of one's own thinking; second, it generates awareness of oneself as a site of unreflected-upon presumptions in general. The second essential practice—that is, thinking through the implications of definitions—has the aim of generating awareness of the reach of one's ideas about the world, and of the fact that those ideas bring with them unforeseen commitments.

Though these practices constitute only the initial stage of philosophical education, each has the logical character of being indeterminate in relation to its end, thus each counts, likewise, as the final stage of philosophical education. The activity of giving account of one's own presumptions is an indeterminate process if indeed one is, simply by living, constantly in the process of generating new presumptions. As was suggested in chapter 2, subjecting one's ideas to scrutiny ought best to be understood not as the finite task of purging oneself of presumptions in order to begin thinking philosophically on a solid foundation, but rather as an act of psychological hygiene, in which the examination of one's own thinking is an ongoing process of purging perpetually accumulated, unreflected-upon ideas. The activity of working through the implications of one's ideas is made more compelling as the ideas become more compelling. We find empirical evidence of this fact in the practice of perpetually returning to the same powerful texts over the course of a lifetime. As we accumulate more experience to apply to our ideas, those ideas become like music played in rooms with increasingly improved acoustics; they resonate more, producing, so to speak, a richer, more satisfying sound. Each of these practices cannot in principle "accomplish" their aim, if by their aim we imagine an end at which the process is completed, and one is compelled to move on to something else. Rather, the only sense in which the aim is to be accomplished is by cultivating the desire and the ability to continue to live in a way that is open to participating in that kind of discourse.

Regarding this accomplishment of the process into which Socrates aims to initiate Theaetetus, I insinuate that it is a "cultivated" state of the soul, which is to say that it is something one is shaped into over a period of time. It would be naive to assume that, having engaged for the first time in these practices, Theaetetus has completely and permanently absorbed them, and even more naive to assume that this will have solidified what I have on several occasions referred to as a wise orientation toward the world. Such a thing is a process undergone over a lifetime. The need for time and the persistent repetition of these lessons in order to move from a merely rational recognition of what the lessons afford to the embedding of those lessons into one's character illustrates the significance of the fact that knowledge is best understood as grounded in character, in human life. Specifically, it illustrates the fact that the cultivation of one's understanding of the world lies not entirely within one's own conscious control, but lies rather within the context of the kind of person one has become. The kind of person one has become *involves* conscious reflection and deliberation, but is not grounded in these conscious capacities. Let us briefly summarize the way in which the critical assessment of the three definitions of knowledge demonstrated the character of knowledge as something grounded in human life, before explicitly restating the conclusions to be drawn from the exercise.

The first definition—that knowledge is perception—is discarded by Socrates and Theaetetus, ultimately, on the grounds that perception alone cannot account for the conceptual edifice that must be assumed for knowledge to occur. Specifically, in the concluding moments of the discussion, they first establish that perception alone—which we should note, again, is perception *abstracted* from its active participation in the integrated whole of the living human being—is only capable of showing the appearance of constant motion. Following the establishment of this, they note that perception is not even capable of establishing this, because the perceiver as much as the perceived object is in motion. The rigorous articulation of constant motion therefore implies a reality in which anything both is and is not, including knowledge. Perception functions as much as a definition of non-knowledge as it does of knowledge (182e10–11). From this, Socrates further points to the fact that perception alone is not capable of accounting for awareness of itself. To sort through and distinguish between perceptions requires something else for which those perceptions occur, namely, the soul (185d7–e2). Perceptions, therefore, are established as inadequate to the task of accounting for knowledge, both because they are incapable of putting to rest their proper object, and because they are not even capable of establishing the fact that they are perceived.

As I mentioned in chapter 4, while this definition of knowledge is rejected, Socrates explicitly points out that it is only under the current terms that perception is disqualified as a candidate for knowledge. It is "at least in terms of the quest for all things to be in motion" that they must reject it (183c3–4). He and Theaetetus never explicitly discard the account of the co-emergence of perceiver and perceived object found in the metaphysical doctrine of infinite motions (156a4–157c1), and never justifiably discard the possibility that perception plays a role in knowledge. Indeed, the account of the philosopher (172c3–177c7) strongly implies that the way in which knowledge is manifest is through what it is that a person perceives in the act of perceiving. In the movement to the second and third definitions, in which perception is excluded from consideration, Socrates and Theaetetus repeat the erroneous practice of abstracting particular human capacities from the whole of the living human being, and therefore repeatedly demonstrate that that abstracted candidate is incapable, on its own, of accounting for our experience of knowledge.

The second definition—that knowledge is true opinion—is ultimately discarded on the grounds that one can hold a true opinion for unjustified reasons. Indeed, as Socrates points out, the whole art of rhetoric is premised on the notion that one can persuade others to hold opinions without adequate grounds (201a8–c8). Though this is the ultimate point at which Socrates and Theaetetus reject the definition of knowledge as true opinion, they arrive at this point by way of arguments that continue to develop the criticism of the abstraction of human capacities. First, Socrates initially excludes from the consideration of opinion both learning and forgetting (188a1–4), with the result that these are shown to be absolutely essential conditions of opinion. The implicit emphasis on the processes by which we arrive at and stray from opinions as necessary for understanding opinions opens the discussion to the centerpiece of this definition, namely the consideration of the two images of knowledge as true opinion, the wax image, and the bird cage image.

The first of these images involved a wax slab representing the soul's ability to receive the impression of what the person perceives. The constitution of the slab—which is insinuated to be a reflection of the character of the person—dictates the extent to which the person is able to hold an accurate and long-lasting impression (i.e., a true opinion) of what has been perceived. In their analysis of this image, Socrates and Theaetetus eventually decide that it is flawed on the grounds that it accounts for error only in the case of the mixture of thinking and perceiving, while error is said to occur also in thinking alone. If it is unable to account for a real phenomenon of our experience of the world, then it is no good. In contrast with their grounds for rejecting the image, I argued that the example of error in thinking presented by Socrates and endorsed by Theaetetus does not occur in thinking independent of perception. Indeed, I argued that the way in which the discussion of the wax image is managed further emphasizes the poverty and erroneousness of the abstraction of thinking from perception. The second image was that of a bird cage, with each bird representing some piece of knowledge. In this second image the intent had been to account for error—and therefore to overcome the inadequacy of the wax image—by first distinguishing between knowledge one has immediately at one's disposal (i.e., the bird in the hand) and in use, and knowledge one has accumulated but of which one is not currently conscious (i.e., the bird in the cage). Error, then, would occur in the space between knowledge as possession (in the cage) and knowledge as having at hand. Though it was explicitly designed for the purpose of better accounting for error, this account failed according to Socrates and Theaetetus because it could not explain, either in the collection of bits of knowledge, and in the recollection of bits of knowledge we have already in our possession, what process guides our collecting if not knowledge itself. For Socrates and Theaetetus, it appeared as though the acquisition of knowledge in this image was question-begging, in the sense that one's knowledge of the "bird" one is pursuing must precede the pursuit. I argued, by contrast, that the problem with the bird cage image, as with the wax image, was that it paid insufficient attention to the natural and constitutive passivity in our acquisition of understanding of the world. The bird cage image insisted on human knowledge as something an active agent is constantly engaged in hunting down. This was an especially egregious error, insofar as they were dealing with the nature of true opinion, something that, when thought of strictly on its own terms, it is easy to identify as having emerged at least in part from passive acquisition.

The discourse surrounding the second definition of knowledge fails because of its insistence on abstracting parts of the human soul from the whole of life. It does so, first, by excluding the conditions by which opinion comes to be and passes away, and second—in each of the two images—by isolating the active agent-like aspects of human activity from the passive shaping of understanding, and third, by isolating the intellectual dimension from the perceptual. Each of these forms of isolation rests on the presumption—one Theaetetus appears to hold sincerely, but one Socrates seems to be *using* for the pedagogical purpose of making Theaetetus think his way to that insight—that knowledge is to be found only in a part of the human experience of the world, rather than in its integrated whole.

The third definition—that knowledge is true opinion with an account—fails for Socrates and Theaetetus on the grounds that, in the analysis of what is meant by "an account," they discover that the characteristic most required in accounting for one's opinion—that is, articulating the differentiating characteristic of the object of knowledge—itself depends upon knowledge of that characteristic. By the end of the account, they find themselves left with a definition of knowledge that amounts to true opinion with knowledge, which appears to be question-begging. In my analysis of their discussion, I argued that the three accounts of the account provided by Socrates, and the failure of each of these to prove adequately that speech can secure knowledge about the world, have the effect of shattering the illusion, the shadow-painting, of knowledge with which one is inclined to operate. That is, through the analysis of what can be accomplished by giving an account—to reflect one's own thoughts back to oneself, to articulate the attributes of the object one seeks to know, and to differentiate the object one seeks to know from all other objects—one discovers that speech is inadequate to the task of securing the exhaustive verification that the opinion one has about the object is an exact reflection of the being of the object. The illusion that this is the accomplishment of philosophical inquiry is dissolved. Insofar as one had been aspiring to accomplish something illusory, though, this insight is profound—though it is not an insight Theaetetus has managed to derive for himself, as this insight takes much more time to develop.

In the examination of the three definitions of knowledge provided by Theaetetus, I have argued that we consistently find the mistake of isolating and abstracting human capacities from the whole of the living human being. The result of this abstraction is the inability to account for the character of our insight into the nature of the world. I have also argued, particularly with respect to the third definition of knowledge, that we find that the human capacity to use language to give account of our opinions about the world cannot provide the guarantee of the correspondence of our psychological resources and the world as it is, and that the dissolution of this illusory appearance of the accomplishment of thinking directs us to what can really be accomplished by thinking.

This last point is worth emphasizing once more. The analysis of the means by which we are able to display for ourselves and others the nature of our own thoughts—that is, the analysis of *logos*—causes the dissolution of the pretense that one can accomplish the very objectively guaranteed, certain knowledge that initially motivates our intellectual pursuits. In its place, what emerges—what the characterization of Socrates in the Platonic corpus *demonstrates* as an attitude that can possibly emerge, and an attitude that one ought to strive to accomplish—is an orientation toward the world that I have mentioned throughout the text, namely the orientation that perceives the world to be something that it is intrinsically desirable to strive to know, and yet one that recognizes that the world is something that one is, at best, able to hold admiringly at a distance. This distance is that between the accumulated understanding that is able to inform a person's cultivated ability to think and to perceive more deeply what is present, and the guarantee of the certainty of the being of what appears that remains elusive. This orientation I have characterized as belonging to the wise, and I have called it an orientation toward the world and toward knowledge of the world that is built on an erotic structure. In this respect, the great insight of the *Theaetetus*, the insight that eludes Theaetetus himself at the end of his conversation with Socrates, is that knowledge is the image of wisdom. The persistent pursuit of the image gives shape to, cultivates the accomplishment of, the process of which it is an image.

NOTES

Introduction

1. See Francis MacDonald Cornford, *Plato's Theory of Knowledge* (New York: Liberal Arts, 1935); David Bostock, *Plato's Theaetetus* (Oxford: Clarendon, 1988); Myles Burnyeat, "Introduction" to *The Theaetetus of Plato* (Indianapolis, Ind.: Hackett, 1990).

2. Kenneth Sayre, *Plato's Literary Garden* (Notre Dame, Ind.: University of Notre Dame Press, 1995).

3. Andrea Tschemplik, *Knowledge and Self-Knowledge in Plato's Theaetetus* (Landham, Md.: Rowman and Littlefield, 2008).

4. See Drew Hyland, *Finitude and Transcendence in the Platonic Dialogues* (Albany: SUNY Press, 1995), 150.

Chapter 1

1. See Ronald M. Polansky, *Philosophy and Knowledge* (Lewisburg: Associated University Presses, 1992), 34–35. Polansky points out that the conversations in the *Theaetetus* and *Phaedo* occurring outside of Athens is significant in part because these frame the dramatic developments surrounding the death of Socrates. They demonstrate its significance by showing people distant in both space and time from the event continuing to discuss it. See also Paul Stern, *Knowledge and Politics in Plato's Theaetetus* (New York: Cambridge University Press, 2008), 14.

2. Stern (*Knowledge and Politics*, 13) emphasizes the significance of this introductory discussion in terms of the way that it "substantively shapes our judgment of that argument."

3. This is the case in the narrative of the *Theaetetus*: whoever we take to be the omniscient author of the preparatory dialogue between Euclides and Terpsion, it is Euclides who authored the dialogue between Socrates, Theodorus, and Theaetetus. Thus we must bear in mind the fact that a different set of motivations were supposed to be operative in the opening discussion as compared to what follows it. Stern (*Knowledge and Politics*, 19) argues that Euclides's editorial decision (to be discussed in detail in section 5 below) to transform the dialogue from indirect to direct discourse aims at obscuring precisely the consideration of the reporter's motivations. See also Jane Harrison, "Plato's Prologue: *Theaetetus* 142a–143c," *Tulane Studies in Philosophy* 27 (1978): 106. By contrast, Plato's introduction of the omniscient author puts Euclides's efforts on display for us, bringing that activity itself potentially under our scrutiny.

4. See the epigraph to this chapter from Aristotle, *Physics*, trans. R. P. Hardie and R. K. Gaye, in *The Complete Works of Aristotle Vol 1*, ed. Jonathan Barnes, 315–446 (Princeton, N.J.: Princeton University Press, 1995), I.1 184a17–19.

5. The uncertainty concerning the date has to do with the fact that battles occurred in Corinth in both time frames, either of which could have been the one in which Theaetetus died. See Seth Benardete, "Theaetetus Commentary," in *The Being of the Beautiful:*

Plato's Theaetetus, Sophist and Statesman: Translation and Commentary (Chicago: University of Chicago Press, 1984), I.184n2. See Debra Nails *The People of Plato: A Prosopography of Plato and Other Socratics* (Indianapolis, Ind.: Hackett, 2002), 276. Nails argues that Theaetetus most likely did not die in 369, in part, because "Athens was almost certainly not mustering forty-six-year old academics for hoplite combat by 369; Theaetetus's skillful soldiering (142b–c) was far more likely to have been exhibited when he was of military age, twenty-four." Moreover, according to Nails, "Euclides' 30–km. walk, from which he has just returned as the dialogue's frame begins, is more likely for a man of fifty-nine than a man of eighty-one."

6. See Aristotle, *Metaphysics*, trans. W. D. Ross, in *The Complete Works of Aristotle Vol 2*, ed. Jonathan Barnes, 1552–1728. (Princeton, N.J.: Princeton University Press, 1995), IX.1 1046a29–33. There we learn about the Megarians that they deny the notion that potential has any reality until it has been realized as actuality. The Megarians deny the existence of a kind of non-being that has any bearing on the domain of reality. In presenting this outer frame of the dialogue, I argue for the relevance of as-yet unrealized potential in the discussion of the development of character.

7. For a good discussion of the various layers of remove from the particular events depicted in what follows from this opening discussion between Terpsion and Euclides, see Seth Benardete, "Plato's *Theaetetus*: On The Way of the Logos," in *The Argument of the Action: Essays on Greek Poetry and Philosophy* (Chicago: University of Chicago Press, 2000), 297–98.

8. Note that the Greek—"*arti ō Terpsion, ē palai ex agrou*?" literally "lately, Terpsion, or long ago out from the country"—gives no indication of whether the "just now" or "lately" in the first part of the disjunction or the "from the country" in its second part has to do with where Terpsion is. If so, this sentence would read transparently as though it were the first of a conversation, as it is translated in the Levett-Burnyeat version: "Are you only just *in from* the country, Terpsion? Or have you *been here* some time? [my emphasis]". By smoothing over the abruptness of this opening line for stylistically understandable reasons, this latter translation ends up obscuring something important.

9. See Hyland, *Finitude and Transcendence*, 158.

10. Stern (*Knowledge and Politics*, 24–25) speculates that perhaps death is rendered so conspicuous here because it is the site of particularity par excellence.

11. See Paul Friedlander, *Plato: The Dialogues, Second and Third Period, Volume 3* (Princeton University Press, 1969), 146. Friedlander points out that the discussion of Theaetetus's character here will only take on its full significance when we see his, still immature though nascent, intelligence at work in the dialogue. We are given the advantage to recognize what foundations have been laid down by his conversation with Socrates, but only in retrospect.

12. Character is the central theme around which Aristotle's *Nicomachean Ethics* is oriented. My discussion of character is drawn heavily from that treatise.

13. Polansky (*Philosophy and Knowledge*, 37) argues that his failure to commit his experience with Socrates to his soul illustrates that Euclides does not really have knowledge of the conversation, and suggests that this foreshadows the commitment to the soul as an important aspect of knowledge. Though he surely is pointing to an important aspect of knowledge, his interpretation of Euclides's failure seems implausible; it is unlikely that Euclides would commit such a lengthy conversation to memory. More importantly, though, it obscures the importance of the passivity of memory, and our lack of complete control over the future uses of our learning experiences. In at least the specific sense of his

need to write down his thoughts in order to recall it years (or decades) later, I take Euclides to be like all of us, and therefore not specifically demonstrative of a kind of failure.

14. See Plato, *Phaedo*, trans. G. M. A. Grube, in *Plato: Complete Works*, ed. John M. Cooper, 49–100 (Indianapolis, Ind.: Hackett, 1997), 59c. Euclides and Terpsion are mentioned as being present at Socrates's death.

15. Socrates here refers to Hesiod's *Theogony*, 915, "and he made love to Mnemosyne with beautiful hair / From whom nine Muses with golden diadems were born." Hesiod, *Works and Days and Theogony* (Indianapolis, Ind.: Hackett, 1993).

16. Compare Plato *Phaedrus*, trans. Alexander Nehamas and Paul Woodruff, in *Plato: Complete Works*, ed. John M. Cooper, 506–56. (Indianapolis, Ind.: Hackett, 1997), 227d6–228e5. Phaedrus describes his editorial choices in representing Lysias's speech in terms of his limited memory.

17. Here again, we are given a subtle reminder of the environmental conditions that facilitate their, and our, access to the text. Were it not for the slave boy—were it not for the political conditions in which Euclides has a slave boy—perhaps the interest in having a long conversation read to them would have waned because of their fatigue.

18. Euclides is here converting the dialogue from narrative to dramatic form. See Aristotle, *Poetics*, trans. I. Bywater, in *The Complete Works of Aristotle Vol. 2*, ed. Jonathan Barnes, 2316–40 (Princeton, N.J.: Princeton University Press, 1995), 1448a19–24. Tschemplik (*Knowledge and Self-Knowledge*, 17) points out that this points to an attribute unique to the *Theaetetus*: though several dialogues have narrative distance between the event and its reporter (Socrates himself reporting in the *Charmides, Lysis* and *Republic*, Apollodorus in the *Symposium*, and Cephalus in *Parmenides*), and though a few have an exterior narrative-framing dialogue (*Phaedo*, *Euthydemus*, *Protagoras*, and *Theaetetus*), among these, only the *Theaetetus* maintains direct dialogue in both frame and framed narrative.

19. Cornford (*Plato's Theory of Knowledge*, 17n1) argues that these editorial decisions by Euclides ought to be taken as representing Plato's own changing views of narrative as "tiresome," pointing to the fact that the *Parmenides*—which uses far less narration—was written later. It is hard to make the claim that Plato came to conclude that narration was tiresome using as the source of evidence an elaborate example of such narrative.

20. Tschemplik (*Knowledge and Self-Knowledge*, 18) offers an interesting account of Euclides's motivations. She argues that Euclides identifies the speakers as trivial as compared to the truths they speak, and that the truths are to be read as objective, rather than to be muddied by too much emphasis on their source. The position Tschemplik attributes to Euclides, whether it is that of Euclides or not, is one I will be explicitly arguing against, in interpreting the dialogue as a reflection on philosophical education.

21. See Amelie Oksenberg Rorty, "A Speculative Note on some Dramatic Elements in the *Theaetetus*," *Phronesis* 17 (1972): 228. Rorty argues that "we are given no indication that the dialogue is unreliable: there is no need to return to Eucleides and Terpsion to close the dialogue." It is not clear what the connection between these two claims is, but more importantly, it seems to me that what we are called to do is precisely to attend to the reliability of Euclides's report, not for the purpose of treating this particular character with suspicion, but rather in order to reflect on what we are deprived of in making our own interpretations. Moreover, it serves as a reminder that we must make interpretive decisions without the luxury of justified certainty.

22. Myles Burnyeat ("Introduction to *The Theaetetus of Plato*, 1990], 127) speculates that perhaps Plato intended Euclides's report on his method of preparation to force us to ask

ourselves whether we should take ourselves to be reading an actual conversation between Socrates, Theaetetus, and Theodorus, or merely a testimony. He suggests that perhaps Plato wants us to make the decision ourselves how to read it. I would agree that we are being put in a situation where our attention is drawn to our interpretive decisions, as well as the responsibilities they entail. It seems to me obvious that Plato intends us to be aware that we are *not* "listening to them directly." Indeed, the deeper point is that whether aware of our restricted access to the events reported or not, we must make decisions we cannot concretely justify.

Chapter 2

1. This definition of wisdom appears rather empty. However, the only way to articulate wisdom in such a way that it appears meaningful is through lived experience. Insofar as the material with which wisdom operates is spontaneous action in the world, merely articulating in the most general terms how it is oriented to and what it does with the world cannot tell the whole story. This is one of the great virtues of the Platonic corpus, because it *shows* us Socrates's wisdom in action. This is also why my discussion of wisdom is developed through the narrative of Socrates's interactions with Theaetetus and Theodorus.

2. See Aristotle, *Nicomachean Ethics*, trans. Joe Sachs (Newburyport, Mass.: Focus, 2002), book 1, chapter 13.

3. This is a point Socrates gets Theaetetus explicitly to gesture to at the end of the analysis of the first definition of knowledge (185e1), when Theaetetus realizes that it is "the soul itself by itself" that is the site of perception. It is at this moment that Socrates declares that Theaetetus is beautiful (185e3).

4. See *Phaedrus* 277b8–c3, where Socrates explicitly states that one's speech must be adapted to respond to the nature of the given person's soul. See also Hyland, *Finitude and Transcendence*, 20–23, for a discussion of the importance of recognizing Socrates's tailoring of his speech for interpreting the Platonic dialogues. For a specific discussion of tailored speech used in this dialogue in relation to Theaetetus the mathematician (as opposed to musician, or literary man), see Rosemary Desjardins, *The Rational Enterprise: Logos in Plato's Theaetetus* (Albany: SUNY Press, 1990), 77–79.

5. Though it is not clearly stated what sort of crowd has gathered, it is insinuated at 146a1–2 that there is one.

6. See Nails (*The People of Plato*, 281).

7. Ibid., 274–78.

8. Tschemplik (*Knowledge and Self-Knowledge*, 25) suggests that Theodorus's clumsy way of speaking here is the result of "the fact that he is in love with Theaetetus after all." This is surely possible, and if this is the case, it would perhaps mitigate to some extent the possibility that Theodorus envies Theaetetus.

9. This is affirmed, first, in the whole dramatic arc of *Alcibiades I*, and at such specific spots in other dialogues as *Charmides*, 153d and *Lysis*, 211e–212a. For a discussion of Socrates's relationship with Alcibiades as it is portrayed in the *Alcibiades I* in particular, see Patricia Fagan, *Plato and Tradition: The Poetic and Cultural Context of Philosophy* (Evanston, Ill.: Northwestern University Press, 2013), 5–20.

10. Socrates's interest in the young men of Athens is elsewhere displayed in the corpus: in the *Charmides*, upon returning from battle, and after having been asked about things related to the battle, Socrates begins asking "about the young men, whether there were any who had become distinguished for wisdom or beauty or both" (153d6–7). In-

deed, the *Charmides* begins with Socrates reflecting on the special relationship one has to one's home.

11. Tschemplik (*Knowledge and Self-Knowledge*, 24) interprets this passage to consist in Socrates claiming that he cares for Athenians as distinct from caring for all young people. This is odd because it seems clear that Socrates is claiming that it is the contingent fact of where he lives that organizes his priorities.

12. One piece of evidence of the extent of Socrates's engagement with the events of the city is his display of knowledge of the financial status of Theaetetus's family (144c8). See Tschemplik. *Knowledge and Self-Knowledge*, 26, for a discussion of this point. See also *Charmides*, 157e–158b, for evidence of Socrates's extensive knowledge of Charmides's family.

13. There are other sources of the development of political institutions, such as mere inheritance (in which case there need not be any deliberation to perpetuate existing policies) and arbitrary contingencies (such as the presence of unexpected natural resources which, when discovered, shape policy in this or that way). Nonetheless, human conscious deliberation does have an important role to play, whether the public recognizes it or not.

14. This is essentially the mechanism that Socrates describes as causing the degeneration of the state in Book VIII of the *Republic*, each generation taking up political life according to terms not present for the previous generation.

15. An issue that I have not discussed here is *philia*. Polansky (*Philosophy and Knowledge*, 40) correctly points out Socrates's conviction that love has a central role in education, pointing specifically to *Phaedrus* 252c ff., and *Symposium* 206b ff. While I agree with Polansky that *philia* is central to philosophical education, I am arguing that this opening discussion about care for the Athenians has more to do with the instrumental and virtuous pursuits associated with political engagement. It is an ethical and political concern of Socrates to make friends. Once he has friends, he is able to engage most powerfully in education, as Polansky correctly points out, but the initial motivation is impersonal and principled.

16. See *The Republic of Plato*, trans. Allan Bloom (New York: Basic Books, 1968), 498b3–c4.

17. See *Apology*, in *Four Texts on Socrates*, trans. Thomas G. West and Grace Starry West, 63–98 (Ithaca, N.Y.: Cornell University Press, 1998), 21b1–22e5. Socrates presents his pursuit and inquiry of Athenians in terms of trying to prove to himself that he was not the wisest person. This characterization might lead one to think that he talks indifferently to everyone, or that his criteria rests solely on whether or not the particular person has yet to be shown to be unwise. This is misleading because he would no doubt have other reasons for engaging in conversations, reasons more related to cultivating relationships with others (as he is characterized as doing in many of the dialogues).

18. Nails, *The People of Plato*, 152–53.

19. See Jan Blitz, "The Holy and the Human: An Interpretation of Plato's *Euthyphro*," *Apeiron* 14 (1980): 24. Blitz points out that Euthyphro's failure to teach Socrates what is pious, according to his own formulation of what is involved in piety, "amounts to a failure to defend publicly his claim to be doing what is holy."

20. It should be noted that one of the themes that comes up in the dialogue is the fact that others openly mock Euthyphro, despite what appears to be some lucky successes at divination (*Euthyphro*, in *Four Texts on Socrates*, trans. Thomas G. West and Grace Starry West, 41–62 [Ithaca, N.Y.: Cornell University Press, 1998]), 3c1–4.

21. The insight that one's life lies not entirely within one's control, due to the web of interrelations within which one inevitably participates, plays a significant role in Gregory Bateson's conception of systems theory. See Gregory Bateson, *Steps to an Ecology of Mind* (Chicago: University of Chicago Press, 2000), 315. See particularly his account of successful forms of therapy used on alcoholics in "The Cybernetics of Self: A Theory of Alcoholism": "We know that no part of such an internally interactive system can have unilateral control over the remainder or over any other part. The mental characteristics are inherent or immanent in the ensemble as a whole."

22. I take the estimated ages of Hippothales, Lysis, and Menexenus from Nails, *The People of Plato*, 174, 195, 202, respectively.

23. Socrates is coaxed over to this discussion by Hippothales and Ctesippus, who name Mikkos, the wrestling instructor and friend of Socrates. See *Lysis*, trans. Stanley Lombardo, in *Plato: Complete Works*, ed. John M. Cooper, 687–707 (Indianapolis, Ind.: Hackett, 1997), 203a1–204a6. It is after this, and only after further questioning what specifically he is getting into (*Lysis*, 204b1–2) that Socrates joins them.

24. This issue of the potential danger of destructiveness in youth is relevant to Socrates. Both Charmides and Alcibiades to varying degress demonstrated themselves to be gifted, and to varying degrees (and in different ways) likewise demonstrated themselves in adulthood to be destructive. For a discussion of the lives of these people see Mark Munn, *The School of History* (University of California Press, 2000). See also Nails, *The People of Plato*. For a historical demonstration of the revolutionary and destructive character of youth, see the speech of Nicias from Thucydides's *History of the Peloponnesian War* (6.12–13). Nicias seeks to persuade the Athenians that to go to war in Sicily would be unwise, and would be the result of having been swayed by those "too young to command" who seek to be admired, and to maintain their private splendor at their country's risk.

25. Theodorus is limited by the narrowness of his interests. See *Republic*, 485d3–4.

26. It appears to be a pattern of Theodorus's to hastily praise, and for Plato to immediately contrast his hastiness with Socrates's more philosophical tendency to examine for himself what has been praised. See, for example, the opening of the *Sophist* in *The Being of the Beautiful*, trans. Seth Benardete, II, 1–68 (Chicago: University of Chicago Press, 2006). After Theodorus calls the Stranger from Elea a true philosopher, Socrates wonders aloud if it is in fact a God coming to judge them (216a), seemingly questioning Theodorus's confident judgment regarding who counts as a philosopher.

27. This is a tendency Socrates will later emphasize in his discussion of the craftspeople in the *Apology*, 22d1–e2.

28. This discussion of Theodorus's lack of expertise concerning the face implies that, because Theodorus is not sufficiently knowledgeable to judge each of them to have ugly appearances, he is a poor judge of the beautiful.

29. See *Laches*, trans. Rosamond Kent Sprague, in *Plato: Complete Works*, ed. John M. Cooper, 664–86 (Indianapolis, Ind.: Hackett, 1997), 187e–188a1. Nicias describes conversing with Socrates: "Whoever comes into close contact with Socrates and associates with him in conversation must necessarily, even if he began by conversing about something quite different in the first place, keep on being led about by the man's arguments until he submits to answering questions about himself concerning both his present manner of life and the life he has lived hitherto." Theodorus appears to be oblivious to this fact, which is certainly borne out in this dialogue, as he will, on several occasions (146b2–3, 162a5–9, 162b5–9, 164e8–165a5, 165b1–2, 168e4–6, 177c5–7) behave as though he has

a choice regarding the extent to which he is required to participate, despite clearly being on display and under scrutiny.

30. See John Russon, "The (Childish) Nature of the Soul in Plato's *Apology*," in *Reexamining Socrates in the Apology*, ed. John Russon and Patricia Fagan (Evanston, Ill.: Northwestern University Press, 2009), 191–94.

31. Stern (*Knowledge and Politics*, 34–36) emphasizes the significance of the fact that Socrates's opening statement's pedagogical tone is juxtaposed with his engaging with an interlocutor who is a mathematician. Though elsewhere Socrates does not deny the intrinsic value of mathematics (see in particular *Republic*, 527b5–c10, where it is characterized as an effective educational cause of turning the soul toward underlying structures), he nonetheless places it in an explicitly subordinate position to dialectics (531d7–e1).

32. See *Symposium*, trans. Alexander Nehamas and Paul Woodruff, in *Plato: The Complete Works*, ed. John M. Cooper, 457–505 (Indianapolis, Ind.: Hackett, 1997). Specifically, in his speech, 185e8–189a1, Eriximachus talks about love in purely material terms, with the result that it is construed as the force causing changes in the body that the physician must manage. While this does indeed speak to an essential aspect of erotic love, in interpreting love strictly in terms of the body, he presumes well-being to be accountable without reference to the soul, and indeed does so by way of a phenomenon—*erōs*—about which it is surely counterintuitive for it to be reduced to a purely somatic event.

33. We will see this very idea come up in our discussion of the bird cage image (196c4–201c7) in chapter 5.

34. For a good discussion of the responsibility that Plato imposes on the reader, see Mitchell Miller, *The Philosopher in Plato's Statesman* (The Hague: Martinus Nijhoff, 1980), xxiii–xxxiii.

35. See *Euthyphro*, 5d9–6e1 and *Meno*, trans. G. M. A., Grube in *Plato: The Complete Works*, ed. John M. Cooper, 870–97 (Indianapolis, Ind.: Hackett, 1997), 71e1–72b6.

36. Indeed, in his commentary on the *Theaetetus*, Heidegger, *The Essence of Truth* (Continuum, 2002), 111–12, claims that what is in fact being first asked for by the question "What is knowledge?" is not the deeper essence of the concept, but rather what its everyday sense is. Thus, for Heidegger, the starting point for Socrates is to make his interlocutor articulate the prejudice so that it can be examined. This practice of first presenting the everyday account of a given concept before moving on to the deeper essence is also the usual analytic method of Aristotle in the opening of his treatises.

37. Though this notion of making one's thoughts known to oneself is the fundamental purpose of midwifery, it will also reappear in chapter 6 when we discuss Socrates's first account of *logos* (206d1–e3).

38. See Sigmund Freud, "Notes Upon a Case of Obsessional Neurosis (1909)," in *Three Case Histories: The "Wolf Man," The "Rat Man," and The Psychotic Doctor Schreber* (Collier Books, 1963), 36. Freud offers a helpful analogy in reference to his own psychoanalytic practice that we can draw upon to show similarities between his practice and Socrates's practice. Freud reports what he told his patient, the rat-man, regarding the unconscious: "everything conscious was subject to a process of wearing-away, while what was unconscious was relatively unchangeable; and I illustrated my remarks by pointing to the antiques standing about in my room. They were, in fact, I said, only objects found in a tomb, and their burial had been their preservation: the destruction of Pompeii was only beginning now that it had been dug up." Freud characterizes psychoanalysis here as extracting from the unconscious preserved neuroses. The desirable effect of causing neuroses to be

"destroyed" can only be caused by "unearthing" them. Likewise, Socrates wishes to extract from Theaetetus unexamined opinions that will be preserved unless made explicit. It is true that later in Freud's "Notes," 44n22, he explicitly refers to the "inefficacy" of rational disputation as a means of combating neuroses, but this does not undermine the similarities between his method and that of Socrates, as the targets of their methods are not the same.

39. A version of this experience of metaphor as a means of being educated is presented by Aristotle in the *Poetics*, 1448b4–20. Aristotle describes the natural inclination human beings have from childhood to representation. We experience representation and then make that representation our own by drawing connections between the representational object and our own experiences. See also Dennis Schmidt, *On Germans and Other Greeks*, (Bloomington: Indiana University Press, 2001), 46–72.

40. Myles Burnyeat, "The Philosophical Sense of Theaetetus' Mathematics," *Isis* 4 (1978): 489–91, draws attention to controversy in the scholarship around whether or not Theaetetus can be credited with having made the discovery of squared and cubed numbers. The standard reading had been that Theaetetus had made this particular discovery, but that he had likely done so later in life, and that Plato was offering this portrayal as a testimonial to an admired figure. By contrast, others had argued that Theaetetus had not in fact accomplished anything more than the appropriation of his teacher's lesson (490–91). Burnyeat argues, persuasively, I think, that this is a fictional presentation intended to demonstrate Theaetetus's intellectual talent. He also takes himself to be providing evidence to support the view that it was Theaetetus's discovery, but that we must distinguish between the actual history and its use in the dialogue. I would add only that we are also being shown Socrates's conviction that such—undoubtedly important—intellectual activity has to be subordinated to the more general activity of reflection on matters applying to all aspects of life, that, in other words, disciplinary knowledge is subordinate to cultivating the philosophical orientation. I exclude from my analysis any claims regarding the actual historical development of mathematics.

41. Note that this is an explicitly geometric sense of roots, and therefore uses only what we would call rational and whole numbers. Thus, the only numbers for which a square root can be found, properly speaking, are those whose root is a whole rational number.

42. For a description of the type of accomplishment Theaetetus has performed, see *Republic*, 525b8–c6, where Socrates suggests to Glaucon that those educated in philosophy take up calculation "not after the fashion of private men, but to stay with it until they come to the contemplation of the nature of numbers with intellection itself." Though Theaetetus has not completed this process, he has clearly begun. See also *Republic*, 526c1–527c3.

43. Burnyeat ("The Philosophical Sense," 509–12) notes that Theaetetus's accomplishment as it is portrayed in the dialogue is not the completion of a proof. Indeed, the mathematical proof is never completed. Burnyeat makes the interesting point that this is of philosophical relevance to the dialogue insofar as what Theaetetus has done in mathematics is to have begun a process that will—we are told—bear great fruit. Correspondingly, this is the place of perception in the story of knowledge, that is, a starting point. We could add, likewise, that the cultivation of a sphere of, and a thirst for, philosophical inquiry is the accomplishment being striven for in conversation with Theatetetus.

44. Nails (*The People of Plato*, 275) points out that there is "scant evidence" that Theaetetus was actually responsible for what has been attributed to him in the development of geometry.

45. For a discussion of the indeterminacy of soul as it is presented in Plato's *Phaedo, Republic*, and *Laws*, see Sara Brill, *Plato on the Limits of Human Life* (Indiana University Press, 2013).

46. Jacob Klein, *Plato's Trilogy: Theaetetus, The Sophists and the Statesman* (London: University of Chicago Press, 1977), 82–83, suggests that perhaps we are being invited to reflect on whether or not Socrates has or had wisdom.

47. Indeed, the very personal nature of the endeavor of articulating one's own tacit concepts offers some explanation for Socrates's admitted discrimination about the people from whom he will deliver intellectual offspring.

48. David Sedley, *The Midwife of Platonism: Text and Subtext in Plato's Theaetetus* (Oxford University Press, 2002), 12, argues that Socrates's barrenness signifies his lack of worked-out metaphysics and physics. I claim that while Socrates speaks only of his personal barrenness, that barrenness points to a formal structure in human beings of the need to perpetually strive for knowledge that cannot be attained.

Sedley notes that the one exception to Socrates's barrenness appears to be his knowledge of midwifery (ibid., 33). This is true, but one has to take Socrates's qualifications of his expertise into account. He claims that he is capable of taking wisdom from others "in a measured way," and that this is "a little bit" of knowledge (161b2–7).

49. Socrates himself cautions against such a higher standard in his characterization of his possession of "human wisdom" in the *Apology*, 23a4–b4.

50. Thomas West, *Plato's Apology of Socrates: An Interpretation, with a New Translation* (Ithaca, N.Y.: Cornell University Press, 1979), 117–24, raises as a puzzle the notion that Socrates's professed "mere" human knowledge does not cohere with the educational character of his interactions with others, not because West presumes him to in fact be dissembling about knowledge, but rather because to engage with someone through this method of questioning requires significant psychological insight. For more discussion of puzzles concerning Socrates's professed ignorance, see Thomas Brickhouse and Nicholas D. Smith, *Routledge Philosophy Guidebook to Plato and The Trial of Socrates* (New York: Routledge, 2004), 98. See also Sean Kirkland, *The Ontology of Socratic Question in Plato's Early Dialogues* (SUNY Press, 2012), 69, where Socrates's human wisdom is presented as marking "what is abidingly beyond our human understanding."

51. In contrast to my interpretation, Cornford (*Plato's Theory of Knowledge*, 27–29) explicitly claims that the purpose of midwifery runs parallel to the recollection characterized in the *Meno*, which is to say that its aim is the extraction of truth, and thus the generation of real knowledge; See also Sedley, *The Midwife of Platonism*, 7–13.

Chapter 3

1. See Martha Nussbaum, *Upheavals of Thought: The Intelligence of Emotions* (Cambridge University Press, 2003), 174–248. Nussbaum provides a rigorous and engaging discussion of how the ways in which infants develop out of these initiating assumptions profoundly determine their psychological health.

2. See Tschemplik, *Knowledge and Self-Knowledge*, 67–69, for a discussion of the erotic nature of perception.

3. This specific formulation of a definition of *erōs* I owe to Seth Benardete, *Socrates and Plato: The Dialectics of Eros* (Munich: Carl Friedrich von Siemens Stiftung, 1999), 19.

4. This characterization of experience is made explicit in Socrates's presentation of Diotima's speech in the *Symposium*.

5. Though the analogy between erotic coupling and perception is the primary thrust of section 2, there is also a secondary discussion of Socrates's positive account of perception, an account that proves invaluable to the discussion in the "digression" concerning the philosopher to be discussed in chapter 4.

6. Burnyeat ("Introduction" to *The Theaetetus of Plato,* 19) characterizes well the way in which the initial definition gets developed: "Thanks to Socrates' skill as a midwife of ideas, Theaetetus' original conception has proved a larger thing than he foresaw. It has grown into a whole theory of knowledge and the world."

7. Specifically, Theaetetus gives his definition at 151e2–3, while Socrates declares the idea delivered at 160e3–4.

8. See Cornford, *Plato's Theory of Knowledge*, 30, where the discussion that occurs over this section and throughout the remainder of the dialogue is called "dialectic," and defined as involving "two minds" discussing something, not for the sake of winning an argument or proving the other wrong, but for the sake of attaining the truth. (See also *Theaetetus* 187d, where Socrates makes this aspect of the conversation explicit.) While this to some extent describes what is happening, and provides the germane distinction Theaetetus is hopefully discovering for himself as a result of Socrates's encouragement, Cornford does not sufficiently acknowledge the importance (and difficulty) of establishing between both parties that this is what is being aimed at.

9. My point here is to draw attention to what a woman pregnant for the first time might feel in anticipating an event she has no direct experience with, in order to connect to roughly to the issues Socrates is concerned with here in dealing with Theaetetus.

10. Theaetetus's use of the term "*aisthēsis*," and the question of what it means, has been much debated. Cornford (*Plato's Theory of Knowledge*, 30) argues that "*aisthēsis*"—perhaps unlike "perception" and certainly unlike "sense-perception"—ought to be understood to refer broadly to bodily responses to what is external, and that this ought to include emotional responses. As evidence of this, he points to 156b, where Socrates includes under the category of perceptions sensations, pleasure and pain, emotion, desire, and fear. See also John McDowell, *Plato: Theaetetus* (New York: Oxford University Press, 1973), 117–18; Klein, *Plato's Trilogy*, 84–85; Benardete, "Theaetetus Commentary," I.103. Against this, Polansky (*Philosophy and Knowledge*, 66) has argued that *aisthēsis* ought, rather, to be understood to encompass aspects of the intellectual sphere. While I will agree with the latter (and, in section 2 of this chapter, will argue that the "digression" about the philosopher is an illustration of the fact that *aisthēsis* is bound to thinking), what I believe is lost in this debate is that Theaetetus probably does not have a very concrete conception of perception, and that his definition is using the term loosely. As Polansky later correctly points out (*Philosophy and Knowledge*, 69), it is through the discussion that the parameters of perception are circumscribed.

11. Tschemplik (*Knowledge and Self-Knowledge*, 70) claims that what is perhaps most striking about Theaetetus's first definition is the fact that a mathematician would first appeal to perception, when mathematics ought to be, for a mathematician, an intuitively plausible example of knowledge *not* involving perception. See also Burnyeat, "Introduction" to *The Theaetetus of Plato*, 4. Compare Aristotle's claim, *Physics*, II.2 193b30–35, that mathematics is the study of separated surfaces of bodies.

12. Sedley (*The Midwife of Platonism*, 49) likewise points out that Socrates chooses not to move immediately to a straightforward criticism or even refutation of the first definition (which Socrates does eventually move to at 184b3–187a3). Sedley goes on to claim

that we are led through the lengthy discussion so that Plato can display Socrates's virtuosic thinking and can therefore display (according to Sedley's interpretation) the way in which Socrates's thinking laid the foundation for his elaborated metaphysical and physical system. Regardless of whether or not that is true, Sedley's reading, in my view, again, pays too little attention to the pedagogical project Socrates is explicitly engaged in.

13. Polansky (*Philosophy and Knowledge*, 81) argues that Protagoras himself was not concerned with ontology, and that the claim Socrates quotes is intended to make a rhetorical point. I am not convinced by his interpretation of Protagoras's claim, primarily because the claim seems to me to be too removed from its context for us to make concrete determinations about its meaning. It also relies too heavily on an appeal to what Polansky imagines Protagoras might be saying: "[What Protagoras said] need amount only to the commonplace observation that each person *trusts* things to be the way they appear to him to be." Even if it were true that Protagoras's claims were purely focused on rhetoric, emphasizing this too much obscures *Socrates's* point in invoking it, which is to draw out the metaphysical implications of those rhetorical claims.

14. All mention of the claims of Protagoras (as well of Heraclitus and others not present for the discussion) are assumed strictly in their characterization by (Plato's) Socrates.

15. Note that this is obviously a preliminary sketch of what will be discussed in great detail later in the chapter. It is brought up here to draw attention to the intuitive plausibility of the equation of Theaetetus's definition with Protagoras's speech.

16. Burnyeat ("Introduction" to *The Theaetetus of Plato*, 10) argues that there are two implicit premises of this definition, especially with Socrates's additional claim, summarizing the definition, that "perception is, after all, always of that which is, and it's without falsehood inasmuch as it is knowledge" (152c5–6). They are, says Burnyeat (1) that all perceiving is knowing, and (2) that all knowing is perceiving. Burnyeat takes this second premise to be the one that the modern reader would want substituted with "knowing *begins* in perceiving."

17. Polansky (*Philosophy and Knowledge*, 8) points out that Socrates's choice of wind is appropriate "because its very being is becoming—motion in air." Contrast this with Cornford (*Plato's Theory of Knowledge*, 33) who claims that the example demonstrates a distinction between sense-object and physical object.

18. For example, one could say that the claim she is making about the draft being cold is more precisely only about the effect of the draft on her body. The draft is not—properly speaking—what is cold. She is cold, and is made cold by virtue of the draft. Thus, she is only the arbiter of the being of her own attribute, namely, experience of body-temperature, not of the cause of that body-temperature, about which she need not make any claims regarding its ontological status.

19. Oded Balaban, *Plato and Protagoras: Truth and Relativism in Ancient Greek Philosophy* (New York: Lexington Books, 1999), 102, characterizes Protagoras as reducing "Being to manifestation" and insinuates that this is due to the fact that "substance has not yet acquired an independent status, as in Aristotle's thought."

20. Note that from what I have just recounted, there is an ambiguity to the meaning of what Socrates has said. This is not surprising; Socrates is claiming to speak on behalf of all of the wise, with the exception of Parmenides, and so therefore would be expected to present a definition general enough to make room for what appears to be a diversity of accounts. The ambiguity lies in whether the flowing and motion are said to be what the diverse things *actually* are, or rather that flowing and motion constitute the *source* of all

that is. In that latter case, things and being might be said to retain legitimately discrete ontological status, but in a wholly derivative, dependent sense, whereas in the former things and being might be said not to be at all, but rather that these are erroneously apprehended on our part.

21. See chapter 6 for a discussion of the namable and the unnamable. There, I discuss in detail the problem of what can and cannot be spoken, and of both the ontological characteristics of each, and the epistemological implications of such a distinction.

22. Tschemplik (*Knowledge and Self-Knowledge*, 75) points out that Socrates gives no account of why these examples demonstrate anything about "the good," and further points out that it could only make sense if the good was equated with becoming.

23. See also Aristotle, *On The Soul*, trans. J. A. Smith, in *The Complete Works of Aristotle, Vol. 1*, ed. Jonathan Barnes, 641–92 (Princeton, N.J.: Princeton University Press, 1995), I.2 405a2–7.

24. This is not to argue that each species of animal must have always existed. My point is merely to draw a distinction between generation and maintenance of a given species or kind.

25. We will see when Socrates presents the myth of infinite motions that this is what he suggests.

26. Polansky (*Philosophy and Knowledge*, 89) points out that in both cases it is surely true that rest is an essential part of health, too. While this is a good point, it seems that what is essential about motion in managing health is that maintaining a state of rest would cause deterioration.

27. Note that we have moved from the denial of independent reality to the claim that all is motion. Desjardins (*The Rational Enterprise*, 20–21) outlines three degrees to which one can interpret the combined Theaetetan-Protagorean-Heraclitean doctrine: First, as claiming merely that sensible qualities are both enacted by, and changeable according to, the perceiver; second, as claiming that because the object admits of opposite qualities depending on instances of perception, no object of perception can be said to have any particular quality; third, that nothing is, in itself, any "strictly identifiable stable object." Desjardins goes on, correctly, to point out that Socrates is directing Theaetetus to recognize that the second of these two versions of the doctrine appears to lead to the third.

28. "First, in connection with the eyes, that which you call white color—don't appoint it to be itself as something other outside your eyes any more than in your eyes or any place for it at all, for otherwise it would surely be in order and abiding and not be becoming in becoming" (*Theaetetus*, 153d9–e4).

29. Polansky (*Philosophy and Knowledge*, 91–92) points out that the other example used by Socrates, along with color, that is, largeness and smallness, does not coincide with it and thus obscures a major threat to this account of perception. Specifically, largeness is not something merely generated by subject and object, but rather by subject and two objects related to each other. For there to be numerically distinct objects to compare to one another would threaten the claim that all is primarily flux, according to Polansky.

30. Cornford (*Plato's Theory of Knowledge*, 44–45) argues that, while Plato, in the *Phaedo*, believed that concepts of "relation between" objects (such as "large" or "loud" or "cold") belong to the objects insofar as they are permanent and unchanging forms, by the *Theaetetus* Plato had changed his view, now claiming that these concepts emerge from relationships. Polansky (*Philosophy and Knowledge*, 93) argues that the distinction between change within the object, and change within the relationship between objects, is presented in

order to deny the reality of the latter. While I disagree with Cornford's interpretation of the evolution of Plato's thinking on the issue of relational identity, I also disagree with Polansky in the implication he draws concerning the distinction between the two kinds of change. That relational identities emerge from the coupling of perceiver and perceptible object does not undermine the reality of the relational identity. Compare this discussion to Aristotle, *Metaphysics*, IV.2 1004b5–1005a8, where he claims it is our poor understanding of the nature of substances that creates these puzzles, and that a better understanding recognizes that substances by their nature admit of contraries, in the form of actuality and privation.

31. For a different reading of the dice example, though not one that in fact conflicts with mine, see Desjardins, *The Rational Enterprise*, 89–95. Desjardins argues that when the dice example is analyzed through the lens of the myth of infinite motions (i.e., the theory of the *kompsoteroi* or the sophisticates) it demonstrates that one must reject the notion that a generated object must either remain the same or become different. I claim that the initial presentation of the dice example is for the purpose of drawing Theaetetus's attention to the fact that he is beholden to the principle of non-contradiction. While this might appear to contradict Desjardins's claim, in fact, the dice example can serve this initial purpose while at the same time ultimately illustrating the commensurability of generated relational attributes allowing the object both to remain the same and to change, provided it is within the confines of the sophisticated version of the principle of non-contradiction.

32. Note that the language used in the text, that is, that the three claims "fight against themselves in our soul" (155b4–5), seems to imply that the three claims contradict one another. Polansky (*Philosophy and Knowledge*, 94) reads this as a fight between versions of these claims that are referring to absolute change and relative change. For example, something becomes greater or less in bulk while being equal to itself *relative to another object*, but does not, absolutely. When the ambiguity of these claims is cleared up, it is obvious that we rely upon their truth absolutely, and their falsehood regarding relative change. Kenneth Dorter, *Form and Good in Plato's Eleatic Dialogues* (Berkeley: University of California Press, 1994), 75, similarly argues that the fight is *within* each of these claims rather than between them.

33. This is the centerpiece of Book Gamma of Aristotle's *Metaphysics*, stated plainly at IV.3 1005b14–23. The argument that those disputing the primacy of the principle of non-contradiction nonetheless rely on it in disputing it, occurs at IV.4 1006a25–30.

34. 1. Nothing becomes greater or less without increasing or decreasing in itself. 2. Whatever neither has anything added nor anything subtracted neither increases nor decreases. 3. What was not before, cannot become later without coming to be (155a3–b2). See also *Republic*, 436b4–7. As for the heading at the beginning of this subsection, note that what I am here calling a "myth" (*muthos*) in the section heading is only explicitly so called at 156c4–5, and in fact ought to be distinguished from a traditional tale. For a clarification on the distinction between myth as a traditional tale that a culture tells itself and Socrates's stories or *muthoi*, see Fagan, *Plato and Tradition*, 81.

35. As we will see, the significance of the reality of relational being lies, at least in part, in the fact that it forces us to reckon with the constant change and thus fundamental instability of relational attributes; a reckoning that undermines common sense notions of being as more or less stable.

36. Polansky (*Philosophy and Knowledge*, 96–7) argues that the uninitiated who are without the muses here are the atomists. I disagree with the notion that Plato uses the

dialogues merely to addresses grievances between himself and others. See also Cornford, *Plato's Theory of Knowledge*, 89–95, for other examples of this interpretation. The point applies more generally to the common sense attitude that relies upon conventional understanding to evade inquiry, and is therefore a much more substantial grievance with unphilosophical human behavior, that is, the very thing out of which Socrates is trying to educate Theaetetus. Were he (or Plato) merely attacking his historical interlocutors, this would be lost on Theaetetus and would apply only to specialized concerns.

37. Desjardins (*The Rational Enterprise*, 34–35) nicely describes what one has to do in order to consider a claim concerning metaphysical reality, and its implications: "What is required is that we try to conceptualize a state prior to, or at least independent of, organizing intelligence—knowing at the same time, of course, that for the mind to focus on a state defined as preceding just such advent of mind can never be more than what we would call a 'thought experiment' . . . such a state—radically prior to the intrusion of organizing mind—will be by definition inherently mindless or irrational; that is to say, it will be as yet undifferentiated, as yet without ratio, as yet indeterminate, as yet uncut by the measuring of mind."

38. Tschemplik (*Knowledge and Self-Knowledge*, 73) argues that there initially appears to be an ambiguity in how one might interpret Protagoras's claim that "man is the measure," but one that is later reconciled in this account of perception as generated by the unity of perceiver and perceived. Specifically, it would appear that one can either interpret it to be concerned with the appearances (*phaenomena*) (i.e., those things external to us) or as being concerned with measurement (*kritēria*) (i.e., that which is internal to us); the myth, however, demonstrates that these concerns are the same.

39. Compare Aristotle, *On The Soul*, II.5 417a15–22.

40. Tschemplik (*Knowledge and Self-Knowledge*, 80) suggests that passive motion ought best to be thought in terms of "reaction." In other words, the activity of motion must be dual because to act, to move, implies a reconfiguration, a reaction, resulting from that motion.

41. Note that in his explanation of what the speech *wants* to say, Socrates begins his description assuming the primordial motion without troubling over the problematic ontological difference between them (157c1–3). For a comparison to a presentation of the nature of primordial flux that is more logically rigorous than the myth (whose purpose as myth is, after all, not absolute logical rigor), see *Timaeus*, trans. Donald J. Zeyl, in *Plato: The Complete Works*, 1224–91 (Indianapolis, Ind.: Hackett, 1997), 47e4–50a4.

42. Desjardins (*The Rational Enterprise*, 43) argues that the movement from the primordial continuum of infinite motion to the perceiver's experience of many discrete objects individuated both from each other and from the perceiver occurs in three stages. The initial stage of infinite activity and passivity is followed by the introduction of measure that, in her words, "cuts the flow" dividing that primordial continuum into "an innumerable number of discrete elements" which is then followed by the third stage, in which, out of the interaction of the discrete elements, is generated "a novel product which is analyzable into, but not reducible to, its constitutive elements." What characterizes the second stage for Desjardins is the introduction of mind into the activity of infinite motion. Mind must be introduced because it is already illicitly presumed in the thought experiment of the initial stage of infinite motions. This means that the under-articulated move, by Socrates, from infinite motions to perceiver and perceived is the move of differentiation that has to have been assumed from the start.

43. We will, below, address the other generated perceptions mentioned by Socrates (pleasure, pain, desire, and fear).

44. By being forced immediately to transform flux into a relationship—or more accurately, by being forced to recognize that to presume flux to be primary means to have already presumed, without yet accounting for it, a relationship—the advocates of flux are forced to predicate of that flux necessary and unchanging structures (i.e., those of activity and passivity), and are thus forced into a tension that demands reconciliation.

45. See also Tschemplik, *Knowledge and Self-Knowledge*, 75: "This idea that reality or being is the result of an interactive process between knower and known will initially be illustrated in Socrates' analysis of motion, which turns out to be a clandestine imitation of the motion of *eros*."

46. Note, though, that the activity of perception that I am describing here is taking into account the intellectual element that is inextricable from perception. This is not something being borne in mind by Theaetetus, although it is implicitly present in the discussion of this definition during Socrates's account of the philosopher (172d3–177b9) and it will be discussed in section 2 of chapter 4.

47. Tschemplik (*Knowledge and Self-Knowledge*, 81) presents the "slower" motion, as I do, as being the activity of what we would retrospectively call "the eye" or "the ears." That is, in the coupling between perceivers and perceptibles is generated—through the activity—what we call the organs of sense: "It is the conjunction of all these motions that constitutes a momentary experience, and the next moment a different experience is in the making. This is precisely all there is—motions on the make. What we call 'eye' is nothing more than a collection of slow motions and the same applies to the so-called seen objects. Indeed as Socrates states the conclusion of the discussion: 'Nothing is itself by itself' (157a); everything is always becoming."

48. See Cornford, *Plato's Theory of Knowledge*, 46n3.

49. I agree with Desjardins (*The Rational Enterprise*, 28n20) that this formulation of the myth is never explicitly rejected by Socrates because he finds it to be a compelling account. My reasons for believing this have to do with the fact that the account draws upon the emergence of relational identities from out of more primordial ones, the latter of which being progressively more amenable to linguistic articulation, that is, to opinion combined with an account, and the former of which being relatively more obscure and opaque to language. This will be a major theme of chapter 6.

50. This is the centerpiece of midwifery. We find evidence elsewhere of this in *Charmides* 159a. Note that Socrates inevitably would have to struggle with the problem of his interlocutors, or at least the ones predisposed to agree with Socrates, uncritically desiring that their own opinions conform to Socrates's. See Sayre, *Plato's Literary Garden* (Notre Dame, Ind.: University of Notre Dame Press, 1995), 119–29, for a discussion of this phenomenon.

51. Aristotle, *Metaphysics*, IV.6 1011a3–14, claims that those who seek a concrete proof that they are not dreaming—just like those who seek an a priori proof that the physician is the better authority than the ignorant person—are confusing demonstration with the starting-point of demonstration, and thus implicitly deny the reality of starting-points.

52. Though we have been shown the complexity of our relationship to independent beings through the recognition that the attributes or relational identities of those objects are in fact co-constituted with us, it is clear that Theaetetus was not successfully shown this insight.

Chapter 4

1. It is here where I would disagree with Tschemplik's formulation (*Knowledge and Self-Knowledge*, 68): "We, as human beings, never stop with sense-awareness, but proceed to form an opinion or judgment about whatever it is that we are sensing." Though it is not certain that this is what she means, it seems that she is arguing that after we take in the world through the senses we "proceed" to form opinions. Though it is surely true that our attitudes about whatever it is that we sense must proceed from what is sensed, I want to claim that the two are experientially inextricable from one another, even if the opinions that emerge from perception are not consciously formulated.

2. See *Theaetetus*, 162a5–9, 164e9–165b2, 168e4–6 and 171c9.

3. My analysis of Theodorus's casual attitude toward the discussion occurs in section 4 of this chapter.

4. Socrates begins speaking as the mouthpiece of Protagoras after announcing at 164e2–4 that Protagoras would have plenty to say in self-defense against their criticism.

5. This is a point noted by Burnyeat, "Introduction" to *The Theaetetus of Plato*, 21.

6. This argument is complimented by Aristotle, *Metaphysics*, IV.4 1006a25.

7. Polansky (*Philosophy and Knowledge*, 110–11) makes the intriguing claim that Theodorus finds Protagoras appealing because the latter, as a sophist, is inclined to appeal to convention over speculation. This would be consistent with Theodorus's essentially anti-philosophical character.

8. In this respect, Theodorus bears some resemblance to the young people Socrates characterizes as hanging around him as spectators to his examination of people who purport to be wise. See *Apology*, 23c1–5.

9. Socrates is picking up the argument where Protagoras's allies fail to. Polansky (*Philosophy and Knowledge*, 114) argues that the purpose of Socrates deciding not to fully devastate Protagoras's positions with complete arguments, but, rather, to defend Protagoras against weaker versions of those arguments, is for the sake of teaching Theaetetus to stand his ground (as he failed to do at 158a8–b4, 162c7–d2, 164b7–c3), and of teaching Theodorus that, whatever one's personal investment, one must examine the argument from all sides. I agree that these are the lessons; however, I am somewhat less convinced that Socrates is interested in teaching Theodorus the second lesson. He is, at least, teaching Theaetetus by using Theodorus as an example.

10. It makes sense that Socrates should be pleased, as this is the first time Theaetetus has decided to defend a position unprompted by Socrates. See Polansky, *Philosophy and Knowledge*, 115.

11. Dorter (*Form and Good*, 80–81) describes knowledge of the understood language as not being "co-extensive with sense perception." I would not put it in those terms, but rather in terms of the meaning in a certain respect obscuring the sensory element of the perceptual experience.

12. Polansky (*Philosophy and Knowledge*, 80) points out that both Theaetetus and Theodorus have been set up as appropriate defenders of Protagoras, Theaetetus claiming to have read his work "and often" (152b5) and Theodorus claiming to be his friend (162a4). However, Polansky compellingly points out that being in Socrates's presence would make it difficult to defend anyone. Socrates is likely holding them to a higher standard than he can reasonably expect of them (or at least expect of Theaetetus), though that standard is perhaps something worthy of one's aspirations.

13. Burnyeat ("Introduction" to *The Theaetetus of Plato*, 24) points out that the relativism of the Protagorean position is threatened unless Protagoras adopts a different definition of truth; otherwise, first, the sense of "better" is going to have an objective measure independent of the subject, and second, the existence of experts is taken as an objective fact too.

14. See *Gorgias*, trans. Donald J. Zeyl, in *Plato: The Complete Works*, ed. John M. Cooper, 791–869 (Indianapolis, Ind.: Hackett, 1997), 495d–499c, for a discussion about the interplay between pleasure and pain, and one that implies the need to cultivate better conscious attitudes toward what is pleasurable.

15. Andrew Barker, "The Digression in the *Theaetetus*," *Journal of the History of Philosophy* 14 (1976): 457.

16. Tschemplik, *Knowledge and Self-Knowledge*, 142. See also Rachel Rue, "The Philosopher in Flight: The Digression (172c–177c) in Plato's *Theaetetus*," *Oxford Studies in Ancient Philosophy* 11 (1993).

17. Gilbert Ryle, *Plato's Progress* (Cambridge University Press, 1966), 158.

18. Cornford, *Plato's Theory of Knowledge*, 89.

19. Burnyeat, "Introduction" to *The Theaetetus of Plato*, 35–36.

20. Polansky, *Philosophy and Knowledge*, 134–38.

21. In his interpretation of the digression, Sedley (*The Midwife of Platonism*, 68) argues that what is created is a sharp distinction between "a lower, civic morality and a higher one of godlike self-distancing." Though the language used by Socrates does indeed imply withdrawal on the part of the philosopher, I argue in what follows that it is to the same world, to the same terms of reality that both the orator and the philosopher are directed. The philosopher *appears* to be withdrawn when in fact the philosopher is more engaged with what is in fact manifestly the case, insofar as the philosopher is directed to reflection on the structural conditions that create the reality that is uncritically taken up by the orator as given, and indeed as the standard bearer for the orator's own conduct.

22. See Plato, *Republic*, 527e4–7.

23. See Plato, *Republic*, 485a10–b3, 521c5–8.

24. See John Russon, *Human Experience: Philosophy, Neurosis and the Elements of Everyday Life* (SUNY Press, 2003), 14–15: "To hear a foreign language is to hear uninterpretable music with magical effects. When I hear someone speak my own language, however, everything changes. Rather than 'conjuring,' one who speaks my language seems to be handing me meanings directly."

25. For a discussion of the role of sykophancy in Athenian society, see Robin Osbourne, "Vexatious Litigation in Classical Athens: Sykophancy and the Sykophant," in *Nomos: Essays in Athenian Law, Politics and Society*, ed. Paul Cartledge, Paul Millet and Stephen Todd, 87 (Cambridge, Eng.: Cambridge University Press, 1990). Athens did not have professional lawyers; particular people educated in public speaking could bring charges against others, and could, in fact, do so for financial gain. At issue in Osbourne's article is whether "sykophant" is an official or merely informal designation. Osbourne claims, 94, that what is designated by the term is "vexatious litigation;" a sykophant was a nuisance, a "pest, causing him and the court unnecessary trouble." For our purposes, the important point is that what is being portrayed is someone who has cultivated the ability to manipulate public opinion, whose skills are determined by the democratic privileging of persuasion.

26. In addition to the clear reference this passage makes to Socrates's claim in the opening moments of the *Apology* that he will appear ridiculous to them because he is

unaccustomed to public speaking, see *Republic*, 487b1–489d5, where Socrates explains to Adeimantus why, in a certain sense, the many are right to claim philosophers are useless to cities; it is not because they could not benefit the cities, but rather because the many of the cities are incapable of identifying how the (true) philosophers would benefit them, because they confuse the true philosophers with their counterfeits.

27. This notion of our encounters with the world directing us to conceptual terrain is a central theme of the Divided Line in Plato's *Republic*, 509d5–511e5, and of Diotima's speech in the *Symposium*, 201d1–212c2.

28. Rue ("The Philosopher in Flight," 79) contrasts the philosopher with Socrates's first lines in the dialogue concerning his interest in the young men of Athens.

29. Dorter (*Form and Good*, 89) suggests that Socrates is characterized in this section as someone who "returns to the Cave from the Islands of the Blessed" with his experience enabling him "to *return* to the corporeal world, in a transformed way" (emphasis in original). I would only distinguish my own view from Dorter's in the sense that I would emphasize that the philosopher, when leaving behind conventional opinions, continues to be directed at the same objects. The return to the cave, in this sense, is engagement with the uninitiated. Benardete ("Plato's *Theaetetus*," 298) claims that "Socrates the gossip, who knows all about Theaetetus' father, cannot possibly be the philosopher whom Socrates describes to Theodorus, whose body alone remains in the city but whose thought flies above and below the earth." I believe that Benardete here misses the mark. Socrates's engagement with the city is not "gossip" and the philosopher's remoteness is not from the city, but from the common understanding of the city.

30. See Ranier Maria Rilke, "Concerning The Poet," in *Selected Works, Vol. 1: Prose* (Hogarth, 1954), 64. Rilke captures this process in describing the facial expression of a rower: "The position of the Poet in the existing world, his 'meaning,' was once shown to me in a fine similitude. It was on board the large sailing vessel in which we crossed from the island of Philae to the wide stretching dams. We went up stream at first and the oarsmen had to exert themselves. I had them all facing me, sixteen of them . . . Occasionally one caught the eye of one or other, but *mostly their eyes saw nothing*, their *open gaze* going out into the air, or their eyes were simply points where the hot vitality of these men lay bare, set in their metallic bodies. But sometimes, looking up quickly, one could catch one of them deep in thought, meditating on the strange disguised phenomenon facing him and on possible situations which might disclose its nature; when noticed, he immediately lost his strenuously thoughtful expression, for a moment all his feelings were in confusion, then, as quickly as he could, he reverted to the watchful gaze of an animal, until the beautiful serious expression became again the usual silly backshish face, with its foolish readiness to assume any required humiliating distortion of thanks."

31. Indeed, with regard to the future, Burnyeat ("Introduction" to *The Theaetetus of Plato*, 42) persuasively argues that the relativist position of Protagoras must be rejected: "an agent who does one thing for the sake of another typically chooses the first because it now seems to them that the second will result. But whether it *will* in fact result or not—that, on the present argument, is something the sense of which can only be given by saying, 'Wait and see.' The very notion of the future makes us submit to objectivity. So, then, does action. That is to say, life itself."

32. Cornford speculates that Plato is expressing his frustration with the Ionian school through the mouth of Theodorus (*Plato's Theory of Knowledge*, 95). I think that one must be

cautious about explaining what happens in the dialogue according to external motivations, as this implies that one can evade responsibility for understanding the philosophical value of the passage within the dramatic context.

33. More precisely, in the *Theaetetus*, Theodorus refers to those driven to madness by the gadfly (*oistrōsin*), while in the *Apology*, Socrates refers to himself as a gadfly (*muōpos*).

34. Note that this structure will be revisited in chapter 6, section 2, subsection b, when we discuss the way in which the unspeakable element is made perceptible through its participation in the whole of which it is made a part.

35. Burnyeat ("Introduction" to *The Theaetetus of Plato*, 53) describes this extension of the doctrine of flux to the dissolution of even the moment of perception, appropriately, the "extended flux doctrine." Sedley (*The Midwife of Platonism*, 97) characterizes this doctrine as requiring that no single act of perceiving can have any duration whatsoever.

36. Homer, *Iliad*, III.172.

37. See Benardete, "Theaetetus Commentary," I.140–I.147, for a discussion of the reference to Helen of Troy.

38. Burnyeat ("Introduction" to *The Theaetetus of Plato*, 33–34), referring to Socrates's previous insistence on returning to focus on Theaetetus rather than on the discussion of justice, argues that the decision not to leave the discussion of Theaetetus's ideas for the "greater" discussion of justice and prudence lies in the fact that Plato believes such questions require their own independent work, and that this discussion must remain focused on the question of knowledge. Though this is possibly true, I find this to be an incomplete explanation, because it fails to attend to why *Socrates* chooses not to discuss the greater issues, but rather to return—admittedly after a lengthy digression concerning the philosopher—to the examination of Theaetetus. Klein (*Plato's Trilogy*, 116), in the context of Socrates's avoidance of the digression concerning Parmenides, similarly points to the importance of returning to the inquiry concerning knowledge and the fear that this inquiry will be lost by the examination of the complexity of Parmenides's ideas, but without, in my view, sufficient emphasis of the purpose of that inquiry for Theaetetus's education.

39. Burnyeat ("Introduction" to *The Theaetetus of Plato*, 61) notes that the senses cannot provide for us the experience of the things we perceive that they *are* anything at all, and that even in the "sensible world" it is the abstract judgments of a thinking soul that gives being to reality. See also Sedley (*The Midwife of Platonism*, 113–14) who describes this discussion of the soul as demonstrating that it is the coherent site of all cognitive operations, rather than the alternative notion that the senses and the intellect somehow perform parallel operations on the world. I will use a version of this notion to criticize the explicit inquiry that proceeds in the discussion of the second definition.

40. Indeed, "tool" and "organ" are the same word (*organon*) in Greek.

41. It is for this reason—that is, that the synthesis of the capacities of a living human being is necessary for the generating of the experience of the being of the things in the world and of the world as a whole—that I prefer the term "soul" to Burnyeat's ("Introduction" to *The Theaetetus of Plato*, 62) use of "mind" as the element missing in perception, that supplements the fact that sensations are "blind." Burnyeat describes the blindness of perception as requiring a "central enduring mind with a unified consciousness capable of far more than the mere reception of isolated data." Where I disagree with this formulation is its obscuring of the role soul is taken to play, namely, as the unifying activity that *is* the consciousness that includes the enduring mind as well as perception.

Chapter 5

1. The relational character of perception is demonstrated in its responsiveness to what one is immediately reflecting on, to what one remembers as one perceives, to how one's desires and perhaps consequent distortions of one's experiences shapes how one perceives, and to the opinions and prejudice that determine one's selective reading of one's environment.

2. Benardete ("Theaetetus Commentary," I.86) says similarly that "the dialogue's most obvious defect seems to consist in its failure to consider knowledge in its relation to learning, intention, and understanding," While I think the spirit of what he says here is correct, I would say that they do not consider knowledge at all, but consider only several of the elements that inform and generate knowledge, included among which are the elements that he lists here.

3. It is for this reason more than any other that one must exercise great caution if one is ever to make claims about Plato. He did not merely remove his own voice from the discussion; he used only conversational voices, which is to say voices operating in circumstances that are to a great extent beyond the complete control of individual participants. The claims one makes for the sake of argument ought not necessarily to be attributed to one; the claims one makes to build up to a larger point that is never reached because of a long digression ought to be remembered as incomplete, and so on. One must remember the immense difficulty of interpreting the greater thrust of these texts.

4. The example I have in mind is Socrates's account of thought and opinion at 189e4–190a7.

5. Some Plato scholars claim that the conclusion drawn from the refutation of the first definition takes the form of the rejection not only of knowledge and perception being one and the same, but also of the rejection of perception having any place in knowledge. See Cornford, *Plato's Theory of Knowledge*, 102. Burnyeat ("Introduction" to *The Theaetetus of Plato*, 62) seems to say more or less the same thing by emphasizing the fact that perception alone can supply no notion of the being of what is perceived. This might find support in Socrates explicitly asking Theaetetus if this is the conclusion that they must draw (186e9–10), but only on the presumption that Socrates is saying what he says absolutely and not provisionally, for pedagogical reasons.

6. In fact, as will be made plain later when we discuss rhetoric (section 2, subsection e) there is a range of motivations that produce the determination no longer to deliberate, some of which are unconscious and, in many contexts, difficult to justify rationally.

7. Socrates will later define thinking as the activity the soul does in conversation with itself, though that later definition does not isolate the soul from the world as this claim does (189e5).

8. Although this is the first explicit invocation of true opinion as part of the definition, Tschemplik (*Knowledge and Self-Knowledge*, 103) points out that in the defense on behalf of Protagoras, opinion was already implicitly invoked when Protagoras moved to questions concerning the city. This is another example of the unacknowledged intermingling of human capacities.

9. Burnyeat ("Introduction" to *The Theaetetus of Plato*, 65–66) notes the intriguing structure of this definition as it relates to the discussion that follows. The definition, it will turn out, is itself an example of false opinion. The bulk of the discussion of the second definition concerns whether or not false opinion is possible. See also Cornford, *Plato's Theory of Knowledge*, 110. Theaetetus's second definition is a false opinion that leads to a discussion that calls into question the possibility of false opinion.

10. One might say Theaetetus is merely demonstrating his willingness to go along with Socrates's line of thought, and that this might be a way to interpret being "shameless." However, it is crucial that Socrates allow Theaetetus to direct the conversation, even when it goes against his own expressed interest. We must consistently take seriously the fact that Socrates is primarily invested in the education of Theaetetus, and that the conversational demands to which he is answering are pedagogical rather than conceptual. See also the discussion of "leisure" in section 2 of chapter 4: it appears that Theaetetus has adopted Theodorus's understanding of leisure. Here, too, we find what could be an implicit criticism of Theodorus as a teacher.

11. Cornford (*Plato's Theory of Knowledge*, 111) suggests that this part of the discussion is a negative presentation on Plato's part, a *reductio* argument against some theories of the nature of error.

12. See chapter 3, section 2, subsection b.

13. Burnyeat ("Introduction" to *The Theaetetus of Plato*, 70) notes that in the passages between 188a-c, Theaetetus tends to answer questions immediately that are highly obscure and that have no examples to aid in clarifying. He cannot possibly be following the line of thought throughout. Indeed, these are passages Burnyeat ("Introduction," 67) characterizes as among those Socrates warns might make them seasick at 190e–191a.

14. Note that Socrates is here invoking the necessary coupling of perceiver and perceptible object that was not rejected before (156a3–c5).

15. Tschemplik (*Knowledge and Self-Knowledge*, 106) points out that despite Socrates's admonishment, Theaetetus's point has some evidence in his own immediate experience. By calling Theaetetus "beautiful" in contrast with Theodorus, Socrates himself appears to be accusing Theodorus of calling the beautiful ugly.

16. Sedley (*The Midwife of Platonism*, 129–30) raises the question, why does Socrates, here (as he did before concerning the account of the soul as that for which perception occurs, 185e3–9) appear to contradict his claim to be intellectually barren? Sedley argues that both the account of the soul as the site of perception and the account of the soul as the site of thinking as a conversation one has with oneself are pieces of knowledge that are necessary conditions of his midwifery.

17. Cornford (*Plato's Theory of Knowledge*, 118) interprets this account of thinking and opining (i.e., *doxa*, which he translates as judgment) as implicitly turning mistaking one thing for another into silently judging that one thing is another. This would mean, in the example previously given, that when one judges a beautiful thing to be ugly, one silently judges that what is beautiful is what is ugly, which appears to be impossible. Burnyeat ("Introduction" to *The Theaetetus of Plato*, 84) criticizes this as too intellectual as a characterization of *doxa*.

18. This is a claim that contributes to the decision to translate *doxa* as opinion rather than as judgment. What is at issue is whether or not a person arrives at true or false *doxa* as a result of the force of her deliberation (i.e., her conversation with herself) or merely as a result of that conversation coming to an end, regardless of whether or not the end that was reached was rationally compelling. I adopt the latter view, in part because I want to emphasize the passive dimension of memory in informing our opinions, and in part because judgment too closely resembles *doxa* with a *logos*, which renders the third definition superfluous. In contrast, see Burnyeat, "Introduction" to *The Theaetetus of Plato*, 69. Burnyeat also ("Introduction," 84) claims one might characterize this account of the generation of judgments as too intellectual.

19. Note that the fact that self-examination leads only to opinion disqualifies it from being on its own sufficient for knowledge. See Tschemplik, *Knowledge and Self-Knowledge*, 105.

20. This notion of being persuaded against one's will insinuates that (in contrast to the hasty Glaucon in Plato's *Republic*) we should adopt the alternative affirmative answer to Polemarchus's question, "Could you really persuade . . . if we don't listen?" (*Republic* 327c11). See John Sallis, *Being and Logos: Reading the Platonic Dialogues,* 3rd ed. (Bloomington: Indiana University Press, 1996), 321–23.

21. Indeed, this is borne out by Socrates's experience of the *daimonion*, and of what we would probably call conscience. See *Alcibiades I*, trans. D. S. Hutchinson, in *Plato: The Complete Works*, ed. John M. Cooper, 557–95 (Indianapolis, Ind.: Hackett, 1997), 103a5–6. Socrates claims to be prevented in his desire to pursue Alcibiades by his divine voice; *Phaedrus*, 242b7–e3, in which Socrates, having been convinced (or having postured himself as though he were convinced) that it was justified to criticize the lover, is prevented from leaving without vindicating the lover against the unjust slight of Lysias's speech; *Apology*, 31d1–5, in which Socrates is prevented from involving himself in public political life.

22. I say here that it seems "superficially" to match Theodorus, primarily because Theodorus himself depends as much as anyone on opinions to grasp and deliberate over, though he espouses (or at least it is strongly suggested that he espouses) a way of thinking that would permit thinking to drift without rest.

23. Cornford (*Plato's Theory of Knowledge*, 121) claims that, with the wax image, a new account of knowledge emerges, one in which I know something when I have had direct acquaintance with it, and also have it stored in my memory. Burnyeat ("Introduction" to *The Theaetetus of Plato*, 76) notes that the wax image amounts to a reformulation on Socrates's part of the proper conditions for making judgments: whereas previously in the discussion of the second definition, knowing the object appeared to be a necessary condition of making judgments about it, now the proper objects of judgment appear to be *either* perception *or* knowledge. By contrast, I claim that the accomplishment of the wax image is to bring into discussion the emergence of opinion through the various faculties of the living human being. It is not, in other words, a matter of knowledge *or* perception generating opinion.

24. Note that the same image might as easily be applied to anything that we are able to commit to memory. The emphasis placed on impressions made by perception makes possible the criticism of this image for failing to account for the reality of errors in the purely intelligible domain (*Theaetetus*, 195c7–196c4). This will be discussed below.

25. Burnyeat ("Introduction" to *The Theaetetus of Plato*, 100) argues that Plato characterizes the activity of examining the wax imprint as the conscious project of committing an impression to memory, referring precisely to the passage at 191d4. While I agree that this is how it appears to be characterized, I disagree with the conclusion that Burnyeat appears to draw that "Plato keeps memory quite separate from perception" (ibid.). The conscious commitment of an idea to memory constitutes only a part of the activity of memory. Memories are formulated without our conscious attention, and play an active, unacknowledged role in the shaping of opinion. In contrast to Burnyeat, Cornford (*Plato's Theory of Knowledge*, 135) takes the wax image to refer simply to the imprint of sense-impressions. This cannot be the case, though, since Socrates explicitly lists "the things we see, hear, or we ourselves think of" as leaving imprints, 191d4–5 (see Sedley, *The Midwife of Platonism*, 135). See also *On the Soul*, II.12 424a17–20 where Aristotle more explicitly connects

the analogy of the wax imprint to perception. Burnyeat ("Introduction" to *The Theaetetus of Plato*, 101) argues that this constitutes an advance by Aristotle on Plato's version of the image.

26. Cornford (*Plato's Theory of Knowledge*, 136) notes that the imprints, representing accumulated experience over a lifetime, cannot possibly count as "bits of knowledge," as is made evident by Socrates's practice of midwifery, whose purpose is to extract from people the recollection of their actual knowledge (see also Cornford, 27.). This contradicts my reading of Socrates's midwifery, taking for granted that what Socrates is aiming at is recollection, whereas I argue that in fact Socrates is oriented in part to the purging of presumptions (see chapter 2).

27. Note that the various forms of "knowledge" translated in this section are *oida* rather than *epistēmē*. Tschemplik (*Knowledge and Self-Knowledge*, 108) notes that in light of this fact, we must take Socrates to be examining not knowledge in the sense around which the dialogue is oriented, but the kind of understanding generated from perception.

28. I take this method of organization of the formal possibilities listed by Socrates from Benardete, "Theaetetus Commentary," I.188, n71.

29. Tschemplik (*Knowledge and Self-Knowledge*, 110) notes that Socrates gives no indication regarding what has shaped the constitution of the wax, first suggesting that it is merely according to the will of the Mother of the Muses, and then asking if it is being suggested that this soul is educated into such a condition. I take it for granted that the latter is precisely what is being suggested by the fact that Socrates describes the different ways in which the shapes of the wax correspond to different kinds of character.

30. It is this set of conditions that compels Aristotle to claim, in the *Nicomachean Ethics*, II.1 1103b23–25, that habituation makes "all the difference."

31. Tschemplik (*Knowledge and Self-Knowledge*, 110) describes the introduction of opinion as the loss of immediacy, and this loss of immediacy "opens up the possibility of error." I would add that, while perception was error-free, on its own it cannot generate knowledge. This is a version of the point that it is out of the combination of capacities in a whole life that knowledge is made possible, *but also* that this possibility is also the possibility of error.

32. Cornford's reading of the wax example as nothing "more than an illustration, a mechanical model which helps us to distinguish a memory-image from a fresh impression of sense," *Plato's Theory of Knowledge*, 127, ignores the way in which knowing is being *directly* linked to the cultivated character of the person.

33. Burnyeat ("Introduction" to *The Theaetetus of Plato*, 101–2) points out that while this appears to be a criticism of the wax image's merits in answering the question "how is false judgment possible?" it is in fact a criticism of the definition of false judgment as that which occurs in the relationship between perception and judgment. Thus, he implies, they could have readjusted the image to fit better with the ameliorated definition of false judgment and maintained the virtues of the image. In what follows, I argue that the concept of strictly intellectual error is more problematic than Socrates and Theaetetus treat it to be, and that therefore, with respect to this objection by Socrates at least, the wax image is better than it appears to be.

34. Though the "second sailing" in this section's title is a reference to the famous passage in the *Phaedo* (99c9–d2), I derive its significance also in part from Benardete, *Socrates' Second Sailing: On Plato's Republic* (Chicago: University of Chicago Press, 1989).

35. See also *Theaetetus* 196d4.

36. This would be one way of interpreting what is meant by Socrates's hope that Theaetetus is "tamer" (*hēmerōteros*) at the end of the dialogue (210c3–5).

37. For a contrasting conception of *hexis* as habit, see Aristotle's *Nicomachean Ethics*, book 2, chapter 1. Aristotle's account of virtuous habits to a significant extent informs my understanding of what Socrates is trying to cultivate in Theaetetus, that is, an active disposition to the world that is questioning, and that is compelled to strive to accomplish knowledge, despite a healthy sense of his own incomplete understanding.

38. Sedley (*The Midwife of Platonism*, 29) interprets the emptiness of the bird enclosure at birth to imply that the Socrates of the *Theaetetus* does not espouse the theory of recollection from the *Meno*, but that—because Socrates uses the term "learning" (*katamanthanein*) to describe the recovery of the birds—Plato subtly alludes to that theory, speaking through Socrates's words. The problem with this interpretation is that it is by no means the case that Socrates is endorsing the bird cage image as true; there is therefore no reason to assume the attributes used in characterizing an image Socrates will reject are attributes Socrates believes must apply to the structure of memory.

39. Analogous to the wax image, one can imagine the size and "storage capacity" of the bird enclosure to be something that is shaped over time. One would also have to imagine, if indeed the enclosure were empty to begin with, that birds inadvertently—or by guidance of a mature person—got "trapped" in the enclosure at the start. Socrates does not, however, pursue the image in this way.

40. One might reasonably be far less sanguine about this distinction. Burnyeat ("Introduction" to *The Theaetetus of Plato*, 106–7) points out that the examples of birds used in the mathematical example are of specific numbers or of even and odd numbers. For Burnyeat, we should ask what the mastery of a whole branch of learning would look like on this model. Is it an infinite number of birds clustered together? Is it a single bird of arithmetical knowledge as a whole? The conceptual tools for addressing these problems, he argues, will not come to us until the third definition is addressed, and specifically in the parts-wholes discussion.

41. Cornford (*Plato's Theory of Knowledge*, 138–9) points out that this is the issue that Socrates ought to be asking about, but that Socrates either chooses not to, or does not think to.

42. The idea that bits of knowledge could breed poorly with one another fits with Socrates's account of midwifery as involving the assessment of good breeding partners (149d5–150a6).

43. This is an idea that Burnyeat makes light of in passing ("Introduction" to *The Theaetetus of Plato*,111). However, the idea that bits of accumulated knowledge interact with each other in creative ways certainly has a history, most conspicuously in book 1 of Hume's *Treatise of Human Nature*. Indeed, Burnyeat himself ("Introduction" to *The Theaetetus of Plato*, 118–21) suggests something similar: if the birds of knowledge were to be reformulated as birds of true judgment, we could imagine their being capable of generating error. Indeed, he characterizes error as resulting from the activity of true judgments without knowledge.

44. One could plausibly present scenarios in which a person too immature to handle the reality of some pieces of information, having been prematurely introduced to them, produces a completely false, distorted set of conclusions.

45. Klein (*Plato's Trilogy*, 133) suggests that the real problem with the proposal of birds of non-knowledge presented by Theaetetus is this proposal continues to fall within

Socrates's equation of the birds with bits of knowledge, when they ought to represent bits of opinion.

46. Note that this passage refers to two distinct possibilities, but that each of them relies on the premise I describe here.

47. Tschemplik (*Knowledge and Self-Knowledge*, 113) offers an interesting suggestion: Might it not be the case that the birds inside the cage have been domesticated? Further, if this is so, what is it that has happened to the knowledge such that it is no longer wild? Has it taken on a different form, thereby perhaps making it something other than what one had initially pursued? Tschemplik does not develop this line of inquiry, but we might add—in a manner corresponding to the variety of constitutions of wax in different souls—that perhaps the degree of domestication has to do with the management of the aviary itself. This, however, is speculation beyond what is made available in the image itself.

48. Desjardins (*The Rational Enterprise*, 119–22) characterizes the problems with the two images as being complimentary, rather than being essentially the same. The wax example, she claims, one-sidedly presents a pure reception through sensation while the aviary example one-sidedly presents intelligence that is detached from perception. While her criticism of the aviary seems right with respect to its diminishment of the role of perception, I believe that she underestimates the characterization of the activity of the interior management of the wax slab. I further claim that the wax image wrongly characterizes the commitment of imprints to memory as a purely conscious activity.

49. Socrates has a history of believing one needs to keep inquiring rather than giving up, perhaps most succinctly stated at the end of the *Laches*, 201a7: "What I don't' advise is that we remain as we are."

50. This is much like the "slower motion" from Socrates's explanation of the myth of infinite motions (see chapter 3, section 2, subsections e–f).

51. Note that the image of being pushed by the river is similar to the one used by Socrates to criticize bad educators in the *Republic*, 492b4–493e1. There, Socrates refers to those who educate only in the "convictions of the many." One who is shaped by such an educator would be "borne by the flood, wherever it tends." The relevant distinction is the cause of the current. In the *Republic*, the flood represents public opinion, whereas in our text, the river is perhaps to be understood as nature, or as the argument.

52. Burnyeat ("Introduction" to *The Theaetetus of Plato*, 125–26) discusses the complexity this example reveals. What the jurors lack is, in his terms, "adequate grounds" for their judgments. Would they have knowledge if more time was available to them to deliberate about the relevant evidence? This, he claims, would insinuate an account of knowledge—which the jurors lack—to which the "modern" reader would be sympathetic. Would they have knowledge only if they were present to witness the event described? This is a conception of knowledge he suggests is insinuated by the *Meno* (97a-b), in which "the difference between someone who knows the road to Larissa and someone who merely has correct opinion about it is due to the former having travelled the road and seen it with their own eyes." It appears that Socrates intends the example of the juror to be one in which, in principle, no knowledge is available, because that juror was not a witness. I suspect, however, that it is not intended to be paradigmatic of all kinds of knowledge, that is, not intended to say "all knowledge depends on being witness to events."

53. See *Gorgias*, 447a–461b, for a discussion of the motive of the orator, as characterized by Socrates in his discussion with Gorgias.

Chapter 6

1. The account I am giving here of knowledge maps well onto Socrates's discussion of the former prisoner who returns to the cave after apprehending the light of the sun and the sun itself. See *Republic*, 516e2–517a2.

2. See *Charmides*, trans. Rosamond Kent Sprague, in *Plato: The Complete Works*, ed. John M. Cooper, 639–63 (Indianapolis, Ind.: Hackett, 1997), 175c1–d7. Socrates discusses, and ultimately rejects, the notion of a person having knowledge of both knowledge and ignorance, with the result that we are *ignorant* (of necessity) of the extent of our ignorance.

3. The way that an orator can convince one that one's opinion is knowledge—which is to say to convince one to mistake one's opinion for a proper end to thinking when it is merely a kind of easy and unjustified end to thinking—is intriguingly similar to Aristotle's claim in the *Politics*, trans. B. Jowett, in *The Complete Works of Aristotle, Vol. 2*, ed. Jonathan Barnes, 1986–2129 (Princeton, N.J.: Princeton University Press, 1995), VII.5 1339b31–35, that "it sometimes happens that men make amusement the end, for the end probably contains some element of pleasure, though not any ordinary pleasure; but they mistake the lower for the higher, and in seeking for the one find the other, since every pleasure has a likeness to the end of action." The orator makes opinions easy to adopt in a way that resembles pleasure insofar as each creates the likeness to an end, and a likeness with the result that it is treated as an end.

4. One could take the fact that activity is necessary for the maintenance of psychic and bodily health the wrong way; one could take activity *simpliciter* as an end in itself, and could spend all of one's time striving simply to act. This is not what I am trying to characterize. My point is to recognize the metaphysical primacy of activity.

5. Note that while we do very often engage in such activities of committing ideas to memory, I was critical of the way Socrates characterized memory exclusively in such terms in the wax image (see chapter 5, section 2).

6. See Burnyeat, "Introduction" to *The Theaetetus of Plato*, 130.

7. Burnyeat ("Introduction," 129) notes that the "dream in exchange for a dream" is presented as hearsay, which Socrates had previously—in the example of the jury—had excluded from knowledge. This point is perhaps not as damaging to the dream that Socrates presents, however, insofar as it is being presented for them to reason through. Hearsay, one must think, is only excluded *in principle* from the domain of knowledge as long as it remains hearsay, that is, remains something one adopts without reflection. Taken up otherwise—that is, as something worthy of deliberation—it does not retain the form of hearsay. Compare to Cornford (*Plato's Theory of Knowledge*, 144), who is convinced the theory presented belongs to an unnamed contemporary of Socrates and Theaetetus, and is equally convinced that Plato does not agree with it.

8. Note that, in this initial statement of the nature of elements, Socrates already insinuates that they cannot be characterized in terms of being, insofar as all that *is* is made up of elements. Burnyeat ("Introduction," 135) takes this attribute of elements to make them "a mystery as dark as anything in the dialogue." See also Heidegger, *The Essence of Truth*, 113: "We ask about what this thing here is, and we answer: a book, i.e. we give the *name* of the thing. But with this latter question we did not actually want to discover the name of the thing, what the thing is called; rather, we wanted to know what it *is*."

9. Burnyeat ("Introduction" to *The Theaetetus of Plato*, 134) argues that whether or not the claim that the elements admit of *logoi* depends on the way in which we translate *logos*. (Compare Cornford, *Plato's Theory of Knowledge*, 144–45, who is confident the sense of

logos is simply "description.") Burnyeat claims that it would be "surprising" if we were to say that the elements cannot be uttered at all in a statement, and much more comprehensible if we were to suggest that they cannot be adequately defined or explained. In a certain respect, it is surely the latter account that best captures the fact that the elements are unspeakable, because, after all, a claim purporting to be true about the elements—that is, that they are unspeakable—is being made. Having said that, though, this is a rather prosaic way of articulating what in fact ought to be a surprising metaphysical fact for us to reflect on. There are, on the account of the unspeakable elements, conditioning "actors" in reality that provide, but are not beholden to, the terms by which we can make reality comprehensible to ourselves. This is remarkable.

10. Cornford (*Plato's Theory of Knowledge*, 146) infers from the invocation of perception that the elements referred to must be material in nature. I believe this to be mistaken in an important sense. We never see the element except by way of *that of which it is an element*. In other words, in perceiving something, the element is insinuated, makes an appearance, *through* that perceived thing. Formulated in this way, the element need not be material, but rather merely implicitly necessary in what is perceived. Mitchell Miller, "Unity and Logos: A Reading of Theaetetus 201c–210a," *Ancient Philosophy* 12 (1992): 93–95, agrees with Cornford that the elements are portrayed as material in nature, but argues that this is the fault of Theaetetus, and that, in fact, conceiving of elements *not* in terms of perceivable objects clarifies how it is possible, in fact, to give an account of the elements. Though I ultimately disagree with Miller, his interpretation is very close to mine. In his view, the elements on their own admit of no account, but through their participation in the structure of the emergent wholes that they combine to make, the possibility of the account emerges. Where I differ from Miller is in my insistence that while the elements are revealed to us through the wholes in which they participate, they can, at best, be identified. Miller ("Unity and Logos," 92) takes the dream to be refuted on the grounds that it requires us to acknowledge knowledge to be impossible (because if we cannot know elements we cannot know wholes emerging from elements that themselves become elements). I claim that the emergent wholes generated in the "plaiting" of elements to be of a fundamentally different character than the elements (as does Miller, ibid., 93), and therefore exempt from the radically skeptical implication. I do, however, take the dream to be announcing the *limits* to knowledge, and identify those limits to be set at the identification of the elements themselves.

11. Burnyeat ("Introduction" to *The Theaetetus of Plato*, 137–39) is clearly troubled by the notion that one can perceive the elements but cannot have a *logos* of them. His problem rests on the assumption that being perceptible means being something that in principle can be spoken of. Once again, I believe that there is a stricter sense of *logos* at work here. We cannot provide a rational explanation justifying what we see when the elements appear for us. The elements do not appear as elements. They appear *in* that which they make possible in their being organized. The elements exist only as relative to whatever they are elements *of*. (It should be noted that Burnyeat himself makes this point, claiming elements appear always as elements *of* (ibid., 210). What distinguishes his insight from the larger point is that, for Burnyeat, the elements *appear* only as elements of, in that appearing their elemental character is obscured.) The purpose of my analogy to the principle of non-contradiction (see section 4, subsection b, below), is that like the elements here, the principle only shows itself in and as rational discourse. It cannot be justified through the method that it makes possible, and so remains necessarily obscure.

12. This characterization of the account anticipates the first of three accounts of *logos*, given by Socrates at the end of the dialogue (206d1–4).

13. Note that there is an ambiguity to this "plaiting" that is impossible to avoid. Are we to take it to mean the parts that together make up the whole of the word, or the parts that are the material with which the words are made? This issue is central to the parts-wholes discussion that follows, so maintaining the ambiguity at this point is appropriate.

14. The initial distinction between syllable and letter is not so clean, because some letters are themselves syllables (203b1–8). However, see Anne Carson, *Eros the Bittersweet* (Princeton University Press, 1986), 53–61. In particular, Carson claims, the "consonant functions by means of an act of imagination in the mind of the user. I am writing this book because that act astounds me. It is an act in which the mind reaches out from what is present and actual to something else. The fact that eros operates by means of an analogous act of imagination will soon be seen to be the most astounding thing about eros" (61). I am grateful to Laura McMahon for drawing my attention to this connection.

15. A similar formulation occurs in the *Republic*. Socrates indicates that he cannot give his opinion of the form of the good—because all opinion without knowledge is ugly (506c6–7)—but that he would, under pressure from Glaucon, describe "what looks like a child of the good and most similar to it" (506e3–4). See also Tschemplik, *Knowlegdge and Self-Knowledge*, 121.

16. In the *Meno*, 99b8–100b6, virtue is characterized as something one cannot know sufficiently to teach it, but that it is, rather, something we can pursue and be given as a gift by the divine power. In *Charmides*, 175c1–d6, Socrates point out that one cannot know things that one does not know with the implication that if we cannot have knowledge of our ignorance, then knowledge of any kind rests on an unknowable foundation of ignorance.

17. Indeed, as Socrates pointed out (196d1–197a1), he himself had been taking for granted knowledge of knowledge in invoking the term repeatedly throughout the discussion.

18. See John Sallis, *Chorology: On Beginning in Plato's Timaeus* (Indiana University Press, 1999). See also Jacques Derrida, "Khora," in *On The Name* (Stanford University Press, 1995). Compare Aristotle, *Physics*, IV.4 212a8–21.

19. See Aristotle, *On the Soul*, III.4 429a18–28.

20. Rorty ("A Speculative Note," 235–36) speculates (with careful qualification) that perhaps the *Theaetetus* constitutes the text with which Plato grapples with the implication of the theory of forms found in the *Republic, Phaedo, Phaedrus* and *Meno*, specifically, that if the forms are "indeed *independent* objects of knowledge, there will be no explaining them." I find the connection to the implications of the theory of forms compelling, though I am less willing to speculate concerning specific motivations on Plato's part.

21. The first example of Socrates exploiting number, discussed in chapter 3 (section 2, subsection d) was the dice example (154c1 ff.) where he drew, for Theaetetus, a distinction between attributes intrinsic to the number six and attributes resulting from its relationship to other numbers. While the example demonstrated that some kind of subsisting identity with itself was necessary for relational identity to emerge at all (six has to *be* six in order to be both "half" and "one plus one half" in relation to twelve and four, respectively), it did not refute the ontological status of relational identity. Rather, it forced the more nuanced account that claims the same being admits both of relative internal subsistence (i.e., "slower motion") *and* with respect to it being, simultaneous to this, a being in relation to others, of perpetual flux in its identity with others (i.e., the "faster motion").

22. Miller ("Unity and Logos," 94) points out that the way in which Socrates formulates the example itself identifies different mathematical equations (i.e., addition and multiplication) that must be differentiated from each other, and from the answer each produces.

23. Plethron and stade are each set units of measure. It would be equivalent to saying "when we say 'one mile' we are also saying '1760 yards,'" and "when we say 'one meter' we are also saying 'one hundred centimeters.'"

24. Edward Gulbekian, "The Origin and Value of the Stadion Unit Used by Eratosthenes in the Third Century BC," *Archive for History of Exact Sciences* 37 (1987): 359–60.

25. Note here two points. First, this is essentially what the metric system is, that is, a construction of identities defined exclusively in relation to other identities within the system of measure. Second, even this example of the metric system is *itself* rooted in an arbitrarily defined empirical measurement. While Socrates's heuristic reduction of the stadion and feet into purely numerical values can conceal their real-world value to Theaetetus, the metric system, had it been available to Socrates to use, would have even more effectively obscured the pre-numeric meaning of measurement, because it is a system which is able to build abstraction on only a single empirical unit.

26. See Burnyeat, "Introduction" to *The Theaetetus of Plato*, 205–7. Burnyeat provides an additional discussion of structure as the factor distinguishing wholes and alls (ibid, 193).

27. Mitchell Miller ("Unity and Logos," 89) provides an illuminating discussion of the apparent jump in the conversation at this point.

28. Theaetetus previously did so at 157c4–6.

29. Burnyeat ("Introduction" to *The Theaetetus of Plato*, 176) notes that Theaetetus's third definition of knowledge is itself merely a list of the parts of knowledge, and is therefore susceptible to this particular criticism right here, insofar as no mention is made of the structural characteristics of the relationship between true opinion and the account.

30. Miller ("Unity and Logos," 99) argues that the second account is not false, but incomplete, requiring the supplement of the third definition, with which it is not combined.

31. To be precise, we should note that in chapter 4 we discussed the different experiences of a language to those who understand it and those who do not. Here, we will be discussing the actual experience of learning a language.

32. Note here that, though this readily applies to harmony in the sense in which it is typically understood in relation to music, this might apply equally to discordant or atonal music, provided there is an identifiable compositional accomplishment one strives to re-enact oneself.

33. Miller ("Unity and Logos," 96) argues that the problem with the way in which the presentation of the three accounts of *logos* is given is that it treats each account of *logos* independent of the others, without relying on the resources provided by the previous account. In other words, each account is shown to be insufficient on its own terms, but Socrates never explores the combination of the accounts of *logos*—one might say, as plaiting for the whole of *logos*—in order to generate a better account. He later suggests that knowledge is a larger whole that emerges from the insufficient parts of true opinion and *logos* (ibid., 103). My claims throughout concerning the three definitions of knowledge are versions of this. That is, the various, limited and limiting human capacities brought together generate knowledge as a potentially ever-developing whole.

34. Cornford (*Plato's Theory of Knowledge*, 162) interprets this aporetic moment as the result of the exclusion of the theory of forms from the attempt to give an account of knowledge. The whole of the *Theaetetus*, for Cornford, is a *reductio* argument which at-

tempts to define knowledge only in reference to what can be extracted from the material world. I disagree with this interpretation on the grounds that it is in the material world as it is presented throughout the dialogue, that we find unchanging concepts, and are led to be capable of perceiving them.

35. Burnyeat ("Introduction" to *The Theaetetus of Plato*, 234 n124) notes that Socrates does not indicate that the improvement in Theaetetus's discourse should necessarily be cashed out in philosophical discussion. Burnyeat infers from this that it might even refer to his future mathematical accomplishments. Though I agree with the emphasis on improvement independent of, or at least not necessarily exclusive to, philosophy, I am inclined to think that it is to the character of Theaetetus that Socrates is directed, insofar as it was the assessment and cultivation of Theaetetus's soul that directed the discussion. By contrast, Cornford (*Plato's Theory of Knowledge*, 163) regards the closing moments of the dialogue as nothing more than the announcement of their failure to define knowledge. Dorter (*Form and Good*, 71) notes that among the thematic parallels between the *Theaetetus* and the *Meno* is the fact that the latter ends with Socrates suggesting that if Meno convinces Anytus of the things of which he has been convinced, he will make the latter calmer, and perhaps benefit the Athenians (*Meno*, 94e). Like the *Theaetetus*, this points both to the future trial of Socrates (insofar as Anytus coauthored the charge against Socrates), and to the desired effect of participation in Socrates's maieutic art.

36. Miller ("Unity and Logos," 104) argues that what Theaetetus has produced is not a wind-egg at all, but rather something to be nurtured and cared for.

Conclusion

1. Dorter (*Form and Good*, 119) suggests that "the next step" after the failure of the three definitions of knowledge would be to emphasize what he argues is implicitly present in the digression concerning the philosopher and implied by the opening discussion between Terpsion and Euclides, but never explicitly thematically developed in the dialogue proper, that being that the pursuit of wisdom entails a change to a new kind of life or a "turning around of the soul" as in the *Republic* (518c6–7). I take this to be made much more explicit in the dialogue as a whole, but otherwise essentially agree. See also Miller, "Unity and Logos," 104.

BIBLIOGRAPHY

Annas, Julia. *Platonic Ethics, Old and New*. Ithaca, N.Y.: Cornell University Press, 1999.

Aristotle. *The Complete Works of Aristotle, Vols. 1 and 2*. Ed. Jonathan Barnes. Princeton, N.J.: Princeton University Press, 1995.

———. *Metaphysics*, in *The Complete Works of Aristotle, Vol 2*. Trans. W. D. Ross. Ed. Jonathan Barnes, 1552–1728. Princeton, N.J.: Princeton University Press, 1995.

———. *Nicomachean Ethics*. Trans. Joe Sachs. Newburyport, Mass.: Focus, 2002.

———. *On the Soul*, in *The Complete Works of Aristotle, Vol 1*. Trans. J. A. Smith. Ed. Jonathan Barnes, 641–692. Princeton, N.J.: Princeton University Press, 1995.

———. *Physics*, in *The Complete Works of Aristotle, Vol 1*. Trans. by R. P. Hardie and R. K. Gaye. Ed. Jonathan Barnes, 315–446. Princeton, N.J.: Princeton University Press, 1995.

———. *Poetics*, in *The Complete Works of Aristotle, Vol 2*. Trans I. Bywater. Ed. Jonathan Barnes, 2316–40. Princeton, N.J.: Princeton University Press, 1995.

———. *Politics*, in *The Complete Works of Aristotle, Vol 2*. Trans. B. Jowett. Ed. Jonathan Barnes, 1986–2129. Princeton, N.J.: Princeton University Press, 1995.

Balaban, Oded. *Plato and Protagoras: Truth and Relativism in Ancient Greek Philosophy*. New York: Lexington Books, 1999.

Barker, Andrew. "The Digression in the *Theaetetus*." *Journal of the History of Philosophy* 14 (1976): 457–62.

Bateson, Gregory. *Steps to an Ecology of Mind*. Chicago: University Of Chicago Press, 2000.

Benardete, Seth. "On Interpreting Plato's *Charmides*." In *The Argument of the Action: Essays on Greek Poetry and Philosophy*. Ed. Ronna Burger and Michael Davis, 231–56. Chicago: University of Chicago Press, 2000.

———. "Plato's *Theaetetus*: On The Way of the Logos." In *The Argument of the Action: Essays on Greek Poetry and Philosophy*. Ed. Ronna Burger and Michael Davis, 297–322. Chicago: University of Chicago Press, 2000.

———. *Socrates and Plato: The Dialectics of Eros*. Munich: Carl Friedrich von Siemens Stiftung, 1999.

———. *Socrates' Second Sailing: On Plato's Republic*. Chicago: University of Chicago Press, 1989.

———. "Theaetetus Commentary" from *The Being of the Beautiful: Plato's Theaetetus, Sophist and Statesman: Translation and Commentary*, I.85–183. Chicago: University of Chicago Press, 1984.

Bensen Cain, Rebecca. *The Socratic Method*. New York: Continuum International, 2007.

Berne, Eric. *Games People Play: The Psychology of Human Relationships*. Ballantine Books, 1996.

Blitz, Jan. "The Holy and the Human: An Interpretation of Plato's *Euthyphro*." *Apeiron* 14 (1980): 19–40.

Bloom, Allan. "Interpretive Essay." In *The Republic of Plato*, 305–436. New York: Basic Books, 1968.

Bostock, David. *Plato's Theaetetus*. Oxford: Clarendon, 1988.

Brickhouse, Thomas, and Nicolas D. Smith. *Routledge Philosophy Guidebook to Plato and the Trial of Socrates*. New York: Routledge, 2004.

Brill, Sara. *Plato on the Limits of Human Life*. Bloomington: Indiana University Press, 2013.

Burnyeat, Myles. "Aristotle on Learning to Be Good." In *Essays on Aristotle's Ethics*. Ed. Amelie Rorty, 69–92. Berkeley: University of California Press, 1980.

———. "Introduction" to *The Theaetetus of Plato*, 1–241. Indianapolis, Ind.: Hackett, 1990.

———. "The Philosophical Sense of Theaetetus' Mathematics." *Isis* 69, no. 4 (1978): 489–513.

Carson, Anne. *Eros the Bittersweet*. Princeton, N.J.: Princeton University Press, 1986.

Cornford, Francis MacDonald. *Plato's Theory of Knowledge*. New York: Liberal Arts, 1935.

Derrida, Jacques. "Khora." In *On The Name*. Trans. David Wood. Stanford, Calif.: Stanford University Press, 1995.

Desjardins, Rosemary. *The Rational Enterprise: Logos in Plato's Theaetetus*. Albany: SUNY Press, 1990.

Dorter, Kenneth. *Form and Good in Plato's Eleatic Dialogues*. Berkeley: University of California Press, 1994.

Fagan, Patricia. *Plato and Tradition: The Poetic and Cultural Context of Philosophy*. Evanston, Ill.: Northwestern University Press, 2013.

Freud, Sigmund. "The Dynamics of Transference." In *The Standard Edition of the Complete Psychological Works of Sigmund Freud, Volume 12 (1911–1913): The Case of Schreber, Papers on Technique and Other Works*. London: Vintage Books, 2001.

———. "Notes Upon a Case of Obsessional Neurosis" (1909). In *Three Case Histories: The "Wolf Man," The "Rat Man," and The Psychotic Doctor Schreber*. Collier Books, 1963.

Friedlander, Paul. *Plato: The Dialogues, Second and Third Period, Volumes 1–3*. Trans. Hans Meyerhoff. Princeton University Press, 1969.

Gonzalez, Francisco J. *Dialectic and Dialogue: Plato's Practice of Philosophical Inquiry*. Evanston, Ill.: Northwestern University Press, 1998.

Gulbekian, Edward. "The Origin and Value of the Stadion Unit used by Eratosthenes in the Third Century BC." *Archive for History of Exact Sciences* 37 (1987): 359–63.

Harrison, Jane. "Plato's Prologue: *Theaetetus* 142a–143c." *Tulane Studies in Philosophy* 27 (1978): 103–23.

Heidegger, Martin. *The Essence of Truth: On Plato's Cave Allegory and Theaetetus*. Trans. Ted Sadler. London: Continuum, 2002.

———. *Plato's Sophist*. Trans. Richard Rojcewicz and Andre Schuwer. Indianapolis: Indiana University Press, 1997.

Hesiod. *Works and Days and Theogony*. Trans. Stanley Lombardo. Indianapolis, Ind.: Hackett, 1993.

Homer. *Iliad*. Trans. Richard Lattimore. University of Chicago Press. 1964.

Hyland, Drew. *Finitude and Transcendence in the Platonic Dialogues*. Albany: SUNY Press, 1995.

Kirkland, Sean. *The Ontology of Socratic Questioning in Plato's Early Dialogues*. SUNY Press, 2012.

Klein, Jacob. *Plato's Trilogy*. Chicago: University of Chicago Press, 1977.

Laing, R. D. *The Divided Self: An Existential Study in Sanity and Madness*. Abingdon, U.K.: Tavistock Publications, 1964.

Lear, Jonathan. *Freud.* New York: Routledge, 2005.

McDowell, John. *Plato: Theaetetus.* New York: Oxford University Press, 1973.

Miller, Mitchell, H. *The Philosopher in Plato's Statesman.* The Hague: Martinus Nijhoff, 1980.

———. *Plato's Parmenides: The Conversion of the Soul.* Penn State University Press, 1991.

———. "Unity and Logos: A Reading of Theaetetus 201c–210a." *Ancient Philosophy* 12 (1992): 87–110.

Minuchin, Salvador. *Families & Family Therapy.* Cambridge, Mass.: Harvard University Press, 1974.

Munn, Mark D. *The School of History: Athens in the Age of Socrates.* Berkeley: University of California Press, 2000.

Nagy, Gregory. *Pindar's Homer: The Lyric Possession of an Epic Past.* Baltimore: Johns Hopkins University Press, 1994.

Nails, Debra. *The People of Plato: A Prosopography of Plato and Other Socratics.* Indianapolis, Ind.: Hackett, 2002.

Nussbaum, Martha. *Upheavals of Thought.* Cambridge University Press, 2004.

Osbourne, Robin. "Vexatious Litigation in Classical Athens: Sykophancy and the Sykophant." In *Nomos: Essays in Athenian Law, Politics and Society*, 83–102. 1990.

Plato. "Alcibiades I." In *Plato: Complete Works.* Trans. D. S. Hutchinson, 557–95. Indianapolis, Ind.: Hackett, 1997.

———. "Apology." In *Four Texts on Socrates.* Trans. Thomas G. West and Grace Starry West, 63–98. Ithaca, N.Y.: Cornell University Press, 1998.

———. "Charmides." In *Plato: Complete Works.* Trans. Rosamond Kent Sprague, 639–63. Indianapolis, Ind.: Hackett, 1997.

———. "Euthyphro." In *Four Texts on Socrates.* Trans. Thomas G. West and Grace Starry West, 41–62. Ithaca, N.Y.: Cornell University Press, 1998.

———. "Gorgias." In *Plato: Complete Works.* Trans. Donald J. Zeyl, 791–869. Indianapolis, Ind.: Hackett, 1997.

———. "Laches." In *Plato: Complete Works.* Trans. Rosamond Kent Sprague, 664–86. Indianapolis, Ind.: Hackett, 1997.

———. "Lysis." In *Plato: Complete Works.* Trans. Stanley Lombardo, 687–707. Indianapolis, Ind.: Hackett, 1997.

———. "Meno." In *Plato: Complete Works.* Trans. G. M. A. Grube, 870–97. Indianapolis, Ind.: Hackett, 1997.

———. "Phaedo." In *Plato: Complete Works.* Trans. G. M. A. Grube, 49–100. Indianapolis, Ind.: Hackett, 1997.

———. "Phaedrus." In *Plato: Complete Works.* Trans. Alexander Nehamas and Paul Woodruff, 506–56. Indianapolis, Ind.: Hackett, 1997.

———. *Plato: Complete Works.* Ed. John M. Cooper. Indianapolis, Ind.: Hackett, 1997.

———. *Platonis Opera.* Vol. 1. Ed. John Burnet. Oxford: Clarendon, 1953.

———. *The Republic of Plato.* 2nd edition. Trans. Allan Bloom. New York: Basic Books, 1968.

———. "Sophist." In *The Being of the Beautiful.* Trans. Seth Benardete, 2:1–68. Chicago: University of Chicago Press, 2006.

———. "Symposium." In *Plato: Complete Works.* Trans. Alexander Nehamas and Paul Woodruff, 457–505. Indianapolis, Ind.: Hackett, 1997.

———. "Theaetetus." In *The Being of the Beautiful: Plato's Theaetetus, Sophist and Statesman: Translation and Commentary*. Trans. Seth Benardete, I-.1–84. Chicago: University of Chicago Press, 1984.

———. "Timaeus." In *Plato: Complete Works*. Trans. Donald J. Zeyl, 1224–91. Indianapolis, Ind.: Hackett, 1997.

Plotinus. *The Enneads*. Trans. Stephen Mackenna. Penguin Books, 1991.

Polansky, Ronald M. *Philosophy and Knowledge*. Lewisburg, Pa.: Associated University Presses, 1992.

Recco, Greg. *Athens Victorious: Democracy in Plato's Republic*. Lexington Books, 2008.

Rilke, Ranier Maria. *Selected Works*, vol. 1: *Prose*. Hogarth, 1954.

Rorty, Amelie Oksenberg. "A Speculative Note on Some Dramatic Elements in the *Theaetetus*." *Phronesis* 17, no. 3 (1972): 227–38.

Rosen, Stanley. *The Quarrel between Philosophy and Poetry*. New York: Routledge, 1988.

Rowe, Christopher. *Plato and the Art of Philosophical Writing*. Cambridge, Eng.: Cambridge University Press, 2007.

Rue, Rachel. "The Philosopher in Flight: The Digression (172c–177c) in Plato's *Theaetetus*." *Oxford Studies in Ancient Philosophy* 11 (1993): 71–100.

Russon, John. "The (Childish) Nature of the Soul in Plato's *Apology*." In *Reexamining Socrates in the Apology*. Ed. John Russon and Patricia Fagan, 191–205. Evanston, Ill.: Northwestern University Press, 2009.

———. *Human Experience: Philosophy, Neurosis and the Elements of Everyday Life*. SUNY Press, 2003.

———. "Just Reading: The Nature of the Platonic Text." In *Retracing the Platonic Text*. Ed. John Russon and John Sallis, ix–xix. Evanston, Ill.: Northwestern University Press, 2000.

———. "We Sense That They Strive: How To Read (the Theory of Forms)." In *Retracing the Platonic Text*. Ed. John Russon and John Sallis, 70–84. Evanston, Ill.: Northwestern University Press, 2000.

Ryle, Gilbert. *Plato's Progress*, Cambridge, Eng.: Cambridge University Press, 1966.

Sallis, John. *Being and Logos: Reading the Platonic Dialogues*, 3rd edition. Bloomington: Indiana University Press, 1996.

———. *Chorology: On Beginning in Plato's Timaeus*. Bloomington: Indiana University Press, 1999.

———. "Traces of the Chora." In *Retracing the Platonic Text*. Ed. John Russon and John Sallis, 57–69. Evanston, Ill.: Northwestern University Press, 2000.

Sayre, Kenneth. *Plato's Literary Garden*. Notre Dame, Ind.: University of Notre Dame Press, 1995.

Schmid, Thomas. "Socratic Moderation and Self-Knowledge." *Journal of the History of Philosophy* 21 (1983), 339–48.

Schmidt, Dennis. *On Germans and Other Greeks: Tragedy and Ethical Life*. Bloomington: Indiana University Press, 2001.

Sedley, David. *The Midwife of Platonism: Text and Subtext in Plato's Theaetetus*. Oxford University Press, 2002.

Seeskin, Kenneth. *Dialogue and Discovery: A Study in Socratic Method*. SUNY Press, 1987.

Sherman, Nancy. "The Habituation of Character." In *Aristotle's Ethics: Critical Essays*. Ed. Nancy Sherman, 231–60. Rowman and Littlefield, 1999.

Sparshott, Francis. *Taking Life Seriously: A Study of the Arguments of the Nicomachean Ethics*. Toronto: University of Toronto Press, 1994.

Stern, Paul. *Knowledge and Politics in Plato's Theaetetus*. New York: Cambridge University Press, 2008.

Strauss, Leo. *The City and Man*. Chicago: Rand McNally, 1964.

Thucydides. *The Landmark Thucydides: A Comprehensive Guide to the Peloponnesian War*. Ed. Robert B. Strassler. Simon and Schuster, 1996.

———. *The Peloponnesian War*. Trans. Steven Lattimore. Hackett, 1998.

Tschemplik, Andrea. *Knowledge and Self-Knowledge in Plato's Theaetetus*. Landham, Md.: Rowman and Littlefield, 2008.

Vlastos, Gregory. *Socrates, Ironist and Moral Philosopher*. Ithaca, N.Y.: Cornell University Press, 1991.

———. *Socratic Studies*. Cambridge, Eng.: Cambridge University Press, 1994.

West, Thomas. *Plato's Apology of Socrates: An Interpretation, with a New Translation*. Ithaca, N.Y.: Cornell University Press, 1979.

Whiting, Jennifer. "Eudaimonia, External Results, and Choosing Virtuous Actions for Themselves." *Philosophy and Phenomenological Research* 65, no. 2 (2002): 270–90.

Zuckert, Catherine. *Plato's Philosphers: The Coherence of the Dialogues*. Chicago: University of Chicago Press, 2009.

INDEX